HP LaserJet
Programming

HP LaserJet
Programming

ANDREW BINSTOCK
DAVID P. BABCOCK
MARV LUSE

▲
▼▼Addison-Wesley Publishing Company, Inc.
Reading, Massachusetts Menlo Park, California New York
Don Mills, Ontario Wokingham, England Amsterdam Bonn
Sydney Singapore Tokyo Madrid San Juan Paris Seoul
Milan Mexico City Taipei

Library of Congress Cataloging-in-Publication Data
Binstock, Andrew.
    HP LaserJet programming / Andrew Binstock, David Babcock, Marvin Luse.
      p. cm.
    Includes bibliographical references and index.
    ISBN 0-201-57736-4
    1. HP LaserJet printers. I. Babcock, David. II. Luse, Marvin.
III. Title.
TK7887.7.B56 1991
686.2′2544526--dc20

90-29111
CIP

Cover design by Joyce Weston
Set in 10-pt Palatino by Carol Woolverton, Lexington, Mass.

ISBN 0-201-57736-4
1 2 3 4 5 6 7 8 9-MW-9594939291
First printing, April 1991

Acknowledgments

It would be improper to write a book such as this and not pause to acknowledge the tremendous contributions of the designers of the two key products that come together in this volume: the C programming language and the LaserJet printer. That both products have known far-reaching success is entirely fitting, for they perform their tasks better than any rivals in their respective areas. For the authors, as for many people, the C language and the LaserJet have enabled so much productivity that an environment without these tools would be impoverished if not completely unappealing. We therefore acknowledge and thank Dennis Ritchie for C, the ANSI committee for standardizing the language, and Hewlett-Packard for the LaserJet. They gave us the raison d'être for this slim volume and the tools necessary for its creation.

A key tool in the production of many of this book's illustrations was Corel Draw. We thank Ms. Mary Lemmex of Corel Systems Corp. for contributing two copies of this excellent package. Also, we thank Lisa McClure at Digi-Fonts who graciously donated several examples of her company's fine HP SoftFont typefaces for inclusion on the disk accompanying this book.

Despite our tools, this book could not have seen light were it not for the inspiration and assistance of many people, some unknown to us, who spent many hours poring over the details of this project or inspiring us in ways subtle or forthright. William Hunt's book *The C Toolbox* provided an extraordinary example of how simply C source code could be presented and how readable it could be made. Joe Savola of Hewlett-Packard provided exemplary technical editing and pointed out areas that were technically incomplete or not precisely worded. Any errors that remain are entirely our own.

Ms. Jenny Kilgore took the twisted tracks of our writing and turned them into high-speed rails capable of carrying our thoughts cleanly, efficiently, without fear of derailment or diversion into dead-end spurs. Again, any questionable English or flat prose is due to our ill-advised tendency to think we know better than she, or to our built-in predilection of making every express train into a local.

The production of any book is the result of a long and, at times, difficult dialogue between author(s) and project editor. Or so we were led to believe. In actual fact, our experiences in working with Elizabeth Rogalin at Addison-Wesley have been so pleasant and so productive that we have never, until this day, paused to think about the many tales of misery we have heard so often from so many authors. Our gratitude to Ms. Rogalin is admixed with the concern that its public expression may have loosed our secret. Such are the risks of embarrassing her publicly with such insufficient mention.

Finally, we *must* thank our spouses and loved ones who so patiently did without us while we hammered at keyboards and manuscripts until the wee hours.

—*ALB, MWL, DPB*

Contents

Preface

Despite the unprecedented success of Hewlett-Packard's line of LaserJet printers, there is a surprising lack of technical information on how to fully exploit the capabilities of the printer. This lack is all the more surprising because of the common availability of sophisticated software that relies in no small part on these very features and abilities.

The LaserJet's secrets are not kept by a cabal of programmers, nor are they the exclusive domain of initiates of a high order; rather they are commonly available from a number of sources. This book for the first time culls these sources and puts forth in a coherent manner the techniques for exploiting the LaserJet hardware. It relies not only on the innate abilities of the printer but also on the application of known techniques for creating fonts and graphics, resulting in a comprehensive guide to extracting from the LaserJet all that it has to offer.

The code is written in C. The only knowledge required of the reader is a comfortable understanding of the C language. Nowhere in this is there any explanation of C per se. The C is ANSI-conforming except where explicitly stated. The programs support the MS-DOS family of systems and UNIX. Where system-dependent material is presented it is carefully marked as such. Beyond knowledge of C, the reader need only have access to a LaserJet (Series II or later) and know how to operate it. Fundamental operations are not discussed in these pages. This book is on programming. Finally, all terms necessary to discuss fonts and graphics are presented as the discussions are undertaken. Although familiarity with these terms is desirable, it is not necessary.

The book is divided into three sections: Chapters 1–3 present an introduction to the LaserJet's PCL language. Veterans of PCL may skip the first chapter. Chapters 2 and 3 are referred to sufficiently by ensuing material that they should be read by veterans and studied by all other readers. Chapters 4–7 form an extensive discussion of fonts and font manipulation. The chapters build sequentially and should be studied as a unit. Chapters 8–10 discuss in considerable depth the techniques for generating useful graphics on the LaserJet. Again, these chapters develop sequentially and should be viewed as a unit. The remaining chapters and appendices provide ancillary information and reference material. The sections on graphics and on fonts do not rely on each other and can be approached independently, although both rely on Chapters 2 and 3 for introductory material.

The question of style was given considerable thought by the authors. It was decided that the first three introductory chapters should stress simplicity of style so as not to distract the reader at all from the material being presented. Subsequent chapters gently move toward code that is more typical of the styles found in real-world programming shops. While the later style does not lack clarity, it supposes greater familiarity with the idioms common in the LaserJet context and tends to rely on more shortcuts than the early chapters. We hope that readers who work through the book from cover to cover will find this approach of evolving rather than uniform style to be useful. If not, please let us know. We have used several conventions in the book that you may want to note now: **boldface** for key terms; `monospace` or `code font` for programs and screen messages; **`boldface code font`** for escape sequences.

The authors have tried to make this volume code-rich: Many programs, some of considerable length, are presented. This approach is grounded in the belief that useful material need be presented as such—that is, as fully developed routines or programs. Nowhere are stubs or snippets of code presented, leaving the full application as "an exercise for the reader." The intent of this volume is to provide solutions rather than new tasks, although we hope it will inspire the latter. To this end, a diskette of the source code in this volume is available from the authors. Information regarding this disk appears at the back of the book. Comments, suggestions, and criticisms are welcome, even encouraged. These should be directed to the authors at the same address specified for the source disk.

Overview of the LaserJet and PCL

Hewlett-Packard's line of LaserJet printers was first brought to market in the early 1980's. The first model, simply called LaserJet, had few of the abilities common in today's models. It simply printed text at a very high quality using laser technology. It supported only level 3 of Hewlett-Packard's printer control language (PCL), giving it little more ability than plain dot matrix printers. The next major model was the LaserJet Plus, which incorporated PCL level 4. (This level is the same found in the hugely successful LaserJet II.) Its major enhancement is the ability to download fonts to the printer. Shortly thereafter followed the LaserJet Plus 500, which was more of a heavy-duty machine. It also carried extensions to PCL 4, which allowed specification of which paper trays to use.

It was not until the advent of the LaserJet Series II or, more commonly, the LaserJet II, that the laser printer industry came into its own. The II was Hewlett-Packard's best-selling product ever. It combined low cost, small size, and all the features of PCL 4. After several years of dominating the market, the II was followed by the IID, which allowed for printing on both sides of the page, and the IIP, a slower, less expensive version of the II (intended for home use).

In 1989, Hewlett-Packard released the LaserJet III, which now supports PCL 5. This printer, mechanically a quicker version of the LaserJet II, is notable because of the new PCL capabilities. These include support for HP-GL/2, scalable resident fonts, reverse printing, resolution enhancement, and a whole host of minor refinements. As was the II, it is currently the flagship of Hewlett-Packard's line of printers. A new model, the IIID, has recently been added to the line. It is a LaserJet III with the ability to print on both sides of the page.

This book, while offering compatibility information for the less popular models, is primarily geared to users of the LaserJets II and III. Discussion of fonts is limited to the downloadable fonts associated with PCL 4 (they are completely compatible with PCL 5). All other topics support both PCL 4 and 5. Where a specific feature is supported only in PCL 5, this fact is noted in the discussion.

1
PCL Basics

Introduction

The advent of dot-addressable printers, such as dot-matrix and laser-based machines, meant that software was actually able to program printers to generate complex representations of data. The new printers superannuated the older **line-based** printers, which were only capable of printing single lines of characters down the length of the page. Dot-addressing technology allowed printers to output graphical data and complex representation which up until then were the exclusive domain of plotters and other analog devices. Dot-addressing also enabled printers to support downloadable fonts. This technology has been so successful that today any inexpensive dot-matrix printer will come with several font options and will easily print graphical images.

Dot-matrix printers, however, still suffer from the main drawback of line-based printers: they can only print down the page. The development of laser-based printers, and the LaserJet in particular, liberated printers (and programmers) from the confines of line-based technology by introducing **page-based** printing. Page-based technology allows printing to occur at any point on the page (except the very edges) at any time until the page is sent as one unit to be printed. In other words, complicated patterns and diagrams can be generated within the printer and then modified endlessly until a page-eject command is issued to force the page to be printed. This new page orientation, combined with the much higher resolution of the laser engine (both in production and location of dots), has made the LaserJet one of the most widely used peripherals in the PC market and the most successful product ever offered by Hewlett-Packard.

Printer Control Language

Page-oriented printers are considerably more programmable than their line-oriented counterparts. Simple single-character commands—line-feeds, carriage returns, form-feeds and so on—were adequte to control line-oriented machines. The commands for manipulating the operation of page-oriented printers are more complicated. With its ability to produce graphics and manipulate downloadable fonts, the LaserJet was designed as the target machine for a complex set of commands referred to as **printer control language**, or more commonly, **PCL**.

PCL commands are sent to the printer exactly like data bytes that are meant to be printed. To distinguish commands from the data, PCL uses an **escape character** to inform the printer that succeeding bytes are a command. The escape character on most printers that use the ANSI character set (this includes the LaserJet and almost all printers for IBM PCs) is assigned to the hexadecimal value 1B. The decimal equivalent is 27. This character is used throughout this book and is printed as **Esc**.

After **Esc** comes one or more characters, which constitute the command. These commands have two basic forms: two-character escape sequences (such as **Esc 9**) and longer, parameterized commands in which data is passed to the printer embedded in the command. An example of the latter is **Esc & a 4 L**. The syntax and use of both kinds of commands will be discussed thoroughly throughout the rest of this book. Notice that the examples we just gave are presented with spaces between the characters. *This is done for clarity only.* There are no spaces in any PCL commands. For example, the command **Esc & a 4 L** would be sent to the LaserJet as the hexadecimal string 1B26614C.

A closer look at this sample command shows its construction. As mentioned earlier, the **Esc** character signals the start of a command. The **&** identifies the command as one of a group that controls page size, spacing, and some other parameters. The **a** further specifies the family of commands being addressed. The **4** is actual data; the **L** indicates that the command applies to the left margin. Taken together, these command parts tell the LaserJet to indent the left margin by four columns. Had we wanted to indent by six columns a 6 would replace the 4. The bytes preceding the data parameter (in this case **Esc & a**) constitute the prefix of the command. Commands that have a common prefix can be combined into one command string, as we shall see shortly.

The last part of this command, **L**, by virtue of being upper case tells the LaserJet that it is the last byte in the command. If this command were just the beginning of a sequence of several commands, the **L** would be lower case and the next command would begin immediately after it. Only commands that have a common prefix, consisting of the first two characters after **Esc**, can be combined. For example, the command to set the right margin at 72 columns is **Esc & a 7 2 M**. If you want to set the left margin to 4 columns and the right margin to 72 columns, you can combine the two commands into the following string:

```
Esc & a 4 l 7 2 M
```

Again, the end of the command string is identified by the capital letter.

Opening the LaserJet

Commands are sent to the printer by standard means: the printer is opened as a file
and data is written to it. When the program terminates, the printer is closed and, as
with most files, this action flushes any data remaining in the buffers maintained by
the operating system. Unfortunately, opening the LaserJet printer for output is not
quite so standard. Since the LaserJet must be able to accept virtually any kind of
data sent to it, including graphics, it is imperative that it be opened in such a way
that the operating system performs no translation on the data sent to it. Under
Unix, this simply consists of opening the printer in binary mode (sometimes referred to as raw mode). Under MS-DOS, selecting binary mode is not enough to ensure that there will be no system interference or translation of bytes. An additional
call must be made to notify MS-DOS not to interfere with the printer data. The C
code for this is shown in Listing 1.1.

This code returns a pointer to FILE, just like fopen(). In fact, for non–DOS applications it simply fopen()s and sends back the return code. For MS-DOS, it calls
the function set_binary_mode() to alert DOS that the file pointed to by fp
should not undergo any translation during I/O operations. In other words, the file
is open in pure, raw binary mode. The file ljmain.h included at the beginning of
Listing 1.1 is a general-purpose header file for use in LaserJet applications. It
#defines a series of useful manifest constants including MSDOS just mentioned.
ljmain.h is called by many of the programs in this book. A complete listing of it
and the other LaserJet-specific headers appears in Appendix A.

Initialization, Esc E

Before starting a print job, it is advisable to clear away any unprinted text remaining from previous jobs and to reset any parameters that may remain in effect. This
reset of the printer environment is performed by the command **Esc E**, which will
print out any unfinished material from the previous job and restore most of the con-
figurable options to the user defaults. Since this command prevents residual commands of previous jobs from affecting the current print job, it should not be omitted
unless there is a specific reason for doing so.

Sending Commands

After opening the printer and resetting it, the programmer can begin sending data
and commands to the LaserJet. After data and commands have been sent, it is important to send a form-feed character to the printer. This will eject the final page of
the job, ensuring that it is not left behind unprinted in the printer RAM. After the
form-feed, it is advisable to reset the printer using **Esc E** once again so that subse-

LISTING 1.1 Opening the LaserJet

```c
/*--------------------- FOPEN_LJ.C ---------------------
 *  Routine to open stream to LaserJet
 *  and handle special MS-DOS requirements.
 *--------------------------------------------------------*/

#include <stdio.h>
#include "ljmain.h"

#if MSDOS
/*-------------------------------------------------------
 * Function to set set device to binary mode. MSDOS only.
 *--------------------------------------------------------*/

void set_binary_mode ( FILE * fptr )
{
    int handle;
    union REGS r;

    handle = fileno ( fptr );

    r.h.ah = 0x44;
    r.h.al = 0x00;
    r.x.bx = handle;
    r.x.dx = 0;
    int86 ( 0x21, &r, &r );

    /* check the device: is it a character device? */
    if ( r.h.dl & 0x80 )
    {
        if ( ! (r.h.dl & 0x20) )  /* cooked mode?   */
        {
            r.h.ah = 0x44;
            r.h.al = 0x01;
            r.x.bx = handle;
            r.h.dh = 0x00;

            /* setting bit 5 forces "raw" mode */
            r.h.dl |= 0x20;

            int86 ( 0x21, &r, &r );
        }
    }
}
#endif /* MSDOS */

/*-------------------------------------------------------
 * Function to actually open LaserJet stream/file
 *--------------------------------------------------------*/

FILE * fopen_laserjet ( char * filename )
{
        FILE * fp;

        fp = fopen ( filename, "wb" );

#if MSDOS
        if ( fp != NULL )
            set_binary_mode ( fp );
#endif

        return (fp);
}
```

quent jobs will not inadvertently inherit the current environment. A typical LaserJet program might well look like the program skeleton in Listing 1.2.

Units of Measure

Before beginning a discussion of page layouts, we need to define some terminology that will arise frequently in discussions of printhead motion—namely the LaserJet's units of measure. The smallest printable unit is the **dot**, which measures $1/300$ of an inch. The LaserJet II constructs images and characters from dots of this size. The LaserJet III, with Resolution Enhancement technology, uses dots of the same resolution, but by slightly changing their location and modifying their size, it can achieve an *apparent* resolution of 600 dpi (dots per inch). The resolution of the LaserJet can be lowered to 150, 100, or 75 dpi, a desirable feature when you want to print graphics quickly. These lower resolutions are achieved by clustering dots of $1/300$ of an inch into arrays. The resolution of 150 dpi is achieved by using a 2×2 array of 300 dpi dots for every printed dot; 100 dpi uses a 3×3 array; and 75 dpi uses a 4×4 array.

Dot-level operations most frequently occur in graphics. In fonts, however, the

LISTING 1.2 A Basic Shell for LaserJet Programs

```
#include <stdio.h>
#include <ljmain.h>

FILE *lj;    /* the LaserJet */

main ( int argc, char *argv[] )
{
        if (( lj = fopen_laserjet ( "PRN" )) == NULL ) /* Open it */
        {
          fputs ( "Error Opening Printer", stderr );
          exit ( 2 );
        }

        fprintf ( lj, "%cE", ESC );   /* ESC is #defined in LJMAIN.H */

        /* The main body of the application goes here */

        /* Closing Up */

        fputc ( FormFeed, lj );      /* FormFeed is #defined in LJMAIN.H */
        fprintf ( lj, "%cE", ESC );  /* Reset the printer */
        fclose ( lj );               /* Close and flush   */

        return ( 1 );
}
```

fundamental unit of measure is the **point**. After many years (centuries, to be correct) of dispute, the size of the point has finally been set at exactly $1/72$ of an inch. Every font has a certain point size associated with it, and that size is measured in 72nds of an inch. Chapter 4 gives further information on the role of points in measuring fonts.

When computing distances, the ROM code in the LaserJet uses a unit called the **decipoint**. Predictably, it is one-tenth the size of a point, or $1/720$ of an inch. This unit is rarely used by programmers because the maximum resolution of the LaserJet is 300 dpi, meaning that decipoint calculations must constantly be rounded to the nearest dot. For this reason, with the exception of a few commands, the point is generally favored over the decipoint.

Finally, the units that are the coarsest and the most familiar are **rows** and **columns**. These terms have their customary meaning: a row is the amount of vertical space required to print one line of text, a column is the width of a monospace letter. A line-feed character generally is interpreted to mean advance one line; in monospace fonts a space character (hex 20) is interpreted as move right one column.

Motion About the Page

The exact distance moved by a line-feed or blank space is set by software. Line spacing, called **leading** by typesetters (rhymes with "heading"), is the vertical distance traveled by the printhead in response to a line-feed. In other words, it is the amount of space from one printed line to the next. It is measured in lines per inch (lpi) and set by the command:

    Esc & l # D

where **#** is the lpi. Allowable values are: 1, 2, 4, 6, 8, 12, 16, 24, and 48. The LaserJet defaults to 6 lpi. Care must be taken not to set lines too close together or printing will overlap. Optimal line spacing depends on the size of the font in use. The LaserJet's built-in courier font looks best at 6 lpi, although it is still readable at 8 lpi. The line-printer font (the small, built-in font) looks excessively spaced at 6 lpi, but quite pleasant at 8 lpi. Aesthetics and readability are the only measures of the "best" line spacing.

Another way to control line spacing is though the LaserJet's Vertical Motion Index (VMI). The command is

    Esc & l # C

where **#** is the line spacing in 48ths of an inch. This number can have up to four decimal places. To show a line spacing of 10 lpi (a spacing not available with the previous lpi command), the command sequence is **Esc & l 4 . 8 C**. (With 10 lines taking up $^{48}\!/_{48}$ths of an inch, each line occupies $^{4.8}\!/_{48}$ths of an inch.) The LaserJet correctly processes new line spacing; all commands that depend on line height (such as **Esc =**, which advances the print location half a line) use the new spacing.

Column width uses the horizontal motion index (HMI). It can be set in a manner similar to that for setting row height. The command is

Esc & k # H

where **#** is the column width measured in 120ths of an inch. In monospace (or fixed-pitch) fonts, where every letter is the same width, this command sets the width allocated to each character. In proportional fonts the characters have different widths, and this command sets the width allocated to a single space. The LaserJet's default is a fixed-pitch font with spacing at 10 characters per inch ($^{12}\!/_{120}$").

> # Warning
>
> If columns are too narrow or line spacing insufficient, the LaserJet will happily print letters on top of each other. Be sure to allow enough white space between letters and lines.

The commands you've seen so far in this section simply set default values for printing text. The LaserJet really comes into its own, however, with commands to perform dot-addressable motion. Two series of commands allow motion to either relative or absolute dot locations. These commands move the current printing location to a new position. Using a regrettable term, Hewlett-Packard calls the current printing location the **cursor**. The cursor corresponds to the printhead on mechanical printers. Our subsequent references to the cursor relate to this printer cursor rather than the more customary video cursor.

Horizontal motion is performed using one of three commands, depending on the unit of measure:

Dots	**Esc * p # X**
Decipoints	**Esc & a # H**
Columns	**Esc & a # C**

As before, the **#** is replaced by the actual value. Vertical motion has its corresponding commands:

Dots	**Esc * p # Y**
Decipoints	**Esc & a # V**
Rows	**Esc & a # R**

The values that replace **#** are expressed in the indicated units. If they are preceded by a **+** or a **–** the move is considered relative; that is, a move of **#** units relative to the current position. As you might expect, horizontal motion to the right is positive. Vertical motion *down* the page is positive. All locations are based on a point located at 0,0, which is the uppermost and leftmost point at which printing can be located. In other words, it is the upper left corner point of the printable area. The location of 0,0 on the page is subject to change depending upon the margin size. Incorrectly setting margins can cause 0,0 to fall in areas on the page where the LaserJet cannot print. The question of margins and their effect on print location will be treated shortly.

Positioning rarely uses decipoints and only occasionally uses columns and rows. The preferred unit for positioning is the dot, since the exact location can be determined with a precision of $1/300$ of an inch. To place the cursor at a specified dot location, two commands must be issued: one to specify the X coordinate (the horizontal motion) and one to specify the Y coordinate (the vertical motion). The following commands will place the cursor at (300,900). This position is 300 dots right of 0,0 and 900 points down from it. At the rate of 300 dpi, this places the cursor 3 inches below and 1 inch to the right of 0,0. Dot-based measurements are always at the rate of 300 dpi. Location is unaffected by print resolution.

```
Esc * p 300 X Esc * p 900 Y
```

Because these two commands have a common prefix they can be combined into one command string:

```
Esc * p 300 x 900 Y
```

Commands of this form are common in LaserJet print files.

Listing 1.3 demonstrates the use of many of the positioning commands discussed here. The program reads up to one page of text and prints it centered both vertically and horizontally. It does this by first reading the entire file and determining how many lines there are to print. Knowing this figure (`lines` in the code), it can determine how much white space there is above and below the text, and, therefore, how far down the page to begin. Notice that there might be an odd number of lines of white space. Splitting an odd number of lines so that they are equal above and below the text requires use of the command to space a half line:

```
Esc =
```

After positioning the cursor at the correct vertical location, the program begins reading lines of text. Each line is stripped of initial and trailing white space. Its length is then computed, so that it can be centered. From this length, the amount of initial white space needed to center the string is calculated. The cursor is then moved across this white space by the commands discussed earlier. As with vertical spacing, the horizontal centering may require positioning to a half column. The

LISTING 1.3 A Demonstration of Vertical and Horizontal Cursor Positioning

```
/*------------------- HPCENTER.C ---------------------
 *  A demonstration of vertical and horizontal
 *  text centering. Will read up to 60 lines
 *  of text from a file specified on the command
 *  line and print it centered on the page.
 *------------------------------------------------*/

#include <stdio.h>
#include <ctype.h>
#include <string.h>

#include "ljmain.h"

FILE * fin, * fout;

#define MAXLINES 61   /* Max. number of lines to print */
#define MAXCHARS 80   /* Max. number of chars in line  */

void center_string ( char * );
FILE * fopen_laserjet ( char * );

void main ( int argc, char * argv[] )
{
   char buffer [ MAXCHARS + 1];
   int i, lines;

   if ( argc < 2 )
   {
      puts ( " Input file must be specified" );
      exit ( 2 );
   }

   if (( fin = fopen ( argv[1], "rt" )) == NULL )
   {
      fprintf ( stderr, "Unable to open %s", argv[1] );
      exit ( 3 );
   }

   fout = fopen_laserjet ( "PRN" );

   fprintf ( fout, "%cE", ESC );               /* Init LaserJet  */

   for ( lines = 0; lines < MAXLINES - 6; lines++ ) /* Count lines*/
   {
      if (( fgets ( buffer, MAXCHARS + 1, fin )) == NULL )
         break;
   }

   i = MAXLINES - lines;

   /* Skip down half the blank lines */

   fprintf ( fout, "%c&a%dR", ESC, i / 2 );

   /* If i is odd, skip 1/2 row.  Esc = is half-line skip */

   if ( i % 2 != 0 )
```

Listing 1.3   continues

Listing 1.3 continued

```
        fprintf ( fout, "%c=", ESC );

    rewind ( fin );                                  /* Start at top of file */

    for ( lines = 0; lines < MAXLINES; lines++ ) /* Read the lines */
    {
        if (( fgets ( buffer, MAXCHARS, fin )) == NULL )
            break;
        center_string ( buffer );                    /* Center the line*/
        fputs ( buffer, fout );                      /* Print the line */
        fputc ( '\n', fout  );
    }

    fputc ( FormFeed, fout );                        /* Flush with FF  */
}

/*-------------------------------------------------------------
 * Place LaserJet printhead where centered string
 * should start printing.
 *-------------------------------------------------*/
void center_string ( char str [] )
{
    int i, j, k;

    k = strlen ( str );

    /*  Find the last character that isn't white space
     *  and mark it as string end
     */

    for ( i = k - 1; i > 0; i-- )
        if ( isgraph ( str[i] ))
            break;
    str [ i+k ] = '\0';

    /* Find the first character that isn't white space */

    for ( i = 0; ; i++ )
        if ( isgraph ( str[i] ) || str[i] == '\0' )
            break;

    /*  If there is initial white space, move
     *  the string to the start of the buffer
     */

    if ( i != 0 )
        memmove ( str, str + i, k - i + 1 );

    k = strlen ( str );
    i = ( MAXCHARS - k ) / 2;                /* The amount to indent */
    fprintf ( fout, "%c&a%dC", ESC, i );  /* Go half the distance */

    /*  If length of new string is an odd number, move
     *  right by half a letter ( 15/300" at 10 cpi ).
     */

    if ( (MAXCHARS - k) % 2 != 0 )
        fprintf (fout, "%c*p+%dX", ESC, 15 );
}
```

LaserJet offers no command to move half a column, so recourse to dot-specific positioning is required.

At the start of the program, the printer is reset using the technique already described. Barring unusual user defaults, this action resets the font to the 10-pitch monospace courier font. A 10-pitch font prints 10 characters per inch. Hence, each character occupies 30 dots of width, and a half-column occupies half of that, or 15 dots. So when centering requires motion of half a column, the cursor is moved to the last full column and then an additional 15 dots (a half column) by the command

```
Esc * p + 15 X
```

Remember, the + sign indicates relative motion from the current printing position. Hence this command moves the cursor one-half column to the right of the current position. At that point printing begins.

Here are a few other notes on the code. Notice that it uses the `fopen_laserjet()` function given in Listing 1.1 and immediately initializes the printer. At program end, it issues a form-feed to make sure the page is printed. These techniques recur frequently in our programs; they should be adopted in all programming for the LaserJet, pursuant to the example given in Listing 1.2.

Page Layout

We have already seen that the page is the basic printing unit of page-based printers such as the LaserJet. The size of the actual sheet of paper, commonly called the **physical page** can be selected by the page-size command. It has the form

```
Esc & l # A
```

where # has the following values:

1	Executive	$7\frac{1}{4}" \times 10\frac{1}{2}"$
2	Letter	$8\frac{1}{2}" \times 11"$
3	Legal	$8\frac{1}{2}" \times 14"$
26	A4	210 mm × 297 mm
80	Monarch envelope	$3\frac{7}{8}" \times 7\frac{1}{2}"$ (letter size)
81	Com-10 envelope	$4\frac{1}{8}" \times 9\frac{1}{2}"$ (business size)
90	DL envelope	110 mm × 220 mm
91	C5 envelope	162 mm × 229 mm

The page-size command will cause the LaserJet to check the current paper tray in use and make sure it is appropriate for the size. This command is not available on the original LaserJet, the LaserJet Plus, or the LaserJet 500 printers. For these models, the page-length command must be used to establish paper size.

Because of mechanical constraints, the LaserJet is not capable of printing at every location on the physical page. Small unprintable areas exist on all four edges of a standard sheet of paper. Regardless of page orientation or paper size, these areas are 50 dots wide on most LaserJet models (see Appendix C for margins on specific LaserJet models); that is, 50 dots at 300 dpi, or ⅙". The area inside these margins is predictably called the **printable area**.

The term **logical page** describes an area the width of the printable area running the full length of the page. In other words, it is the size of the printable area plus the top and bottom unprintable margins. Even though it contains unprintable areas, the logical page is the basis for cursor positioning. In fact, the logical page is defined as the area of the page in which the printer cursor can be positioned.

In practice, the useful area of the page is restricted to a subset of the printable area by means of margins. Margins indent text and can be set from any edge of the *logical* page. The early examples of PCL commands in this chapter showed how to set the left and right margins. Top and bottom margins will be discussed shortly. The printable area between margins is called the **text area**. The text area is the area within which all text is printed unless specific commands are issued to move the cursor outside of it. Figure 1.1 illustrates the areas of a page.

Top and Bottom Margins

The top margin defaults to a height of half an inch. If some other setting is desired, the top margin can be set by a command of the form

```
Esc & l # E
```

where # represents the desired number of lines of margin space. Notice that line spacing will affect the top margin setting. For example, if the LaserJet is set to print at 8 lpi, a value of 8 will create a margin of 1"; if the LaserJet is set to 6 lpi, the same value will generate a top margin of 1⅓". Once the margin is set, changing the lpi setting does not affect the location of the top margin. Printing will occur at the first line below the top margin. The baseline of this first line occurs at a distance of 72 to 75% of VMI below the top margin. (See Appendix C for the specific distance for each LaserJet model.)

The bottom margin of the text area is computed from the sum of the top margin and the number of printing lines on the page. The number of printing lines, called **text length**, is set by the command

```
Esc & l # F
```

where # is the number of lines in the text area.

FIGURE 1.1 Page Areas Used by LaserJet

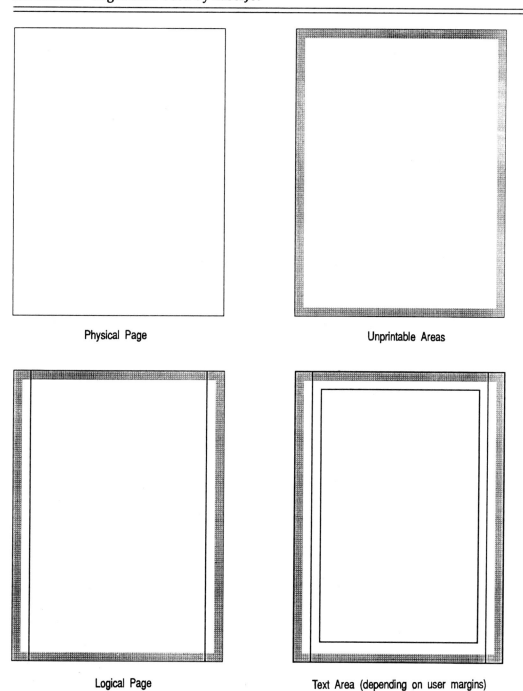

Physical Page

Unprintable Areas

Logical Page

Text Area (depending on user margins)

Perforation Skip

The **perforation area** refers to the space between the bottom of the text area of one page and the top of the text area of the next page. On continuous forms, this is the most common location for perforation lines, hence the name. Of course, LaserJets cannot accept continuous forms, but it is important to discuss the perforation area anyway. This area, which falls below the bottom margin, can still be written to provided it falls within the printable area. To print there we need to disable **perforation skip**. This is controlled through the command

```
Esc & l # L
```

where **#** is 0 to disable perforation skip and 1 to enable it. Disabling perforation skip means that cursor movement below the bottom text margin is allowed. Enabling perforation skip means that attempts to print below the bottom text margin will result in a page-eject and printing will continue at the top of the next page.

Warning
Printing below the bottom margin (with perforation skip disabled) can lead to printing loss if printing is attempted in the unprintable areas of the logical page.

Because changing perforation skip resets the top margin and the page length to the user defaults, it is unwise to reset perforation skip in the middle of a job.

Printing Outside the Text Area

The text area is simply the established printing area within all the defined margins. It is possible to violate the margins and print outside the text area by moving the cursor outside the text area. The commands for moving the cursor were discussed in the section Motion About the Page earlier in the chapter. It is important to remain within the printable area, otherwise characters or even whole lines might not print.

You can maximize the text area by setting it equal to the logical page. This is done by setting the top margin to 0, disabling perforation skip, and resetting any left/right margins. Extending the text area to the maximum is not recommended, as it will include the unprintable areas at the top and bottom of the page. To do it, however, use the following command string:

```
Esc & l 0 e 0 L Esc 9
```

Notice that the first two commands are combined since they have a common prefix.

Programming Project: PCL Debugger

In this book, and probably in your work programming the LaserJet, you will write or generate hundreds of PCL commands. Most commands are straightforward, easy to write, and quick to verify. However, a number of commands and settings can be difficult to verify, much less debug. This is because the LaserJet will simply ignore invalid or unsupported PCL commands. Hence, slight errors can result in mispositioned printing, garbage output, or, most frustrating of all, no output at all.

To assist in debugging PCL files, the following programming project presents a utility that reads a PCL file and prints the PCL commands in regular English. Any print data is passed through as regular data. This utility, in effect, permits you to read and dump a PCL file. It has a few fairly minor limitations. It only does limited error checking. It will flag all illegal PCL commands (commands with invalid syntax) and most unsupported commands (valid syntax but not a recognized command). When these errors are detected, an error message and the command itself are written to `stderr` (almost always the screen) and the command is passed as data to the output file. The utility will accept any valid PCL file and handle all commands except those whose parameters use a decimal point, a very rare occurrence.

The utility itself, called `pclparse`, is designed to be extensible. It consists of two modules: `pclparse.c` (Listing 1.4), which reads through the PCL file and identifies command strings, and `pclprint.h` (Listing 1.5), which acts upon the commands once they have been identified. This separates the PCL command recognizer (in compiler-writing terms, the **parser**) from the actions, which allows a different set of actions to be attached to the parser. For example, if you want to translate PCL into commands suitable for a dot-matrix printer, you would only need to replace `pclprint.h`.

Design of the Debugger

The debugger is presented in the listings that follow. Each module is approximately 850 lines long. The routines in `pclprint.h` are pretty much self-documenting since they simply print a description of their activity in English. By contrast, `pclparse.c` is a fairly involved piece of code. The remainder of this section describes this code. It is primarily of interest to readers who wish to study the code. If you just want to use the utility or simply look at the code briefly, you should proceed to the next section where usage and output are described.

After opening the input and output files, the parser reads through the PCL file byte by byte, looking for an **Esc** character. Until one is found, all bytes are passed as data to the output file. It is assumed that **Esc** signals the start of a PCL string. When **Esc** is found, the command is read into `buffer`. While moving the command bytes to `buffer`, the parser checks them to make sure they fit within the HP-specified rules for PCL commands. This verification is performed in the function `get_command_string`. The values used to verify the string are set forth in HP's *LaserJet Technical Reference* (a different version comes with each model of the Laser-Jet). If the command string does not fit within the parameters or if the string is longer than 128 characters (way beyond the maximum useful length), an error is returned, and the command is passed as data to the output file. The program then resumes its search for the next **Esc** character.

If a valid command string is found, it is processed by `parse_command_-string()`. Two-character commands are handled on the spot and the appropriate routine in `pclprint.h` is called. The first character following **Esc** is handed to a `switch` statement, which calls the appropriate routine based on the value of the character.

Parameterized commands, although considerably more complex, are handled using the same approach. The first character after **Esc** (pointed to by `buf_ptr`) is handed to a very long `switch` statement. This first character identifies the family of commands to which a given PCL instruction belongs. In the case of **Esc %**, for example, the **%** is sufficient information to know which family of functions handles this command. In the case of **Esc ***, however, the next character determines the family, so this character is also evaluated before the command can be processed. Commands whose family cannot be identified with two characters after the **Esc** are currently unsupported in PCL, and a warning to this effect is printed. Once again, the invalid command is passed as data to the output file.

When functions process families of commands, the program must be able to recognize whether a command is a combined command—that is, the concatenation of two commands with a common prefix. As stated previously, combined commands use lower-case letters rather than capitals to separate commands. When a lowercase letter is detected at the end of a command, the `combined_command` variable is set to 1. At the end of the parsing and processing of a single command, the `combined_command` variable is queried. If it is set (to 1), the unprocessed part of the command string is moved forward to the head of `buffer` where it overlays the processed command. The function `reset_buffer` moves the remaining command into place. The parsing process is then resumed by jumping to the beginning of the parsing cycle. This jump is accomplished by use of a `goto` statement. (Purists shocked by this technique may rewrite the code to their standards. However, they will find the rewritten material more cumbersome and far less clear. Parsers and compilers often contain `goto` statements, the clarity of the code being prized more than dogged adherence to stylistic dogma.)

The function `font_management`, which handles all commands with the prefix **Esc * c**, contains code to step around an unusual feature of PCL. In what can only be termed a deplorable design decision, creators of PCL allowed the command **Esc * c 2 G** to have two distinct meanings: it can fill a rectangular area with vertical lines or fill a rectangular area with a very light gray. How the two meanings are distinguished is discussed in the next chapter. The rest of the code, we hope, should be clear from the comments and from the source code itself.

FIGURE 1.2 Debugger Output from the Initialization Commands for Printing Chapter 1 Manuscript

```
[Perforation Skip Off][Spacing at 6 lines/inch][Normal Portrait
Orientation][Top Margin: 0 Lines][Font Assigned #2018][Download Font:
Futura][1][2][3][4][5][6][7][8][9][A][B][C][D][E][F][10][11][12][13][14]
[15][16][17][18][19][1A][1B][1C][1D][1E][1F][21][22][23][24][25][26][27

...font download continues through next line...

[EE][EF][F0][F1][F2][F3][F4][F5][F6][F7][F8][F9][FA][FB][FC][FD][FE]
[Make Font Permanent][IBM-PC Symbol Set][Proportional Spacing]
[Primary Height: 12 Points][Semi Light Stroke Weight][Typeface
14][Paper Size: Letter][Top Margin: 0 Lines][Make 1 Copy][Position to
Y 343 Dots][Position to X 874 Dots]
```

Using the Debugger

To use the debugger you need to generate a PCL file. You can do this by writing your own or redirecting printer output intended for the LaserJet to a disk file. Once the file exists, run the debugger with the following command line:

```
pclparse filename.in filename.out
```

where `filename.in` is the name of the PCL file to be analyzed, and `filename.out` is the resulting file. Figure 1.2 shows the first portion of the output that results from running `pclparse` on a sample of the manuscript for this chapter. Notice that PCL commands are enclosed in brackets: [`PCL command`]. A long series of initialization commands follows. These commands are generated by Word-Perfect, as was the file. They should provide an interesting example of how extensively an application can initialize the LaserJet before setting to work.

This chapter has presented the basic syntax of PCL commands with examples to show cursor movement and definition of page size. Chapter 2 continues the exploration of PCL commands and the LaserJet's abilities.

LISTING 1.4 pclparse.c: The Parsing Engine

```
/*---------------- PCLPARSE.C ------------------
*    Parser for PCL version 5 and earlier.
*    Once a command is known, it is acted upon by
*    routines in <pclprint.h> which write out a
*    description of the PCL commands. Replace
*    pclprint.h with your own routines as needed.
*
*    Usage: PCLPARSE infile outfile
*
*    Errors are printed to stderr, and the data
*    is passed to outfile untouched.
*--------------------------------------------------*/
```

Listing 1.4 continues

Listing 1.4 continued

```c
#define MS_DOS 1

#include <stdio.h>
#include <ctype.h>

#undef islower     /* Make sure they're functions,  */
#undef isupper     /*  NOT macros with side-effects */
#undef isdigit
#undef isgraph

void do_resolution ( void );
void eol_pitch_family ( void );
void eol_wrap_family ( void );
void font_management ( void );
int  get_command_string ( void );
void graphics_pcl_family ( void );
void macro_family ( void );
int  our_atoi ( void );
void page_control_family ( void );
void parse_command_string ( int );
void pcl_err ( int );
void pos_margin_family ( void );
void print_imaging ( void );
void raster_compression ( void );
void raster_graphics ( void );
void reset_buffer ( int );
void underline_family ( void );

FILE *fin, *fout;

int combined_command;    /* = YES if several commands in one string */
int saved_char;

#define PCL_BUF_SIZE   128
#define UNSUPPORTED    200    /* error codes  */
#define ILLEGAL        201
#define TOO_LONG       202

char buffer [PCL_BUF_SIZE + 1];
char * buf_ptr = buffer;      /* Where are we in buffer?  */

#include "ljmain.h"
#include "pclprint.h"   /* header with actions for each command */
                        /* should change with every application */

main ( int argc, char *argv[] )
{
    int c, i;

    if ( argc > 2 )
    {
        fin = fopen ( argv[1], "rb" );
        if ( fin == NULL )
        {
            printf ( "Cannot open %s\n", argv[1] );
            exit ( 5 );
        }
    }
```

Listing 1.4 continues

Listing 1.4 continued

```
    else
    {
        fputs ("Usage: HPPCLINT file_in.ext file_out.ext", stderr);
        exit ( 6 );
    }

    pcl_init( argc, argv );

    while (( c = fgetc( fin )) != EOF )
    {
        if ( c != ESC )
            pcl_reg_char ( c );
        else
        {
            if ((( i = get_command_string()) == ILLEGAL) ||
                     i == UNSUPPORTED || i == TOO_LONG )
            {
                pcl_err ( i );
                continue;
            }
            else
                parse_command_string ( i );
        }
    }
    wrapup:
    fclose ( fout );
    return ( 2 );
}       /* end of main() */

/*------------------------------------------------------------
 * Get the PCL command string after ESC detected
 * Returns length of command (excluding Esc) or error code
 *-----------------------------------------------------------*/
int get_command_string ( void )
{
    int c, i;
    i = 0;

    memset ( buffer, '\0', PCL_BUF_SIZE+1 ); /* set buffer to 0's */
    buffer [i++] = c = fgetc ( fin );

    if ( c == EOF )                    /* 2nd char cannot be EOF */
        return ILLEGAL;

    if ( c >= 0x30 && c <= 0x7E )     /* a 2-character command  */
        return ( 2 );     /* length of command */

    if ( c >= 0x21 && c <= 0x2F )    /* Paramaterized Command  */
    {
        buffer[i++] = c = fgetc ( fin );
        if (( c >= 0x60 && c <= 0x7E ) || isdigit ( c ))
        {              /* Valid char, so get rest of command string */
            while ( i < PCL_BUF_SIZE && c != EOF )
            {
                buffer[i++] = c = fgetc ( fin );

                if ( c >= 0x40 && c <= 0x5E )   /* end of command */
                    break;
```

Listing 1.4 continues

Listing 1.4   continued

```
                }
                if ( i == PCL_BUF_SIZE  && ( c < 0x40 || c > 0x5E ))
                    return ( TOO_LONG ); /* 128 chars was not enough! */
            }
            clse
                return ( ILLEGAL );
        }
        else
            return ( ILLEGAL );

        return ( strlen( buffer ));   /* Valid command */
}

/*-----------------------------------------------------------
 * Parses command strings and calls action routine.
 * While a string may be valid by HP standards it might
 * not be supported by the current PCL (now at Level 5).
 * In these cases, the command is passed on as print data.
 * Note the main loop has a goto destination at top. This
 * is for use in combined commands, to process the next command.
 *-----------------------------------------------------------*/
void parse_command_string ( int len )
{
    if ( len < 2 )        /* It's not PCL, so just pass it on */
    {
        fprintf ( fout, "\n%c%s", ESC, buffer );
        return;
    }

    if ( len == 2 )       /* Handle 2-char commands here */
    {
        switch ( buffer[0] )
        {
            case '9':
                pcl_reset_margins();        break;
            case 'E':
                pcl_reset();                break;
            case 'Y':
                pcl_display_codes ( ON );  break;
            case 'Z':
                pcl_display_codes ( OFF ); break;
            case '=':
                pcl_half_line_feed ();      break;
            default:
                pcl_err ( UNSUPPORTED );
        }
    }
    else    /* Parameterized commands from here on in */
    {
    parse_loop:            /* destination of subsequent goto's */
        combined_command = NO;
        buf_ptr = buffer;

        switch ( *buf_ptr )
        {
            case '%':
                graphics_pcl_family ();  break;
```

Listing 1.4   continues

Listing 1.4   continued

```
    case '&':
    {
        switch ( *(++buf_ptr) )
        {
            case EOF:
                pcl_finish();               break;
            case 'a':
                pos_margin_family();        break;
            case 'd':
                underline_family();         break;
            case 'f':
                macro_family();             break;
            case 'k':
                eol_pitch_family();         break;
            case 'l':
                page_control_family();      break;
            case 'p':
                pcl_transparent_data();     break;
            case 's':
                eol_wrap_family();          break;
            default:
                pcl_err ( UNSUPPORTED ); break;
        }
        if ( combined_command == YES )
           goto parse_loop;
        else
           return;
    }
    case '*':
    {
        switch ( *(++buf_ptr) )
        {
            case 'b':
                raster_compression ();    break;
            case 'c':   /* Fonts and shading areas */
                font_management ();       break;
            case 'p':
                pcl_dot_position ();      break;
            case 'r':
                raster_graphics ();       break;
            case 't':
                do_resolution ();         break;
            case 'v':
                print_imaging ();         break;
            default :
                pcl_err ( UNSUPPORTED ); break;
        }
        if ( combined_command == YES )
           goto parse_loop;
        else
           return;
    }
    case ')':
    case '(':
    {
        int i, ch, e;

        ch = *buf_ptr;   /* save the ) or ( */
```

Listing 1.4   continues

Listing 1.4   continued

```
if (( e = *(++buf_ptr)) == 's' )
{
    i = our_atoi();
    e = *buf_ptr;          /* get last char in string */
    switch ( e )
    {
    case 'W':
        if ( ch == ')' )
            pcl_download_font_header ( i );
        else
            pcl_download_font_char ( i );
        combined_command = NO;
        break;
    case 'p': case 'P':
        pcl_spacing_type ( i );
        break;
    case 'h': case 'H':
        pcl_primary_pitch ( i );
        break;
    case 't': case 'T':
        pcl_typeface ( i );
        break;
    case 'v': case 'V':
        pcl_primary_height ( i );
        break;
    case 'b': case 'B':
        pcl_stroke_weight ( i + 7 );
        break;

    }
    if ( islower( e )) /* combined command */
    {
        combined_command = YES;
        reset_buffer ( 2 );
    }
    break;
}
else
{
    char *save_buf_ptr = buf_ptr; /* see below at */
                                  /* special case */
    i = our_atoi();
    e = *buf_ptr;

    switch ( e )
    {
        case '@':
                pcl_default_font (SECONDARY);
                break;
        case 'x': case 'X':
                pcl_select_font (SECONDARY, i);
                break;
        case 'd': case 'D':
        case 'e': case 'E':
        case 'f': case 'F':
        case 'g': case 'G':
        case 'i': case 'I':
        case 'k': case 'K':
```

Listing 1.4   continues

Listing 1.4 continued

```
                        case 'n': case 'N':
                        case 's': case 'S':
                        case 'u': case 'U':
                        {
                        /* Special case:
                            prefix on these combined commands
                            is only 1 char, so our_atoi() and
                            reset_buffer() must be done specially,
                            since those functions depend on the
                            more common 2-char prefix.
                        */
                            buf_ptr = save_buf_ptr - 1;
                            i = our_atoi();

                            pcl_symbol_set ( i, e );

                            if ( islower ( e ))
                            {
                                reset_buffer ( 1 );
                                goto parse_loop;
                            }
                        }
                            break;
                    }
                    if ( islower( e )) /* combined command */
                    {
                        combined_command = YES;
                        reset_buffer ( 2 );
                    }
                    break;
                }
            }
            default:
                pcl_err ( UNSUPPORTED );  break;
        }
        if ( combined_command == YES )
            goto parse_loop;
    }
}

/*-------------------------------------------------------------
 *   Command Prefix: Esc %
 *   Switching between graphics and PCL modes
 *-----------------------------------------------------------*/
void graphics_pcl_family ( void )
{
    int parameter, type;

    parameter = *(++buf_ptr); /* get the data/parameters */
    type      = *(++buf_ptr); /* get the type of command */

    if ( type == 'A' )
        pcl_enter_pcl_mode ( parameter );
    else
    if ( type == 'B' )
        pcl_enter_hpgl_mode( parameter );
    else
        pcl_err ( UNSUPPORTED );
}
```

Listing 1.4 continues

Listing 1.4 continued

```
/*-----------------------------------------------------------
 *   Command Prefix: Esc & d
 *   Underlining handled here.
 *-----------------------------------------------------------*/
void underline_family ( void )
{
    switch ( *(++buf_ptr ))
    {
        case '@':
            pcl_disable_underline();        return;

        case '0':
            pcl_enable_fixed_underline(); break;
        case '3':
            pcl_enable_float_underline(); break;
        default:
            pcl_err ( UNSUPPORTED );        return;
    }

    if ( *buf_ptr == 'd' )
    {
        combined_command = YES;  reset_buffer ( 2 );
    }
}

/*-----------------------------------------------------------
 *   Command prefix: Esc & a
 *   Set cursor position, right and left margins,
 *       and print rotation.
 *-----------------------------------------------------------*/
void pos_margin_family ( void )
{
    int i;

    i = our_atoi();

    switch ( *buf_ptr )
    {
        case 'v':     case 'V':
            pcl_vert_position ( i , DECIPOINTS); break;
        case 'r':     case 'R':
            pcl_vert_position ( i , ROWS);       break;
        case 'c':     case 'C':
            pcl_horz_position ( i , COLUMNS);    break;
        case 'h':     case 'H':
            pcl_horz_position ( i , DECIPOINTS); break;

        case 'l':     case 'L':
            pcl_set_left_margin ( i );    break;
        case 'm':     case 'M':
            pcl_set_right_margin ( i );   break;

        case 'P':                      /* note absence of 'p' */
            pcl_rotate_print ( i );       break;
        default:
            pcl_err ( UNSUPPORTED );      return;
    }
```

Listing 1.4 continues

Listing 1.4 continued

```
    if ( islower ( *buf_ptr ))
    {
        combined_command = YES;  reset_buffer ( 2 );
    }
}

/*------------------------------------------------------------
 *   Command Prefix: Esc & k
 *   Set line-termination sequence, pitch,
 *      and HMI (i.e., line height)
 *-----------------------------------------------------------*/
void eol_pitch_family ( void )
{
    int c;
    int i = our_atoi();
    switch ( *buf_ptr )
    {
        case 'G': case 'g': /* Esc & k # G */
        {
            enum {Cr = 1, Lf = 2, Ff = 4}; /* Possible EOL actions*/

            char CR_LF_FF[3];         /* Array of process switches */
            CR_LF_FF[0] = Cr;         /* for CR LF FF respectively */
            CR_LF_FF[1] = Lf;
            CR_LF_FF[2] = Ff;

            switch ( i )
            {
                case 0: break;
                case 1: CR_LF_FF[0] |= Lf;  break; /* CR = CR+LF      */

                case 3: CR_LF_FF[0] |= Lf;         /* fall through    */
                case 2: CR_LF_FF[1] |= Cr;         /* LF = LF+CR      */
                        CR_LF_FF[2] |= Cr;  break; /*  and FF = FF+CR */
            }
            pcl_line_termination ( CR_LF_FF );
            break;
        }
        case 'H': case 'h':  /* Esc & k # H */
            pcl_horz_move ( i );
            break;
        case 'S': case 's':  /* Esc & k # S */
        {
            switch ( i )
            {
                case 0:
                    pcl_set_10_pitch ();  break;
                case 4:
                    pcl_set_12_pitch ();  break;
                case 2:
                    pcl_set_compressed_mode(); break;
            }
            break;
        }
        default:
            pcl_err ( UNSUPPORTED );        return;
    }
```

Listing 1.4 continues

Listing 1.4 continued

```
    if ( islower ( *buf_ptr ))
    {
        combined_command = YES;  reset_buffer ( 2 );
    }
}

/*-------------------------------------------------------
 *  Command Prefix: Esc & s
 *  Set whether long lines should wrap at EOL
 *-----------------------------------------------------*/
void eol_wrap_family ()
{
    if ( *(++buf_ptr) == '0' )
        pcl_eol_wrap ( ON );
    else
        pcl_eol_wrap ( OFF );

    if ( islower ( *(++buf_ptr) ))
    {
        combined_command = YES;  reset_buffer ( 2 );
    }
}

/*-------------------------------------------------------
 *  Command Prefix: Esc & l
 *  Sets most page-related parameters, including:
 *      page size, top margin, perforation skip,
 *      orientation, number of copies, etc.
 *-----------------------------------------------------*/
void page_control_family()
{
    int i = our_atoi();

    switch ( *buf_ptr )
    {
        case 'A': case 'a':
            pcl_page_size ( i );           break;
        case 'C': case 'c':
            pcl_vert_move ( i );           break;
        case 'D': case 'd':
            pcl_line_spacing ( i );        break;
        case 'E': case 'e':
            pcl_top_margin ( i );          break;
        case 'F': case 'f':
            pcl_text_length ( i );         break;
        case 'H': case 'h':
            pcl_paper_source ( i );        break;
        case 'L': case 'l':
            pcl_perforation_skip ( i ); break;
        case 'O': case 'o':
            pcl_orientation ( i );         break;
        case 'P': case 'p':
            pcl_page_length ( i );         break;
        case 'U': case 'u':
            pcl_registration (i, LEFT); break;
        case 'X': case 'x':
            pcl_make_copies ( i );         break;
        case 'Z': case 'z':
```

Listing 1.4 continues

Listing 1.4 continued

```
            pcl_registration ( i, TOP );break;
    }

    if ( islower ( *buf_ptr ))
    {
        combined_command = YES;  reset_buffer ( 2 );
    }
}
/*-------------------------------------------------------
 *   Command Prefix: Esc & f
 *   All macro handling done here.
 *-----------------------------------------------------*/
void macro_family()
{
    int i, c;

    i = our_atoi();

    switch ( *(++buf_ptr) )
    {
        case 'S': case 's':
            pcl_push_pop_position ( i );            break;
        case 'X': case 'x':
        {
            switch ( i )
            {
                case 0:    pcl_start_macro_def(); break;
                case 1:    pcl_stop_macro_def();  break;
                case 2:    pcl_execute_macro();   break;
                case 3:    pcl_call_macro();      break;
                case 4:    pcl_enable_overlay();  break;
                case 5:    pcl_disable_overlay(); break;
                case 6:    pcl_delete_macros();   break;
                case 7:    pcl_delete_temp_macros(); break;
                case 8:    pcl_delete_macro_id(); break;
                case 9:    pcl_make_macro_temp(); break;
                case 10:   pcl_make_macro_perm(); break;
            }
        }
        case 'Y': case 'y':
            pcl_identify_macro( i );
    }

    if ( islower ( *buf_ptr ))
    {
        combined_command = YES;  reset_buffer ( 2 );
    }
}

/*-------------------------------------------------------
 *   Command Prefix: Esc * t
 *   Set graphics print resolution
 *-----------------------------------------------------*/
void do_resolution ( void )
{
    pcl_resolution ( our_atoi() );

    if ( islower ( *buf_ptr ))
```

Listing 1.4 continues

Listing 1.4   continued

```
    {
        combined_command = YES;  reset_buffer ( 2 );
    }
}

/*------------------------------------------------------------
 * Command Prefix: Esc * c
 * Handle some font and many shading functions
 *----------------------------------------------------------*/
void font_management ( void )
{

    static int fill_type;
    enum { Shade = 1, CrossHatch };

    int i = our_atoi();

    switch ( *buf_ptr )
    {
        case 'A': case 'a':
            pcl_rectangle ( i, POINTS, HORIZ );         break;
        case 'B': case 'b':
            pcl_rectangle ( i, POINTS, VERT  );         break;
        case 'D': case 'd':
            pcl_assign_font_id ( i );                   break;
        case 'E': case 'e':
            pcl_announce_next_char ( i );               break;
        case 'F': case 'f':
        {
            switch ( i )
            {
                case 0:
                    pcl_delete_fonts ( ALL_FONTS );   break;
                case 1:
                    pcl_delete_fonts ( TEMPORARY );   break;
                case 2:
                    pcl_delete_last_font ( );         break;
                case 3:
                    pcl_delete_last_char ( );         break;
                case 4:
                    pcl_font_status ( TEMPORARY );    break;
                case 5:
                    pcl_font_status ( PERMANENT );    break;
                case 6:
                    pcl_assign_font_temp ( );         break;
            }
            break;
        }
        case 'G':   case 'g':
        {
            if ( fill_type == CrossHatch )
                pcl_select_pattern ( i );
            else
            if ( fill_type == Shade )
                pcl_select_shading ( i );
            else                    /* It hasn't been defined, so we */
            if ( i <> 6 )           /* do our best. Shade < 6 is     */
                pcl_select_pattern ( i );     /* so unlikely that*/
```

Listing 1.4   continues

Listing 1.4 continued

```
            else                            /* we assume it's  */
                pcl_select_shading ( i );   /* a pattern.      */
            break;
        }
        case 'H':   case 'h':
            pcl_rectangle ( i, DECIPOINTS, HORIZ );   break;
        case 'P':   case 'p':

            pcl_fill_rectangle ( i );

            if ( i == 3 )
                fill_type = CrossHatch;
            else
            if ( i == 2 )
                fill_type = Shade;                    break;

        case 'V':   case 'v':
            pcl_rectangle ( i, DECIPOINTS, VERT );    break;
        default:
            pcl_err ( UNSUPPORTED );                  return;
    }

    if ( islower ( *buf_ptr ))
    {
        combined_command = YES;  reset_buffer ( 2 );
    }
}

/*----------------------------------------------------------
 *  Command Prefix: Esc * r
 *  Set various raster graphics parameters
 *----------------------------------------------------------*/
void raster_graphics ( void )
{
    int i = our_atoi();

    switch ( *buf_ptr )
    {
        case 'A': case 'a':
            pcl_start_raster_graphics ( i );     break;
        case 'B': case 'b':
            pcl_end_raster_graphics ();          break;
        case 'F': case 'f':
            pcl_graphic_presentation ( i );      break;
        case 'S': case 's':
            pcl_raster_width ( i );              break;
        case 'T': case 't':
            pcl_raster_height ( i );             break;
    }

    if ( islower ( *buf_ptr ))
    {
        combined_command = YES;  reset_buffer ( 2 );
    }
}
```

Listing 1.4   continues

Listing 1.4   continued

```
/*-----------------------------------------------------------
 *   Command Prefix: Esc * v
 *   Set miscellaneous raster functions:
 *      compression mode, offset, actual rasters
 *---------------------------------------------------------*/
void raster_compression ( void )
{
    int i = our_atoi();

    switch ( *buf_ptr )
    {
        case 'M':   case 'm':
            pcl_raster_compress ( i );  break;
        case 'W':
            pcl_send_raster_data ( i ); break;
        case 'Y':   case 'y':
            pcl_raster_Y_offset ( i );  break;
    }

    if ( islower ( *buf_ptr ))
    {
        combined_command = YES;  reset_buffer ( 2 );
    }
}

/*-----------------------------------------------------------
 *   Command Prefix: Esc * v
 *   Set transparency mode and imaging pattern
 *---------------------------------------------------------*/
void print_imaging ( void )
{
    int i = our_atoi();

    switch ( *buf_ptr )
    {
        case 'T':
            pcl_imaging_pattern ( i );         break;
        case 'N':
            pcl_source_transparency ( i );   break;
        case 'O':   /* the letter O */
            pcl_pattern_transparency ( i );  break;
    }
}

/* =============== Utility Functions ============ */

/*-----------------------------------------------------------
 *    Returns atoi() on characters at buf_ptr + 1.
 *    at end, buf_ptr points to the first char after digits
 *---------------------------------------------------------*/
int our_atoi ( void )
{
    char num_str [6];        /* max size of int string is 5 + '\0' */
    int c, i;
    int sign = 0;

    buf_ptr += 1;
```

Listing 1.4   continues

Listing 1.4 continued

```c
    for ( i = 0; i < 5; )          /* Get the digits as a string */
    {
        c = *(buf_ptr++);
        if ( isdigit( c ) || c == '-' || c == '+' )
        {
            if ( c == '-' || c == '+' )
            {
                if ( sign != 0 )        /* Sign already seen, so   */
                {                       /* new sign is not part of */
                    buf_ptr -= 1;       /* this string of digits   */
                    break;
                }
                else
                    sign = 1;
            }
            num_str[i++] = c;
        }
        else
        {   /* buf_ptr currently points past non-digit char */
            buf_ptr -= 1;
            break;
        }
    }
    num_str[i] = '\0';

    i = atoi ( num_str );
    return ( i );
}

/*------------------------------------------------------------
 *  Prints an error message and the incorrect command,
 *  then writes the data to the output file.
 *------------------------------------------------------------*/
void pcl_err ( int type )
{
    int c;

    if ( type == TOO_LONG )
    {
        fprintf ( stderr, "\nCommand Too Long : [Esc%s", buffer );
        fputs ( buffer, fout );

        while (( c = fgetc ( fin )) != EOF && !isupper ( c ))
        {
            fputc ( c , stderr );
            fputc ( c , fout );
        }
    }
    else
    {
        fprintf ( stderr, "\n%s Command : [Esc%s]",
                ( type == UNSUPPORTED ? "Unsupported" : "Illegal" ),
                buffer );
        fprintf ( fout, "%c%s", ESC, buffer );
    }
}
```

Listing 1.4 continues

Listing 1.4 continued

```
/*-----------------------------------------------------------
 * Resets parsing buffer so that the next parsing operation
 * will look at the next command in a combined command.
 * Combined commands have prefix_length chars after the Esc
 * as a common prefix, so the rest of the string is moved
 * forward in the buffer to follow right behind the prefix
 *---------------------------------------------------------*/
void reset_buffer ( int prefix_length )
{
    buf_ptr += 1;  /* point to the next command */
    memmove ( buffer + prefix_length , buf_ptr,
            strlen ( buf_ptr ) + 1 );
}
```

LISTING 1.5 pclprint.h: The Interpreter of PCL Commands

```
/*-------------------- PCLPRINT.H -----------------------
 *    Functions to print the meanings
 *    of PCL code sequences in English
 *
 *    Function names are in alphabetical order
 *
 *    This module requires access to
 *    our_atoi() and reset_buffer() in PCLPARSE.C
 *---------------------------------------------------------*/

void pcl_announce_next_char ( int );
void pcl_assign_font_id ( int );
void pcl_assign_font_temp ( void );
void pcl_call_macro ( void );
void pcl_default_font ( int );
void pcl_delete_fonts ( int );
void pcl_delete_last_char ( void );
void pcl_delete_last_font ( void );
void pcl_delete_macro_id ( void );
void pcl_delete_macros ( void );
void pcl_delete_temp_macros ( void );
void pcl_disable_overlay ( void );
void pcl_disable_underline ( void );
void pcl_display_codes ( int );
void pcl_dot_position ( void );
void pcl_download_font_char ( int );
void pcl_download_font_header ( int );
void pcl_enable_fixed_underline ( void );
void pcl_enable_float_underline ( void );
void pcl_end_raster_graphics ( void );
void pcl_enable_overlay ( void );
void pcl_enter_hpgl_mode ( int );
void pcl_enter_pcl_mode ( int );
void pcl_eol_wrap ( int );
void pcl_execute_macro ( void );
void pcl_fill_rectangle ( int );
void pcl_finish ( void );
void pcl_font_status ( int );
void pcl_graphic_presentation ( int );
```

Listing 1.5 continues

Listing 1.5 continued

```
void pcl_half_line_feed ( void );
void pcl_horz_move ( int );
void pcl_horz_position ( int , long int );
void pcl_identify_macro ( int );
void pcl_imaging_pattern ( int );
void pcl_init ( int, char *[] );
void pcl_line_spacing ( int );
void pcl_line_termination ( char [] );
void pcl_make_macro_perm ( void );
void pcl_make_macro_temp ( void );
void pcl_make_copies ( int );
void pcl_orientation ( int );
void pcl_page_length ( int );
void pcl_page_size ( int );
void pcl_paper_source ( int );
void pcl_pattern_transparency ( int );
void pcl_perforation_skip ( int );
void pcl_push_pop_position ( int );
void pcl_raster_compress ( int );
void pcl_raster_graphics ( void );
void pcl_raster_height ( int );
void pcl_raster_width ( int );
void pcl_raster_Y_offset ( int );
void pcl_reg_char ( int );
void pcl_registration ( int, int );
void pcl_reset ( void );
void pcl_reset_margins ( void );
void pcl_resolution ( int );
void pcl_rotate_print ( int );
void pcl_select_font ( int, int );
void pcl_select_pattern ( int );
void pcl_select_shading ( int );
void pcl_send_raster_data ( int );
void pcl_set_10_pitch ( void );
void pcl_set_12_pitch ( void );
void pcl_set_compressed_mode ( void );
void pcl_set_left_margin ( int );
void pcl_set_right_margin ( int );
void pcl_source_transparency ( int );
void pcl_spacing_type ( int );
void pcl_start_macro_def ( void );
void pcl_start_raster_graphics ( int );
void pcl_stop_macro_def ( void );
void pcl_symbol_set ( int, int );
void pcl_text_length ( int );
void pcl_top_margin ( int );
void pcl_transparent_data ( void );
void pcl_typeface ( int );
void pcl_vert_move ( int );
void pcl_vert_position ( int, long int );

static void get_unit_name ( int, char * );
void pcl_enter_pcl_mode ( int );


void pcl_announce_next_char ( next_char )
{
```

Listing 1.5 continues

Listing 1.5 continued

```
    fprintf ( fout, "[%X]", next_char );
}

void pcl_assign_font_id ( int id )
{
    fprintf ( fout, "[Font Assigned #%d]", id );
}

void pcl_assign_font_temp ( void )
{
    fputs ( "[Last Font Assigned as Temporary]", fout );
}

void pcl_call_macro ( void )
{
    fputs ("[Call Macro]", fout);
}

void pcl_default_font ( int which_one )
{
    fprintf ( fout, "[Default to %s Font]",
             which_one == PRIMARY ? "Primary" : "Secondary" );
}

void pcl_delete_last_char ( void )
{
    fputs ( "[Delete Last Character]", fout );
}

void pcl_delete_last_font ( void )
{
    fputs ( "[Delete Last Font]", fout );
}

void pcl_delete_fonts ( type )
{
    fprintf ( fout, "[Delete %s Fonts]",
             type == TEMPORARY ? "Temporary" : "All" );
}

void pcl_delete_macro_id ( void )
{
    fputs ( "[Delete Macro ID]", fout );
}

void pcl_delete_macros ( void )
{
    fputs ( "[Delete Macros]", fout );
}

void pcl_delete_temp_macros ( void )
{
    fputs ( "[Delete Temp Macros]", fout );
}

void pcl_disable_overlay ( void )
{
    fputs ( "[Disable Macro Overlay]", fout );
```

Listing 1.5 continues

Listing 1.5 continued

```c
}

void pcl_disable_underline (void )
{
    fputs ( "[Turn Off Underline]", fout );
}

void pcl_display_codes ( int state )
{
    fprintf ( fout, "[Turn %s Function Display]",
        ( state == ON ? "ON" : "OFF" ));
}

void pcl_dot_position ( void )   /* Move cursor to dot position */
{
    int i, c, d, x;

    x = *( ++buf_ptr );
    if ( isdigit (x) || x == '-' ||   /* digit = absolute move */
        x == '+' )
            --buf_ptr;                   /* sign = relative move  */
                                         /* if digit, push it back*/
    i = our_atoi ();
    c = *buf_ptr;                    /* X = horiz , Y = vert  */
    d = toupper ( c );

    if ( isdigit ( x ))
        fprintf ( fout, "[Position to %c %d Dots]", d, i );
    else
        fprintf ( fout, "[Position to %c %c%d Dots]", d, x, i );

    if ( islower ( c ))
    {
        combined_command = YES;
        reset_buffer ( 2 );
    }
}

void pcl_download_font_char ( int bytes )      /* Just eat 'em */
{
    for ( ; bytes > 0; bytes-- )
        fgetc ( fin );
}

void pcl_download_font_header ( int bytes )
{
    char name [16];   /* store the font name */
    int i;

    ++buf_ptr;                       /* Get rid of trailing byte in */
                                     /*          PCL command.       */
    for ( i = 0; i < 48; i++ )    /* Eat the first 48 characters */
        fgetc ( fin );
    for ( i = 0; i < 15; i++ )    /* Next 15 chars are font name */
        name[i] = fgetc ( fin );
    for ( i = 14; i > 0; i-- )    /* Null-terminate name after   */
        if ( isgraph (name[i]) ) /* last character              */
        {
            i += 1; break;
```

Listing 1.5 continues

Listing 1.5 continued

```
        }
    name [i] = '\0';

    fprintf ( fout, "[Download Font: %s]", name );

    for ( i = 0; i < (bytes - 63); i++ )
        fgetc ( fin );          /* Eat rest of header */
}

void pcl_enable_fixed_underline ( void )
{
    fputs ( "[Fixed Underline Enabled]", fout );
}

void pcl_enable_float_underline ( void )
{
    fputs ( "[Float Underline Enabled]", fout );
}

void pcl_enable_overlay ( void )
{
    fputs ( "[Enable Macro Overlay]", fout );
}

void pcl_end_raster_graphics ( void )
{
    fputs ( "[End of Raster Graphics]", fout );
}

void pcl_enter_hpgl_mode ( int position )
{
    int c, i;
    char num [7];

    fprintf ( fout, "[Enter HPGL Mode Using % Position]",
            position == '0' ? "Previous HPGL " : "Current PCL " );

    /* Continue reading bytes looking for one of five legitimate
     * Esc commands available in HP-GL/2. If it's not one of them,
     * discard the data. Keep going until EOF or the beginning of
     * "enter PCL mode" command is found. At that point, call pcl_
     * enter_pcl_mode (function below) and return to the parser.
     */

    while (( i = fgetc ( fin )) != EOF )
    {
        if ( i != ESC )
            continue;
        if (( i = fgetc ( fin )) != '*' || i != '%' )
            continue;
        if ( i == '%' )  /* start of "return to PCL" command */
        {
            i = fgetc ( fin ); /* s/b 0 or 1 */
            c = fgetc ( fin ); /* s/b A       */
            if ( c == 'A' )
            {
                pcl_enter_pcl_mode ( i );
                break;
```

Listing 1.5 continues

Listing 1.5   continued

```
        }
    }   /* otherwise, keep looping for chars */
    else
    {                    /* start of HP-GL/2 command */
        if (( i = fgetc ( fin )) != 'c' )
            continue;
        for ( i = 0; i < 6; i++ )  /* load digits into num */
        {
            num [ i ] = c = fgetc ( fin );
            if ( c == EOF )
                return;
            if ( ! isdigit ( c ))
                num [ i ] = '\0';
        }
        i = atoi ( num );

        switch ( c )
        {
            case 'K':
                fprintf ( fout,
                    "[HP-GL/2 Horiz. size: %d inches]", i );
                break;
            case 'L':
                fprintf ( fout,
                    "[HP-GL/2 Vert. size: %d inches]", i );
                break;
            case 'T':
                fprintf ( fout,
                    "[HP-GL/2 Set anchor point to CAP");
                break;
            case 'X':
                fprintf ( fout,
                "[HP-GL/2 Picture Fame Horiz. Size %d Decipoints]",
                i);
                break;
            case 'Y':
                fprintf ( fout,
                "[HP-GL/2 Picture Fame Vert. Size %d Decipoints]",
                i);
                break;
        }
    }
    }
}

void pcl_enter_pcl_mode ( int position )
{
    fprintf ( fout, "[Enter PCL Mode Using % Position]",
        position == '0' ? "Previous PCL " : "Current HPGL " );
}

void pcl_eol_wrap ( int toggle )
{
    fprintf ( fout, "[EOL Wrap Set %s]",
        toggle == ON ? "On" : "Off" );
}

void pcl_execute_macro ( void )
{
```

Listing 1.5   continues

Listing 1.5 continued

```
    fputs ( "[Execute Macro]", fout );
}

void pcl_fill_rectangle ( int style )
{
    static char *fills [] =
    {
        "Solid Black", "Solid White", "Shaded Fill",
        "Cross-Hatched", "User-Defined", "Current Pattern"
    };

    fprintf ( fout, "[Fill Area with %s]", fills [style] );
}

void pcl_finish ( void )   /* The end of the interpretation */
{
    fflush ( fout );
    fcloseall();
    exit ( 1 );
}

void pcl_font_status ( int type )
{
    fprintf ( fout, "[Make Font %s]",
                type == TEMPORARY ? "Temporary" : "Permanent" );
}

void pcl_graphic_presentation ( int mode )
{
        fprintf ( fout, "[Print Raster Image %s]",
            mode == 0 ? "Along Orientation of Logical Page"
                      : "Along Page Width" );
}

void pcl_half_line_feed ( void )
{
    fputs ( "[Half-Line Feed]", fout );
}

void pcl_horz_move ( int units )
{
    fprintf ( fout, "[Horiz. Move %d / 120\"]", units );
}

void pcl_horz_position ( int num, long int units )
{
    char unit_name [11];

    get_unit_name ( units, unit_name );

    fprintf ( fout, "[Horizontal Position to %d %s]",
        num, unit_name ) ;
}

void pcl_identify_macro ( int id )
{
    fprintf ( fout, "[Macro ID # %d]", id );
```

Listing 1.5 continues

Listing 1.5 continued

```c
}

void pcl_imaging_pattern ( pattern )
{
    static char *style [] =
    {
        "Solid Black", "Solid White",
        "HP Defined Shading", "HP Defined Cross-Hatch"
    };

    fprintf ( fout, "[Imaging Pattern: %s]",
                style [ pattern ] );
}

void pcl_init ( int argc, char *argv[] )
{
    /* argc is not used in this function, but it is
     * included as a parameter for good measure and
     * for future replacement functions. Simply
     * passing argv with no argc is strange coding
     * practice anyway.
     */

    fout = fopen ( argv[2], "wb" );

    if (fout == NULL)
    {
        fprintf ( stderr, "Cannot open %s for ouput\n", argv[2] );
        exit ( 7 );
    }
}

void pcl_line_spacing ( int spacing )
{
    fprintf ( fout, "[Spacing at %d lines/inch]", spacing );
}

void pcl_line_termination ( char switches [3] )
{
    int i;
    static const char *terminator [] =
        { "CR", "LF", "FF"};

    fputc ( '[', fout );

    for ( i = 0; i < 3; i++ )
    {
        int j;
        j = 0;

        fprintf ( fout, "%s=", terminator[i] );

        if ( switches[i] & 0x04 )
        {
            fputs( "FF", fout );
            j += 1;
        }
        if ( switches[i] & 0x02 )
```

Listing 1.5 continues

Listing 1.5   continued

```
        {
            if ( j )  fputc ( '+', fout );
            fputs( "LF", fout );
            j += 1;
        }
        if ( switches[i] & 0x01 )
        {
            if ( j )  fputc ( '+', fout );
            fputs( "CR", fout );
        }
        if ( i < 2 )
            fputc ( ',', fout );
    }
    fputc ( ']', fout );
}

void pcl_make_copies ( int copies )
{
    fprintf ( fout, "[Make %d %s]", copies,
            copies == 1 ? "Copy" : "Copies" );
}

void pcl_make_macro_perm ( void )
{
    fputs ( "[Make Macro Permanent]", fout );
}

void pcl_make_macro_temp ( void )
{
    fputs ( "[Make Macro Temporary]", fout );
}

void pcl_orientation ( int j )
{
    fprintf ( fout, "[%s ", j > 1 ? "Reverse" : "Normal" );
    fprintf ( fout, "%s Orientation]",
                    j & 0x01 ? "Landscape" : "Portrait" );
}

void pcl_page_length ( int lines )
{
    fprintf ( fout, "[Page Length: %d Lines]", lines );
}

void pcl_page_size ( int size )
{
    int i, j;
    enum { Paper, Envelope };

    static char *name [] =
    {
        "Executive", "Letter", "Legal", "A4",
        "Monarch", "COM 10", "DL", "C5"
    };

    switch ( size )
    {
```

Listing 1.5   continues

Listing 1.5 continued

```
        case  1:   i = 0; j = Paper;        break;
        case  2:   i = 1; j = Paper;        break;
        case  3:   i = 2; j = Paper;        break;
        case 26:   i = 3; j = Paper;        break;
        case 80:   i = 4; j = Envelope;     break;
        case 81:   i = 5; j = Envelope;     break;
        case 90:   i = 6; j = Envelope;     break;
        case 91:   i = 7; j = Envelope;     break;
    }

    fprintf ( fout, "[%s Size: %s]",
                ( j == Paper ? "Paper" : "Envelope"), name [i] );
}

void pcl_paper_source ( int source )
{
    static char *paper_sources[] =
    {
        "Eject Page",   "Paper Tray Auto Feed",
        "Manual Feed", "Manual Envelope Feed"
    };

    fprintf ( fout, "[Paper Source: %s]",
                paper_sources[source] );
}

void pcl_pattern_transparency ( int opacity )
{
    fprintf ( fout, "[Pattern is %s]",
                opacity == 0 ? "Transparent" : "Opaque" );
}

void pcl_perforation_skip ( int toggle )
{
    fprintf ( fout, "[Perforation Skip %s]",
                ( toggle == 0 ? "Off" : "On" ));
}

void pcl_primary_height ( int points )
{
    fprintf ( fout, "[Primary Height: %d Points]", points );
}

void pcl_primary_pitch ( int pitch )
{
    fprintf ( fout, "[Primary Pitch %d]", pitch );
}

void pcl_push_pop_position ( int toggle )
{
    fprintf ( fout, "[%s Position]",
                toggle == 0 ? "Push" : "Pop" );
}

void pcl_raster_compress ( int method )
{
    static char * compression [] =
    {
        "Uncoded", "RLE", "TIFF", "Delta Row"
```

Listing 1.5 continues

Listing 1.5 continued

```
    };

    fprintf ( fout, "[Raster Compression: %s]",
              compression [method] );

    buf_ptr++;
}
void pcl_raster_height ( int rows )
{
    fprintf ( fout, "[Raster Height %d Rows]", rows );
}

void pcl_raster_width ( int pixels )
{
    fprintf ( fout, "[Raster Width %d Pixels]", pixels );
}

void pcl_raster_Y_offset ( int lines )
{
    fprintf ( fout, "[Vertical Movement: %s Raster Lines]",
              lines );
}

void pcl_rectangle ( int qty, int units, int direction )
{
    char name [11];
    get_unit_name ( units, name );

    fprintf ( fout, "[Rectangle %s of %d %s]",
              direction == VERT ? "Height" : "Width",
              qty, name );
}

void pcl_reg_char ( int c )   /* char that is not PCL */
{
    if ( c == FormFeed )
        fputs ( "[FormFeed]", fout );
    else
        fputc ( c, fout );
}

void pcl_registration ( int distance, int margin )
{
    fprintf ( fout, "[%s Registration: %d Decipoints]",
              margin == TOP ? "Top" : "Left", distance );
}

void pcl_reset ( void )
{
    fputs ( "[Reset Printer]", fout );
}

void pcl_reset_margins ( void )
{
    fputs ( "[Reset Margins]", fout );
}
```

Listing 1.5 continues

Listing 1.5 continued

```c
void pcl_resolution ( int resolution )
{
    fprintf ( fout, "[Resolution: %d DPI]", resolution );
}

void pcl_rotate_print ( int rotation )
{
    fprintf ( fout, "[Print Rotated %d Degrees]", rotation );
}

void pcl_select_font ( int type, int number )
{
    fprintf ( fout, "[Select %s Font # %d]",
            type == PRIMARY ? "Primary" : "Secondary", number );
}

void pcl_select_pattern ( int pattern )
{
    static char * built_in [] =
    {
        "Horiz. Lines", "Vert. Lines",
        "Right Diag.",  "Left Diag.",
        "Square Grid",  "Diag. Grid"
    };

    fprintf ( fout, "[Fill with %s]", built_in [pattern - 1] );
}

void pcl_select_shading ( int shade )
{
    fprintf ( fout, "[Shading of %d %%]", shade );
}

void pcl_send_raster_data ( int bytes )
{
    int i;

    fprintf ( fout, "[Receive %d Bytes Raster Data]", bytes );

    for ( i = 0; i < bytes; i++ )   /* Eat up the data bytes */
        fgetc ( fin );
}

void pcl_set_10_pitch ( void )
{
    fputs ( "[Set to 10 Pitch]", fout );
}

void pcl_set_12_pitch ( void )
{
    fputs ( "[Set to 12 Pitch]", fout );
}

void pcl_set_compressed_mode ( void )
{
    fputs ( "[Compressed Mode On]", fout );
}
```

Listing 1.5 continues

Listing 1.5 continued

```c
void pcl_set_left_margin ( int column )
{
    fprintf ( fout, "[Set Left Margin to %d]", column );
}

void pcl_set_right_margin (int column )
{
    fprintf ( fout, "[Set Right Margin to %d]", column );
}

void pcl_source_transparency ( int opacity )
{
    fprintf ( fout, "[Source is %s]",
              opacity == 0 ? "Transparent" : "Opaque" );
}

void pcl_spacing_type ( int type )
{
    fprintf ( fout, "[%s Spacing]",
              type == 1 ? "Proportional" : "Fixed" );
}

void pcl_start_macro_def ( void )
{
    fputs ( "[Start of Macro Definition]", fout );
}

void pcl_start_raster_graphics ( int position )
{
    fprintf ( fout, "[Start Raster Graphics at %s]",
              position == 1 ? "Current Cursor" :
                              "Left Graphic Margin" );
}

void pcl_stop_macro_def ( void )
{
    fputs ( "[End of Macro Definition]", fout );
}

void pcl_stroke_weight ( int weight )
{
    static char * weight_name [] =
    {
        "Ultra Thin",  "Extra Thin",   "Thin",
        "Extra Light", "Demi Light",   "Semi Light",
        "Medium",
        "Semi Bold",   "Demi Bold",    "Bold", "Extra Bold",
        "Black",       "Extra Black", "Ultra Black"
    };

    fprintf ( fout, "[%s Stroke Weight]", weight_name [weight] );
}

void pcl_symbol_set ( int id_num, int id_ltr )
{
    if ( id_ltr == 'U' || id_ltr == 'u' )
    {
        if ( id_num == 8 )
            fputs ( "[Roman-8 Symbol Set]", fout );
```

Listing 1.5 continues

Listing 1.5 continued

```c
        if ( id_num == 10 )
            fputs ( "[IBM-PC Symbol Set]", fout );
        return;
    }

    fprintf ( fout, "[Symbol Set %2d%c]", id_num,
            toupper( id_ltr ));
}

void pcl_text_length ( int length )
{
    fprintf ( fout, "[Text Length: %d Lines]", length );
}

void pcl_top_margin ( int margin )
{
    fprintf ( fout, "[Top Margin: %d Lines]", margin );
}

void pcl_transparent_data ( void )
{
    /* Prints characters that normally are  */
    /* commands to the LaserJet. Ex: Esc, FF */

    char num_str[6];
    int c, i, j;

    j = our_atoi ();

    fprintf ( fout, "[Transparent Print of Next %d Bytes]", j );

    for ( i = 0; i < j; i++ )   /* Output the transparent data */
    {
        c = fgetc ( fin );
        fputc ( c, fout );
    }

    combined_command = NO;
}

void pcl_typeface ( int face )
{
    fprintf ( fout, "[Typeface %d]", face );
}

void pcl_vert_move (int units )
{
    fprintf ( fout, "[Vert. Move of %d / 48\"]", units );
}

void pcl_vert_position ( int num, long int units )
{
    char unit_name [11];

    get_unit_name ( units, unit_name );

    fprintf ( fout, "[Vertical Position to %d %s]",
            num, unit_name );
```

Listing 1.5 continues

Listing 1.5 continued

```
}

/*============== PCL_ support Functions ==============*/

static void get_unit_name (int unit, char *unit_name)
{
    switch (unit)
    {
        case POINTS:
            strcpy ( unit_name, "Points" );     break;
        case DECIPOINTS:
            strcpy ( unit_name, "Decipoints" ); break;
        case ROWS:
            strcpy ( unit_name, "Columns" );    break;
        case COLUMNS:
            strcpy ( unit_name, "Columns" );    break;
        default:
            strcpy ( unit_name, "? Units" );    break;
    }
}
```

2
Built-in Graphics

Introduction

Chapter 1 showed how the page is laid out in the world of the HP LaserJet, how the margins are set, and how the printhead or cursor is moved. This chapter presents the built-in graphics capabilities of the LaserJet printers.

The LaserJet comes with certain simple pattern-drawing features available directly through PCL commands. These abilities, coded into the LaserJet firmware, are limited to defining rectangular areas and filling them in with either patterns or shading. While these features appear at first blush to offer little value in terms of substantial graphics capabilities, they can be manipulated imaginatively to produce a wide range of special effects. They are also important in creating forms, generating bar codes, and many other business applications. Graphics that exceed the built-in commands have to be programmed using techniques that will be introduced in Chapter 3 and developed in detail in Chapters 7 through 10.

The techniques we present in this chapter all rely on the ability to define a rectangular area in which the graphical activity will occur. Defining the rectangle requires placing the cursor at the upper left corner of the area. Cursor positioning was discussed in Chapter 1 and should be reviewed as needed.

Once the cursor has been positioned, the dimensions of the rectangle must be specified by stating the horizontal and vertical dimensions. To specify the horizontal dimension (the width), two commands may be used:

    Esc * c # H

where # is the width in decipoints, and

    Esc * c # A

where # is the width in dots. Likewise, the vertical dimension can be specified using a pair of commands that differ only in the choice of the unit of measure (dots or decipoints):

```
Esc * c # V
```

where **#** is the height in decipoints, and

```
Esc * c # B
```

where **#** is the height in dots.

A decipoint (1/720") can be specified with a precision of up to two decimal places. A dot (1/300") can be specified only in whole numbers. The added precision of decipoints is a bit deceptive, since the measurement in decipoints will be converted to points at print time. To obtain exact sizing, therefore, it is better to specify sizes in dots, since no rounding or conversion will occur.

Establishing the location and size of a rectangle does not result in any printing. Next you must specify what is to be printed inside the rectangle. The choices are fairly straightforward; the area can be shaded using various shades of gray or solid black, or filled with one of six predefined patterns called **cross-hatches**.

Cross-hatch Patterns

The term cross-hatch usually connotes a pattern of intersecting lines. On the Laser-Jet cross-hatch patterns comprise intersecting lines, parallel vertical lines, and parallel horizontal lines. Figure 2.1 shows the six possible cross-hatch patterns.

Selecting a particular pattern is a two-step process. Once the rectangle has been defined, a command must identify what kind of graphic will fill the rectangle. The command is:

```
Esc * c # P
```

FIGURE 2.1 Samples of the Six Built-in Cross-hatch Patterns

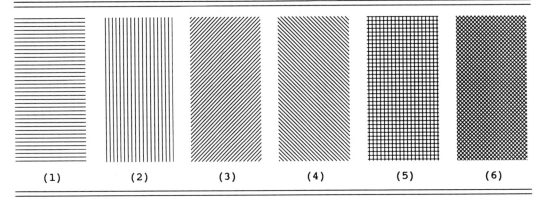

(1)   (2)   (3)   (4)   (5)   (6)

where # can have one of the following values:

0 fill with black
1 fill with white (erase)
2 shaded fill
3 cross-hatch fill
5 current-pattern fill

To generate cross-hatches, select the value **3**. (The other values in this command are discussed later in this chapter.)

Once a cross-hatch fill has been specified, it is necessary to identify which of the six cross-hatch patterns to use. They are numbered 1 through 6, as illustrated in Figure 2.1. The command that identifies which cross-hatch to use is:

Esc * c # G

where # is the cross-hatch number. The code that generates Figure 2.1 appears in Listing 2.1. Note that the dimensions of the panels in the illustrations have been re-

LISTING 2.1 Creating the Cross-hatch Patterns in Figure 2.1

```
/*-------------------- XHATCH1.C --------------------
 * Generate a sample page of the six cross-hatch patterns.
 * Uses FOPEN_LJ and must be linked to this routine.
 *
 * Usage:   XHATCH1
 *-----------------------------------------------------*/

#include <stdio.h>
#include "ljmain.h"

void fill_type ( int );
void pattern ( int );
void position_cursor ( int, int );
void rect_height ( int );
void rect_width ( int );

void main ( void )
{
    int i;
    int x, y;  /* the x and y coordinates of cursor */

    if (( prt = fopen_laserjet ( "PRN" )) == NULL )
    {
        fputs ( "Unable to open printer", stderr );
        exit();
    }

    fprintf ( prt, "%cE", ESC );    /* reset the printer */
```

Listing 2.1 continues

Listing 2.1 continued

```
    /*-------------------------------------------------------
     *   position the cursor 1/2" from the left, 1" from top
     *   using dots as the units of measure (300/inch);
     *   then cycle through the six patterns, printing
     *   the rectangles 1" wide, 2" high, 1/4" apart.
     *-----------------------------------------------------*/

    x = 150; y = 300;   /* start at x = 1/2", y = 1" */

    for ( i = 1; i <= 6; i++ )
    {
        position_cursor ( x, y );
        rect_width ( 300 );
        rect_height ( 600 );
        pattern ( i );
        fill_type ( 3 );                /* use cross-hatch    */
        x += 375;                       /* move 1.25" to right */
    }

    /*-------------------------------------------------------
     *   position under each cross-hatch panel and print the
     *   cross-hatch pattern identification number.
     *-----------------------------------------------------*/

    x = 260; y = 975;
    for ( i = 1; i <= 6; i++ )
    {
        position_cursor ( x, y );
        fprintf ( prt, "(%d)", i );
        x += 375;
    }

    fprintf ( prt, "%c", FormFeed );   /* print it! */
}

/*-----------------------------------------------------------
 * Position the cusor (using dot units) at x, y
 *---------------------------------------------------------*/
void position_cursor ( int x, int y )
{
    fprintf ( prt, "%c*p%dx%dY", ESC, x, y );
}

/*-----------------------------------------------------------
 * Specify the rectangle width in dots
 *---------------------------------------------------------*/
void rect_width ( int width )
{
    fprintf ( prt, "%c*c%dA", ESC, width );
}

/*-----------------------------------------------------------
 * Specify the rectangle height in dots
 *---------------------------------------------------------*/
void rect_height ( int height )
{
    fprintf ( prt, "%c*c%dB", ESC, height );
```

Listing 2.1 continues

Listing 2.1 continued

```
}
/*------------------------------------------------------------
 * Select the pattern # to print
 *---------------------------------------------------------*/
void pattern ( int selection )
{
    fprintf ( prt, "%c*c%dG", ESC, selection );
}

/*------------------------------------------------------------
 * Select the type of fill: shading, cross-hatch, etc.
 *---------------------------------------------------------*/
void fill_type ( int type )
{
    fprintf ( prt, "%c*c%dP", ESC, type );
}
```

duced somewhat to fit into the book's page size. Running the code in Listing 2.1 will produce full-size panels 2 inches high and 1 inch wide.

Let us examine some aspects of the code. Notice that, after printing each pattern, the cursor must be moved across the area just printed to begin printing the next pattern. This is important. When you define and print patterns, the cursor position remains unchanged. The cursor is originally placed in the upper left corner of the rectangle and remains there while the rectangle is defined, filled, and printed. To begin a new rectangle, therefore, the cursor must be moved across the printed rectangle to its new position.

Cursor positioning for printing rectangles is an exception to the positioning rules set forth in Chapter 1. Even though cursor position is limited to the logical page, rectangles can be printed outside the text area and without regard to the perforation skip setting. Attempting to print outside the logical page, however, will cause the rectangular area to be clipped at the boundaries of the logical page.

Combining Cross-Hatch Patterns

Cross-hatch patterns can be combined by printing two or more different patterns within the same rectangle. To do this, do not move the cursor after printing the first pattern. Select a second pattern and print it using the same rectangle defined for the first pattern. Figure 2.2 gives three examples of the novel effects that can be obtained using this technique. The code for printing the patterns in Figure 2.2 is given in Listing 2.2. This replaces the main printing loop in Listing 2.1; all other code remains the same.

Refer to the patterns printed in Figure 2.1 and note that combining patterns 1

FIGURE 2.2 The Effects Generated by Combining Cross-hatch Patterns

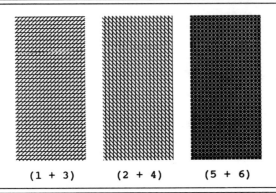

(1 + 3)   (2 + 4)   (5 + 6)

and 2 will generate pattern 5 and combining patterns 3 and 4 will generate pattern 6.

Shading

Shading is the technique of filling an area with a given color. Because in the LaserJet the color is black, shading is generally expressed as a percentage, where 0 percent represents no color (white) and 100 percent represents solid color (black). On the LaserJet the percentages in between are often referred to as gray. Remember, though, when discussing gray or shading with professionals in the graphics industry, that the professionals refer to all shadings strictly by percentages and that terms like light gray have little meaning. In fact, to graphics professionals, gray represents a different color from one mixed strictly of black and white; it may often contain hints of blue or some other color.

Shading on the LaserJet can be rendered in eight steps of increasing darkness. Figure 2.3 illustrates these shades. Each shade covers a range of percentages. The percentage of shade is specified with the following command:

    Esc * c # G

where **#** represents the percentage. Percentages that fall within a given range all print at the same level of shading. For example, any shading between 21 and 35 percent prints like the fourth panel in Figure 2.3.

Note that the command for specifying shading is exactly the same as that for specifying a cross-hatch pattern. This dual meaning was touched on briefly in the comments for the PCL interpreter presented in Chapter 1. The critical question is: how does the LaserJet know which of the two meanings is intended? The answer

LISTING 2.2 Main Printing Code for Examples in Figure 2.2

```
position_cursor ( x, y );    /* Patterns 1 & 3 */
rect_width ( 300 );
rect_height ( 600 );
pattern ( 1 );
fill_type ( 3 );
pattern ( 3 );
fill_type ( 3 );
x += 375;

position_cursor ( x, y );    /* Patterns 2 & 4 */
rect_width ( 300 );
rect_height ( 600 );
pattern ( 2 );
fill_type ( 3 );
pattern ( 4 );
fill_type ( 3 );
x += 375;

position_cursor ( x, y );    /* Patterns 5 & 6 */
rect_width ( 300 );
rect_height ( 600 );
pattern ( 5 );
fill_type ( 3 );
pattern ( 6 );
fill_type ( 3 );
x += 375;

/*---------------------------------------------------------
 *   position under each cross-hatch panel and print the
 *   cross-hatch pattern identification number.
 *-----------------------------------------------------*/

x = 200; y = 975;
position_cursor ( x, y );
fprintf ( prt, "(1 + 3)", i );
x += 375;

position_cursor ( x, y );
fprintf ( prt, "(2 + 4)", i );
x += 375;

position_cursor ( x, y );
fprintf ( prt, "(5 + 6)", i );
x += 375;
```

comes in the form of the PCL command presented at the beginning of the section on cross-hatches:

Esc * c # P

To generate the cross-hatch patterns, **#** is assigned a value of **3**. To generate shading, **#** is assigned a value of **2**. Hence by use of a **2** or a **3** in this command, the LaserJet knows whether shading or cross-hatching is being selected.

FIGURE 2.3   Samples of the Eight Levels of Shading on the LaserJet

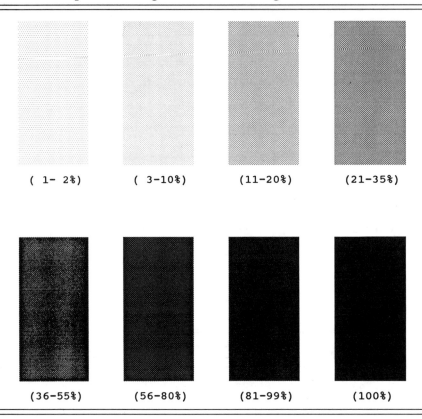

(1- 2%)   (3-10%)   (11-20%)   (21-35%)

(36-55%)   (56-80%)   (81-99%)   (100%)

The code in Listing 2.3 shows how to generate the shading examples shown in Figure 2.3. It calls the same routines given in Listing 2.1. These routines are not presented a second time. (Note that the source code diskette that accompanies this book [see coupon at back] contains the full source code for all these examples.)

The panels in Figure 2.3 illustrate some difficulties in using shading darker than 35 percent. The most notable difficulty of the darker panels is that text becomes difficult to read when placed on a background this dark. Graphic artists generally use shading greater than 35 percent to print white letters on a dark background. Another drawback of the darker shading as printed on the LaserJet is that it tends to be uneven. Unless a brand new printer is used with a completely fresh cartridge and just the right kind of paper, chances are good that the black (especially at 100 percent) will not be uniformly dark. Lighter areas such as patches or faint lines will generally appear, spoiling the black and making for an unattractive appearance. Finally, note how little difference exists between the 35 percent panel and the 100 per-

LISTING 2.3   The Main Program to Generate Shading Examples in Figure 2.3

```
/*-------------------- SHADING.C --------------------
 * Generate a sample page of the eight shading panels.
 * Uses FOPEN_LJ and must be linked to this routine.
 *
 * Usage:   SHADING
 *-----------------------------------------------------*/

#include <stdio.h>
#include "ljmain.h"

void fill_type ( int );
void pattern ( int );
void position_cursor ( int, int );
void rect_height ( int );
void rect_width ( int );

#define shading(x) pattern(x)   /* same command on the LJ */

FILE *prt, *fopen_laserjet();

void main ( void )
{
    int i;
    int x, y;   /* the x and y coordinates of cursor */

    /* shading percentages */
    static int levels [] = { 1, 3, 11, 21, 36, 56, 81, 100 };

    if (( prt = fopen_laserjet ( "PRN" )) == NULL )
    {
        fputs ( "Unable to open printer", stderr );
        exit();
    }
    fprintf ( prt, "%cE", ESC );    /* reset the printer */

    /*-----------------------------------------------------
     *  position the cursor 1/2" from the left, 1" from top
     *  using dots as the units of measure (300/inch);
     *  then cycle through four shadings, printing
     *  the rectangles 1" wide, 2" high, 1/2" apart.
     *-----------------------------------------------------*/

    x = 300; y = 300;  /* start at x = 1", y = 1" */

    for ( i = 1; i <= 4; i++ )
    {
        position_cursor ( x, y );
        rect_width ( 300 );
        rect_height ( 600 );
        shading ( levels[i-1] );
        fill_type ( 2 );                /* use shading       */
        x += 450;                       /* move 1.5" to right */
    }

    /*-----------------------------------------------------
     *  position under each shading panel and print the
     *  shading percentage.
     *-----------------------------------------------------*/
```

Listing 2.3   continues

Listing 2.3 continued

```
    x = 338; y = 975;
    for ( i = 1; i <= 4; i++ )
    {
        position_cursor ( x, y );
        if ( levels[i - 1] != 100 )
            fprintf ( prt, "(%2d-%2d%%)", levels[i-1], levels[i] - 1 );
        else
            fprintf ( prt, "(100%%)" );

        x += 450;
    }

    /*-----------------------------------------------------------
     * Now repeat the previous cycle for the second row
     *---------------------------------------------------------*/

    x = 300; y = 1200; /* start at x = 1", y = 4" */

    for ( i = 5; i <= 8; i++ )
    {
        position_cursor ( x, y );
        rect_width ( 300 );
        rect_height ( 600 );
        shading ( levels[i-1] );
        fill_type ( 2 );                /* use shading     */
        x += 450;                       /* move 1.5" to right */
    }

    x = 338; y = 1875;
    for ( i = 5; i <= 8; i++ )
    {
        position_cursor ( x, y );
        if ( levels[i - 1] != 100 )
            fprintf ( prt, "(%2d-%2d%%)", levels[i-1], levels[i] - 1 );
        else
        {
            x += 30; position_cursor ( x, y );
            fprintf ( prt, "(100%%)" );
        }
        x += 450;
    }

    fprintf ( prt, "%c", FormFeed );  /* print it! */
}

/* There follow the called routines from XHATCH1.C */
```

cent panel. The human eye is more capable of detecting variations in light shadings than in dark; another reason for avoiding heavy use of the darker shadings.

Because of these difficulties we make the following suggestions on shadings. Use shading below 35 percent for most graphical applications and all text applications. Shading at 100 percent should be used only in small, preferably narrow areas, where variations in print density will not show. Shadings between 36 and 99 percent should rarely be used except to frame a lighter area. In such cases, use only one dark shading since it is difficult to detect variations in shading above 35 percent.

Although a shading of 100 percent tells the LaserJet to print a solid black rectangle, this command is not the best one for this purpose. The following section shows a more efficient alternative.

Straight Lines

There is no built-in PCL command for printing straight lines. Rather, straight lines are printed as very long thin rectangles filled in with black. A very thin line across a standard size sheet, for example, can be defined as a rectangle 2400 dots wide (8" × 300 dots per inch) and 1 dot high. Once it is filled in, a line is printed. Likewise a vertical line might be defined as 3000 dots high and 1 dot wide.

Before looking at some examples, let us examine an efficient command to fill rectangles with black. In the printing trade, a black line is called a **rule**. Specifically, a rule is a solid-filled rectangular area; in other words, a straight line with 100 percent shading. In the section on shading, commands were presented for creating rules by defining a rectangle, selecting shading as a fill, and then specifying the degree of shading. Since shading at 100 percent is such a common activity, a PCL command exists for that purpose alone. The command is already familiar from discussion of its other variations.

Esc * c # P

where **#** can have these values:

0   black fill, or rule
1   erase or white fill
2   shaded fill (discussed previously)
3   cross-hatch fill (discussed previously)
5   current pattern fill

We will rely on value **0** for rules. Drawing a simple horizontal line with the thickness of 2 dots (straight lines of 1 dot generally don't work well since any lightness in the printing will make parts appear to be missing) requires only the following code (presuming the cursor has been positioned):

```
/* print a line 2 dots high and 5" long */

rect_width ( 1500 );
rect_height ( 2 );
fill_type ( 0 )
```

Given that lines are printed as flattened rectangles, it is easy to see that a frame, or box, is itself printed as four lines which meet at the ends; or as four rectangles each of which constitutes a side. An illustration of two frames, one within the other, appears in Figure 2.4. The code to generate them appears in Listing 2.4. Again, it relies on the functions presented in Listing 2.1, so those functions will not be repeated.

A quick examination of the code shows that the technique is straightforward to the point of being prosaic. A rule is printed for each side of the frame. By making sure the rules meet at the ends, a rectangular frame is formed. This technique is intuitive and effective, but laborious. It is, however, the only technique for drawing rectangles available on LaserJet printers such as the LaserJet II, which do not support PCL level 5. Later printers can utilize erasing, discussed next.

Erasing

With the advent of PCL level 5 on the LaserJet III, a new feature became available: erasing. Erasing consists of filling an area with white; the term **white fill** is used in LaserJet manuals. In fact, there is no "white" to fill with; instead, dots that are set to print are actually cleared. An area without print appears white. Obviously if blue paper is being used, the white area will be blue not white.

Erasing a rectangular area is achieved by the command we have used already:

```
Esc * c # P
```

FIGURE 2.4 Two Frames Drawn by the Code in Listing 2.4 (Shown at Half Size)

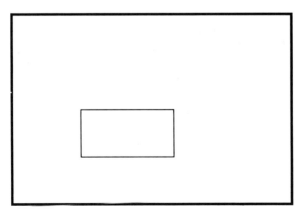

LISTING 2.4   Drawing Frames with Each Side Defined as a Rectangle

```
/*--------------------  FRAME1.C  --------------------
 * Create a set of frames by drawing each side as a rectangle
 * Uses FOPEN_LJ and must be linked to this routine.
 *
 * Usage:    FRAME1
 *-------------------------------------------------------*/

#include <stdio.h>
#include "ljmain.h"

void draw_frame ( int, int, int, int, int );
void fill_type ( int );
void pattern ( int );
void position_cursor ( int, int );
void rect_height ( int );
void rect_width ( int );

#define shading(x) pattern(x)   /* same command on the LJ */

FILE *prt, *fopen_laserjet();

void main ( void )
{
    int x, y;  /* the x and y coordinates of cursor */
    int height, width, border;

    if (( prt = fopen_laserjet ( "PRN" )) == NULL )
    {
        fputs ( "Unable to open printer", stderr );
        exit();
    }

    fprintf ( prt, "%cE", ESC );     /* reset the printer */

    x = 300; y = 300;   /* start at x = 1", y = 1" */
    height = 1200;      /* 4" high */
    width  = 1800;      /* 6" wide */
    border = 15;        /* border 1/20" wide */

    draw_frame ( x, y, height, width, border );

    draw_frame ( 750, 900, 300, 600, 5 ); /* draw inner frame */

    fprintf ( prt, "%c", FormFeed );  /* print it! */
}

/*----------------------------------------------------------
 * Draw a frame using technique of drawing a rectangle for
 * each side. Passed arguments are (all units in dots):
 *   x, y :   location of upper left corner
 *   height:  height of frame;
 *   width:   width of frame;
 *   border:  width of border
 *----------------------------------------------------------*/
void draw_frame ( int x, int y,
                  int height, int width,
                  int border )
```

Listing 2.4   continues

Listing 2.4 continued

```
{
    /*--- Left Vertical ---*/

    position_cursor ( x, y );
    rect_width ( border );
    rect_height ( height );
    fill_type ( 0 );               /* use black rule    */

    /*--- Right Vertical ---*/.

    position_cursor (( x + width - border ), y );
    rect_width ( border );
    rect_height ( height );
    fill_type ( 0 );

    /*--- Top Horizontal ---*/

    position_cursor ( x, y );
    rect_width ( width );
    rect_height ( border );
    fill_type ( 0 );

    /*--- Bottom Horizontal ---*/

    position_cursor ( x, ( y + height - border ));
    rect_width ( width );
    rect_height ( border );
    fill_type ( 0 );
}
/*** There follow called routines from Listing 2.1 ***/
```

where # is 1 to erase. The technique is the same as that used to draw rules: a rectangle is defined and then filled with white (rather than black) using this command. Note that erasing a rectangle only clears it at that specific moment. If writing later occurs in an area that was previously erased, printing *will* occur.

By use of erasing it is possible to draw frames more simply than the earlier method of drawing four rectangles each representing one side. Now the full rectangle can be drawn and filled in with black. Then a second, slightly smaller rectangle is defined within the black rectangle and it is filled with white. The result is a border around a white-filled rectangle, creating the effect of a frame. Said another way: take a black square, put a small white square inside it; what is left is a black frame. This technique is faster, requires fewer PCL commands, and is more elegant. It is also less portable, since PCL level 5 must be on the printer in question. If PCL 5 is not available on the LaserJet, the command to white-fill the inner rectangle will be ignored and you will see a black rectangle instead. If you know that the output will be sent to a LaserJet III or later model, use the erase technique, otherwise build your borders piece by piece.

LISTING 2.5 Drawing a Frame Using the White Fill Technique

```
/*-----------------------------------------------------------
 * Draw a frame using technique of drawing the outer rect.
 * and erasing an inner rectangle. Requires PCL 5 or later.
 *  x, y :    location of upper left corner
 *  height:   height of frame;
 *  width:    width of frame;
 *  border:   width of border
 *-----------------------------------------------------*/
void draw_frame ( int x, int y,
                  int height, int width,
                  int border )
{
    position_cursor ( x, y );
    rect_width ( width );
    rect_height ( height );
    fill_type ( 0 );    /* fill outer rect. with black */

    position_cursor ( x + border, y + border );
    rect_width ( width - 2 * border );
    rect_height ( height - 2 * border );
    fill_type ( 1 );    /* fill inner rect. with "white" */
}
```

Listing 2.5 presents the relevant code for printing a rectangle using the erase technique. It is a drop-in replacement for the `draw_frame` function in Listing 2.4.

Programming Project: Postal Bar Code

If you live in the United States, you probably have noticed the bar code that appears along the bottom of many pieces of mail you receive. This bar code is an encrypted representation of the addressee's zip code. An example is shown in Figure 2.5.

At the post office, incoming mail is scanned for this bar code. If none is found, the scanner attempts to read the zip code. If it can be recognized, the scanner con-

FIGURE 2.5 A Postal Bar Code for 90401-1066

```
Barcode for 90401-1066 is:
```

II.I..II....I..III.....II...IIII....II...II....III

verts the number to bar code and prints it on the face of the letter along the bottom edge. All subsequent sorting, bundling, and delivery processes look for this bar code. When it is found, processing continues apace. If it is absent, the letter is routed to another, less efficient process that reads the zip code. Using postal bar codes whenever possible expedites delivery, and in large mailings, slightly reduces the cost per piece of mail.

Printing these bar codes requires knowledge of the postal bar-coding scheme and the requirements for size and placement of the bar codes. This information is available free of charge from local post offices in "Publication 12: Preparing Business and Courtesy Mail." Before launching into the programming code to generate these bar codes, we give an overview of the bar code system and its requirements for our implementation.

The bar codes represent zip codes, which can consists of either five or nine digits. Each digit is encoded as a series of five vertical lines, some of which are short and others of which are long. Long bars are assigned a value of 1, short bars a value of 0. Each digit in the zip code is represented by five bars, two of which must be ones (long bars). The five positions occupied by bars are assigned values of (from left to right): 7, 4, 2, 1, and 0. (This scheme is very different from traditional computer models where the 1 and 0 occupy the same position.)

Under this model, 1 is assigned the value 00011, that is, $1 + 0 = 1$. Two is 00101; 6 is 01100. Zero is rendered by a special value: 11. In other words, the bar code 11000 is recognized as a special value, zero. The list of bar codes appears as the **static** array of strings **code** in **main( )** in Listing 2.6. Each bar code begins and ends with

LISTING 2.6 Generating Postal Bar Codes from a Zip Code

```
/*--------------------- BARCODE.C ---------------------
 *  Prints postal barcodes for zip codes per USPS specs
 *  Must be linked to fopen_laserjet() routine.
 *  Usage:
 *              BARCODE zipcode
 *
 *  where zipcode can use 99999 or 99999-9999 formats
 *----------------------------------------------------*/

#include <stdio.h>
#include <stdlib.h>

#include "ljmain.h"

#define LONG   '1'
#define SHORT  '0'

FILE *prt, *fopen_laserjet();

void print_bar ( char );
void print_bar_code ( char * );
void print_digit_barcode ( char * );
```

Listing 2.6 continues

Listing 2.6 continued

```c
void print_bar_code ( char *zip )
{
    static char * code [10] =
    {
                    /* 74210 */   /* The value of each position */
        /* 0 */     "11000",
        /* 1 */     "00011",
        /* 2 */     "00101",
        /* 3 */     "00110",
        /* 4 */     "01001",
        /* 5 */     "01010",
        /* 6 */     "01100",
        /* 7 */     "10001",
        /* 8 */     "10010",
        /* 9 */     "10100"
    };
    char *p;
    int i, j, len, sum;
    i = sum = 0;

    len = strlen ( zip );
    if ( len != 5 && len != 10 )
    {
        fprintf ( stderr, "zip %s must be 5 or 10 characters", zip );
        exit ( EXIT_FAILURE );
    }

    while ( *zip )
    {
        if ( *zip == '-' )              /* skip the dash in ZIP+4 */
        {
            zip += 1;
            continue;
        }

        j = *zip - '0';                 /* convert to a number */

        if ( i == 0 )                   /* no digits done yet? */
            print_bar ( LONG );         /* then do initial bar */

        p = code [ j ];                 /* point p at the pattern */

        print_digit_barcode ( p );      /* print it */

        i   += 1;                       /* count digits processed */
        sum += j;                       /* k = sum of zip code */
        zip += 1;                       /* go on to next digit */
    }

    sum %= 10;                          /* remainder of sum/10 */

    p = code [ sum ? 10 - sum : 0 ];/* check digit = 10 - sum */
    print_digit_barcode ( p );

    print_bar ( LONG );                 /* closing bar */
}
```

Listing 2.6 continues

Listing 2.6 continued

```c
void print_digit_barcode ( char * p )
{
    while ( *p )
    {
        print_bar ( *p );
        p += 1;
    }
}

void print_bar ( char size )
{
    if ( size == SHORT )
        fprintf ( prt, "%c*p+21Y", ESC );

    /* bar width is .015 - .025 inch */
    /* 6 dots = .020 inch            */

    fprintf ( prt, "%c*c%dA", ESC, 6 );

    /* bar height is:
        LONG:    .115 - .135 inch  or   35 - 41 dots
        SHORT:   .040 - .060 inch  or   14 - 20 dots

        we use: LONG 38 dots, SHORT 17 dots
     */

    fprintf ( prt, "%c*c%dB", ESC,
                ( size == SHORT ? 17 : 38 ));

    /* specify print as black */

    fprintf ( prt, "%c*c0P", ESC );

    /* spacing from start of one bar to start of next bar
       is .045 - .050 inch or 14 - 15 dots
       we'll use a relative move of 15 dots.
     */

    fprintf ( prt, "%c*p+15X", ESC );

    if ( size == SHORT )
        fprintf ( prt, "%c*p-21Y", ESC );

}

main ( int argc, char * argv[] )
{
    if ( argc < 2 )
    {
        fputs ( "Usage: BARCODE zipcode", stderr );
        exit ( EXIT_FAILURE );
    }

    prt = fopen_laserjet ( "PRN" );
    if ( prt == NULL )
    {
        fputs ("Error opening printer\n", stderr );
        exit ( EXIT_FAILURE );
    }
```

Listing 2.6 continues

Listing 2.6 continued

```
    fprintf ( prt, "\n\r\tBar code for %s  ", argv[1] );
    print_bar_code ( argv[1] );
    fprintf ( prt, "%c", FormFeed );    /* eject the page */
    return ( EXIT_SUCCESS );
}
```

a single long line (a 1). The last digit of each bar code is a check digit. This check digit is computed by first summing all the digits in the zip code. This sum is then subtracted from the next highest number evenly divisible by 10. The result is the check digit. For example, if the sum of the digits in the zip code is 63, this number is subtracted from the next highest multiple of 10 (70), and the result (7) is the check digit. The check digit is printed after the zip code but before the closing long bar.

The postal specifications relating to size and position of the individual bars are embedded as comments in the source code in Listing 2.6, along with explanations of how these specifications are converted into suitable LaserJet units. The program itself, **barcode.c**, accepts a zip code on the command line and then prints the zip code beside its corresponding bar code. It is assumed that in a real-world application, the reader would take the bar code routines and apply them against zip code data read from a file.

The bar codes are a series of bars (or rules) of uniform width and one of two heights. Printing the bar code consists of converting the digits into bars and printing the bars as small black-filled rules. Most of the techniques used in this project were explained in this chapter. Notice that the y component of the cursor position changes with long and short bars, since the cursor is always placed in the upper left corner of the rule. Although it appears that the bars all start at a common baseline, they in fact start from the two top positions and the common baseline.

A final note regarding postal bar codes: It is expected that in 1991 the U.S. Postal Service will begin using scanners that will recognize these bar codes when they appear anywhere on the face of the envelope. Presently they must be printed no more than 4 inches and no less than 3⅞ inches from the right edge of the envelope. The baseline of the bar code must be ⅛ to ⅜ of an inch from the bottom edge of the envelope.

Now that we've examined the built-in graphics capabilities, we can move on to discuss raster graphics, the heart and soul of LaserJet technology.

3

Introduction to Raster Graphics

Introduction

The first two chapters illustrated the use of printer-control-language (PCL) commands to move and position the cursor, print text, set margins, draw straight lines, shade boxes, and exploit basic built-in graphics features of the LaserJet. These commands are sufficient for straightforward kinds of applications: designing and printing forms, shading and boxing text (such as sidebars in magazines), adding or creating imaginative frames, and so on. To unleash the LaserJet's true graphics abilities, you have to drop down to the level of raster graphics.

Raster graphics are images constructed by specifying the dots required to print them. In raster graphics, you are at the lowest level of operation in a dot-addressing mode, and every action must be manually specified. In many ways, raster graphics is the assembly language of LaserJet programming. It is low-level and requires a lot of code, but it handles tasks that cannot be handled any other way. It (unlike assembly language) is much slower and far less compact than the higher-level functions. Because of this, raster graphics should be used only when no other means are available.

This chapter presents an introduction to the basic techniques of raster graphics. Chapters 7 through 10 present in-depth discussions of raster images with examples for generating polygons, curves, and so on, as well as many useful techniques for optimizing raster performance. You need to be conversant with the information presented in this chapter in order to understand the techniques presented in Chapters 7 through 10.

Basics

The technique for printing raster graphics is simple and straightforward. Raster images are printed one line at a time, each line being one dot high. The size of the dot can be set by software and is generally specified just before printing begins. Allowable values are 75, 100, 150, or 300 dots per inch. After specifying print resolution (the size of the dot), a PCL command tells the LaserJet to switch to raster-graphics mode. A second command tells the printer how many bytes of raster data occur in the raster line about to be sent. The raster line is then sent. Once the line is sent, the process begins again: a new command gives the length of the next raster line, and the line is sent to the printer. The cycle continues until the last line has been sent. When the raster image is complete, a command is issued to switch the LaserJet out of raster-graphics mode.

The raster line consists of a series of bits, each of which controls one LaserJet dot. If the bit is set to 1, a dot prints; if it is set to 0, the dot does not print. The bits are in the same order as the dots on the page. For example, if the first bit in a raster line is set to 1, a dot will print at the leftmost end of the printed line.

Let us now look at the printing process in detail.

Setting Print Resolution

Setting print resolution for raster graphics is done with the following command:

```
Esc * t # R
```

where # specifies the resolution in dpi (dots per inch). # can be 75, 100, 150, or 300.

Resolutions below 300 dpi are achieved by using clusters of 300-dpi dots. 150 dpi uses a 2×2 matrix of dots, 100 dpi uses a 3×3 matrix, and 75 dpi uses a 4×4 matrix. Examples of these appear in Figure 3.1. If no resolution is specified, the Laser-Jet defaults to 75 dpi. Which resolution to use? Figure 3.1 shows the dramatic differences in output quality and size when different resolutions are used. Resolutions also differ dramatically in printing speed and memory requirements. For example, a 2" × 3" graphics image requires 34,200 bits at 75 dpi, but 540,000 bits at 300 dpi. The disparity in printing times reflects the data sizes. Hence, the application should determine resolution: If a quick look (a rough draft, for example) at an image is sufficient, 75 dpi or 100 dpi should be used. For higher-grade work, use a finer resolution.

Entering Raster-Graphics Mode

After the resolution has been set and the cursor positioned to the upper left corner of the graphic area (Chapter 1 discusses cursor positioning), the command to enter raster-graphics mode is sent:

FIGURE 3.1 Output of Listing 3.1 Showing the Effects of Resolution on a PCL
Graphic Image

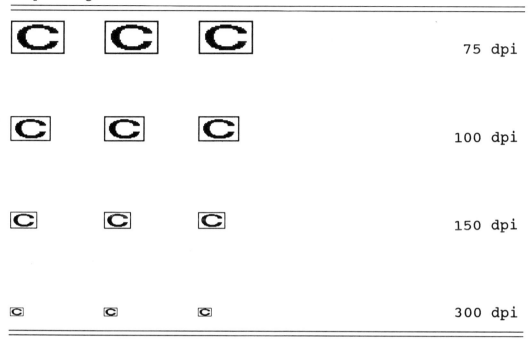

<pre>
Esc * r # A
</pre>

where # indicates the type of cursor positioning. If # is 1, the current cursor position
is used; if it is 0, printing begins at the left margin.

Since most raster graphics begin after a cursor-positioning command, # most
often has a value of 1. While in graphics mode, the LaserJet takes on a unique be-
havior pattern: it correctly responds only to the following commands: transfer raster data, set raster compression mode, and raster Y offset (these commands are
discussed later in this chapter). The following commands are ignored by the Laser-
Jet while it is in raster-graphics mode: start raster graphics, set raster width, set raster height, set raster presentation mode, and set raster graphics resolution. Any
other PCL command not mentioned here, rather than being ignored, will cause the
printer to exit graphics mode. From these restrictions, it is clear that once it is in
graphics mode, the LaserJet expects to receive only raster data. You will notice that
the printing-resolution command is ignored in raster-graphics mode; to change resolution in the middle of a raster graphic it is necessary to exit graphics mode, reset
resolution, and re-enter graphics mode.

Sending Raster Data

The next step is to send the data. This is done with the command

Esc *b # W

where **#** is the number of bytes of raster data that follow. The raster data follows immediately after this command, a 1 indicating that the corresponding dot should be printed. For example, if a byte with bits of 1000000 is sent, a leftmost dot is printed, and that is all. All data until **#** bytes have been received is treated as raster data. If the raster graphic does not fit exactly in an eight-bit byte, the last bits should be padded with zeros (which do not print). The preceding command specifies the number of bytes for a single raster row. After the raster row is printed, the cursor is moved to the position one dot below the beginning of the row just printed.

Exiting Raster-Graphics Mode

Once the last row has been sent, a command to indicate the end of the raster graphics is sent. It is

Esc * r B

This command switches the LaserJet back into standard PCL mode.

Listing 3.1, which generates the illustration in Figure 3.1, demonstrates the use of these commands.

The code in Listing 3.1 contains one item that bears repetition. The image to be

LISTING 3.1 Print a LaserJet Graphic at Four Levels of Resolution

```
/*-------------------  GRAPHRES.C  ---------------------
 * Print a PCL graphic at various resolutions.
 * Uses FOPEN_LJ and must be linked to this routine.
 *
 * Usage:   GRAPHRES.C
 *-----------------------------------------------------*/

#include <stdio.h>
#include <limits.h>
#include "ljmain.h"

#ifndef CHAR_BIT            /* Ostensibly for portability, but */
#define CHAR_BIT 8          /* the LaserJet expects 8-bit bytes*/
#endif

#define Rows 26
#define Cols (6 * CHAR_BIT)
```

Listing 3.1 continues

Listing 3.1 continued

```
char image [Rows] [Cols+1] =  /* the image to print: a 'C' in a box */
    {
      "111111111111111111111111111111111111111111100000", /* 6 x 8 */
      "100000000000000000000000000000000000000000100000",
      "100000000000000000000000000000000000000000100000",
      "100000000000000011111111000000000000000000100000",
      "100000000000001111111111111111100000000000100000",
      "100000000011111111111111111111111100000000100000",
      "100000000111111000000000011111111100000000100000",
      "100000011111110000000000000011111110000000100000",
      "100000111111100000000000000001111110000000100000",
      "100000111111100000000000000001111110000000100000",
      "100001111111000000000000000000000000000000100000",
      "100001111111000000000000000000000000000000100000",
      "100001111111000000000000000000000000000000100000",
      "100001111111000000000000000000000000000000100000",
      "100001111111000000000000000000000000000000100000",
      "100000111111100000000000000000000000000000100000",
      "100000111111100000000000000011111110000000100000",
      "100000011111110000000000000011111110000000100000",
      "100000001111111000000000011111111100000000100000",
      "100000000011111111000000001111111100000000100000",
      "100000000011111111111111111111111110000000100000",
      "100000000000011111111111111111111000000000100000",
      "100000000000000011111111111110000000000000100000",
      "100000000000000000000000000000000000000000100000",
      "100000000000000000000000000000000000000000100000",
      "111111111111111111111111111111111111111111100000"
    };

FILE *prt, *fopen_laserjet();

void raster_res (res)
int res;
{
    fprintf(prt, "%c*t%dR", ESC, res);
}

void set_rast_mrgn_left()        /* Set raster margin to current cursor   */
{
    fprintf (prt, "%c*r1A", ESC);
}

/*-------------------------------------------------------------
 * Send the raster bits from the image
 *--------------------------------------------------------*/
void send_image ( int rows, int cols, char * source )
{
    int  i, j;
    char k;
    for ( i = 0; i < rows; i++ )
    {
        fprintf ( prt, "%c*b%dW", ESC, cols/CHAR_BIT ); /* # of bytes coming */
        for ( j = 0; j < ( Cols / CHAR_BIT ); j++ )
        {
            k = do_a_char ( source );    /* Sends 8 bits at once */
            fputc ( k, prt );
```

Listing 3.1 continues

Listing 3.1 continued

```
            source += CHAR_BIT;
        }
        source += 1;                    /* Skip the NULL at EOS */
    }
}

/*-----------------------------------------------------------
 * Turn off raster graphics
 *---------------------------------------------------------*/
void end_graphics()
{
    fprintf ( prt, "%c*rB", ESC );
}

/*-----------------------------------------------------------
 * Converts a sequence of '1' and '0' into a raster byte
 *---------------------------------------------------------*/
int do_a_char ( char * ptr )
{
    int i, r;
    r = 0;

    for ( i = 0; ; i++ )
    {
        if ( *(ptr++) == '1' )          /* Add if it's a '1' */
            r += 1;                     /* then shift left.  */
        if ( i < CHAR_BIT - 1 )         /* Repeat 7 times    */
            r <<= 1;                    /* then do last bit. */
        else
            break;
    }
    return ( r );
}

/*-----------------------------------------------------------
 * Position the cursor (using dot units) at x, y
 *---------------------------------------------------------*/
void position_cursor ( int x, int y )
{
    fprintf ( prt, "%c*p%dx%dY", ESC, x, y );
}


/*------------------- MAIN LINE STARTS HERE ---------------------*/
void main ( void )      /* Print examples of raster graphic images */
{
    char * pic = &image[0][0];
    int i, j, x, y;
    static int resolution [4] = { 75, 100, 150, 300 };

    if (( prt = fopen_laserjet ( "PRN" )) == NULL )
    {
        fputs ( "Unable to open printer", stderr );
        exit();
    }

    fprintf ( prt, "%cE", ESC );        /* reset the printer */
```

Listing 3.1 continues

Listing 3.1 continued

```
/* Draw 4 images on a line, 1" apart. Start at 100, 400 */

x = 100;
y = 400;

for ( j = 0; j < 4; j++ )            /* for each level of resolution,  */
{
    for ( i = 0; i < 3; i++, x += 300 ) /* print a row of 3 images  */
    {
                                      /* This is a typical cycle: */
        position_cursor ( x, y );         /* 1) Position the cursor,  */
        raster_res ( resolution[j] );     /* 2) Set print resolution, */
        set_rast_mrgn_left();             /* 3) Set left margin,      */
        send_image ( Rows, Cols, pic );   /* 4) Send raster image,    */
        end_graphics();                   /* 5) Exit graphics mode.   */
    }
    position_cursor ( x + 300 , y );
    fprintf ( prt, "%3d dpi", resolution[j] );

    x  = 100;
    y += 300;
}
fprintf ( prt, "%c", FormFeed );  /* print it! */
}
```

printed takes up only 43 bits of width (or, as printed, 43 dots of space). Since we are required to tell the LaserJet how many *bytes* are to be printed and since the number of bits in each row must therefore be a multiple of 8, the rows in `image` are padded with five zero-bits, which do not print. You must make certain that raster lines contain a multiple of 8 bits.

Figure 3.1 shows the effect resolution has on the appearance of a printed image. Notice that the quality is much better at higher resolutions: the jagged curves at 75 dpi are almost completely gone at 300 dpi. Even more striking is the difference in dot size. At 75 dpi, each dot is four times taller and four times wider than a dot at 300 dpi. The effect is that at 75 dpi, images are 16 times larger (4 × 4) than at 300 dpi. Likewise, images printed at 150 and 100 dpi are respectively 4 and 9 times larger than their 300 dpi equivalents. Hence, selection of printer resolution should involve assessment of graphic quality, graphic size, and printing speed.

Macros

Our discussion of raster-image creation implies that a major consideration in the handling of LaserJet images is the size of the image in memory. Size is important for two reasons: It is difficult to store and manipulate large blocks of data, and the LaserJet requires more time to process large blocks of data. Storing large blocks of data is treated at length in Chapter 7. The matter of processing time is never fully resolved—except for a handful of techniques that diminish data size. Most available optimizations in PCL involve the use of high-level commands to replace multiple low-level commands. The effect is to send fewer bytes to the LaserJet. This brings us to the fundamental rules of LaserJet performance:

- Use the highest-level commands possible
- Use built-in graphics wherever possible
- Download repeated images only once

The third rule is the one most likely to confer significant savings. If you examine the code in Listing 3.1, you will see that the image of a boxed C is downloaded *twelve* times! Were the image larger and more complicated, Figure 3.1 would take a long time to print and occupy a substantial amount of memory.

Rather than downloading the image so many times, we can download it once and simply refer to it later when it must be printed. This technique is accomplished by use of **macros**. A macro is a shorthand expression for a series of PCL commands. Macros are created using the following sequence of actions:

- Assign an ID number to the macro
- Issue the start-macro command: **Esc & f 0 X**
- Send the data that makes up the macro
- Issue an end-of-macro command: **Esc & f 1 X**

Macro **invocation** is the process of performing the commands in the macro. First you specify which macro is to be invoked. This is done with the command

```
Esc & f # Y
```

where **#** is the macro ID assigned at creation. The number must be in the range 0–32767. Subsequent macro commands use the macro specified by this command. The command for invoking a macro is:

```
Esc & f # X
```

where **#** has the following meanings:

2   Execute last macro specified
3   Call last macro specified
4   Use last macro specified as an overlay

When a macro is *executed*, any changes it makes in the print environment are retained after completion of the macro. When a macro is *called*, changes it makes to the print environment are discarded after macro completion. When a macro is used as an **overlay**, it will be called as the last action before a page is printed. In this manner, an overlay macro can serve to draw such elements as footers, headers, and letterhead images. Notice that overlay macros are called rather than executed, so that changes they make to the print environment are discarded upon macro completion.

Macros can invoke other macros to a nesting level of two. In other words, macro A can invoke macro B which can invoke macro C. Macro C cannot invoke any further macros. Let us look at a new way of generating Figure 3.1 using macros. Listing 3.2 shows the main routine from Listing 3.1 adapted for macros.

LISTING 3.2 Listing 3.1 Altered to Use Macros

```
/*-------------------------------------------------------------
 * Select a macro for subsequent use/definition
 *-----------------------------------------------------*/
void select_macro ( int macro )
{
    fprintf ( prt, "%c&f%dY", ESC, macro );
}

/*-------------------------------------------------------------
 * Call a macro
 *-----------------------------------------------------*/
void call_macro ( void )
{
    fprintf ( prt, "%c&f3X", ESC );
}

/*-------------------- MAIN LINE STARTS HERE ----------------------*/

void main ( void )        /* Print examples of raster graphic images */
{
    char * pic = &image[0][0];
    int i, j, x, y;
    static int resolution [4] = { 75, 100, 150, 300 };

    if (( prt = fopen_laserjet ( "PRN" )) == NULL )
    {
        fputs ( "Unable to open printer", stderr );
        exit();
    }

    fprintf ( prt, "%cE", ESC );        /* reset the printer */

    select_macro ( 1 );                 /* select_macro ID: 1 */
    fprintf ( prt, "%c&f0X", ESC );     /* start macro definition */
    send_image ( Rows, Cols, pic );     /* send raster data */
    fprintf ( prt, "%c&f1X", ESC );     /* end macro definition */

    /* Draw 3 images on a line, 1" apart. Start at 100, 400 */

    x = 100;
    y = 400;

    for ( j = 0; j < 4; j++ )           /* for each level of resolution,  */
    {
        for ( i = 0; i < 3; i++, x += 300 ) /* print a row of 3 images  */
```

Listing 3.2 continues

Listing 3.2 continued

```
    {
                                            /* This is a typical cycle: */
        position_cursor ( x, y );           /* 1) Position the cursor,  */
        raster_res ( resolution[j] );       /* 2) Set print resolution, */
        set_rast_mrgn_left();               /* 3) Set left margin,      */
        call_macro ();                      /* 4) Call macro,           */
        end_graphics();                     /* 5) Exit graphics mode.   */
    }
    position_cursor ( x + 300 , y );
    fprintf ( prt, "%3d dpi", resolution[j] );

    x  = 100;
    y += 300;
}

fprintf ( prt, "%c", FormFeed );  /* print it! */
}
```

This code replaces all the code after the function `position_cursor()` in List-ing 3.1. Notice that after we open the LaserJet printer and reset it, we define a macro that simply sends the raster lines to the printer. Then in the main `for` loop, rather than calling the print routine, we call the macro. Notice that since the macro in question was the last macro specified (when we created it), it is the one referred to by the call command. The output from Listing 3.2 is identical to that from Listing 3.1—that is, identical in appearance, not in size (see Figure 3.1). Listing 3.1 gener-ates 3840 bytes of PCL commands and data, while Listing 3.2 generates only 769 bytes. The same image uses one fifth the amount of data and prints considerably faster. Macros are efficient.

To use macros effectively you should consider a few other commands. Macros can be made temporary or permanent. Permanent macros will survive a printer reset, whereas temporary macros will not (by default, macros are temporary). Mac-ros can also be selectively deleted. The command to manage macros in this way is:

Esc & f # X

where # has the following meanings:

6	Delete all macros
7	Delete all temporary macros
8	Delete a macro (last ID specified)
9	Make macro temporary (last ID specified)
10	Make macro permanent (last ID specified)

A final macro command, which is useful in conjunction with overlays, turns off the overlay printing. That is, it stops calling a macro at the end of each page. This command has the same form as the commands just examined, but # has the value **5**.

Saving the Cursor Position

When you use macros you need to be aware of a potential problem: The cursor position is never saved in the print environment. Whether a macro is called or executed, if the macro changes the cursor's position, the cursor will retain the new location at macro completion. Most of the time this is helpful. However, you may occasionally need to run several macros with the cursor in the same position, or you may want to run a macro just before some other activity without having to reposition the cursor. The LaserJet has the following built-in command for saving the current cursor position:

Esc & f # S

where **#** has the following meanings:

0   Store current cursor position
1   Recall a cursor position

Storing and recalling cursor positions are done on a LIFO basis (last in, first out). That is, the last position stored is the first position recalled. (To programmers familiar with stacks, these actions are equivalent to pushing and popping cursor positions.) Up to twenty positions may be stored at one time; attempts to have more than twenty positions stored at one time are ignored.

Transparency Modes

With the advent of PCL level 5, the LaserJet acquired the capability of printing images in an overlaid fashion. This facility, known as **transparency mode** in LaserJet parlance, allows an image to be printed on a patterned area (see Chapter 2 for a discussion of patterns) using a second pattern; for example, a cross-hatched maple leaf on a black background.

The techniques for doing this involve a complex series of steps and a set of new terms. We will continue to use the example of the cross-hatched maple leaf on a black background. First, we download the **destination image**. This is the image upon which another image, the **source image**, will be overlaid. Then we select the transparency modes. Two transparency modes are required: one for the source image, one for the pattern. In our example we have a pattern (cross-hatch) in the shape of a source image (a maple leaf) being printed on a destination image (a black area).

The transparency modes control how the bits of the pattern and the two images interact. When **source transparency** is set to 0 (transparent) only the black pixels (the bits that are set to 1) will provide ports through which the pattern can print. So, with the source transparency mode set to 0, you turn on the bits in those areas where you want the patttern to print on the destination image. If you set the source transparency to 1 (opaque), the effects of the transparent setting are retained, but in addition, white pixels (the bits that are set to 0) print as white on the destination image. In the transparent mode, white pixels had no effect on the destination image.

Pattern transparency determines how the pattern, as shaped by the source image, is applied to the destination image. When pattern transparency is set to 0 (transparent), the pattern is printed wherever the final image is not black. In other words, it appears only in the white areas of the destination image. If pattern transparency is set to 1 (opaque), the pattern prints over any areas of the destination image whether it is white or black. Consider our cross-hatched maple leaf. If we set pattern transparency to transparent, the result is black cross-hatch patterns on a black square—giving us a black square on which no maple leaf is visible. To force the pattern onto the black area, we set the pattern transparency to opaque, and now both the white and black areas of the pattern are visible on the black destination area. In other words, we are making the white areas of the pattern visible—they have become opaque on the black background.

Figure 3.2 shows the effects of combinations of transparency modes. It is taken from the *LaserJet Technical Reference*.

Using the effects of transparency mode demands an exact sequence of downloads:

1. Download the destination raster image (discussed earlier in the chapter)
2. Select the transparency modes (discussed next)
3. Select area fill ID and pattern (discussed in Chapter 2)
4. Download the source raster image (discussed earlier in the chapter)

The command for selecting source transparency mode is:

```
Esc * v # N
```

where **#** is **0** (transparent) or **1** (opaque).

The command for selecting pattern transparency mode is:

```
Esc * v # O
```

where **#** is **0** (transparent) or **1** (opaque) (the last letter of this command is the letter "oh," not the digit zero).

The code in Listing 3.3 prints a boxed C in solid white on a black background. In effect, this creates reversed (white on black) graphics on the LaserJet. Once again, only the main line is given; the ancillary routines are unchanged. Figure 3.3 shows the output from the program.

These first three chapters have laid the foundation for study of the advanced features of the LaserJet and Printer Control Language. The following chapters address

FIGURE 3.2   The Effects of Source and Transparency Modes

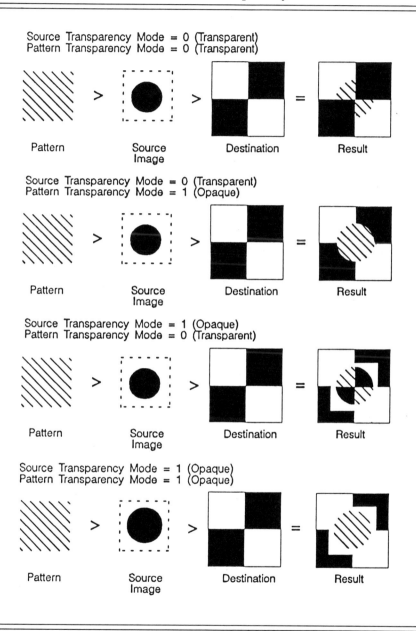

LISTING 3.3 Using Transparency Modes to Create Reverse Graphics

```c
void main ( void )               /* Print example of reverse printing */
{
    char * pic = &image[0][0];
    int i, j, x, y;
    int   resolution = 75;

    if (( prt = fopen_laserjet ( "PRN" )) == NULL )
    {
        fputs ( "Unable to open printer", stderr );
        exit();
    }

    fprintf ( prt, "%cE", ESC );        /* reset the printer */

    /* Draw 3 images on a line, 1" apart. Start at 100, 400 */

    x = 100;
    y = 400;

    position_cursor ( x, y );             /* Position the cursor,  */
    raster_res ( resolution);             /* Set print resolution, */
    set_rast_mrgn_left();                 /* Set left margin,      */

    fprintf ( prt, "%c*c600H",  ESC );  /* define an area and   */
    fprintf ( prt, "%c*c600V",  ESC );  /* make it black        */
    fprintf ( prt, "%c*c0P",    ESC );

    position_cursor ( x + 30, y + 30 );  /* move inside square   */

    fprintf ( prt, "%c*v1O", ESC );       /* opaque pattern trans*/
    fprintf ( prt, "%c*v0N", ESC );       /* transp. source      */

    fprintf ( prt, "%c*v1T", ESC );       /* select solid white  */
                                          /* pattern (on black)  */
    send_image ( Rows, Cols, pic );       /* Send raster image   */

    end_graphics();                       /* Exit graphics mode  */

    fprintf ( prt, "%c", FormFeed );  /* print it! */
}
```

the construction, manipulation, and use of fonts (Chapters 4–7) and the manipulation of raster graphics and HP-GL/2 (Chapters 8–10). Chapter 11 presents a discussion of file formats germane to LaserJet programming. Appendices A–E provide reference material.

FIGURE 3.3 Sample Output Showing Reverse Graphics

4

The HP Soft Font Format

Introduction

If the HP LaserJet printer inspired the desktop publishing revolution on DOS computers, then it is surely true that the widespread use and availability of fonts for the LaserJet ensured the revolution's success. Today, the HP Soft Font format is easily the most widely used printer font format in the world. Fonts are available from a large number of vendors in a seemingly endless array of typeface styles. And the good news is that they are generally of high quality and reasonable price.

The Soft Font format itself is well designed for typographic applications, yet remains accessible to the average developer. It is possible to deal with the format from a program with a minimum of fuss and still achieve some very striking results. An otherwise mundane page of printed output can be elevated to almost artistic status through the use of high-resolution typefaces. This is the kind of stuff that raises the developer's status to magician in the eyes of the end user!

The LaserJet III is the first member of the LaserJet family to support scalable typefaces. This feature uses AGFA Compugraphic's Intellifont technology with their Font Access Interchange Standard, and soft font outlines in this format can be directly downloaded to the printer. The printer then performs all the necessary scaling and rasterization to produce individual fonts as they are requested.

We will not cover the FAIS format here for two reasons. First, the format is rather complex, and a suitably detailed discussion of it would fill a respectably sized book. Secondly, since it is not applicable to the entire LaserJet family, its usefulness to the average developer is limited. Interested readers can obtain additional information on the FAIS format from AGFA Compugraphic.

In this chapter we present a detailed look at the font format itself and, along the way, introduce typographic terms and concepts with which the developer should be familiar. The next chapter will cover basic font manipulations, and the following chapter will present some advanced techniques. We begin with a discussion of some of the terminology.

A Font Primer

Nearly everyone uses the word **font** to indicate a **typeface**. Typeface refers to the particular style, or look, that is apparent in all of the individual characters in an alphabet or character set. Thus, we make reference to the **Helvetica font** or **Times Roman typeface**. **Type style** refers to alterations of the basic face, such as bold or italic. Strictly speaking, the word font refers to a specific size of a specific typeface. Thus, Helvetica is a typeface, and 12-point Helvetica is a font, and "a Helvetica font" is correct usage while "the Helvetica font" is not. The latter should read "the Helvetica typeface."

Font sizes are expressed in points, and there are 72 points to the inch. Note that when referring to the size of a font it is the font's height that is being referenced. The widths of individual characters in a proportionally spaced font vary, so it makes no sense to refer to the font's width. Do not confuse **point sizes** with **resolution**. LaserJet fonts are rendered at a resolution of 300 dots per inch. Thus, a character designed on a one-inch cell will have a bitmap up to 300 dots high, while the cell's point size will be 72.

There are a number of terms that are used to express qualitative differences among fonts, and it is useful to be conversant with them. Perhaps the most basic distinction is between serif and sans serif faces. A **serif** refers to the small lines that cross the ends of individual strokes within a character and results in a more ornate face. **Sans serif**, of course, means without serif. An example of a serif and a sans serif "E" is shown in Figure 4.1. The examples are shown in Times Roman, a serif face, and Helvetica, a sans serif face.

Another common typeface classification scheme is by the **weight**, or thickness, of the strokes that make up each character. Some adjectives commonly used to describe weight are light, book, medium, demi, bold, heavy, and black. These are listed roughly in order from thinnest to thickest. Fonts can also be compressed, condensed, expanded, oblique, italic, ornate, or script. There is an almost limitless pal-

FIGURE 4.1 Examples of Serif and Sans Serif Characters

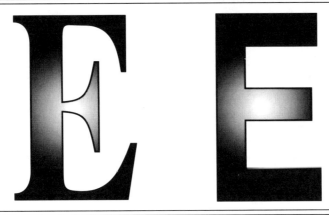

ette of weights that can be achieved within a single typeface family through typestyle modifications such as these.

Note that the use of serifs is a fundamental characteristic of a typeface, so you would seldom encounter serif and sans serif versions of the same typeface. By contrast, the other qualities listed are less fundamental and can occur within a given typeface in much the same sense that changing a font's size does not alter the distinctive identity of a particular typeface.

Having discussed the notions of font and typeface, we now turn to the individual characters that comprise a font. Figure 4.2 illustrates the anatomy of a character using a number of terms with which the developer should be familiar. Characters are placed on a page with reference to an imaginary line referred to as the **baseline**. This baseline is functionally equivalent to the rules found on ordinary notebook paper. Note that a character can extend above and below the baseline.

A design cell to accommodate all of the characters of a font will generally consist of a rectangle in which the baseline intersects the rectangle in its lower half. The distance from the baseline to the top of the cell is referred to as the **ascent** distance; the distance from the baseline to the bottom of the cell is referred to as the **descent** distance. As you might expect, the sum of the ascent and descent is the character's (and font's) height, which is normally expressed in points. The terms ascent and

FIGURE 4.2 The Anatomy of a Character

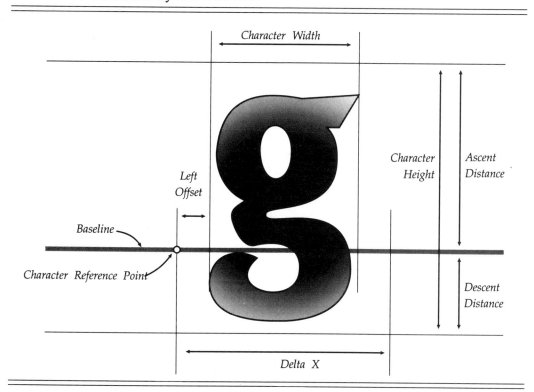

descent are also used to qualify individual characters. Thus, a lower case "g," which normally extends below the baseline, is a **descender** character, while a lower case "h," which normally extends above other lower case letters, is an **ascender** character.

It is customary to render consecutive lines of text with some white space between the lines for legibility. This white space is referred to as leading, which is pronounced as lead, the metal. Indeed, the term derives from the days of metal typesetting, when space between lines of set type was filled with strips of metallic lead.

The width of characters in a proportionally spaced font varies from one character to the next. In a monospaced font all characters occupy the same width, and it then makes sense to speak of the font's **pitch** as being so many characters per inch. Use of the word pitch in a font's name is a sure sign of a monospaced font, such as the LaserJet's built-in default font, Courier 10 pitch.

The terms discussed so far constitute a basic typographer's vocabulary. In the discussion of the HP Soft Font format that follows, additional terminology will be introduced that, in most cases, is specific to the HP format itself.

An Overview of the HP Format

Considered as a whole, an HP Soft Font file is a data stream containing three types of objects: escape sequences; data descriptors, which can be read or written with a suitable C structure; and character bitmaps.

Escape Sequences

An **escape sequence** is nothing more than a PCL command string. The name derives from historical usage, in which a given character code was designated as the escape character, used to introduce and distinguish a command string from actual data. The decimal value 27 is universally recognized as the escape character, and this is always the first character in an escape sequence. In PCL, all characters following the escape character up to and including the first occurrence of a capital letter constitute the command string. For a more detailed discussion, refer back to Chapter 1.

Data Descriptors

There are only two types of data descriptors used in a Soft Font file. There is one **font descriptor** for the font being defined and one **character descriptor** for each character defined in the font. A descriptor is a fixed-length data structure that is normally read or written using a C structure definition (more on this later).

Character Bitmaps

A character **bitmap** consists of a sequence of bytes (unsigned char) that define the individual dots that make up the character's image. A 1 bit represents a black dot (the foreground) and a 0 bit represents a white dot (the background). The bytes are ordered as a series of lines from top to bottom, and within each line the bytes are ordered from left to right. The very first bit of the first byte thus represents the upper left corner of the character's image. Scan lines in a character bitmap always begin on a byte boundary, whether or not the scan line length is a multiple of eight.

It is important to note that each line, or row, is always an integral number of bytes in length, even if the dot width of the character's image is not a multiple of eight. The last byte of each line is thus padded, if necessary, with unused bits to fill out the width to a multiple of eight. These unused bits should always be cleared (zero). An example of a character bitmap and its corresponding byte values is illustrated in Figure 4.3.

A font of a given size has defined to it a design cell that is large enough to contain any character in the font. The dimensions of this cell are contained in the font descriptor. Note that individual character bitmaps can be any size up to but not greater than the design cell dimensions. Thus, it is only necessary to provide as many rows and columns in a character's bitmap as are necessary to contain the character's image. Remember, however, that the width must be padded to a multiple of eight. The actual dimensions of a character bitmap are contained in the character descriptor for that character.

FIGURE 4.3 Example of a Character Bitmap

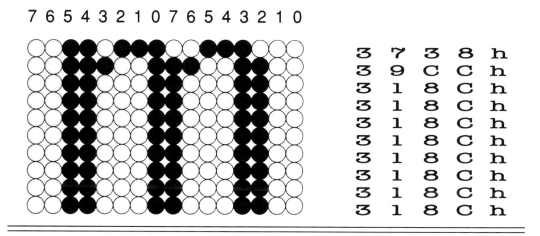

The Data Stream

As we noted above, the font file consists of a stream of escape sequences, data descriptors, and character bitmaps. Escape sequences precede the other components and serve to identify the item to follow and specify its length in bytes. This structure is diagrammed in Figure 4.4.

FIGURE 4.4   Schematic of a Bitmapped Font File

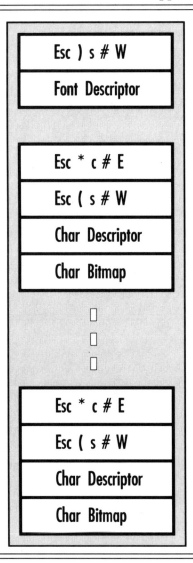

Font-Definition Escape Sequences

There are generally only three different escape sequences found in a font file. A fourth sequence, specify font ID, is required to download the font, but is usually supplied by the software performing the download. The following sections describe these escape sequences.

Specify Font ID

The specify-font-ID sequence is used to assign a font ID number to the font that is about to be downloaded. The font ID is a positive 16-bit integer that is used to identify the font in any operation requiring the specification of a font, such as selecting the active font, deleting a font, and so on. The format of this sequence is

```
Esc * c # D
```

where # is replaced by the ASCII string representing the numeric value of the font ID, for example:

```
Esc * c 1 2 D
```

for a font to be assigned the ID 12. This escape sequence is not generally placed in the font file itself, but is sent by a program just prior to performing the download. (Note that in this, as in all escape sequences listed in this book, blanks are inserted between characters for readability but do not occur in the actual string sent to the printer.)

Define Font Descriptor

The define-font-descriptor escape sequence indicates that the data immediately following constitutes a font descriptor and also indicates the size of the descriptor in bytes. Note that this size should be at least `sizeof( font_desc )` bytes in length. The final field of the font descriptor, the `font_name member`, is frequently extended to include additional information, such as the vendor's name or a copyright statement. The format of the sequence is

```
Esc ) s # W
```

where # is replaced by the ASCII string giving the length of the font descriptor in bytes. Note that if the final field, the font name, is not extended then the length is 64 bytes, that is:

```
Esc ) s 6 4 W
```

Specify Character Code

The specify-character-code sequence is used to indicate the decimal value of the next character to be downloaded. This sequence means, in effect, "here comes the definition of character *n*." The format of the sequence is

```
Esc * c # E
```

where **#** is replaced by the **ASCII decimal equivalent (ADE)** of the character code to be defined. For, example, the capital "A" has an ADE value of 65 and the corresponding specify-character-code sequence is

```
Esc * c 6 5 E
```

Define Character Descriptor

This sequence is used to introduce a combined character descriptor and character bitmap. The format of the sequence is

```
Esc ( s # W
```

where **#** is replaced by the ASCII string giving the combined length, in bytes, of the character descriptor and character bitmap. Note that this value would be computed by a program using an expression such as `sizeof( char_-desc ) + nbytes`, where `nbytes` is the number of bytes in the character bitmap. The bitmap follows the character descriptor immediately and can be thought of as being part of the descriptor itself.

Units

There are two character measurement units found in a font file, dots and **quarter-dots**. There are 300 dots per inch and 1200 quarter-dots per inch. Quarter-dot units are used where the normal 300 dots per inch do not provide adequate precision. Be sure not to confuse the dot coordinate system with measurements expressed as points or **decipoints**. These latter units are used in other contexts.

Warning
Fonts are always displayed at a resolution of 300 dots per inch, regardless of the current graphics resolution, which can range from 75 to 300 dots per inch.

Data Types

Numeric values in the font and character descriptor data structures can be either 8 bits (a byte) or 16 bits (a word) in length. Furthermore, a value can be either signed or unsigned. The *LaserJet Technical Reference* also makes use of a Boolean type, which is nothing more than a byte with a value of zero (false or off) or one (true or on). Word values are stored backward relative to the byte ordering used on Intel processors, in the order high byte to low byte (most significant byte, or MSB, first); so the bytes in a word must be swapped before being used in a program that runs on the 80x86 processor family. Most C compilers provide a library function, `swab()`, which can be used for this purpose. Alternatively, a macro such as the following can be used:

```
#define REV_WRD( w )   ( ((w>>8) & 0xFF) | (w<<8) )
```

Warning

Don't leave out the AND with 0xFF! Otherwise, a negative signed integer will be shifted with sign extension, resulting in a high-order byte of 0xFF regardless of the value of the low order byte that is being shifted into the high-order position.

The Font Descriptor

The font descriptor data structure provides information about the font as a whole. Recall that it is preceded in the font file by the define-font-descriptor escape sequence, **Esc) s # W**. A suitable C structure for reading or writing a font descriptor is illustrated in Listing 4-1.

Warning

Determine the length of the font descriptor from the define-font-descriptor escape sequence—do not assume that it will be 64 bytes in length, as it generally is not!

As defined in the *LaserJet Technical Reference*, the length of the `font_name` member is 16 bytes, and `sizeof( font_desc )` yields a value of 64. However, the `font_name` member can be of any length in practice, so the true length of the font descriptor should be determined from the define-font-descriptor escape sequence.

LISTING 4.1 LJFONT.H, HP Soft Font Types Header File

```
/*----------------------------------------------------------*/
/* FILE:       LJFONT.H                                     */
/* DESC:       HP Soft Font types header file               */
/* VERSION:    1.0                                          */
/* DATE:       June, 1990                                   */
/*----------------------------------------------------------*/

/* these define structures within an HP font file */
typedef struct _font_desc               /* font descriptor */
{
    unsigned short fd_size;              /* descriptor size */
    unsigned char  fd_fmt;             /* descriptor format */
    unsigned char  font_type;                /* font type */
    unsigned char  style_msb;          /* style word msb */
            char   resv_1;                    /* reserved */
    unsigned short bl_dist;        /* baseline distance */
    unsigned short cell_wid;             /* cell width */
    unsigned short cell_hgt;             /* cell height */
    unsigned char  orient;          /* 0=por, 1=land */
    unsigned char  spacing;     /* 0=fixed, 1=propnl */
    unsigned short sym_set;             /* symbol set */
    unsigned short pitch;                   /* pitch */
    unsigned short height;                 /* height */
    unsigned short xheight;              /* x height */
            char   wid_typ;             /* width type */
    unsigned char  style_lsb;          /* style word lsb */
            char   stk_wgt;          /* stroke weight */
    unsigned char  typeface;             /* typeface */
    unsigned char  vendor;          /* vendor-version */
    unsigned char  serif;              /* serif style */
    unsigned char  quality;              /* quality */
            char   placement;          /* placement */
            char   ul_dist;        /* underline dist */
    unsigned char  ul_hgt;       /* underline height */
    unsigned short txt_hgt;             /* text height */
    unsigned short txt_wid;              /* text width */
    unsigned short min_ch;           /* 1st ADE in font */
    unsigned short max_ch;           /* last ADE in font */
    unsigned char  pitch_ext;         /* pitch extended */
    unsigned char  height_ext;        /* height extended */
    unsigned short cap_hgt;          /* cap letter hgt */
    unsigned long  font_id;          /* font ID code */
            char   font_name[16];       /* font name */
    /*      vendor-dependent data follows...   (optional)   */
}
font_desc;

typedef struct _char_desc          /* character descriptor */
{
    unsigned char  format;                    /* LJII=4 */
            char   continued;          /* 0=cd, 1=data */
    unsigned char  cd_size;          /* des+data size */
    unsigned char  cd_class;                 /* LJII=1 */
    unsigned char  orient;           /* 0=por, 1=land */
            char   resv_1;                  /* reserved */
            short  left_ofs;           /* left offset */
            short  top_ofs;             /* top offset */
```

Listing 4.1 continues

Listing 4.1 continued

```
    unsigned short char_wid;              /* char wid in dots */
    unsigned short char_hgt;              /* char hgt in dots */
            short delta_x;                /* cur pos change */
    /*     character bitmap data follows...   (required)   */
}
char_desc;

/*-----------------------------------------------------------*/

/* these define structures used within the book's code */

typedef int width_tbl[256];        /* array of char widths */

typedef struct _font_hdr        /* font file data structure */
{
        char      name[18];                  /* name of font */
        short     family;               /* typeface family */
        short     orient;          /* portrait or landscape */
        short     spacing;         /* proportional or fixed */
        short     posture;            /* upright or italic */
        short     weight;          /* light, med, bold, etc */
        short     pitch;                   /* default pitch */
        short     height;                /* default leading */
        short     bldist;          /* cell top to baseline */
        width_tbl wtbl;            /* array of char widths */
}
font_hdr;

typedef struct _string_metric       /* string measurements */
{
        double   width;               /* full width, inches */
        double   height;              /* max height, inches */
        double   nb_width;         /* width excluding blanks */
        double   ascent;                     /* max ascent */
        double   descent;                   /* max descent */
}
string_metric;

/*-----------------------------------------------------------*/

/* macros... */

/* reverse the two bytes in a word */
#define REV_WRD(w)    ( ((w >> 8) & 255) | (w << 8) )

/* a two-character, non-parameterized seq begins with... */
#define IS_SMPL_SEQ(c)  (((c >= 48) && (c <= 126)) ? 1 : 0)

/* a parameterized escape seq begins with... */
#define IS_PARM_SEQ(c)  (((c >= 33) && (c <= 47)) ? 1 : 0)

/* a parameter character is from this range... */
#define IS_PARM_CHR(c)  (((c >= 96) && (c <= 126)) ? 1 : 0)

/* termination character (end-of-sequence) */
#define IS_TERM_CHR(c)  (((c >= 64) && (c <= 94)) ? 1 : 0)

/*-----------------------------------------------------------*/
```

Listing 4.1 continues

Listing 4.1 continued

```
/* constants... */

/* escape sequence identifiers */
#define   eUNKNOWN        0               /* anything else */
#define   eFONTDESC       1        /* define font descriptor */
#define   eCHARDESC       2        /* define char descriptor */
#define   eCHARCODE       3             /* specify char ADE */

/* units */
#define   uDPI          300              /* dots per inch */
#define   uQDPI        1200      /* quarter-dots per inch */

/* spacing */
#define   sFIXED          0               /* fixed width */
#define   sPROPORTIONAL   1          /* proportional width */

/* orientation */
#define   oPORTRAIT       0        /* portrait orientation */
#define   oLANDSCAPE      1       /* landscape orientation */

/* font formats */
#define   fBITMAP         0             /* bitmapped font */
#define   fSCALABLE      10               /* outlined font */

/*--------------- End of File LJFONT.H ------------------*/
```

The length of the `font_name` member is then determined by subtracting the length of the fixed part of the font descriptor, 47, from the size indicated by the define-font-descriptor escape sequence. It is customary among vendors of HP Soft Fonts to extend the font name field to include all sorts of miscellaneous information, such as copyright statements.

There are up to nine reserved fields in a font descriptor, depending upon the PCL release number. Later versions use some of these to add members to the font descriptor, but all can be safely ignored and should be zero filled. The remaining fields are discussed below. Note that the field data type is indicated in parentheses after the name, and will be one of the following:

Abbreviation	Meaning
B	Byte value indicating true (1) or false (0)
SB	Signed byte (–128..127)
UB	Unsigned byte (0..255)
SI	Signed int (–32768..32767)
UI	Unsigned int (0..65535)
ASCn	Character array of *n* bytes

    `fd_size`   Font descriptor size—UI. This field contains the size of the font descriptor in bytes. This value should be the same as that indicated by the define-font-descriptor escape sequence.

`font_type`
Font type—UB. The value of this field indicates the defined character range for the font. Valid values and their meaning are as follows:

Value	Font Type
0	7-bit, values 32–127 are printable
1	8-bit, values 32–127 and 160–255 are printable
2	PC-8, all codes printable except 0, 7–15, and 27

`bl_dist`
Baseline distance—UI. This specifies the distance, in dot units, from the top of the character cell to the baseline.

`cell_wid`
Cell width—UI. This specifies the width of the character cell in dot units. The width of individual characters must be less than or equal to this value. The maximum permissible value is printer dependent; for a LaserJet II, it is 4200 dots (1008 points).

`cell_hgt`
Cell height—UI. This specifies the height of the character cell in dot units. The height of individual characters must be less than or equal to this value. The maximum permissible value is printer dependent; for a LaserJet II, it is 4200 dots (1008 points).

`orient`
Orientation—UB. Specifies the font's orientation. A value of 0 indicates portrait and 1 indicates landscape.

`is_prop`
Proportional spacing—B. A value of 0 indicates a fixed width font and a value of 1 indicates a proportionally spaced font.

`sym_set`
Symbol set—UI. Specifies the symbol set for the font. For the standard PC-8 set this value should be 341. For other symbol sets refer to the *LaserJet Technical Reference*. There is also a formula for computing the symbol set value. To quote the *Laserjet Technical Reference*, "This value is computed by taking the PCL escape sequence value field, multiplying it by 32, adding the ordinal value (ASCII decimal value) of the PCL escape sequence termination character, and subtracting 64." What this sentence actually means is not clear, but the *LaserJet Technical Reference* fortunately provides a table of values for all of the commonly used symbol sets.

`pitch`
Default pitch—UI. This value defines the default pitch of the font in quarter-dot units. It is also referred to as the default HMI (for Horizontal Motion Index). For monospaced fonts this is the distance between consecutive characters. For proportionally spaced fonts this defines the size of a blank space.

Warning
Font files generally do not provide a character definition for the space character (hex 20 or decimal 32). For the size of a blank in width computations, use the pitch field from the font descriptor.

height   Design height—UI. Specifies the design height of the font in quarter-dot units. When selecting a font by point size, this is the value that should be used (as opposed to the cell height).

xheight   X height—UI. Specifies the height of the lower-case "x" in quarter-dot units. This value is not actually used by the printer, but can be used by the application if, for example, a line touching the tops of lower-case characters must be drawn.

wid_typ   Width type—SB. This is a value that indicates the general proportionate width of a font. Valid values include the following:

Value	Width Type
–2	Condensed
–1	Semicondensed
0	Normal
1	Semiexpanded
2	Expanded

style   Style—UB. This value specifies the style of the font. Valid values include the following:

Value	Style
0	Upright
1	Italic

stk_wgt   Stroke weight—SB. A relative signed value that indicates the thickness of the strokes used in designing the font. The range is –7 through 7, from lightest to thickest. A normal book face would have a value of 0. A bold font would have a value of 3, and a light font would have a value of –3.

typeface Typeface—UB. A code indicating a specific typeface. Valid values include the following (partial list):

Value	Face
0	Line Printer
3	Courier
4	Helvetica
5	Times Roman

6	Letter Gothic
23	Century Schoolbook
24	University Roman

serif
: Serif style—UB. A code indicating the style of serifs or the stroke cap style for sans serif faces. Valid values include the following:

Value	Serif Style
0	Sans serif, square
1	Sans serif, round
2	Serif, line
3	Serif, triangular
4	Serif, swath
5	Serif, block
6	Serif, bracket
7	Rounded bracket
8	Flair stroke

ul_dist
: Underline distance—SB. Specifies the distance from the character cell baseline to the top dot row of the underline in dots. Positive values are above the baseline and negative values are below the baseline.

ul_hgt
: Underline height—UB. Specifies the thickness of the underline in dots. Note that the LaserJet II ignores this value, using a fixed value of three dots instead.

txt_hgt
: Text height—UI. This value provides an optimum interline spacing for the font in quarter-dot units. It can be used by a program to position consecutive lines of text if desired. This value is not used by the printer.

txt_wid
: Text width—UI. This value provides an optimum character spacing delta in quarter-dot units. HP recommends setting this to the average width of the lower-case letters. It is ignored by the printer and is not particularly useful in a program.

pitch_ext
: Pitch extended—UB. This value is used to extend the precision of the font's pitch field and is added to the pitch field to obtain the true pitch. The units for this field are $1/1024$ of a dot. In most applications this value can be ignored.

height_ext
: Height extended—UB. This value is used to extend the precision of the font's height field and is added to the height field to obtain the true height. The units for this field are $1/1024$ of a dot. In most applications this value can be ignored.

font_name
: Font name—ASC16. This field provides a slot for attaching a 16-character name to the font. As we noted previously, this field is

often extended to provide additional information, such as vendor name or a copyright message.

The Character Descriptor

The character descriptor is a data structure that applies to individual characters in the same manner that a font descriptor applies to an individual font. It serves as a header to the character's bitmap and provides metric information on the character. Most of the fields in the character descriptor are illustrated in Figure 4.2. A suitable C structure for reading or writing a character descriptor is presented in Listing 4-1.

There is one unusual situation that occurs with character descriptors when the size of the character descriptor plus the size of the character bitmap, in bytes, exceeds 32,767. Since the maximum value that can be indicated in an escape sequence value field is 32,767, whenever the size of a character definition exceeds this value it must be downloaded using two or more character descriptors. This situation is indicated when a nonzero value appears in the continuation field of the character descriptor and the continuation of the character bitmap immediately follows this byte; that is, the remainder of the character descriptor structure is omitted. A little arithmetic reveals that a bitmap larger than 512 by 512 dots square will cause this to happen. Since this corresponds to a 123-point character (a size seldom called for), the chances of this happening are slim, but certainly not impossible. This anomaly should therefore be considered in the design of any software that will deal directly with the font format.

A discussion of the individual fields in the character descriptor follows.

`format`	Descriptor format—UB. This is a code indicating the format of the descriptor. For the LaserJet II this value is 4.
`continued`	Continuation flag—B. Specifies whether the following data are a character descriptor (zero) or a continuation of the bitmap for the last previous descriptor (one). This was just discussed.
`cd_size`	Descriptor size—UB. Indicates the size of the descriptor structure in bytes, minus the size of the format and continuation flag. This value should be 14.
`cd_class`	Data class—UB. Specifies the format of the character bitmap. It should be set to 1.
`orient`	Character orientation—UB. Specifies the orientation of the character, where 0 implies portrait and 1 implies landscape. This value must match the orientation field in the font descriptor.
`left_ofs`	Left offset—SI. This value indicates the offset in dots from the current character reference point to the left edge of the character

bitmap. Note that the value is orientation dependent. Valid values are in the range −4200 to 4200.

`top_ofs`   Top Offset—SI. This value indicates the offset in dots from the current character reference point to the top edge of the character bitmap. Note that the value is orientation dependent. Valid values are in the range −4200 to 4200.

`char_wid`   Character width—UI. Specifies the width of the character bitmap in dots. Note that the number of bytes in one row of the bitmap are computed from this value by rounding up to the next multiple of 8. That is,

```
rowbytes = (char_wid + 7) / 8
```

`char_hgt`   Character height—UI. Specifies the height of the character bitmap in dots. The number of bytes in the character bitmap will be equal to this value multiplied by the rowbytes value mentioned under `char_wid`.

`delta_x`   Delta x—SI. Specifies the number of quarter-dot units by which the current page position is incremented after printing the character. This value is used only with proportionally spaced font. Valid values are 0 to 16800, corresponding to 0 to 4200 dots.

The Character Bitmap

The data for a character's bitmap immediately follows the character's descriptor in the font file data stream. If the descriptor's continuation field is zero, then this is the start of the bitmap and it follows the `delta_x` member. If the descriptor's continuation field is nonzero, then this is a continuation of the previous descriptor's bitmap, and the descriptor structure consists only of the format and continuation fields. Be sure to test the continuation field of the character descriptor in order to interpret the data stream properly. If the continuation field is nonzero then only a partial descriptor structure is present.

The bitmap data represents horizontal rows of dots. These are commonly referred to as scan lines from analogy with television and monitor operation. The scan lines are presented in consecutive order starting with the top row and proceeding downward to the last row. Note that these physical references are absolute and do not bear any relation to the font's orientation. Thus, with a portrait font, the first scan line coincides with the top row of the character's image. With a landscape font, however, the character image is rotated counterclockwise 90 degrees, and the first scan line represents the last column of the character's image. This is illustrated in Figure 4.5.

FIGURE 4.5 Portrait Versus Landscape Characters

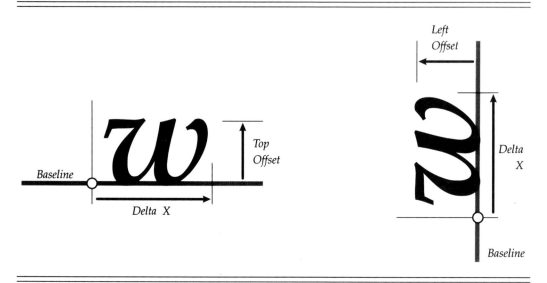

Remember that bitmap scan lines are padded to an integral number of bits. For example, if a character is 21 dots wide, then the last bit of the first scan line occurs at bit 4 of byte 3, and the first bit of the second scan line occurs at bit 0 of byte 4. Bits 5–7 of byte 3 are ignored and are present only to pad the end of the scan line. While it is not essential, it is always a good practice to clear (zero) the unused padding bits in a character bitmap. If you are writing a bitmap, construct an end-of-line mask that is and-ed with the last byte in each row, as follows:

```
unsigned char eol_mask;
    :
eol_mask = 0xFF << (char_wid & 7);
```

Portrait versus Landscape

Most of the metric quantities associated with a character image are relative to the physical page and thus do not rotate with the character image when it is in landscape orientation. This means that the left offset for a portrait character is the distance from the current physical reference point to the leftmost column of the character image, while the same measurement for a landscape character defines the distance from the top of the character bitmap to the baseline.

The one exception to this rule is the `delta_x` member of the character descriptor, which defines the distance to move the current position after a character is printed. For a portrait character this is measured horizontally from left to right. For a landscape character `delta-x` is measured vertically from bottom to top. In other words, `delta_x` is measured relative to the text drawing direction.

Programming Project: A Font Query Utility

We now turn to some actual code and present a utility for producing a formatted listing of information obtained from a font file's data descriptors. The program, HPQFONT, has the following command line syntax:

```
HPQFONT   font_file_path   [ /n | /f | /c ] [ /wXXX ]
```

where:

`font_file_path`	Specifies the `[drv:][\dir]name.ext` for the font file to be inspected. There is no default for the extension.
`/n`	Print nothing (typically used with /w).
`/f`	Print information on the font descriptor only.
`/c`	Print information on the character descriptors only.
`/w`	Create a binary width table as XXX.

The code is straightforward, and most of the program needs no explanation. The following notes, however, should be helpful.

(1) In many cases a descriptor member value is used as an index to an array of strings so that text is printed instead of the actual numeric value. For example, orientation can be either 0 or 1, but "Portrait" and "Landscape" are printed instead.

(2) Values expressed in quarter-dots are converted to dots by right-shifting by 2 (that is, division by 4). This makes all metric quantities expressed as dots, which is preferable for value comparisons. Note, however, that there is a slight loss of precision, since the two low-order bits are lost.

(3) The /w option causes the creation of a font header file with a width table. This file contains important information on a font (a binary image of a `font_hdr` structure; see Listing 4.1) and is used with the font handling functions described in Chapter 6. The width table contains the print width of each character in the font in quarter-dot units. Note that it is common practice to omit a definition for the space character (32 decimal, 20 hex); its width should be set to the default pitch for the font.

The HPQFONT program (see Listing 4.2) can be used on any commercially available HP Soft Font file and is also useful for validating the contents of a modified or newly created font. In the following chapters we will consider the processes of font modification and font creation.

LISTING 4.2   HPQFONT.C, HP Soft Font File Query Utility

```
/*-------------------------------------------------------------*/
/* FILE:     HPQFONT.C                                         */
/* DESC:     HP Soft Font File Query Utility                  */
/*-------------------------------------------------------------*/

#include "stdlib.h"
#include "stdio.h"
#include "string.h"

#include "ljfont.h"

#define BUF_LEN   80                      /* i/o buffer size */
#define MAX_ESEQ 80            /* largest permissible esc seq */

/*-------------------------------------------------------------*/
/* global variables...                                        */
/*-------------------------------------------------------------*/

int   list_fd = 1,         /* flag - list font descriptor */
      list_cd = 1,         /* flag - list char descriptors */
      make_wt = 0;         /* flag - output width table */

char  eseq[MAX_ESEQ];          /* escape sequence buffer */

font_desc fd;                      /* a font descriptor */

char_desc cd;                      /* a char descriptor */

char  *font_file,                    /* font file name */
      *wtbl_file;              /* width table file name */

font_hdr fh;               /* font info and width table */

char  *ftyp[] =                     /* font type strings */
{
   "7-bit, 32-127 are printable",
   "8-bit, 32-127 and 160-255 are printable",
   "PC-8, all codes printable except 0, 7-15, 27",
   "Unknown"
};

char  *frot[] =             /* font orientation strings */
{
   "Portrait",
   "Landscape"
};

char  *fspc[] =                 /* font spacing strings */
{
   "Fixed",
   "Proportional"
};

char  *fwid[] =                  /* font width strings */
{
   "Ultra Compressed",
   "Extra Compressed",
```

Listing 4.2   continues

Listing 4.2 continued

```
    "Compressed",
    "Condensed",
    "Semi-Condensed",
    "Normal",
    "Semi-Expanded",
    "Expanded",
    "Extra Expanded",
};

#define MAX_IND 45

char *type_names[MAX_IND+1] =
{
    /* 00 */ "Line Printer",
    /* 01 */ "Pica",
    /* 02 */ "Elite",
    /* 03 */ "Courier",
    /* 04 */ "Helvetica",
    /* 05 */ "Times Roman",
    /* 06 */ "Letter Gothic",
    /* 07 */ "Script",
    /* 08 */ "Prestige",
    /* 09 */ "Caslon",
    /* 10 */ "Orator",
    /* 11 */ "Presentation",
    /* 12 */ "Helvetica Condensed",
    /* 13 */ "Serifa",
    /* 14 */ "Futura",
    /* 15 */ "Palatino",
    /* 16 */ "ITC Souvenir",
    /* 17 */ "Optima",
    /* 18 */ "ITC Garamond",
    /* 19 */ "Cooper Black",
    /* 20 */ "Coronet",
    /* 21 */ "Broadway",
    /* 22 */ "Bauer Bodini Black Condensed",
    /* 23 */ "Century Schoolbook",
    /* 24 */ "University Roman",
    /* 25 */ "Helvetica Outline",
    /* 26 */ "Futura Condensed",
    /* 27 */ "ITC Korinna",
    /* 28 */ "Naskh",
    /* 29 */ "Cloister Black",
    /* 30 */ "ITC Galliard",
    /* 31 */ "ITC Avant Garde Gothic",
    /* 32 */ "Brush Script",
    /* 33 */ "Blippo",
    /* 34 */ "Hobo",
    /* 35 */ "Windsor",
    /* 36 */ "Helvetica Compressed",
    /* 37 */ "Helvetica Extra Compressed",
    /* 38 */ "Peignot",
    /* 39 */ "Baskerville",
    /* 40 */ "ITC Garamond Condensed",
    /* 41 */ "Trade Gothic",
    /* 42 */ "Goudy Old Style",
    /* 43 */ "ITC Zapf Chancery",
    /* 44 */ "Clarendon",
```

Listing 4.2 continues

Listing 4.2 continued

```
    /* 45 */ "ITC Zapf Dingbats",
};

char *cd_cl_names[] =
{
    "Undefined",
    "Bitmap",
    "Compressed Bitmap",
    "Contour (Scalable)",
    "Compound Contour (Scalable)",
};

/*----------------------------------------------------------*/
/* explain program usage...                                 */
/*----------------------------------------------------------*/

void explain_pgm( void )
{
    printf( "HPQFONT  [drv:][dir]name.ext  [sw...]\n" );
    printf( "\n" );
    printf( "-c       : list char descriptors only\n" );
    printf( "-f       : list font descriptor only\n" );
    printf( "-n       : no listing\n" );
    printf( "-wXXX.X : output width table file XXX.X\n" );
}

/*----------------------------------------------------------*/
/* write a message and quit...                              */
/*----------------------------------------------------------*/

void exit_pgm( char *msg )
{
    printf( "%s\n", msg );
    exit( 0 );
}

/*----------------------------------------------------------*/
/* process command line args...                            */
/*----------------------------------------------------------*/

void process_args( int argc, char *argv[] )
{
    int  i;
    char c;

    /* establish initial values */
    font_file = NULL;
    wtbl_file = NULL;

    /* look at command line args */
    for( i=1; i<argc; i++ )
    {
        if( (*argv[i] == '/') || (*argv[i] == '-') )
        {
            c = *(argv[i] + 1);
            switch( c )
            {
                /* char descriptors only */
```

Listing 4.2 continues

Listing 4.2 continued

```
                case 'c' :
                case 'C' :
                    list_cd = 1;
                    list_fd = 0;
                    break;

            /* font descriptors only */
                case 'f' :
                case 'F' :
                    list_cd = 0;
                    list_fd = 1;
                    break;

            /* list nothing */
                case 'n' :
                case 'N' :
                    list_cd = 0;
                    list_fd = 0;
                    break;

            /* width table */
                case 'w' :
                case 'W' :
                    make_wt = 1;
                    wtbl_file = argv[i] + 2;
                    if( *wtbl_file == 0 )
                        exit_pgm( "No width table file name." );
                    break;

            /* help */
                case 'h' :
                case 'H' :
                    explain_pgm();
                    exit( 0 );
            }
        }
        else
            font_file = argv[i];
    }

    /* do we have a font file name? */
    if( font_file == NULL )
        exit_pgm( "No font file name." );
}

/*------------------------------------------------------------*/
/* skip next nbytes in a file...                              */
/*------------------------------------------------------------*/
void fskip( FILE *fptr, int nbytes )
{
    int  n;
    char buf[BUF_LEN];

    while( nbytes > 0 )
    {
        n = (nbytes > BUF_LEN) ? BUF_LEN : nbytes;
        fread( buf, n, 1, fptr );
```

Listing 4.2 continues

Listing 4.2 continued

```
        if( feof(fptr) )
            exit_pgm( "Unexpected EOF in function fskip" );
        nbytes -= n;
    }
}

/*------------------------------------------------------------*/
/* list vendor info following font descriptor...            */
/*------------------------------------------------------------*/

void flist( FILE *fptr, int nbytes )
{
    int  i, n;
    char buf[BUF_LEN];

    if( nbytes < 1 )
        return;
    printf( "\nVendor Info:\n" );
    printf( "----------------------------------------" );
    printf( "---------------------------------------\n" );
    buf[BUF_LEN-1] = 0;
    while( nbytes > 0 )
    {
        n = (nbytes > BUF_LEN-1) ? BUF_LEN-1 : nbytes;
        fread( buf, n, 1, fptr );
        if( feof(fptr) )
            exit_pgm( "Unexpected EOF in function flist" );
        /* remove any ctl chars and add a null */
        for( i=0; i<n; i++ )
            if( buf[i] < ' ' )
                buf[i] = ' ';
        buf[n] = 0;
        printf( "%s\n", buf );
        nbytes -= n;
    }
}

/*------------------------------------------------------------*/
/* print a formatted listing of a font descriptor...        */
/*------------------------------------------------------------*/

void print_fd( font_desc *fd )
{
    char fnam[18];

    printf( "\nFont Descriptor\n" );
    printf( "----------------------------------------" );
    printf( "---------------------------------------\n" );

    printf( "desc size:        %u\n",
            REV_WRD(fd-fd_size) );

    /* descriptive fields... */

    memcpy( fnam, fd->font_name, 16 );
    fnam[16] = 0;
    printt( "name:             %s\n",
            fnam );
```

Listing 4.2   continues

Listing 4.2 continued

```
if( fd->typeface <= MAX_IND )
    printf( "typeface:        %s\n",
            type_names[fd->typeface] );
else
    printf( "typeface:        %d\n",
            fd->typeface );
printf( "vendor code:     %d\n",
        fd->vendor );
printf( "serif:           %d\n",
        fd->serif );
printf( "quality:         %d\n",
        fd->quality );
printf( "placement:       %d\n",
        fd->placement );
printf( "type:            %s\n",
        ftyp[(fd->font_type & 3)] );
printf( "symbol set:      %d\n",
        REV_WRD(fd->sym_set) );
printf( "style word:      %02X%02Xh\n",
        fd->style_msb, fd->style_lsb );
printf( "font ID dword:   %08Xh\n",
        fd->font_id );
printf( "orientation:     %s\n",
        frot[(fd->orient & 1)] );
printf( "spacing:         %s\n",
        fspc[(fd->spacing & 1)] );

/* metric fields... */

printf( "char code range: %d to %d\n",
        REV_WRD(fd->min_ch),
        REV_WRD(fd->max_ch) );
printf( "cell size:       %dW x %dH (dots)\n",
        REV_WRD(fd->cell_wid),
        REV_WRD(fd->cell_hgt) );
printf( "text size:       %dW x %dH (dots)\n",
        REV_WRD(fd->txt_wid)>>2,
        REV_WRD(fd->txt_hgt)>>2 );
printf( "default pitch:   %d (dots)\n",
        REV_WRD(fd->pitch)>>2 );
printf( "pitch extended:  %d (1/1024 dots)\n",
        fd->pitch_ext );
printf( "height extended: %d (1/1024 dots)\n",
        fd->height_ext );
printf( "baseline dist:   %d (dots)\n",
        REV_WRD(fd->bl_dist) );
printf( "underline dist:  %d (dots)\n",
        fd->ul_dist );
printf( "underline hgt:   %d (dots)\n",
        fd->ul_hgt );
printf( "design height:   %d (dots)\n",
        REV_WRD(fd->height)>>2 );
printf( "x height:        %d (dots)\n",
        REV_WRD(fd->xheight)>>2 );
printf( "width type:      %s\n",
        fwid[fd->wid_typ+5] );
printf( "stroke weight:   %d\n",
        fd->stk_wgt );
```

Listing 4.2   continues

Listing 4.2 continued

```
    printf( "cap height:        %d (dots)\n",
            REV_WRD(fd->cap_hgt) );
}

/*----------------------------------------------------------*/
/* print a char descriptor header...                        */
/*----------------------------------------------------------*/

void print_cd_header( void )
{
    printf( "\n" );
    printf( "\nChar Descriptors:\n" );
    printf( "\nChar (Dec)  Fmt  Size  Class  Orient" );
    printf( " Left Ofs  Top Ofs   Wid    Hgt    DX" );

    printf( "\n---- -----  ---  ----  -----  ------" );
    printf( " --------  -------   -----  -----  -----" );
}

/*----------------------------------------------------------*/
/* print a 1-line listing of a char descriptor...           */
/*----------------------------------------------------------*/

void print_cd( unsigned char ch, char_desc *cd )
{

    printf("\n %c    %3d   %2d    %2d     %d        %c",
            ch, ch, cd->format, cd->cd_size,
            cd->cd_class, (cd->orient ? 'L' : 'P') );

    /* metric fields... */

    printf( "    %5d      %5d   %5d  %5d  %5d",
            REV_WRD(cd->left_ofs),
            REV_WRD(cd->top_ofs),
            REV_WRD(cd->char_wid),
            REV_WRD(cd->char_hgt),
            REV_WRD(cd->delta_x) > 2 );
}

/*----------------------------------------------------------*/
/* gather the next escape sequence...                       */
/*----------------------------------------------------------*/

int get_eseq( FILE *fptr, char ebuf[], int esiz )
{
    int  i;
    char c;

    /* If the first byte read is not an escape character */
    /* (dec 27), then either the file is not a font file */
    /* or the file is not readable - damaged, etc. Also,  */
    /* should encounter end-of-file at this point.        */

    fread( &c, 1, 1, fptr );
    if( feof(fptr) )
       return( 0 );
    if( c != 27 )
```

Listing 4.2 continues

Listing 4.2 continued

```
      exit_pgm( "Sync error, or file not a font file." );

   i = 0;
   do
   {
      fread( &c, 1, 1, fptr );
      if( feof(fptr) )
         exit_pgm( "Sync error reading escape sequence." );
      if( i == esiz )
         exit_pgm( "Escape sequence buffer overflow." );
      ebuf[i++] = c;
   }
   while( ! IS_TERM_CHR( c ) );

   return( 1 );
}

/*------------------------------------------------------------*/
/* parse an escape sequence...                                */
/*------------------------------------------------------------*/

void parse_eseq( char eseq[], int *etyp, int *eval )
{
   int  i;
   char pchar, gchar, tchar;

   /* since we are dealing only with font-file related */
   /* sequences we limit the scope of this function as */
   /* follows: only single-valued parameterized seqs.  */
   /* also, passed buffer omits the esc char, 1B (27).  */

   /* establish some initial values */
   *etyp = eUNKNOWN;
   *eval = 0;

   /* eseq[0] == parameterized character */
   /* eseq[1] == group character         */
   /* eseq[2] == start of value field    */
   /* :                                  */
   /* eseq[n] == termination character   */

   pchar = eseq[0];

   gchar = eseq[1];

   *eval = atoi( eseq+2 );

   i = 2;
   while( (! IS_TERM_CHR( eseq[i] )) && (i < MAX_ESEQ) )
      i++;
   tchar = eseq[i];

   if( (pchar==')') && (gchar=='s') && (tchar=='W') )
      *etyp = eFONTDESC;
   else if( (pchar=='(') && (gchar=='s') && (tchar=='W') )
      *etyp = eCHARDESC;
   else if( (pchar=='*') && (gchar=='c') && (tchar=='E') )
      *etyp = eCHARCODE;
```

Listing 4.2 continues

Listing 4.2 continued

```
}
/*-----------------------------------------------------------*/
/* scan the font file...                                     */
/*-----------------------------------------------------------*/

void scan_font( char *path )
{
     FILE     *fptr;
     int       eval, etyp, elast, cur_ch, cd_cnt;

     fptr = fopen( path, "rb" );
     if( fptr == NULL )
        exit_pgm( "Font file not found." );

     printf( "Scanning %s...\n\n", path );

     cur_ch = -1;
     cd_cnt = 0;
     elast  = eUNKNOWN;

     /* loop while escape sequences are found */
     while( get_eseq( fptr, eseq, MAX_ESEQ ) )
     {
        parse_eseq( eseq, &etyp, &eval );

        switch( etyp )
        {
           case eFONTDESC :

                fread( &fd, sizeof(font_desc), 1, fptr );

                /* we will deal only with bitmapped fonts */
                if( fd.fd_fmt != fBITMAP )
                     exit_pgm( "Font not bitmapped - cannot scan." );

                /* save important values for width table, */
                if( make_wt )
                {
                     strncpy( fh.name, fd.font_name, 16 );
                     fh.name[16] = 0;
                     /* family is a 9-bit value! */
                     fh.family   = ((fd.vendor & 1) << 8) |
                                        fd.typeface;
                     fh.orient   = fd.orient;
                     fh.spacing  = fd.spacing;
                     fh.posture  = fd.style_lsb & 0x03;
                     fh.weight   = fd.stk_wgt;
                     fh.pitch    = REV_WRD( fd.pitch );
                     fh.height   = REV_WRD( fd.height );
                     fh.bldist   = REV_WRD( fd.bl_dist );
                     /* initialize the width table */
                     memset( fh.wtbl, 0, sizeof( width_tbl ) );
                }

                if( list_fd )
                {
                     print_fd( &fd );
```

Listing 4.2 continues

Listing 4.2 continued

```
                    /* vendor-specific information */
                    flist( fptr, eval-sizeof(font_desc) );
              }
              else
                    fskip( fptr, eval-sizeof(font_desc) );
              break;

        case eCHARDESC :

              /* if last etyp is the same then this */
              /* is a continuation of previous cd.  */
              if( elast == eCHARDESC )
                    fskip( fptr, eval );
              else
              {
                    fread( &cd, sizeof(char_desc), 1, fptr );
                    if( list_cd )
                    {
                        if( cd_cnt == 0 )
                            print_cd_header();
                        print_cd( cur_ch, &cd );
                    }
                    fskip( fptr, eval - sizeof(char_desc) );
                    cd_cnt++;
                    /* if width table requested, save char width */
                    if( make_wt )
                        fh.wtbl[cur_ch] = REV_WRD(cd.delta_x);
              }
              break;

        case eCHARCODE :

              cur_ch = eval;
              break;
        }

        elast  = etyp;
    }

    fclose( fptr );
}

/*-----------------------------------------------------------*/
/* write width table array to specified file...             */
/*-----------------------------------------------------------*/

void write_wtbl( char *path )
{
    FILE *fptr;

    printf( "\nWriting width table '%s'...", path );

    fptr = fopen( path, "wb" );
    if( fptr == NULL )
        exit_pgm( "Error opening width table." );

    if( fwrite( &fh, sizeof( font_hdr ), 1, fptr ) != 1 )
        exit_pgm( "Error writing width table." );
```

Listing 4.2 continues

Listing 4.2 continued

```
     fclose( fptr );
}

/*-----------------------------------------------------*/
/*                    M A I N                          */
/*-----------------------------------------------------*/

void main( int argc, char *argv[] )
{
    /* sign-on */
    printf( "\nHPQFONT - HP Soft Font Query Utility\n\n" );

    /* help indicated? */
    if( (argc < 2) || (*argv[1] == '?') )
    {
        explain_pgm();
        exit( 0 );
    }

    /* process command line... */
    process_args( argc, argv );

    /* scan the font file... */
    scan_font( font_file );

    /* write the width table file if requested... */
    if( make_wt )
        write_wtbl( wtbl_file );

    /* sign-off */
    printf( "\nend-of-pgm" );
}

/*--------------- End of File HPQFONT.C -----------------*/
```

5
Downloading Fonts

Introduction

The LaserJet III was the first member of the LaserJet family to support **outlined** (or **stroked**) fonts. By contrast, the LaserJet family has supported **bitmapped** fonts since its inception. Of the two types of fonts, bitmapped are by far the more important to the developer. A number of reasons can be cited.

- The wide availability of bitmapped fonts. There are many sources for bitmapped fonts, both commercial and in the public domain; the typeface selection is quite large. (Sources for fonts are listed in Appendix E.)
- Bitmapped fonts do not require additional processing. While a bitmapped font consists of ready-to-use character images, outlined fonts must first be converted to character images (a process referred to as **rasterization**). This is seldom a simple task and adds computational overhead to an application.
- Ease of access and use. A bitmapped font can be thought of as pure data. In contrast, an outlined font is a mixture of data, structures, and methods. This mixture can be complex.

For these reasons, the discussion of font usage on the LaserJet will concentrate mainly on the bitmapped variety. Interested readers can obtain information on outlined font technology from one of the sources cited in the bibliography.

There are three categories of bitmapped fonts, distinguishable by their physical location. There are the printer's **built-in fonts**, which reside as a component of the printer's firmware (ROM). There are **cartridge fonts**, which also reside in ROM; however, the ROM for these fonts is located in a separate cartridge that is plugged into the printer. Finally, there are **soft fonts**, which reside on disk. These are transferred to the printer's on-board memory (RAM) by software over a communications link to the printer, typically a parallel or serial port. The process of transferring the font data to the printer is referred to as **downloading** the font.

Downloading a Font

In its most basic implementation, downloading a font is a simple three-step process: assigning an ID number to the font via an escape sequence, transferring the contents of the font file to the printer, and specifying additional directives such as selecting the font as the current active font or making the font temporary or permanent.

Fonts are explicitly referenced on the LaserJet via a unique nonnegative 16-bit integer termed the **font ID**. Valid values for the font ID range from 0 through 32767. This value is assigned to the font when it is downloaded by indicating the ID of the font to follow. The font ID number is specified by the escape sequence

```
Esc * c # D
```

where # is replaced by the ID number to be assigned to the font. For example, to specify an ID number of 101 for a font you would send

```
Esc * c 1 0 1 D
```

After you specify a font ID, all subsequent font management commands apply to that ID. Thus, a subsequent font download is presumed to define the font with that ID, and the font definition replaces any existing definition associated with that ID.

Since a soft font file contains a complete font definition, it is only necessary to transmit the contents of the file to the printer in order to define the font. This can, in fact, be accomplished directly from DOS via the COPY command. For example, assuming a font file named HELV012.SFP and a printer on LPT1, the following code does the trick:

```
COPY HELV012.SFP /B LPT1:
```

Note the /B switch, which indicates that the file's contents are **binary data**, as opposed to **text data**. This switch is always required; otherwise, byte values of 9 (tab character) and 26 (^Z, or end-of-file) are interpreted as indicated. This is fine for text documents but never correct for a font file data structure or character bitmap.

Warning

Under MS-DOS all character devices are opened in "cooked" mode, regardless of the mode specified in an `fopen()` call. It is necessary to modify the mode to raw (binary) explicitly using the IOCTL function (function 44h of interrupt 21h). See Chapter 1 for further details.

While it is possible to utilize operating system services such as DOS's COPY command, this is not generally done from an application program. Rather, the data transfer is typically effected by reading from disk and writing to the printer, as in the following:

```
#define BUF_SIZE 1024
    :
unsigned char io_buf[BUF_SIZE];
int nbytes;
FILE *inp, *outp;
    :
inp = fopen( "HELV012.SFP", "rb" );
outp = fopen( "LPT1", "wb" );
#if MSDOS
/* force binary mode under MS DOS */
set_binary_mode( outp );
#endif
nbytes = fread( io_buf, 1, BUF_SIZE, inp );
while( nbytes > 0 )
{
    fwrite( io_buf, 1, nbytes, outp );
    nbytes = fread( io_buf, 1, BUF_SIZE, inp );
}
```

This is all that is necessary if the application needs to print only unformatted or pre-formatted text files using a given font. For example, this technique can be used to replace the printer's default font (10-pitch Courier) temporarily, which will affect the output of subsequent PRINT commands. Note that the contents of the font file are not inspected, so the application does not know anything about the font.

Once a font has been downloaded, there are font-specific parameters that can be set by sending additional escape sequences to the printer. In particular, the font can be made **temporary** or **permanent**, and the font can be **selected** (so that subsequent text printing utilizes the font).

As we noted, downloaded fonts are stored in the printer's RAM, so these fonts are lost once the printer is turned off. The next time the printer is powered on it is necessary to download a given soft font again in order to utilize it. However, it is possible to control whether or not a downloaded soft font survives a printer reset. Fonts marked temporary (which is the default) are purged whenever a printer reset occurs; fonts marked permanent are retained and remain usable following a reset. Fonts are made permanent via the **font control** escape sequence, as follows:

Esc * c 5 F

This command makes permanent the font associated with the last referenced font ID. This sequence can be combined with the specify-font-ID sequence. For example, to mark the font with an ID of 101 as permanent you send the following:

Esc * c 101 d 5 F

TABLE 5.1 Functions of the Font-Control Command

Value	Function
0	Delete all soft fonts
1	Delete all temporary soft fonts
2	Delete specific font (last ID specified)
3	Delete character (last ID and character code)
4	Make soft font temporary (last ID specified)
5	Make soft font permanent (last ID specified)
6	Copy font (last ID to this ID)

The value field of the font-control escape sequence specifies the particular font management command to be performed. In this example, the value field is 5. This and other functions are summarized in Table 5.1.

Intelligent Font Downloading

In the font download described in the preceding section, the font file is treated like a "black box" whose contents remain unknown. If, however, the individual components making up the font file are individually extracted and sent to the printer, then an application can obtain information about the font or modify the font for its own uses. This is where knowledge of a font file's structure can pay dividends—in the form of additional capabilities.

In effect, the application must parse the font file to perform an intelligent font download. A suitable algorithm, presented as pseudo-code, is as follows:

```
while( get_escape_sequence() )
   perform_escape_sequence();
```

A program must perform the instructions indicated by the file's escape sequences. For this reason it is an error to read anything from the file that is not either an escape sequence or data being processed as a result of an escape sequence. Thus, the first character read by `get_escape_sequence()` should always be the escape character, 27 decimal or 1B hex. The `get_escape_sequence()` function continues to read characters from the file until a termination character is encountered. A suitable macro to test for a termination character, `IS_TERM_CHR()`, is defined in LJFONT.H (Listing 4.1). Note that the test is almost, but not quite, identical to the standard C function `isupper()`.

Once extracted, the escape sequence is interpreted, and its prescribed task is performed. There are currently only three such tasks, and the body of the `perform_escape_sequence()` function looks something like the following:

```
    case eFONTDESC : /* define font descriptor */
        nbytes = sequence_value_field();
        send_sequence();
        read_and_send( nbytes );
        break;

    case eCHARDESC : /* define character descriptor */
        nbytes = sequence_value_field();
        send_sequence();
        read_and_send( nbytes );
        break;

    case eCHARCODE : /* specify character code */
        send_sequence();
        break;

    default :    /* unknown, or an error */
          :
        break;
```

In this code fragment the `sequence_value_field()` function returns an escape sequence's value field as an integer, for example:

```
sequence_value_field( "Esc)s64W" ) = 64
```

The `send_sequence()` function transmits the sequence itself to the printer, and the `read_and_send()` function transfers a specified number of bytes from the file to the printer.

The defined constants are specified in LJFONT.H (Listing 4.1). Note that this code fragment does nothing more than perform the black-box transfer described in the previous section, but it provides the groundwork needed to alter or inspect the font as it is downloaded. Some of these capabilities are covered in the next sections.

Partial Downloading

One of the primary drawbacks of 300-dpi bitmapped fonts is the relatively large amount of data they generate, particularly at large point sizes. For example, a complete 72-point font file can run 300K to 500K in size, depending upon the typeface and symbol set employed. Bear in mind, too, that font point size and font file size are related by a square-law: doubling a given point size results in a file that is approximately four times larger. Since a downloaded font consumes RAM on the printer, it is certainly possible to exceed the printer's capacity to print a given page of text when large numbers of large-sized fonts are employed.

Fortunately, the LaserJet does not require that a font definition be complete; it is possible to download just those characters actually needed. This is particularly useful with large, headline fonts, in that the full character set is seldom employed. The only catch is that you must know in advance which characters are required.

To implement a partial downloading capability, an array of byte flags can be created for each font. Each array contains 256 elements initialized to zero. The ADE (ASCII decimal equivalent) value of a character is used to index into the array, and if a given character is needed its flag is set to a nonzero value, for example:

```
flags[ 65 ] = 1
```

which is of course equivalent to

```
flags[ 'A' ] = 1
```

Then, as each character descriptor is encountered during the download, the decision to actually send the data to the printer is determined from the table.

From a design standpoint, the only complication to this process arises from dealing with the font as a packet-oriented data stream. The decision to use or not to use affects three separate packets: specify-character-code escape sequences, define-character-descriptor escape sequences, and character descriptors and data. While it is possible to invalidate a given character download intentionally, a cleaner approach is to maintain a current character variable and either send all three items or send none of them.

Many commercial applications utilize a similar scheme to support partial downloading. The technique is generally triggered by a request for a font above a given threshold point size. It is best to make the threshold size user controllable or to provide an option to turn off the feature altogether.

Fixed-Width Conversion

Judging by their scarcity, fixed-width fonts (as opposed to proportionally spaced fonts) are a thing of the past. Most type foundries offer fewer than one percent of their faces in fixed-width versions, and commercial applications tend to overlook them as well. One well known drawing program offers 100 high-quality typefaces, of which only one, a mundane, typewriter-style face, can be used at a fixed pitch.

However, fixed-width faces have many applications, such as source code listings or columnar data presentation, where their fancier, proportionally spaced cousins are less appropriate. While a proportional font can be used at a fixed pitch, the technique is both computation and data intensive, requiring that a cursor position be computed and specified for every printed letter.

A better approach is to convert a proportional font's spacing information as it is downloaded to simulate a fixed-pitch font. As long as width table information is concurrently generated, both the printer and the program are using the same spacing information, and no anomalies result.

The only problematic side-effect of this technique arises when the range of widths among the font's characters is great. In order to guarantee that no two consecutive letters ever overlap, it is necessary to set the font's pitch low enough so that the character spacing width is at least the width of the font's widest letter. This frequently results in an unattractively low pitch, with too much white space between letters. In most fonts it is the capital "W" and capital "M" that cause this problem. Figure 5.1 illustrates the problem using the Avant Garde typeface. Note that the best result is obtained with the reduced-pitch version in which consecutive capital W's overlap.

Font Descriptor Modifications

To convert a font to fixed pitch, two fields in the font descriptor structure must be modified. First, the **proportional spacing flag** must be set to zero. Second, the **default pitch** member must be changed to the desired pitch. A third field is the font's **design cell width**. In the unlikely event that the desired pitch results in a character-spacing width that exceeds the font's design cell width, then the design cell width must be modified, as a character's width cannot exceed the font's design cell width. Attempting to download a character with a width greater than the design cell width invalidates the character definition.

FIGURE 5.1 Example of Three Spacings of the Same Font

This is 12pt Avant Garde, proportionally spaced
(the font's designed spacing).

AAAAA   IIIII   WWWWW

T h i s   i s   1 2 p t   A v a n t   G a r d e ,
m o d i f i e d   f o r   f i x e d   p i t c h ,
p i t c h   s e t   t o   d e s i g n   w i d t h .

A A A AA   I I I I I   W W W W W W

T h i s   i s   1 2 p t   A v a n t   G a r d e ,
m o d i f i e d   f o r   f i x e d   p i t c h ,
p i t c h   r e d u c e d   t o   8   c p i .

AAAAA I I I I I WWWWWW

Character Descriptor Modifications

Two fields in the character descriptor must be modified. First, the **delta x** member must be set to achieve the desired pitch. This holds for both portrait and landscape orientation. The original setting is actually sufficient to get the font to print at a fixed pitch, but the character images will generally be left justified within this distance, which does not look correct visually. The character image looks better if it is centered within the character spacing distance. This is accomplished by computing a new **left offset** value for a portrait font and a new **top offset** value for a landscape font. For a portrait font the code is

```
left_ofs = ((300/pitch) - char_width) / 2
```

For a landscape font the code is

```
top_ofs = ((300/pitch) + char_height) / 2
```

The expression `(300/pitch)` yields the character spacing distance in dot units. This computation should be performed using reals, since fractional pitches such as 8.5 are commonly employed. The relationships of these various metrics are illustrated by Figure 5.2.

FIGURE 5.2 Relationship of Pitch to Character Metrics

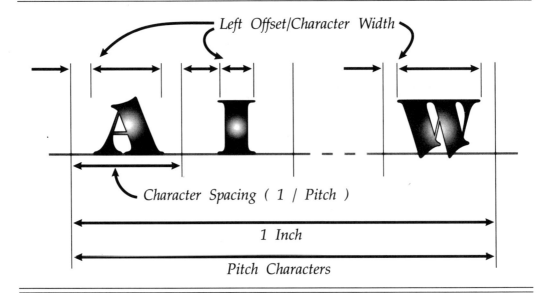

Programming Project: A Font Download Utility

We end the chapter with a font download utility that implements the features just discussed. The program source code is presented in Listing 5.1. The program takes as input any standard HP bitmapped font file and will download it to a LaserJet or compatible printer with any of the following options.

- Download a subset of the font by specifying a string containing the needed characters, for example:

  ```
  DLFONT HELV12.SFP /{The Story of My Life}
  ```

- Convert a proportionally spaced font to fixed width as it is being downloaded, for example:

  ```
  DLFONT HELV12.SFP /F
  ```

- Force a font being converted to monospacing to print at a specified pitch, for example:

  ```
  DLFONT HELV12.SFP /F /W8.0
  ```

- Allow the font to be selected or marked as temporary or permanent, for example:

  ```
  DLFONT HELV12.SFP /S /P
  ```

Note that the code fragments quoted in the text are from the program presented in Listing 5.1, but are adapted with changes to enhance their clarity or appropriateness to the discussion. Thus, you will see such things as function names in Listing 5.1 that are similar but not necessarily identical to those in the excerpts. Other than this, the program's flow and the techniques used should be easy to follow. Finally, note that the program contains DOS-specific code that is conditionally included whenever the MS-DOS symbol is defined to be nonzero. On non-DOS systems this symbol should be defined to zero.

In this chapter we covered the task of getting fonts to the printer. In the next chapter we turn to the more complex task of using fonts within an application. This topic includes the capabilities of the DLFONT program as a set of C-callable functions and also addresses such issues as text justification and formatting.

LISTING 5.1 DLFONT.C, A Font Download Utility for HP Soft Font Files

```
/*---------------------------------------------------------*/
/* FILE:  DLFONT.C                                         */
/* DESC:  A Font Download Utility for HP Soft Font Files.  */
/*---------------------------------------------------------*/

#include "stdlib.h"
#include "stdio.h"
#include "string.h"
#include "ctype.h"

/* define the following for MS DOS systems */
#define MSDOS 1

#if MSDOS
#include "dos.h"
#endif

#include "ljfont.h"

/*---------------------------------------------------------*/
/* Globally referenced variables...                       */
/*---------------------------------------------------------*/

char   *fnt_file,                      /* font file name */
       *prt_port,                      /* printer port name */
       *prt_def = "LPT1";      /* default printer port name */

FILE   *fnt_fp,                          /* font stream */
       *prt_fp;                          /* printer stream */

int    font_id,                          /* font id number */
       make_fixed,         /* flag- convert to monospaced */
       select_fnt,              /* flag- select this font */
       reset_prt,              /* flag- reset printer */
       is_perm,                     /* flag- perm font */
       cellW, cellH,         /* design cell dimensions */
       cur_chr;            /* ascii value of current char */

double cpi;               /* if != 0, force this pitch  */

long   bytes_read,                    /* read from font */
       bytes_written;             /* sent to printer */

#define BUF_SIZ 512
#define ESQ_SIZ 512

char io_buf[BUF_SIZ],                  /* file i/o buffer */
     esq_buf[ESQ_SIZ+1],        /* escape seq holding area */
     dld_chr[256];              /* flags - set ==> download */

/*---------------------------------------------------------*/
/* Font Control escape sequences...                       */
/*---------------------------------------------------------*/

char   *pRESET  = "\033E";                /* printer reset */
char   *fPERM   = "\033*c5F";        /* make font permanent */
```

Listing 5.1   continues

Listing 5.1 continued

```c
char  *fSETID  = "\033*c???D";        /* set font id to ??? */
char  *fSELECT = "\033(???X";     /* make font ??? primary */

/*------------------------------------------------------------*/
/* Print a message and exit the pgm...                        */
/*------------------------------------------------------------*/

void exit_pgm( int retc, char *msg )
{
    printf( "\n%s", msg );
    exit( retc );
}

/*------------------------------------------------------------*/
/* Explain ourselves...                                       */
/*------------------------------------------------------------*/

void explain_pgm( void )
{
    printf( "\n" );
    printf( "\nusage:" );
    printf( "\n" );
    printf( "\n DLFONT font_file [prt_port] [switches]" );
    printf( "\n" );
    printf( "\n        font_file = path to HP font file" );
    printf( "\n        prt_port  = prt port (def=LPT1)" );
    printf( "\n" );
    printf( "\nswitches:" );
    printf( "\n" );
    printf( "\n /F     = convert font to fixed width" );
    printf( "\n /In    = set font id to n (def=1)" );
    printf( "\n /P     = make font permanent (def=temp)" );
    printf( "\n /R     = reset printer before download" );
    printf( "\n /S     = select font (make current)" );
    printf( "\n /Wd.d  = force width (pitch) to d.d cpi" );
    printf( "\n /{xxx} = specify chars to download" );
}

/*------------------------------------------------------------*/
/* Set variables and override from command line...            */
/*------------------------------------------------------------*/

void process_args( int argc, char *argv[] )
{
    int   i, j;
    char  sw, *swval;

    /* set defaults */
    fnt_file  = NULL;
    prt_port  = prt_def;
    font_id   = 1;
    is_perm   = 0;
    reset_prt = 0;
    select_fnt = 0;
    make_fixed = 0;
    cpi       = 0.0;
    for( j = 0; j < 256; j++ )
```

Listing 5.1 continues

Listing 5.1 continued

```
      dld_chr[j] = 1;

 /* inspect command line */
 for( i = 1; i < argc; i++ )
 {
    /* a switch... */
    if( (*argv[i] == '/') || (*argv[i] == '-') )
    {
       sw    = *(argv[i] + 1);
       swval =   argv[i] + 2;

       switch( toupper(sw) )
       {
          /* force fixed width font */
          case 'F' :
               make_fixed = 1;
               break;

          /* set font id */
          case 'I' :
               sscanf( swval, "%d", &font_id );
               break;

          /* make font permanent */
          case 'P' :
               is_perm = 1;
               break;

          /* reset printer */
          case 'R' :
               reset_prt = 1;
               break;

          /* select font at printer */
          case 'S' :
               select_fnt = 1;
               break;

          /* force width of d.d cpi */
          case 'W' :
               sscanf( swval, "%lf", &cpi );
               break;

          /* specify chars to download */
          case '{' :
               for( j = 0; j < 256; j++ )
                  dld_chr[j] = 0;
               while( *swval && (*swval != '}') )
                  dld_chr[*swval++] = 1;
               break;

          /* undefined */
          default  :
               printf( "undefined switch '%s'",
                       argv[i] );
               exit_pgm( 4, "program terminated" );
               break;
       }
```

Listing 5.1 continues

Listing 5.1 continued

```c
        }

        /* font file name */
        else if( fnt_file == NULL )
            fnt_file = argv[i];

        /* printer destination */
        else
            prt_port = argv[i];
    }

    /* make sure we have a font name */
    if( fnt_file == NULL )
        exit_pgm( 8, "Error - no file name specified" );

    /* check for a valid font id */
    if( font_id < 0 )
        exit_pgm( 8, "Error - font id must be >= zero" );
}

#if MSDOS
/*------------------------------------------------------------*/
/* Use DOS func 44h to set raw mode if a char device...   */
/*------------------------------------------------------------*/

void set_binary_mode ( FILE *fptr )
{
    int hand;
    union REGS r;

    /* get file handle */
    hand = fileno(fptr);

    /* get device info */
    r.h.ah = 0x44;
    r.h.al = 0x00;
    r.x.bx = hand;
    r.x.dx = 0;
    int86(0x21, &r, &r);

    /* check the device... */
    if( (r.h.dl & 0x80) )              /* char device ? */
    {
        if( ! (r.h.dl & 0x20) )        /* cooked mode ? */
        {
            r.h.ah  = 0x44;
            r.h.al  = 0x01;
            r.x.bx  = hand;
            r.h.dh  = 0x00;
            r.h.dl |= 0x20;            /* set raw mode */
            int86(0x21, &r, &r);
        }
    }
}
#endif
```

Listing 5.1 continues

Listing 5.1 continued

```
/*------------------------------------------------------------*/
/*  Open files, set device mode...                            */
/*------------------------------------------------------------*/

void open_files( void )
{
    fnt_fp = fopen( fnt_file, "rb" );
    if( fnt_fp == NULL )
        exit_pgm( 8, "Could not find font file" );
    prt_fp = fopen( prt_port, "wb" );
    if( prt_fp == NULL )
        exit_pgm( 8, "Error opening printer" );
    #if MSDOS
    set_binary_mode( prt_fp );
    #endif
    printf( "\ndownloading '%s' to '%s'...",
                fnt_file, prt_port );
}

/*------------------------------------------------------------*/
/*  Close all files...                                        */
/*------------------------------------------------------------*/

void close_files( void )
{
    fclose( fnt_fp );
    fclose( prt_fp );
    printf( "done" );
}

/*------------------------------------------------------------*/
/*  Modify fd, save any values needed...                      */
/*------------------------------------------------------------*/

void modify_fd( font_desc *fd )
{
    int w;

    /* if forcing fixed-width, set fd flag */
    if( make_fixed )
        fd->orient = 0;

    /* save cell dimensions in quarter-dot units */
    cellW = REV_WRD( fd->cell_wid ) * 4;
    cellH = REV_WRD( fd->cell_hgt ) * 4;

    /* if cpi is nonzero, force specified pitch */
    if( cpi > 0.0 )
    {
        /* save actual cell width */
        w = cellW;

        /* compute required cell width */
        cellW = (int) ((1200.0 / cpi) + 0.5);

        /* design width must be at least this value, */
        /* otherwise char defs will be invalidated.  */
        /* update value if needed (units = dots).    */
```

Listing 5.1 continues

Listing 5.1 continued

```
        if( w < cellW )
            fd->cell_wid =  REV_WRD( (cellW+3)/4 );
    }

    /* set font's default pitch from cell size.  */
    /* note that pitch is expressed in qtr-dots. */
    if( fd->orient )  /* landscape font */
        fd->pitch = REV_WRD( cellH );
    else                /* portrait font */
        fd->pitch = REV_WRD( cellW );
}

/*------------------------------------------------------*/
/*  Modify cd for use as monospaced font...             */
/*------------------------------------------------------*/

void modify_cd( char_desc *cd )
{
    int ofs, wid;

    if( cd->orient ) /* char is for landscape mode */
    {
        wid = REV_WRD( cd->char_hgt );
        /* ofs is in dots, cellH is in qtr-dots */
        ofs = ((cellH>>2) + wid) / 2;
        cd->delta_x  = REV_WRD( cellH );
        cd->top_ofs  = REV_WRD( ofs );
    }
    else                 /* char is for portrait mode */
    {
        wid = REV_WRD( cd->char_wid );
        /* ofs is in dots, cellW is in qtr-dots */
        ofs = ((cellW>>2) - wid) / 2;
        cd->delta_x  = REV_WRD( cellW );
        cd->left_ofs = REV_WRD( ofs );
    }
}

/*------------------------------------------------------*/
/*  Send prefix escape sequences to the printer...      */
/*------------------------------------------------------*/

void send_pfx( void )
{
    /* if requested, reset printer */
    if( reset_prt )
        if( fwrite(pRESET,strlen(pRESET),1,prt_fp ) != 1 )
            exit_pgm( 8, "Error writing to printer" );

    /* set id for font to follow if not writing to disk */
    if( strchr( prt_port, '.' ) == NULL )
    {
        sprintf( fSETID, "\033*c%dD", font_id );
        if( fwrite(fSETID,strlen(fSETID),1,prt_fp) != 1 )
            exit_pgm( 8, "Error writing to printer" );
    }
```

Listing 5.1 continues

Listing 5.1 continued

```
}
/*------------------------------------------------------------*/
/*  Send suffix escape sequences to the printer...            */
/*------------------------------------------------------------*/

void send_sfx( void )
{
    /* if requested, make font permanent */
    if( is_perm )
        if( fwrite(fPERM,strlen(fPERM),1,prt_fp) != 1 )
            exit_pgm( 8, "Error writing to printer" );

    /* if requested, make font the current font */
    if( select_fnt )
    {
        sprintf( fSELECT, "\033(%dX", font_id );
        if( fwrite(fSELECT,strlen(fSELECT),1,prt_fp) != 1 )
            exit_pgm( 8, "Error writing to printer" );
    }
}

/*------------------------------------------------------------*/
/*  Skip next nbytes from input...                            */
/*------------------------------------------------------------*/

void skip_inp( int nbytes )
{
    int nout;

    while( nbytes > 0 )
    {
        nout = (nbytes > BUF_SIZ) ? BUF_SIZ : nbytes;
        nbytes -= nout;
        if( fread(io_buf, 1, nout, fnt_fp) != nout )
            exit_pgm( 8, "Unexpected EOF reading font" );
        bytes_read += nout;
    }
}

/*------------------------------------------------------------*/
/*  Copy next nbytes from input to printer...                 */
/*------------------------------------------------------------*/

void copy_inp( int nbytes )
{
    int nout;

    while( nbytes > 0 )
    {
        nout = (nbytes > BUF_SIZ) ? BUF_SIZ : nbytes;
        nbytes -= nout;
        if( fread(io_buf, 1, nout, fnt_fp) != nout )
            exit_pgm( 8, "Unexpected EOF reading font" );
        bytes_read += nout;
        if( fwrite(io_buf, 1, nout, prt_fp) != nout )
            exit_pgm( 8, "Error writing to printer" );
        bytes_written += nout;
```

Listing 5.1 continues

Listing 5.1 continued

```
    }
}
/*-----------------------------------------------------------*/
/*  Read nbytes from input into passed buffer...             */
/*-----------------------------------------------------------*/

void read_buf( void *buf, int nbytes )
{
    if( fread( buf, 1, nbytes, fnt_fp ) != nbytes )
        exit_pgm( 8, "Unexpected EOF reading font" );
    bytes_read += nbytes;
}

/*-----------------------------------------------------------*/
/*  Send passed buffer to printer...                         */
/*-----------------------------------------------------------*/

void send_buf( void *buf, int nbytes )
{
    if( fwrite( buf, 1, nbytes, prt_fp ) != nbytes )
        exit_pgm( 8, "Error writing to printer" );
    bytes_written += nbytes;
}

/*-----------------------------------------------------------*/
/*  Determine esq type and its numeric argument...           */
/*-----------------------------------------------------------*/

void get_esq_values( char esq_buf[], int *type, int *parm )
{
    int i;
    char  c1, c2, clast;

    /* extract group char and terminating char */
    c1 = esq_buf[1];
    c2 = esq_buf[2];
    i = 0;
    while( esq_buf[i] ) i++;
    clast = esq_buf[i-1];

    /* determine type */
    if( (c1==')') && (c2=='s') && (clast=='W') )
        *type = eFONTDESC;
    else if( (c1=='(') && (c2=='s') && (clast=='W') )
        *type = eCHARDESC;
    else if( (c1=='*') && (c2=='c') && (clast=='E') )
        *type = eCHARCODE;
    else
        *type = eUNKNOWN;

    /* get the sequence's value field */
    *parm = 0;
    i     = 0;
    while( (esq_buf[i]) && (! isdigit(esq_buf[i])) ) i++;
    if( isdigit(esq_buf[i]) )
        sscanf( esq_buf+i, "%d", parm );
}
```

Listing 5.1 continues

Listing 5.1 continued

```
/*-----------------------------------------------------------*/
/*  Process the escape seq now in the buffer...              */
/*-----------------------------------------------------------*/

void do_esq( char esq_buf[] )
{
    font_desc  fd;
    char_desc  cd;
    int        esq_type, esq_parm;

    /* get the escape sequence type and its */
    /* numeric value field...               */
    get_esq_values( esq_buf, &esq_type, &esq_parm );

    bytes_read += strlen( esq_buf );

    /* process the sequence */
    switch( esq_type )
    {

      case eFONTDESC:  /* font descriptor */

            /* send the sequence */
            send_buf( esq_buf, strlen(esq_buf) );

            /* if cvt to fixed, read-modify-write */
            if( make_fixed )
            {
              /* read the descriptor */
              read_buf( &fd, sizeof(font_desc) );
              /* modify as necessary */
              modify_fd( &fd );
              /* send the descriptor */
              send_buf( &fd, sizeof(font_desc) );
              /* send any trailing info */
              if( esq_parm > sizeof(font_desc) )
                 copy_inp( esq_parm-sizeof(font_desc) );

            }
            /* otherwise, just send the descriptor */
            else
              copy_inp( esq_parm );
            break;

      case eCHARDESC:  /* char descriptor */

            /* are we using this char ? */
            if( dld_chr[cur_chr] )
            {
              /* send the sequence */
              send_buf( esq_buf, strlen(esq_buf) );

              /* if cvt to fixed, read-modify-write */
              if( make_fixed )
              {
                /* read the descriptor */
                read_buf( &cd, sizeof(char_desc) );
                /* modify as necessary */
```

Listing 5.1 continues

Listing 5.1 continued

```
                    modify_cd( &cd );
                    /* send the descriptor */
                    send_buf( &cd, sizeof(char_desc) );
                    /* send the bitmap which follows */
                    if( esq_parm > sizeof(char_desc) )
                       copy_inp( esq_parm-sizeof(char_desc) );
               }
               /* otherwise, just send the descriptor */
               else
                  copy_inp( esq_parm );
            }
            else
               /* skip the descriptor */
               skip_inp( esq_parm );
            break;

         case eCHARCODE:  /* specify character code ADE */

            cur_chr = esq_parm;

            /* send the sequence */
            if( dld_chr[cur_chr] )
               send_buf( esq_buf, strlen(esq_buf) );
            break;

         caseeUNKNOWN:  /* unexpected sequence - ignore it */

            printf( "Unexpected sequence '%s' ignored",
                    esq_buf );
            send_buf( esq_buf, strlen(esq_buf) );
            break;
      }
}

/*------------------------------------------------------------*/
/*  Read the next esc seq from the font file...               */
/*------------------------------------------------------------*/

int get_esq( char esq_buf[], int buf_len )
{
     int i, nbytes;

     nbytes = 0;
     while( (i=fgetc(fnt_fp)) != EOF )
     {
       esq_buf[nbytes] = (char) i;
       nbytes++;
       /* cap letter signals last character in sequence */
       if( IS_TERM_CHR( i ) ) break;
       if( nbytes == buf_len )
         exit_pgm( 8, "Error - esc seq buffer overflow" );
     }

     /* validity check - first char should be decimal 27 */
     if( (nbytes > 0) && (esq_buf[0] != 27) )
       exit_pgm( 8, "Error - esc seq expected, not found" );

     /* add a terminating null */
```

Listing 5.1   continues

Listing 5.1 continued

```
    esq_buf[nbytes] = 0;
    return( nbytes );
}

/*-----------------------------------------------------------*/
/*  Send the font file to the printer...                     */
/*-----------------------------------------------------------*/

void send_fnt( void )
{
    while( get_esq( esq_buf, ESQ_SIZ ) > 0 )
      do_esq( esq_buf );
}

/*-----------------------------------------------------------*/
/*                      M  A  I  N                            */
/*-----------------------------------------------------------*/

void main ( int argc, char *argv[] )
{
    char msg[80];

    /* sign on */
    printf("\n----- HP Font File Download Utility -----");

    /* enough args ? */
    if( (argc < 2) || (*(argv[1]) == '?') )
    {
        explain_pgm();
        exit_pgm( 0, "" );
    }

    /* set values from command line */
    process_args( argc, argv );

    /* init counters */
    bytes_read    = 0;
    bytes_written = 0;

    /* do the download... */
    open_files();
    send_pfx();
    send_fnt();
    send_sfx();
    close_files();

    /* summarize activity and exit */
    sprintf( msg,
            "%ld bytes downloaded out of %ld bytes read",
            bytes_written, bytes_read );
    exit_pgm( 0, msg );
}
```

6

Using Fonts from
Application Programs

Introduction

The LaserJet family has long been noted for its text capabilities, yet there is surprising little commercial software available to the developer that truly exploits those capabilities. Here, we are referring to developer tools such as callable functions libraries, not to stand-alone applications; the latter category is, by contrast, quite extensive. This dearth of software is all the more curious when you consider that a PCL-based toolkit would provide access to a rather substantial family of printers.

In this chapter we implement just such a toolkit, a library of functions to provide a calling program access to the text-rendering capabilities of the LaserJet. We begin with the design of some needed data structures.

Font Data Structures

For a program to utilize a font properly, it must have access to some information about that font. As a minimum, it would need access to a width table holding the widths of the individual characters in the font. Beyond this, it is handy for the program to know the name of the font and some of its basic characteristics.

One way to gather this information is to make copies of the font's data descriptors as the font is being downloaded. However, since much of the information contained in the descriptors is of interest only to the printer and since the combined size of all of a font's descriptors is significant enough to pose a memory management problem to the developer, this method isn't useful. We will therefore construct a more suitable structure and fill it from the font's descriptors as they are encountered during the downloading process. Here is a reasonable implementation. A brief description of each member follows.

```
typedef short width_tbl[256]; /* array of char widths */

typedef struct _font_hdr      /* font data structure */
{
     char        name[18];      /* name of font */
     short       family;        /* typeface family */
     short       orient;        /* portrait or landscape */
     short       spacing;       /* proportional or fixed */
     short       posture;       /* upright or italic */
     short       weight;        /* light, med, bold, etc */
     short       pitch;         /* default width */
     short       height;        /* default leading */
     width_tbl   wtbl;          /* array of char widths */
     }
font_hdr;
```

name   Name of the font. Note that the font name member of the font
                descriptor is 16 characters in length. The name member of the
                font header structure is 2 bytes larger: 1 byte for a terminating
                null and an additional byte for padding to a word boundary.
                Without the padding, the size of the structure can vary depend-
                ing upon compiler alignment switches.

family   Typeface family. This field can be used to process bold and italic
                codes. To find a bold version of a given font we look for another
                font from the same family that has a bold weight. Note that with
                the Series II and earlier printers this value is an 8-bit quantity. It
                has subsequently been enlarged to a word value in which the
                typeface family comprises 9 bits. The remaining bits serve to
                specify vendor and version codes.

orient   Font orientation. 0 = portrait, 1 = landscape.

spacing   Font spacing. 0 = fixed width, 1 = proportionally spaced.

posture   Font posture. 0 = upright, 1 = italic. An additional value, 2 for
                alternate italic, is seldom encountered. Note that the posture is
                a bit field within the LSB (least significant byte) of the style
                word.

weight   Font stroke weight. This is a signed value in the range −7 to 7,
                where normal weight is zero, lighter weights are less than zero,
                and heavier weights are greater than zero. For example, bold is
                defined as a weight of 3.

pitch   The font's default pitch in quarter-dots. For a fixed-width font this is the character width of all characters. For a proportionally spaced font this defines the size of the space character.

height   The font's default height in quarter-dots. This defines the font's height characteristic, which, converted to points, is the font's point size. It also provides the default leading (line spacing).

bldist   The font's baseline distance in dots. This is measured from the top of the cell.

wtbl   The font's character width table. Each value is expressed in quarter-dots. The character code is used to index into this array to find the width of a particular character. Note that character definitions for some codes cannot be utilized, for example, the escape character, decimal 27. A corresponding width-table entry is present but is not used and should be set to zero.

When you deal with strings from an application it is often necessary to make various measurements of a string—its width and height, for example. It is useful to gather these different measurements into a single structure, which we will term a **string metrics** structure, defined as follows.

```
typedef struct _string_metric
{
     double width;          /* full width */
     double height;         /* max height */
     double nb_width;       /* non-blank width */
     double ascent;         /* max ascent dist */
     double descent;        /* max descent dist */
}
string_metric;
```

Note that the three height members, height, ascent, and descent, are maximums for all characters in a string and allow for the possibility of multiple fonts within the same string. The two width measurements are the full string width including blanks and the same width minus all blanks. The latter measurement represents the combined width of all words in the string. All values are expressed in inches.

Width-Table Generation

Any application generating text on the LaserJet almost certainly needs to be able to determine the sizes of strings and characters. With a fixed-width font only a single quantity is needed, the font's pitch. With proportionally spaced fonts, however, character widths can vary from character to character, and a width table is required.

This is nothing more than an array of widths, where the character's ADE value is used to index into the array.

The width table can be generated on the fly as the font is downloaded, or it can be generated once and saved as a disk file. The table remains valid as long as the original font is not modified in any way. The second approach was touched upon briefly in Chapter 4, in the discussion of the HPQFONT program. The HPQFONT program (Listing 4.2) will write the binary image of the font_hdr structure defined in the preceding section. A suitable font download function must also be able to create this data structure.

From a programming standpoint it does not matter whether widths are stored as inches or dots. However, using inches requires the use of floating point arrays, which can contribute to a program's memory overhead. From a resource standpoint, it is best to work with integer dot units, converting dots or quarter-dots to inches as a last step before using the value. Note that physical character widths are computed using the delta_x member from the character descriptor, not the char_width member. Also keep in mind that delta_x is specified in quarter-dot units, while the other descriptor members are given in dots.

The Font Download Function

Let us modify the perform_escape_sequence() code fragment presented in Chapter 5 to gather font and width-table information. We will need to add some static variables, as follows:

```
int       cur_ch;      /* current character code */
font_hdr  fh;          /* header with width table */
font_desc fd;          /* font descriptor structure */
char_desc cd;          /* current char descriptor */
```

The body of the function then looks like the following:

```
case eFONTDESC : /* define font descriptor */
    nbytes = sequence_value_field();
    send_sequence();
    read_fd( &fd );
        :
    /* fill in font-hdr structure */
        :
    send_fd( &fd );
    read_and_send( nbytes-sizeof(font_desc) );
    break;

case eCHARDESC : /* define character descriptor */
    nbytes = sequence_value_field();
```

```
            send_sequence();
            read_cd( &cd );
            /* save character width */
            fh.wtbl[cur_ch] = cd.delta_x;
            send_cd( &cd );
            read_and_send( nbytes-sizeof(char_desc) );
            break;

    case eCHARCODE : /* specify character code */
            cur_ch = sequence_value_field();
            send_sequence();
            break;

    default :   /* unknown, or an error */
            :
            break;
```

Note that the value field of the specify-character-code sequence is saved to index into the width-table array. Then, when a character descriptor is encountered, its **delta_x** member is placed in the array. Once the character descriptor has been read and forwarded on to the printer, the remainder of the character definition, the character's bitmap, is also read and sent.

The width table should be initialized to zeroes. It is then a simple process to determine if a character is defined—its width will be nonzero. Recall that fonts generally do not provide a character definition for the space character, so no width-table entry for this character will be generated. This value should be set to the font's default pitch, that is,

```
fh.wtbl[32] = fd.pitch;
```

The actual download function and its supporting functions are presented in the listings at the end of this chapter. Note that word values from descriptors must have their byte order reversed before being used in a program. In the code fragments we presented, this was omitted for the sake of illustration.

The Font Register Function

It is often more convenient to download a font once and make it permanent, rather than downloading the same font at every program execution. This case is handled by the **register_font()** function, which can be used in lieu of the **download_font()** function.

The **register_font()** function loads a binary image of a **font_hdr** structure that was previously created by the HPQFONT program (see Listing 4.2). It assumes that the font has already been downloaded. Note that an application has no means of verifying that this is indeed the case, and must rely upon the program user to manage downloaded fonts. If a registered font is not resident on the printer then the escape sequence to select that font will be ignored, and the printed output will not be correct.

Computing Character and String Sizes

Once a font is downloaded and its width table is constructed, it is possible to implement functions to determine the sizes of individual characters and strings. Although the table is stored in integer units of quarter-dots, these functions will be most useful returning values in inches, as in the following:

```
double chr_width( int ch )
{
     return( ((double) fh.wtbl[ch]) / 1200.0 );
}

double str_width( char *str )
{
     int sum;
     sum = 0;
     while( *str )
          sum += fh.wtbl[*str++];
     return( ((double) sum) / 1200.0 );
}
```

For working with other units, the following constants can be used to convert quantities from quarter-dot units:

Conversion	Multiply By
Quarter-dots to inches	0.000833
Quarter-dots to centimeters	0.00212
Quarter-dots to points	0.06

Note that, as coded in the preceding paragraph, the `str_width` function assumes that all characters in a string are from the same font. If your application must support arbitrary font changes within a string then some additional coding is necessary. The most straightforward approach to handling arbitrary font changes is to implement a select-font code that can be embedded directly into strings. Then, when the width function encounters a font change code it can switch width tables. This is the approach used by our toolkit.

Character Heights and Line Spacing

Unlike width information, individual character heights are not normally needed. A single leading value applies to the font as a whole, and this value is specified by the height member of the font descriptor (which is saved as the height member of the font header structure). This value, converted to inches, is returned by the font_hgt() function:

```
double font_hgt( void )
{
     return( ((double) fh.height) / 1200.0 );
}
```

When the LaserJet receives a carriage-return/line-feed pair, the printer's cursor X position is updated to the current left margin, and the cursor Y position is moved down the page by an amount determined from the currently active line spacing. Note that line spacing is independent of the current font's leading value, and that the printer's default line spacing is 6 lines per inch. If, for example, you download and select an 18 point font and then print a file without altering the line spacing, the lines of text will overlap vertically. For this reason—and because the available printer-supported line spacings are limited—it is best for an application to manage line spacing itself and explicitly set the printer's cursor position at each new line.

The scheme used by many word-processing programs is to define a line spacing variable that is multiplied by the current font's character height to obtain a line spacing increment. The variable is set to 1.0 initially, corresponding to single spacing. If, for example, double spacing is requested, the line spacing variable is set to 2.0, and the distance between consecutive lines of text is computed as font_hgt() * 2.0. By making the line spacing multiplier a real value, we can support fractional line spacings as well.

Cursor Positioning

This material was discussed in Chapter 1 but is summarized here for the reader's convenience.

The LaserJet uses a printer cursor that defines the current position on the physical page and determines where the next printed output will occur. This cursor position is used for all printed output, including text, bitmapped graphics, and **rules** (a rule is nothing more than a filled rectangular area).

As each text character is printed, the cursor position is automatically adjusted to the right by an amount equal to the delta_x value for the character just printed. This is the *only* position management that the printer performs. Any other position changes must be explicitly specified by the application. As we continue to output printable characters, eventually the right margin is reached. At that point any additional printable characters are clipped and discarded unless there is input from the application.

A new line can be forced by sending a carriage-return/line-feed pair to the printer (byte values 13 and 10 decimal, or 0D and 0A hex). Note that these byte commands function exactly as indicated by their names: a carriage return (13) moves the cursor's X position to the left margin; a line-feed (10) advances the cursor's Y position by an amount determined from the currently active line spacing.

As we said, it is best for applications to reposition the printer's cursor manually. There are a number of PCL commands provided for this purpose; they vary in the units employed and whether the position is relative or absolute. The most commonly employed commands specify absolute positions in dot coordinates.

To specify a new X position, we send

Esc * p # X

where # is replaced by the number of dots from the left edge of the logical page area to the desired position. For example, to position the cursor 1 inch to the right of the left page boundary we send

Esc * p 3 0 0 X

To specify a new Y position, we send

Esc * p # Y

where # is replaced by the number of dots from the top edge of the logical page area to the desired position. For example, to position the cursor 2 inches below the top page boundary we send

Esc * p 6 0 0 Y

If you want, you can combine the two commands, as in the following:

Esc * p 3 0 0 x 6 0 0 Y

(Note that in the combined form only the final parameter character, the Y, is capitalized.)

We can now implement a set-cursor-position function taking arguments in units of inches as illustrated in the following code.

```
void set_cursor_posn( double xi, double yi )
{
    int    xd, yd;
    char   cmd[20];

    /* convert inches to dots */
    xd = (int) ((xi * 300.0) + 0.5);
    yd = (int) ((yi * 300.0) + 0.5);
```

```
        /* fabricate the escape sequence */
        sprintf( cmd, "\033*p%dx%dY", xd, yd );

        /* and send the sequence to the printer */
        send_to_printer( cmd );
}
```

The `send_to_printer()` function should be treated as pseudo-code at this point. For its actual implementation refer to the source code listings presented at the end of this chapter.

Finally, remember that coordinates are relative to the logical page, not the physical page. To reference a position relative to the physical edge of the page, the logical page starts approximately a quarter inch from the left and a half inch from the top of the paper. The actual offsets can vary slightly as a result of inaccuracies in the mechanical process of the paper moving through the printer.

Word and String Justification

Justification refers to how an object is oriented, or placed, with respect to a given position. The most commonly used justification for text is *(left, base)*, meaning that the referenced location lies at the intersection of the left edge and baseline of the word or string being justified.

There are three commonly used horizontal justifications, left, center, and right. There are four commonly used vertical justifications, top, center, base, and bottom. Of these, only vertical justification with reference to a font's baseline can vary from font to font. A font's baseline will generally be positioned in the bottom half of the character cell, but this is not guaranteed. Recall that the baseline position sets the font's ascent and descent distances. Examples of various justifications are illustrated in Figure 6.1.

Differing vertical justifications are not used very often in typical page layout applications. For this reason we will work with baseline justification only. The rare situation requiring fine control of vertical placement can be handled by a function to place a string on the page at an arbitrary (X, Y) position.

Line Justification

In most cases, an application that prints text must be concerned with line justification—how the lines of text making up a paragraph are positioned between a page's left and right margins. Two schemes are commonly employed, termed **ragged-right justification** and **full justification**.

In ragged-right mode, lines of text always begin at the left margin, and the space between words is fixed, typically set to the width of the space character, decimal 32.

FIGURE 6.1 Examples of Text Justification

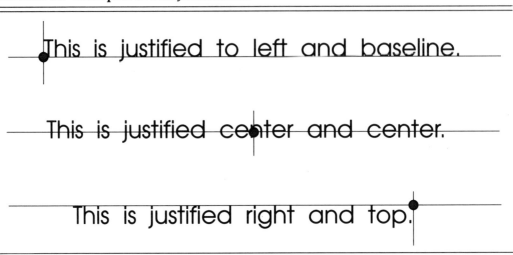

Words are output on the current line until the end of a word would protrude beyond the right margin. At that point a new line is started, and the protruding word becomes the first word on the next line. A result of this algorithm is that, while the left side of the text body is a straight line, the right side of the text body presents a line that zig-zags left and right down the page, giving the ragged appearance for which it is named. Ragged-right implies left justification; the two terms are interchangeable.

In full justification mode, the spacing between words is variable and is adjusted so that the right side of the text body also presents a straight line. Note that in order to implement variable word spacing it is necessary to defer outputting the words of a line until the entire line has been collected.

Kerning

Kerning refers to the process of overlapping the images of two consecutive characters to reduce the spacing between them. It is employed to make the visual spacing of characters within a word appear more uniform. Kerning is an advanced technique that is normally required only in the most stringent typesetting situations. The amount of overlap depends upon the characters involved; in many cases it will be zero; that is, the two characters are not kerned. In cases where an overlap is used, the two characters involved are referred to as a **kerning pair**.

To implement kerning, it is necessary to construct a table of kerning pairs that contains an offset to be applied to the normal spacing between the letters in each pair. Then, as the characters of a word are output to the printer, a table lookup is performed to determine if the current character and the following character constitute a kerning pair. If so, the current character is output and the printer's cursor position is adjusted by the quantity `cur_char_width + kern_offset` before the next character is output.

Figure 6.2 illustrates the use of kerning. Depending upon a number of factors, including typeface, type style, point size, and the characters involved, the effect can vary from barely discernable to very noticeable. On the whole, however, kerning is a subtle effect and quite acceptable results can be obtained without it.

Underlining

The LaserJet printer will perform text underlining on its own, so it is not necessary to implement this feature in software. It is only necessary to provide functions to turn underlining on and off. To turn underlining on, the following escape sequence is sent:

```
Esc & d # D
```

where **#** is 0 for fixed underlining or 3 for floating underlining. **Fixed underlining** places the underline 5 dots below the baseline (using a line that is 3 dots thick). **Floating underlining** uses the greatest underline distance found among the fonts used on the current line, where the underline distance is taken from the font descriptor.

When underlining is enabled, an action resulting in positive horizontal movement causes an underline to be drawn. There are two such actions: outputting text and positive cursor positioning.

To disable underlining, the following escape sequence is sent:

```
Esc & d @
```

FIGURE 6.2 Example of Normal and Kerned Text

Normal Spacing   After Kerning

Text Management Codes

A text-printing application that supports features beyond those of the DOS print spooler must have a scheme for indicating font changes, formatting specifications, justification settings, and the like. The most flexible approach—the one used by most word-processing software—is to embed commands directly into the text being dealt with. A text file so modified is called a **document file**, consisting of an ordered stream of data (text) and commands. In this sense, a document file is not unlike a font file.

The document file approach has been implemented in many different ways. For example, both the Unix NROFF text formatting utility and IBM's SCRIPT product work with a plain ASCII (or EBCDIC) text file in which commands of the form .xx are embedded. WordPerfect also uses embedded codes, which are displayed as commands between square brackets, for example, [BOLD].

Early word-processing software for the IBM PC, such as the original WordStar, also used embedded codes. In many cases byte values with the high bit set were used as formatting codes. This corresponds to values above 127 if bytes are unsigned or values less than zero if they are signed. Nowadays this is not a good approach, because it limits a font's naturally expressible character set to less than 127 characters.

For our purposes here, we want formatting codes to be easily embedded within an existing file using a typical text editor or word processor. We also want to minimize keystrokes and, at the same time, make formatting codes visually easy to distinguish and interpret. These are perhaps contradictory goals, but we will attempt a solution with them in mind. Here, then, are the rules:

1. All formatting codes appear between curly braces, for example,

    ```
    { xxx }
    ```

2. All codes consist of a single alphabetical character. Codes that require a numeric parameter will be followed by the parameter value. For example,

    ```
    X Y1 Z234
    ```

3. Most codes are toggles that turn a feature on or off. A capital letter turns the corresponding feature on, a lower-case letter turns that feature off. As an example, to bold the phrase "hello, world" you use

    ```
    {B}hello, world{b}
    ```

4. Multiple codes can be combined within one pair of braces. Embedded blanks can be used for readability and will be ignored. For example:

    ```
    {BiU} or {B i U}
    ```

TABLE 6.1 Supported Toolkit Formatting Codes

Code	Meaning
B-b	Bold on-off
C-c	Center justify on-off
F*nnn*	Select font with ID *nnn*
I-i	Italic on-off
J-j	Full justify on-off
L or l	Left justify
N or n	Normal face (no bold or italic)
R-r	Right justify on-off

Table 6.1 lists the codes that are implemented here.

The Text Processing Toolkit

A look at the supported codes given in Table 6.1 provides a general idea of the toolkit's capabilities. These represent a minimal function set for obtaining useful results and can be used as a starting point in the implementation of a page layout program for the LaserJet printer.

Note that there are no codes for indicating specific fonts, only for selecting fonts by ID and for specifying face style changes. A program using the toolkit handles this aspect by downloading the fonts to be used and specifying the font IDs that select each font.

Additional page layout parameters such as margins and tab settings are also set outside the body of the document being printed. While there are functions provided to control these parameters there are no corresponding format codes for setting these parameter values within the document itself. These can be handled separately by using a startup initialization file or by implementing additional formatting codes.

The toolkit comprises three modules. These are:

FNTMGMT.C   Functions for managing fonts, implementing PCL commands, and controlling the printer interface. See Listings 6.1 and 6.2.

DOCGMT.C   Functions for managing the document: controlling margins, tabs, line spacing, selecting fonts, and so forth. See Listings 6.3 and 6.4.

TOKEN.C   Functions for processing input lines as token strings. This is used when you format lines in full justification mode. See Listings 6.5 and 6.6.

Also provided is a sample application program, PRTDOC.C, Listing 6.7. This illustrates the toolkit in actual practice. Finally, SAMPLE.DOC, Listing 6.8, provides a typical excerpt from a document file and shows the format codes embedded within the text.

There are two basic input functions, `line_store()` and `line_out()`. The `line_store()` function is used when in full justification mode, and `line_out()` is used for all remaining justification modes. The `line_out()` function accepts a line of text as a parameter and then outputs the line appropriately to the printer. By contrast, `line_store()` parses each input line, extracts individual format tokens, and stores them in a circular token queue. The position of the format token is marked in the input string by placing an escape character at that point in the string. When the combined widths of all stored characters exceeds the current line width, the `line_flush()` function is called to format a line of output, using as many characters as are needed. Any excess is moved to the front of the character buffer to serve as the start of the next line.

Note that `line_flush()` will not normally empty the buffer/queue. This occurs only with the last line of a paragraph (signaled by an empty input line) or with an abrupt justification change.

Formatting codes are interpreted by the `process_fmt()` function. This function is called twice for each format code, once when the code is queued and again when the code is unqueued. Note that only in the latter case do we actually want any escape sequences to be sent to the printer.

A complete page layout program is beyond the scope of this book. As a result, there are some basic capabilities that are not addressed by the toolkit. The developer may consider adding such capabilities as tab character processing, page numbering, page headers and footers, and margin-related functions such as indent and inset.

LISTING 6.1 FNTMGMT.H, Font Management Function Prototypes

```c
/*----------------------------------------------------------*/
/* FILE:   FNTMGMT.H                                        */
/* DESC:   Font management function prototypes.             */
/*----------------------------------------------------------*/

/* fmt code delimiters */
#define  BGN_FMT   '{'
#define  END_FMT   '}'

/* args to str_width() */
#define  W_FULL   1                        /* with blanks */
#define  W_NB     0                     /* without blanks */

/* args to str_height() */
#define  H_FULL   0                        /* full height */
#define  H_ASC    1                        /* ascent only */
#define  H_DSC    2                       /* descent only */

/* function prototypes */
void       assert_error( char *msg );
int        open_printer( char *dev_name );
void       close_printer( int eject_page );
int        send_buf( char *buf, int len );
int        send_str( char *str );
int        send_chr( char chr );
int        copy_inp( FILE *inp, int nbytes );
void       download_font( char *path, int font_id );
void       register_font( char *path, int font_id );
int        create_wtl( char *path, int font_id );
void       select_font( int font_id, int notify );
void       delete_font( int font_id );
font_hdr  *get_font_hdr( int font_id );
font_hdr  *cur_font_hdr( void );
int        cur_font_id( void );
int       *cur_width_tbl( void );
double     cur_height( void );
double     cur_ascent( void );
double     cur_descent( void );
double     cur_pitch( void );
double     get_height( int font_id );
double     get_ascent( int font_id );
double     get_descent( int font_id );
double     get_pitch( int font_id );
int        is_bold( int font_id );
int        is_italic( int font_id );
int        find_bold( int font_id );
int        find_italic( int font_id );
int        find_normal( int font_id );
int        new_font_id( int id, int face );
double     chr_width( int ch );
double     fch_width( int ch, int font_id );
double     str_width( char *str, int full );
double     str_height( char *str, int full );
void       str_size( char *str, string_metric *sm );
void       set_ixy( int ix, int iy );
void       set_ix( int ix );
void       set_iy( int iy );
void       set_xy( double x, double y );
void       set_x( double x );
void       set_y( double y );
void       set_underlining( int state );
void       eject_pg( void );
```

LISTING 6.2 FNTMGMT.C, Font Management Functions for Text Toolkit

```
/*------------------------------------------------------------*/
/* FILE:  FNTMGMT.C                                           */
/* DESC:  Font management functions for text toolkit          */
/*------------------------------------------------------------*/

#include "stdlib.h"
#include "stdio.h"
#include "string.h"
#include "ctype.h"

/* define the following for MS DOS systems */
#define MSDOS 1

#if MSDOS
#include "dos.h"
#endif

#include "ljfont.h"
#include "fntmgmt.h"

/*------------------------------------------------------------*/
/* Defines and such specific to this module...               */
/*------------------------------------------------------------*/

#define  MAX_FONTS  16       /* controls table sizes, etc. */
#define  ESQ_SIZE   64       /* size of escape seq buffer */
#define  BUF_SIZE   256         /* size of i/o buffer */

/*------------------------------------------------------------*/
/* Global data and such...                                   */
/*------------------------------------------------------------*/

static FILE     *prt;          /* file pointer for printer */

static font_hdr *fnt_tbl[MAX_FONTS],      /* header table */
                *cur_hdr;                /* current header */

static int      fnt_ids[MAX_FONTS];         /* id table */

static int      is_open = 0,      /* flag - printer open */
                fnt_cnt = 0,      /* active tbl entry cnt */
                cur_id = -1,         /* current font id */
                cur_ch,           /* var to save chr code */
                e_last,           /* last sequence type */
                x_bias = -60,        /* fine tune origin */
                y_bias = -120;

/*------------------------------------------------------------*/
/* Function to terminate with an error...                    */
/*------------------------------------------------------------*/

void assert_error( char *msg )
{
    printf( "%s\n", msg );
    exit( 8 );
}
```

Listing 6.2 continues

Listing 6.2 continued

```
#if MSDOS
/*----------------------------------------------------------*/
/* Use DOS func 44h to set raw mode if a char device...   */
/*----------------------------------------------------------*/

void set_binary_mode ( FILE *fptr )
{
    int hand;
    union REGS r;

    /* get file handle */
    hand = fileno(fptr);

    /* get device info */
    r.h.ah = 0x44;
    r.h.al = 0x00;
    r.x.bx = hand;
    r.x.dx = 0;
    int86(0x21, &r, &r);

    /* check the device... */

    if( (r.h.dl & 0x80) )            /* char device ? */
    {
       if( ! (r.h.dl & 0x20) )       /* cooked mode ? */
       {
          r.h.ah  = 0x44;
          r.h.al  = 0x01;
          r.x.bx  = hand;
          r.h.dh  = 0x00;
          r.h.dl |= 0x20;            /* set raw mode */
          int86(0x21, &r, &r);
       }
    }
}
#endif

/*----------------------------------------------------------*/
/* Open a stream to the printer...                        */
/*----------------------------------------------------------*/

int open_printer( char *dev_name )
{
    if( (prt=fopen(dev_name, "wb")) != NULL )
    {
       #if MSDOS
       set_binary_mode( prt );
       #endif
       is_open = 1;
    }
    else
    {
       is_open = 0;
    }
    return( is_open );
}
```

Listing 6.2 continues

Listing 6.2 continued

```
/*----------------------------------------------------------*/
/* Close the printer stream...                              */
/*----------------------------------------------------------*/

void close_printer( int eject_page )
{
    if( is_open )
    {
        if( eject_page )
            send_str( "\014" );
        fclose( prt );
        is_open = 0;
    }
}

/*----------------------------------------------------------*/
/* Write a buffer to the printer...                         */
/*----------------------------------------------------------*/

int send_buf( char *buf, int len )
{
    return( fwrite( buf, len, 1, prt ) );
}

/*----------------------------------------------------------*/
/* Write a string to the printer...                         */
/*----------------------------------------------------------*/

int send_str( char *str )
{
    return( fwrite( str, strlen(str), 1, prt ) );
}

/*----------------------------------------------------------*/
/* Write a char to the printer...                           */
/*----------------------------------------------------------*/

int send_chr( char chr  )
{
    return( fputc( chr, prt ) );
}

/*----------------------------------------------------------*/
/* Copy n bytes from a file to the printer...               */
/*----------------------------------------------------------*/

#define INP_SIZE 64

int copy_inp( FILE *inp, int nbytes )
{
    int  n;
    char buf[INP_SIZE];

    while( nbytes > 0 )
    {
        n = nbytes > INP_SIZE ? INP_SIZE : nbytes;
        if( fread(buf, n, 1, inp) != 1 )
            assert_error( "Unexpected EOF in copy_inp" );
```

Listing 6.2 continues

Listing 6.2 continued

```
        send_buf( buf, n );
        nbytes -= n;
    }
    return( 1 );
}

/*----------------------------------------------------------*/
/* Return ptr to new tbl entry with passed id...            */
/*----------------------------------------------------------*/

font_hdr *get_font_hdr( int font_id )
{
    int i;

    /* Find an existing table entry */

    for( i=0; i<fnt_cnt; i++ )
        if( fnt_ids[i] == font_id )
            return( fnt_tbl[i] );

    return( NULL );
}

/*----------------------------------------------------------*/
/* Return ptr to new tbl entry with passed id...            */
/*----------------------------------------------------------*/

static font_hdr *new_font_hdr( int font_id )
{
    font_hdr *fh;

    /* Is there room for a new entry? */

    if( fnt_cnt == MAX_FONTS )
        assert_error( "Font header table overflow" );

    /* Create the new table entry */

    fh = (font_hdr *) malloc( sizeof(font_hdr) );
    if( fh == NULL )
        assert_error( "Out of memory allocating font header" );
    fnt_tbl[fnt_cnt] = fh;
    fnt_ids[fnt_cnt] = font_id;
    fnt_cnt++;

    return( fh );
}

/*----------------------------------------------------------*/
/* Delete tbl entry with passed id...                       */
/*----------------------------------------------------------*/

static int del_font_hdr( int font_id )
{
    int      i, j;

    /* Find entry to delete */
```

Listing 6.2   continues

Listing 6.2 continued

```
    j = -1;
    for( i=0; i<fnt_cnt; i++ )
        if( fnt_ids[i] == font_id )
        {
            j = i;
            break;
        }

    /* Free it, remove its slot in table */

    if( j != -1 )
    {
        free( fnt_tbl[j] );
        for( i=j+1; i<fnt_cnt; i++ )
        {
            fnt_tbl[i-1] = fnt_tbl[i];
            fnt_ids[i-1] = fnt_ids[i];
        }
        fnt_cnt--;
    }

    return( (j==-1) ? 0 : 1 );
}

/*----------------------------------------------------------*/
/*  Init a font header from a font descriptor...            */
/*----------------------------------------------------------*/

static void init_font_hdr( font_desc *fd, font_hdr *fh )
{
    strncpy( fh->name, fd->font_name, 16 );
    fh->name[16] = 0;
    /* family is a 9-bit value! */
    fh->family   = ((fd->vendor & 1) << 8) |
                     fd->typeface;
    fh->orient   = fd->orient;
    fh->spacing  = fd->spacing;
    fh->posture  = fd->style_lsb & 0x03;
    fh->weight   = fd->stk_wgt;
    fh->pitch    = REV_WRD( fd->pitch );
    fh->height   = REV_WRD( fd->height );
    fh->bldist   = REV_WRD( fd->bl_dist );
    /* initialize the width table */
    memset( fh->wtbl, 0, sizeof( width_tbl ) );
}

/*----------------------------------------------------------*/
/*  Determine esq type and its numeric argument...          */
/*----------------------------------------------------------*/

static void get_esq_values( char esq_buf[], int *type, int *parm )
{
    int i;
    char  c1, c2, clast;

    /* extract group char and terminating char */
    c1 = esq_buf[1];
    c2 = esq_buf[2];
```

Listing 6.2 continues

Listing 6.2 continued

```
        i = 0;
        while( esq_buf[i] ) i++;
        clast = esq_buf[i-1];

        /* determine type */
        if( (c1==')') && (c2=='s') && (clast=='W') )
            *type = eFONTDESC;
        else if( (c1=='(') && (c2=='s') && (clast=='W') )
            *type = eCHARDESC;
        else if( (c1=='*') && (c2=='c') && (clast=='E') )
            *type = eCHARCODE;
        else
            *type = eUNKNOWN;

        /* get the sequence's value field */
        *parm = 0;
        i     = 0;
        while( (esq_buf[i]) && (! isdigit(esq_buf[i])) ) i++;
        if( isdigit(esq_buf[i]) )
            sscanf( esq_buf+i, "%d", parm );
}

/*------------------------------------------------------------*/
/*  Process the escape seq now in the buffer...               */
/*------------------------------------------------------------*/

static void do_esq( FILE *inp, char esq_buf[], font_hdr *fh )
{
        font_desc  fd;
        char_desc  cd;
        int        esq_type, esq_parm;

        /* get the escape sequence type and its */
        /* numeric value field...               */
        get_esq_values( esq_buf, &esq_type, &esq_parm );

        /* process the sequence */
        switch( esq_type )
        {

          case eFONTDESC:  /* font descriptor.............. */

                /* send the sequence */
                send_str( esq_buf );

                /* read the descriptor */
                if( fread( &fd, sizeof(font_desc), 1, inp ) != 1 )
                    assert_error( "Read on font file failed" );

                /* collect header info for this font */
                init_font_hdr( &fd, fh );

                /* send the descriptor */
                send_buf( (char *) &fd, sizeof(font_desc) );

                /* send any trailing info */
                if( esq_parm > sizeof(font_desc) )
```

Listing 6.2 continues

Listing 6.2 continued

```
                copy_inp( inp, esq_parm-sizeof(font_desc) );

        break;

    case eCHARDESC:  /* char descriptor.............. */

        /* send the sequence */
        send_buf( esq_buf, strlen(esq_buf) );

        /* if not a continuation... */
        if( e_last != eCHARDESC )
        {
           /* read the descriptor */
           if( fread( &cd, sizeof(char_desc), 1, inp ) != 1 )
              assert_error( "Read on font file failed" );

           /* set width table entry */
           fh->wtbl[cur_ch] = REV_WRD( cd.delta_x );

           /* send the descriptor */
           send_buf( (char *) &cd, sizeof(char_desc) );

           /* send the bitmap which follows */
           if( esq_parm > sizeof(char_desc) )
              copy_inp( inp, esq_parm-sizeof(char_desc) );
        }
        /* continuation of previous descriptor */
        else
        {
           copy_inp( inp, esq_parm );
        }

        break;

    case eCHARCODE:  /* specify character code........ */

        cur_ch = esq_parm;

        /* send the sequence */
        send_str( esq_buf );

        break;

    case eUNKNOWN:  /* unknown seq - ignore it........ */

        send_str( esq_buf );

        break;
    }

    /* save the sequence type */
    e_last = esq_type;
}

/*------------------------------------------------------*/
/*  Read the next esc seq from the font file...         */
/*------------------------------------------------------*/
```

Listing 6.2 continues

Listing 6.2 continued

```c
static int get_esq( FILE *inp, char esq_buf[], int buf_len )
{
    int i, nbytes;

    nbytes = 0;

    while( (i=fgetc( inp )) != EOF )
    {
        esq_buf[nbytes++] = (char) i;

        /* check for end of sequence */
        if( IS_TERM_CHR( i ) ) break;

        if( nbytes == buf_len )
            assert_error( "Download - esc seq buffer overflow" );
    }

    /* validity check - first char should be decimal 27 */
    if( (nbytes > 0) && (esq_buf[0] != 27) )
        assert_error( "Download - esc seq expected, not found" );

    /* add a terminating null */
    esq_buf[nbytes] = 0;
    return( nbytes );
}
/*-----------------------------------------------------------*/
/*  Download a font file, create font header record...       */
/*-----------------------------------------------------------*/

void download_font( char *path, int font_id )
{
    FILE     *inp;
    font_hdr *fh;
    char      esq_buf[ESQ_SIZE];

    if( (inp = fopen( path, "rb" )) == NULL )
        assert_error( "Open for font file download failed" );

    /* initialize static globals */
    cur_ch = 0;
    e_last = eUNKNOWN;

    /* setup a new table entry */
    fh = new_font_hdr( font_id );

    /* specify the ID to the printer */
    sprintf( esq_buf, "\033*c%dD", font_id );
    send_str( esq_buf );

    /* scan the file and download */
    while( get_esq( inp, esq_buf, ESQ_SIZE )  0 )
        do_esq( inp, esq_buf, fh );

    /* set width of blank */
    if( fh->wtbl[' '] == 0 )
        fh->wtbl[' '] = fh->pitch;
```

Listing 6.2 continues

Listing 6.2 continued

```
        fclose( inp );
}
/*------------------------------------------------------------*/
/*  Register a font file, create font header record...   */
/*------------------------------------------------------------*/

void register_font( char *path, int font_id )
{
        font_hdr *fh;
        FILE     *inp;

    /*
     * This function can be used in lieu of download_font()
     * to load a .WTL file for a font that is already
     * resident on the printer.
     */

        if( (inp = fopen( path, "rb" )) == NULL )
            assert_error( "Open for font file register failed" );

        /* setup a new table entry */
        fh = new_font_hdr( font_id );

        /* read the header record */
        if( fread( fh, sizeof(font_hdr), 1, inp ) != 1 )
            assert_error( "Read on font header file failed" );

        /* set width of blank */
        if( fh->wtbl[' '] == 0 )
          fh->wtbl[' '] = fh->pitch;

        fclose( inp );
}

/*------------------------------------------------------------*/
/*  Create a .WTL file from downloaded font...            */
/*------------------------------------------------------------*/

int  create_wtl( char *path, int font_id )
{
        int    i;
        FILE *fp;

    /*
     * This function can be used to create a .WTL file
     * for a font that has already been downloaded.
     */

        fp = fopen( path, "wb" );
        if( fp == NULL )
            return( 0 );
        i = fwrite( get_font_hdr(font_id), sizeof( font_hdr ),
                    1, fp );
        fclose( fp );
        return( i );
}
```

Listing 6.2 continues

Listing 6.2 continued

```
/*------------------------------------------------------------*/
/*  Set active font by id...                                  */
/*------------------------------------------------------------*/

void select_font( int font_id, int notify )
{
    char cmd[12];

    cur_id  = font_id;
    cur_hdr = get_font_hdr( font_id );

    /* if notify, send font change to printer */
    if( notify )
    {
        sprintf( cmd, "\033(%dX", font_id );
        send_str( cmd );
    }
}

/*------------------------------------------------------------*/
/*  Delete a font from the table...                           */
/*------------------------------------------------------------*/

void delete_font( int font_id )
{

    /*
     * Note: because of a LaserJet firmware bug we do
     * not delete the font on the printer. This will
     * not normally cause problems, because a new font
     * downloaded with this ID will replace the
     * existing font definition.
     */

    if( font_id == cur_id )
    {
        cur_id  = -1;
        cur_hdr = NULL;
    }

    del_font_hdr( font_id );
}

/*------------------------------------------------------------*/
/*  Return current font's id...                               */
/*------------------------------------------------------------*/

int cur_font_id( void )
{
    return( cur_id );
}

/*------------------------------------------------------------*/
/*  Return current font's header record...                    */
/*------------------------------------------------------------*/

font_hdr *cur_font_hdr( void )
{
```

Listing 6.2 continues

Listing 6.2 continued

```c
        return( cur_hdr );
}

/*----------------------------------------------------------*/
/*  Return current font's width table...                    */
/*----------------------------------------------------------*/

int *cur_width_tbl( void )
{
        return( cur_hdr->wtbl );
}

/*----------------------------------------------------------*/
/*  Return current font's height...                         */
/*----------------------------------------------------------*/

double cur_height( void )
{
        return( ((double)cur_hdr->height) / 1200.0 );
}

/*----------------------------------------------------------*/
/*  Return current font's ascent...                         */
/*----------------------------------------------------------*/

double cur_ascent( void )
{
        return( ((double)cur_hdr->bldist) / 1200.0 );
}

/*----------------------------------------------------------*/
/*  Return current font's descent...                        */
/*----------------------------------------------------------*/

double cur_descent( void )
{
        return( ((double)(cur_hdr->height-cur_hdr->bldist))
                / 1200.0 );
}

/*----------------------------------------------------------*/
/*  Return current font's pitch...                          */
/*----------------------------------------------------------*/
double cur_pitch( void )
{
        return( ((double)cur_hdr->pitch) / 1200.0 );
}

/*----------------------------------------------------------*/
/*  Return a specified font's height...                     */
/*----------------------------------------------------------*/

double get_height( int font_id )
{
        font_hdr *fh;
        fh = get_font_hdr( font_id );
        return( ((double)fh->height) / 1200.0 );
}
```

Listing 6.2 continues

Listing 6.2 continued

```c
/*----------------------------------------------------------*/
/*  Return a specified font's ascent...                     */
/*----------------------------------------------------------*/

double get_ascent( int font_id )
{
    font_hdr *fh;
    fh = get_font_hdr( font_id );
    return( ((double)fh->bldist) / 1200.0 );
}

/*----------------------------------------------------------*/
/*  Return a specified font's descent...                    */
/*----------------------------------------------------------*/

double get_descent( int font_id )
{
    font_hdr *fh;
    fh = get_font_hdr( font_id );
    return( ((double)(fh->height-fh->bldist)) / 1200.0 );
}

/*----------------------------------------------------------*/
/*  Return a specified font's pitch...                      */
/*----------------------------------------------------------*/

double get_pitch( int font_id )
{
    font_hdr *fh;
    fh = get_font_hdr( font_id );
    return( ((double)fh->pitch) / 1200.0 );
}

/*----------------------------------------------------------*/
/*  Returns true if passed font_id is a bold font...        */
/*----------------------------------------------------------*/
int is_bold( int font_id )
{
    font_hdr *fh;
    fh = get_font_hdr( font_id );
    return( fh->weight > 1 ? 1 : 0 );
}

/*----------------------------------------------------------*/
/*  Returns true if passed font_id is an italic font...     */
/*----------------------------------------------------------*/

int is_italic( int font_id )
{
    font_hdr *fh;
    fh = get_font_hdr( font_id );
    return( fh->posture == 0 ? 0 : 1 );
}

/*----------------------------------------------------------*/
/*  Return font id of a bold form of passed font id...      */
/*----------------------------------------------------------*/
```

Listing 6.2 continues

Listing 6.2 continued

```
int find_bold( int font_id )
{
      int       i;
      font_hdr *fh;

      fh = get_font_hdr( font_id );

      /* first look for an exact match */
      for( i=0; i<fnt_cnt; i++ )
         if( fnt_ids[i] != font_id )
         {
            if( (fnt_tbl[i]-family  == fh->family)  &&
                (fnt_tbl[i]-orient  == fh->orient)  &&
                (fnt_tbl[i]-height  == fh->height)  &&
                (fnt_tbl[i]-spacing == fh->spacing) &&
                (fnt_tbl[i]-posture == fh->posture) &&
                (fnt_tbl[i]-weight  >  fh->weight)  )
               return( fnt_ids[i] );
         }

      /* now a close match */
      for( i=0; i<fnt_cnt; i++ )
         if( fnt_ids[i] != font_id )
         {
            if( (fnt_tbl[i]-orient  == fh->orient)  &&
                (fnt_tbl[i]-height  == fh->height)  &&
                (fnt_tbl[i]-posture == fh->posture) &&
                (fnt_tbl[i]-weight  >  fh->weight)  )
               return( fnt_ids[i] );
         }
      /* no good match, used the passed id */
      return( font_id );
}

/*----------------------------------------------------------*/
/*  Return font id of an italic form of passed font id... */
/*----------------------------------------------------------*/

int find_italic( int font_id )
{
      int       i;
      font_hdr *fh;

      fh = get_font_hdr( font_id );

      /* first look for an exact match */
      for( i=0; i<fnt_cnt; i++ )
         if( fnt_ids[i] != font_id )
         {
            if( (fnt_tbl[i]->family  == fh->family)  &&
                (fnt_tbl[i]->orient  == fh->orient)  &&
                (fnt_tbl[i]->height  == fh->height)  &&
                (fnt_tbl[i]->spacing == fh->spacing) &&
                (fnt_tbl[i]->weight  == fh->weight)  &&
                (fnt_tbl[i]->posture != 0)           )
               return( fnt_ids[i] );
         }
```

Listing 6.2 continues

Listing 6.2 continued

```
      /* now a close match */
      for( i=0; i<fnt_cnt; i++ )
         if( fnt_ids[i] != font_id )
            {
               if( (fnt_tbl[i]->orient  == fh->orient)  &&
                   (fnt_tbl[i]->height  == fh->height)  &&
                   (fnt_tbl[i]->posture != 0)           )
               return( fnt_ids[i] );
            }

      /* no good match, used the passed id */
      return( font_id );
}

/*------------------------------------------------------------*/
/*  Return font id of a normal form of passed font id...  */
/*------------------------------------------------------------*/

int find_normal( int font_id )
{
      int      i;
      font_hdr *fh;

      fh = get_font_hdr( font_id );
      /* first look for an exact match */
      for( i=0; i<fnt_cnt; i++ )
         if( fnt_ids[i] != font_id )
            {
               if( (fnt_tbl[i]->family  == fh->family)  &&
                   (fnt_tbl[i]->orient  == fh->orient)  &&
                   (fnt_tbl[i]->height  == fh->height)  &&
                   (fnt_tbl[i]->spacing == fh->spacing) &&
                   (fnt_tbl[i]->weight < 2)             &&
                   (fnt_tbl[i]->posture == 0)           )
               return( fnt_ids[i] );
            }

      /* now a close match */
      for( i=0; i<fnt_cnt; i++ )
         if( fnt_ids[i] != font_id )
            {
               if( (fnt_tbl[i]->orient  == fh->orient)  &&
                   (fnt_tbl[i]->height  == fh->height)  &&
                   (fnt_tbl[i]->weight < 2)             &&
                   (fnt_tbl[i]->posture == 0)           )
               return( fnt_ids[i] );
            }

      /* no good match, used the passed id */
      return( font_id );
}

/*------------------------------------------------------------*/
/*  Determine a new font id from current and face chg...  */
/*------------------------------------------------------------*/

int new_font_id( int id, int face )
{
```

Listing 6.2 continues

Listing 6.2 continued

```
    int new_id;

    switch( face )
    {
        case 'B' : /* bold on */
                   new_id = find_bold( id );
                   break;

        case 'b' : /* bold off */
                   new_id = find_normal( id );
                   if( is_italic(id) )
                       new_id = find_italic( new_id );
                   break;

        case 'I' : /* italic on */
                   new_id = find_italic( id );
                   break;

        case 'i' : /* italic off */
                   new_id = find_normal( id );
                   if( is_bold(id) )
                       new_id = find_bold( new_id );
                   break;

        case 'n' : /* normal - cancels BI */
        case 'N' :
                   new_id = find_normal( id );
                   break;

        default  : /* no change */
                   new_id = id;
                   break;
    }
    return( new_id );
}

/*------------------------------------------------------------*/
/*  Return width of a char in inches (uses cur font)...   */
/*------------------------------------------------------------*/

double chr_width( int ch )
{
    int i;

    i = ch & 255;
    return( ((double) cur_hdr->wtbl[i]) / 1200.0 );
}

/*------------------------------------------------------------*/
/*  Return width of a char in inches (specified font)... .*/
/*------------------------------------------------------------*/

double fch_width( int ch, int font_id )
{
    font_hdr *fh;
    int       i;

    i  = ch & 255;
```

Listing 6.2 continues

Listing 6.2 continued

```
    fh = get_font_hdr( font_id );
    return( ((double) fh->wtbl[i]) / 1200.0 );
}

/*-----------------------------------------------------------*/
/*  Width of a string in inches (full or no blanks)...    */
/*-----------------------------------------------------------*/

double str_width( char *str, int full )
{
    font_hdr *fh;
    char      dig[8];
    int       i, id, *wt, sum;

    /*
     * This function computes the width in inches of the
     * passed string, and will handle a string with embedded
     * format codes.  The format codes will be honored, and
     * the codes' characters will not contribute to the
     * string's width.  The flag "full" controls whether
     * or not space characters are to be counted.
     */

    id  = cur_id;
    fh  = cur_hdr;
    wt  = cur_hdr->wtbl;
    sum = 0;

    while( *str )
    {
        /* format code of form {...} */
        if( *str == BGN_FMT )
        {
            /* literal curly brace : {{ */
            if( *(str+1) == BGN_FMT )
                sum += wt[(unsigned char)*str];
            /* format code to be scanned */
            else
            {
                while( *str && (*str != END_FMT) )
                {
                    if( (*str=='f') || (*str=='F') )
                    {
                        str++;
                        i = 0;
                        while( isdigit(*str) && (i < 7) )
                            dig[i++] = *str++;
                        dig[i] = 0;
                        id = atoi(dig);
                    }
                    else
                        id = new_font_id( id, *str++ );
                }
                if( *str == 0 ) break;
                fh  = get_font_hdr( id );
                wt  = fh->wtbl;
            }
        }
    }
```

Listing 6.2 continues

Listing 6.2 continued

```c
        /* literal in string */
        else if( (full == W_FULL) || (*str != ' ') )
           sum += wt[(unsigned char)*str];
        str++;
    }

    return( ((double) sum) / 1200.0 );
}

/*------------------------------------------------------------*/
/*  Return max of height, ascent, or descent...              */
/*------------------------------------------------------------*/

double str_height( char *str, int full )
{
    font_hdr *fh;
    char      dig[8];
    int       i, id, hgt, asc, dsc;

    /*
     * This function determines the max char height in a
     * string by font, and will handle multiple fonts
     * caused by embedded format code.  If the flag
     * "full" is zero (don't count blanks), and the
     * string only contains blanks, then its height is
     * zero, otherwise it's the height for the font.
     */

    id  = cur_id;
    fh  = cur_hdr;
    hgt = 0;
    asc = 0;
    dsc = 0;

    while( *str )
    {
        /* format code of form {...} */
        if( *str == BGN_FMT )
        {
            /* literal curly brace : {{ */
            if( *(str+1) == BGN_FMT )
            {
               hgt = (hgt > fh->height) ? hgt : fh->height;
               asc = (asc > fh->bldist) ? asc : fh->bldist;
               i   = fh->height - fh->bldist;
               dsc = (dsc > i) ? dsc : i;
            }
            /* format code to be scanned */
            else
            {
               while( *str && (*str != END_FMT) )
               {
                  if( (*str=='f') || (*str=='F') )
                  {
                     str++;
                     i = 0;
                     while( isdigit(*str) && (i < 7) )
                        dig[i++] = *str++;
```

Listing 6.2 continues

Listing 6.2 continued

```
                    dig[i] = 0;
                    id = atoi(dig);
                }
                else
                    id = new_font_id( id, *str++ );
            }
            if( *str == 0 ) break;
            fh  = get_font_hdr( id );
        }
    }
    /* literal in string - blanks don't count */
    else if( *str != ' ' )
    {
        hgt = (hgt > fh->height) ? hgt : fh->height;
        asc = (asc > fh->bldist) ? asc : fh->bldist;
        i   = fh->height - fh->bldist;
        dsc = (dsc > i) ? dsc : i;
    }
    str++;
    }

    switch( full )
    {
        case H_FULL :  i = hgt;  break;
        case H_ASC  :  i = asc;  break;
        case H_DSC  :  i = dsc;  break;
    }

    return( ((double) i) / 1200.0 );
}
/*----------------------------------------------------------*/
/*  Fill in string metrics structure...                     */
/*----------------------------------------------------------*/

void str_size( char *str, string_metric *sm )
{
    font_hdr *fh;
    char     dig[8];
    int      i, id, *wt, sum, nb_sum, hgt, asc, dsc;

    /*
     * A string_metric structure contains all useful
     * measurements of a string's dimensions.  All
     * values are in inches.
     */

    id  = cur_id;
    fh  = cur_hdr;
    wt  = cur_hdr->wtbl;
    sum = nb_sum = 0;
    hgt = asc = dsc = 0;
    while( *str )
    {
        /* format code of form {...} */
        if( *str == BGN_FMT )
        {
            /* literal curly brace : {{ */
```

Listing 6.2 continues

Listing 6.2 continued

```
          if( *(str+1) == BGN_FMT )
          {
             sum    += wt[(unsigned char)*str];
             nb_sum += wt[(unsigned char)*str];
             hgt = (hgt > fh->height) ? hgt : fh->height;
             asc = (asc > fh->bldist) ? asc : fh->bldist;
             i   = fh->height - fh->bldist;
             dsc = (dsc > i) ? dsc : i;
          }
          /* format code to be scanned */
          else
          {
             while( *str && (*str != END_FMT) )
             {
                if( (*str=='f') || (*str=='F') )
                {
                   str++;
                   i = 0;
                   while( isdigit(*str) && (i < 7) )
                      dig[i++] = *str++;
                   dig[i] = 0;
                   id = atoi(dig);
                }
                else
                   id = new_font_id( id, *str++ );
             }
             if( *str == 0 ) break;
             fh = get_font_hdr( id );
             wt = fh->wtbl;
          }
       }
       /* literal in string */
       else
       {
          sum += wt[(unsigned char)*str];
          if( *str != ' ' )
             nb_sum += wt[(unsigned char)*str];
          hgt = (hgt > fh->height) ? hgt : fh->height;
          asc = (asc > fh->bldist) ? asc : fh->bldist;
          i   = fh->height - fh->bldist;
          dsc = (dsc > i) ? dsc : i;
       }
       str++;
    }

    sm->width    = ((double) sum) / 1200.0;
    sm->nb_width = ((double) nb_sum) / 1200.0;
    sm->height   = ((double) hgt) / 1200.0;
    sm->ascent   = ((double) asc) / 1200.0;
    sm->descent  = ((double) dsc) / 1200.0;
}

/*------------------------------------------------------------*/
/*  Set cursor position using dot units...                  */
/*------------------------------------------------------------*/

void set_ixy( int ix, int iy )
{
```

Listing 6.2 continues

Listing 6.2 continued

```
      char cmd[24];

      sprintf( cmd, "\033*p%dx%dY", ix+x_bias, iy+y_bias );
      send_str( cmd );
}

void set_ix( int ix )
{
      char cmd[24];

      sprintf( cmd, "\033*p%dX", ix+x_bias );
      send_str( cmd );
}

void set_iy( int iy )
{
      char cmd[24];

      sprintf( cmd, "\033*p%dY", iy+y_bias );
      send_str( cmd );
}

/*-----------------------------------------------------------*/
/*  Set cursor position using inch units...                  */
/*-----------------------------------------------------------*/

void set_xy( double x, double y )
{
      int ix, iy;

      x *= 300.0;  x += 0.5;  ix = (int) x;
      y *= 300.0;  y += 0.5;  iy = (int) y;
      set_ixy( ix, iy );
}

void set_x( double x )
{
      int ix;

      x *= 300.0;  x += 0.5;  ix = (int) x;
      set_ix( ix );
}

void set_y( double y )
{
      int iy;

      y *= 300.0;  y += 0.5;  iy = (int) y;
      set_iy( iy );
}

/*-----------------------------------------------------------*/
/*  Turn underlining on or off...                            */
/*-----------------------------------------------------------*/

void set_underlining( int state )
{
```

Listing 6.2   continues

Listing 6.2 continued

```
    /*
     * Note: there are two underline methods, fixed
     * and floating.  See LJ reference manual for
     * details.  To select floating, change the 'd0D'
     * in the following string to 'd3D'.
     */

    if( state ) /* turn on fixed underline */
         send_str( "\033&d0D" );
    else         /* turn off underlining */
         send_str( "\033&d@" );
}

/*------------------------------------------------------------*/
/*   Eject the current page...                                */
/*------------------------------------------------------------*/

void eject_pg( void )
{
    /* send a formfeed character (dec 12, hex 0C) */
    send_str( "\014" );
}
```

LISTING 6.3   DOCMGMT.H, Document Management for LJ Text Toolkit

```
/*------------------------------------------------------------*/
/* FILE:   DOCMGMT.H                                          */
/* DESC:   Document management module for LJ text toolkit. */
/*------------------------------------------------------------*/

/* justifications */
#define  J_LEFT     -1
#define  J_CENTER    0
#define  J_RIGHT     1
#define  J_FULL      2

/* line spacings */
#define  LS_FIXED    0
#define  LS_AUTO     1

/* function prototypes */
void    init_pg( void );
void    term_pg( void );
void    set_ln_spacing( int type );
int     get_ln_spacing( void );
void    set_just( int just );
int     get_just( void );
void    set_ln_height( double hgt );
double  get_ln_height( void );
void    set_leading( double leading );
double  get_leading( void );
void    set_margins( double lm, double tm,
                     double rm, double bm );
void    set_doc_font( int font_id );
double  get_lm( void );
double  get_rm( void );
double  get_bm( void );
double  get_tm( void );
int     process_fmt( char *fmt, int notify );
void    new_line( int nlines );
void    line_out( char *str );
void    line_store( char *str );
void    line_flush( char *buf, int nch, double bscl );
void    process_ln( char *ln_of_txt );
void    flush_txt( void );

/*--------------- End of File DOCMGMT.H -----------------*/
```

LISTING 6.4 DOCMGMT.C, Document Management for LJ Text Toolkit

```
/*------------------------------------------------------*/
/* FILE:   DOCMGMT.C                                    */
/* DESC:   Document management module for LJ text toolkit. */
/*------------------------------------------------------*/

#include "stdlib.h"
#include "stdio.h"
#include "string.h"
#include "ctype.h"

/* define the following for MS DOS systems */
#define MSDOS 1

#if MSDOS
#include "dos.h"
#endif

#include "ljfont.h"
#include "fntmgmt.h"
#include "docmgmt.h"
#include "token.h"

/*------------------------------------------------------*/
/* Defines and such specific to this module...          */
/*------------------------------------------------------*/

#define  WK_SIZE   256                    /* buffer size */
#define  FMT_MARK   27            /* fmt code place holder */

/*------------------------------------------------------*/
/* Global data and such...                              */
/*------------------------------------------------------*/

static
double  pg_wid  = 8.5,           /* page width in inches */
        pg_hgt  = 11.0,         /* page height in inches */
        t_mgn   = 1.0,                    /* top margin */
        b_mgn   = 1.0,                 /* bottom margin */
        l_mgn   = 1.0,                   /* left margin */
        r_mgn   = 1.0,                  /* right margin */
        ln_rem  = 6.5,              /* width remaining */
        w_sum   = 0.0,           /* sum of word widths */
        w_asc   = 0.0,             /* max word ascent */
        w_dsc   = 0.0,            /* max word descent */
        w_sp    = 0.0,          /* sum of blank widths */
        f_hgt   = 0.125,        /* fixed line spacing */
        v_hgt   = 0.0,       /* variable line spacing */
        v_asc   = 0.0,           /* ascent for v_hgt */
        v_dsc   = 0.0,          /* descent for v_hgt */
        ln_scl  = 1.2,       /* leading - times f or v */
        x_cur   = 1.0,          /* current x position */
        y_cur   = 1.0;          /* current y position */

static
int     pg_num  = 0,            /* current page number */
        wk_ptr  = 0,           /* work buffer pointer */
        j_cur   = J_LEFT,      /* current justification */
```

Listing 6.4   continues

Listing 6.4 continued

```
        ls_type = LS_AUTO,              /* line spacing type */
        ul_flag = 0;                   /* underlining flag */

static
char    wk_buf[WK_SIZE];               /* work buffer */
/* These are local, and don't reflect the printer state.  */
/* They are used in computing widths when saving chars in */
/* full justification mode.                               */

static
int     doc_id,                        /* font id */
        *doc_wt;                       /* width table */

static
font_hdr *doc_fh;                      /* font header */

/*----------------------------------------------------------*/
/* Initialize a line prior to use...                        */
/*----------------------------------------------------------*/

void init_ln( void )
{
    /*
     * Amt of usable width in line. This is decremented
     * as we go until < 0, thus is "line remaining".
     */

    ln_rem = pg_wid - l_mgn - r_mgn;

    /*
     * w_sp is running sum of blanks in current line.
     * w_sum is running sum of all printable chars in
     * line.  w_sum is redundant with ln_rem, but is
     * carried along for debug use, etc...
     */

    w_sp    = 0.0;
    w_sum   = 0.0;

    /*
     * The following track the largest heights in the
     * current line and are used to find y_cur for the
     * following line when line spacing is LS_AUTO.
     */

    w_asc   = 0.0;
    w_dsc   = 0.0;
    v_hgt   = 0.0;
}

/*----------------------------------------------------------*/
/* Initialize a page prior to use...                        */
/*----------------------------------------------------------*/

void init_pg( void )
{
    /* reset cursor to upper left */
    x_cur = l_mgn;
```

Listing 6.4 continues

Listing 6.4 continued

```
        y_cur = t_mgn;

        /* page number of this page */
        pg_num++;

        /* other values */
        init_ln();
}

/*------------------------------------------------------------*/
/* Cleanup required after a page is complete...          */
/*------------------------------------------------------------*/

void term_pg( void )
{
    /*
     * Page numbering could be processed here, as
     * well as page headers and footers.
     * The present function only does a page eject.
     */

    eject_pg();
}

/*------------------------------------------------------------*/
/* Set or get line spacing style (fixed or auto)...      */
/*------------------------------------------------------------*/

void set_ln_spacing( int type )
{
    ls_type = type;
}

int  get_ln_spacing( void )
{
    return( ls_type );
}

/*------------------------------------------------------------*/
/* Set or get leading factor - scales f_hgt ro v_hgt...  */
/*------------------------------------------------------------*/

void set_leading( double ld )
{
    ln_scl = ld;
}

double get_leading( void )
{
    return( ln_scl );
}
/*------------------------------------------------------------*/
/* Set or get line hgt for fixed spacing...              */
/*------------------------------------------------------------*/

void set_ln_height( double hgt )
{
    f_hgt = hgt;
```

Listing 6.4 continues

Listing 6.4 continued

```c
}

double get_ln_height( void )
{
    return( f_hgt );
}

/*----------------------------------------------------------*/
/* Set or get current justification...                      */
/*----------------------------------------------------------*/

void set_just( int just )
{
    j_cur = just;
}

int  get_just( void )
{
    return( j_cur );
}

/*----------------------------------------------------------*/
/* Set or get current margins...                            */
/*----------------------------------------------------------*/

void set_margins( double lm, double tm, double rm, double bm )
{
    l_mgn = lm;
    t_mgn = tm;
    r_mgn = rm;
    b_mgn = bm;
    ln_rem = pg_wid-l_mgn-r_mgn;
}

double get_lm( void )
{
    return( l_mgn );
}

double get_rm( void )
{
    return( r_mgn );
}

double get_tm( void )
{
    return( t_mgn );
}

double get_bm( void )
{
    return( b_mgn );
}

/*----------------------------------------------------------*/
/* Set local font vars...                                   */
/*----------------------------------------------------------*/
```

Listing 6.4   continues

Listing 6.4 continued

```
void set_doc_font( int id )
{
    double v;

    /*
     * "doc font" tracks the current font used by
     * line_store, which will not normally be in sync
     * with "cur font" on the printer
     */

    doc_id = id;
    doc_fh = get_font_hdr( id );
    doc_wt = doc_fh->wtbl;
    v      = get_ascent( doc_id );
    v_asc  = v > v_asc ? v : v_asc;
    v      = get_descent( doc_id );
    v_dsc  = v > v_dsc ? v : v_dsc;
    v_hgt  = v_asc + v_dsc;
}

/*-----------------------------------------------------------*/
/* Set or clear an underlining semaphore...                  */
/*-----------------------------------------------------------*/

static void set_ul_flag( int ul_state )
{
    ul_flag = ul_state;
}

static void clear_ul_flag( void )
{
    switch( ul_flag )
    {
        case 'U' : set_underlining( 1 ); break;
        case 'u' : set_underlining( 0 ); break;
    }
    ul_flag = 0;
}

/*-----------------------------------------------------------*/
/* Process a formatting code (w or w/o curly braces)...      */
/*-----------------------------------------------------------*/

int process_fmt( char *fmt, int cur_id )
{
    char dig[8];
    int  i, id, done;

    id = cur_id;
    done = 0;
    while( ! done )
    {
        switch( *fmt )
        {
            /* justifications on... */

            case 'J' :      j_cur = J_FULL;
```

Listing 6.4 continues

Listing 6.4 continued

```
                            break;

        case 'C' :      j_cur = J_CENTER;
                        break;

        case 'R' :      j_cur = J_RIGHT;
                        break;

        /* justifications off... */

        case 'j' :
        case 'c' :
        case 'r' :
        case 'L' :      j_cur = J_LEFT;
                        break;

        /* set font by ID... */

        case 'F' :
        case 'f' :      fmt++;
                        i = 0;
                        while( isdigit(*fmt) && (i<7) )
                            dig[i++] = *fmt++;
                        dig[i] = 0;
                        id = atoi(dig);
                        break;

        /* underlining on or off... */

        case 'U' :
        case 'u' :      set_ul_flag( *fmt );
                        break;

        /* end of fmt code (case 0 is an error, but */
        /* is included to prevent infinite loops. */

        case END_FMT :
        case 0       : done = 1;
                        break;

        /* skip the starting curly brace */

        case BGN_FMT : break;

        /* font change by face code */

        default  :      id = new_font_id( id, *fmt );
                        break;
        }
        fmt++;
    }

    return( id );
}
/*-----------------------------------------------------------*/
/* Send text to printer, removing formatting codes...      */
/*-----------------------------------------------------------*/
```

Listing 6.4 continues

Listing 6.4 continued

```
void send_txt( char *str )
{
    int id;

    wk_ptr = 0;
    while( *str )
    {
        if( *str == BGN_FMT )
        {
            str++;
            if( *str == BGN_FMT )
            {
                wk_buf[wk_ptr++] = *str++;
                if( wk_ptr == WK_SIZE )
                {
                    send_buf( wk_buf, wk_ptr );
                    wk_ptr = 0;
                }
            }
            else
            {
                /* flush buffer */
                if( wk_ptr > 0 )
                    send_buf( wk_buf, wk_ptr );

                /* extract formatting code */
                wk_ptr = 0;
                while( (*str != 0) && (*str != END_FMT) )
                    wk_buf[wk_ptr++] = *str++;
                wk_buf[wk_ptr] = 0;
                if( *str == END_FMT )
                    str++;

                /* process formatting code */
                id = process_fmt( wk_buf, cur_font_id() );
                if( id != cur_font_id() )
                {
                    select_font( id, 1 );
                    set_doc_font( id );
                }

                /* reset buffer pointer */
                wk_ptr = 0;
            }
        }
        else
        {
            wk_buf[wk_ptr++] = *str++;
            if( wk_ptr == WK_SIZE )
            {
                send_buf( wk_buf, wk_ptr );
                wk_ptr = 0;
            }
        }
    }
    if( wk_ptr > 0 )
    {
        send_buf( wk_buf, wk_ptr );
```

Listing 6.4 continues

Listing 6.4 continued

```
         wk_ptr = 0;
     }
}

/*------------------------------------------------------------*/
/* Perform 1 or more new lines...                            */
/*------------------------------------------------------------*/

void new_line( int cnt )
{
    double h;

    if( cnt < 1 ) return;

    /* do the first */
    cnt--;
    x_cur = l_mgn;
    if( v_hgt == 0.0 )
       v_hgt = cur_height();
    y_cur += (ls_type==LS_AUTO) ? v_hgt*ln_scl : f_hgt*ln_scl;
    if( y_cur >= pg_hgt-b_mgn )
    {
        term_pg();
        init_pg();
    }

    /* do any remaining */
    h = (ls_type==LS_AUTO) ? cur_height()*ln_scl : f_hgt*ln_scl;
    while( cnt-- > 0 )
    {
        y_cur += h;
        if( y_cur >= pg_hgt-b_mgn )
        {
            term_pg();
            init_pg();
        }
    }

    /* initialize vars */
    init_ln();
}

/*------------------------------------------------------------*/
/* Output a line of text with given justification...        */
/*------------------------------------------------------------*/

void line_out( char *str )
{
    double      x, h;
    string_metric sm;

    /*
     * This function is for use when not in full just
     * mode.  Full just is handled by line_store
     */

    /* measure string */
    str_size( str, &sm );
```

Listing 6.4 continues

Listing 6.4 continued

```
    h = sm.ascent + sm.descent;

    /* determine x position */
    switch( j_cur )
    {
        case J_CENTER :
                x = (l_mgn + pg_wid - r_mgn - sm.width) / 2.0;
                break;

        case J_RIGHT :
                x = pg_wid - r_mgn - sm.width;
                break;

        default : /* J_LEFT */
                x = l_mgn;
                break;
    }

    /* will this line fit ? */
    if( y_cur+h > pg_hgt-b_mgn )
    {
        term_pg();
        init_pg();
    }

    /* position cursor, draw string */
    set_xy( x, y_cur+sm.ascent );
    send_txt( str );

    /* update max hgt for this line, start new line */
    v_hgt = (h > v_hgt) ? h : v_hgt;
    new_line( 1 );
}
/*------------------------------------------------------------*/
/* Output a line of text from saved array of chars...    */
/*------------------------------------------------------------*/

void line_flush( char *buf, int nch, double bscl )
{
    double    wsp;
    int       id;

    /*
     * This function flushes the char buffer saved by
     * line_store and starts a new line on the page.
     * Space characters scaled by "bscl" to force
     * the line width to fit the current margins
     */

    /* position cursor at left margin */
    set_xy( x_cur, y_cur+v_asc );

    while( nch > 0 )
    {
        if( *buf == FMT_MARK ) /* fmt code place holder */
        {
            buf++;
```

Listing 6.4 continues

Listing 6.4 continued

```
            nch--;
            id = process_fmt( get_token(), cur_font_id() );
            if( id != cur_font_id() )
                select_font( id, 1 );
            if( ul_flag )
                clear_ul_flag();
        }
        else if( *buf == ' ' )
        {
            wsp = chr_width( ' ' ) * bscl;
            while( *buf == ' ' )
            {
                buf++;
                nch--;
                x_cur += wsp;
            }
            set_x( x_cur );
        }
        else
        {
            x_cur += chr_width( *buf );
            send_chr( *buf++ );
            nch--;
        }
    }

    new_line( 1 );
}

/*------------------------------------------------------------*/
/* Process text line when in full just mode...                */
/*------------------------------------------------------------*/

void line_store( char *str )
{
    int     n, id, sv_ptr, sv_cnt;
    double  w, bscl, dw;

    /*
     * This function is the counterpart of line_out when
     * in full just mode.  Chars are saved in "wk_buf"
     * until enough for a line are accumulated, the
     * line_flush is called to print the line.
     */

    while( *str )
    {
        /* check for start of a format code */
        if( *str == BGN_FMT )
        {
            str++;
            if( *str != BGN_FMT )
            {
                /* save format */
                str--;
                str = put_token( str );

                /* place mark in buffer */
```

Listing 6.4 continues

Listing 6.4 continued

```
        wk_buf[wk_ptr++] = FMT_MARK;

        /* process the format code */
        id = process_fmt( rd_tail(), doc_id );
        if( id != doc_id )
            set_doc_font( id );
    }
}

/* this char's width */
w = ((double) doc_wt[(unsigned char)*str]) / 1200.0;

/* process the character */
if( *str == ' ' )
    w_sp += w;
wk_buf[wk_ptr++] = *str;
ln_rem -= w;
w_sum  += w;

/* time to flush ? */
if( ln_rem < 0.0 )
{
    dw = 0.0;
    sv_cnt = 0;

    /* while last char nonblank, backup & save */
    n = wk_ptr-1;
    while( (wk_buf[n]!=' ') && (n > 0) )
    {
        w = ((double) doc_wt[(unsigned char)wk_buf[n]])
                 / 1200.0;
        ln_rem += w;
        w_sum -= w;
        dw += w;
        sv_cnt++;
        n--;
        wk_ptr--;
    }
    sv_ptr = wk_ptr;

    /* while last char blank, backup & discard */
    w = ((double) doc_wt[' ']) / 1200.0;
    while( (wk_buf[n]==' ') && (n > 0) )
    {
        ln_rem += w;
        w_sum -= w;
        w_sp -= w;
        n--;
        wk_ptr--;
    }

    /* compute blank scaling factor */
    bscl = (w_sp==0.0) ? 1.0 : (w_sp+ln_rem)/w_sp;

    /* and flush the line */
    line_flush( wk_buf, wk_ptr, bscl );

    /* if any chars saved, prime the buffer */
```

Listing 6.4 continues

Listing 6.4 continued

```
            wk_ptr = 0;
            ln_rem -= dw;
            w_sum += dw;
            while( wk_ptr < sv_cnt )
            {
                wk_buf[wk_ptr] = wk_buf[sv_ptr+wk_ptr];
                wk_ptr++;
            }
        }

        str++;
    }
}

/*------------------------------------------------------------*/
/* Function to flush any pending text...                      */
/*------------------------------------------------------------*/

void flush_txt( void )
{
    if( wk_ptr > 0 )
        line_flush( wk_buf, wk_ptr, 1.0 );
    wk_ptr = 0;
}

/*------------------------------------------------------------*/
/* Generic entry point for processing a line of text...       */
/*------------------------------------------------------------*/

void process_ln( char *ln )
{
    /*
     * This is a "generic" entry point that calls
     * either line_out() or line_store(), depending
     * upon the current justification.  It anticipates
     * justification changes by looking at the start
     * at start of each line for formatting code.
     */

    if( (*ln == BGN_FMT) && (*(ln+1) != BGN_FMT) )
        process_fmt( ln, cur_font_id() );

    /* process the line */

    if( j_cur == J_FULL )
    {
        /* Check for new paragraph. */
        if( *ln == 0 )
        {
            flush_txt();
            new_line( 1 );
        }
        else
        /* Process the line. */
            line_store( ln );

        /*
         * end of input line may occur in middle of output
```

Listing 6.4 continues

Listing 6.4 continued

```
         * line, so a blank is required to separate it
         * from start of following line.
         */

        if( wk_ptr > 0 )
            line_store( " " );
    }
    else
    {
        if( wk_ptr  0 )
            flush_txt();
        if( *ln )
            line_out( ln );
        else
            new_line( 1 );
    }
}

/*--------------- End of File DOCMGMT.C ----------------*/
```

LISTING 6.5 TOKEN.H, Word and Fmt Code Token Management Functions

```
/*-----------------------------------------------------*/
/* FILE:   TOKEN.H                                     */
/* DESC:   Word and fmt code token management functions. */
/*-----------------------------------------------------*/

void  init_queue( void );
int   token_cnt( void );
char *put_token( char *str );
char *get_token( void );
char *unput_token( void );
void  unget_token( void );
char *rd_head( void );
char *rd_tail( void );

/*--------------- End of File TOKEN.H ----------------*/
```

LISTING 6.6 TOKEN.C, Format Code Token Management Functions

```
/*------------------------------------------------------------*/
/* FILE:   TOKEN.C                                            */
/* DESC:   Format code token management functions.            */
/*------------------------------------------------------------*/

#include "stdlib.h"
#include "stdio.h"
#include "string.h"
#include "ctype.h"

/* define the following for MS-DOS systems */
#define MSDOS 1

#if MSDOS
#include "dos.h"
#endif

#include "ljfont.h"
#include "fntmgmt.h"
#include "token.h"


/*------------------------------------------------------------*/
/* allocation sizes */
#define B_SIZE 256                /* size of token buffer */
#define Q_SIZE 64                 /* size of token ptr queue */

static char  tok_buffer[B_SIZE];     /* buffer for tokens */
static int   b_head = 0,              /* buffer tail pointer */
             b_tail = 0;              /* buffer head pointer */
static char *tok_queue[Q_SIZE];      /* token access queue */
static int   q_head = 0,              /* queue tail pointer */
             q_tail = 0;              /* queue head pointer */

/*------------------------------------------------------------*/
/* Initialize the queue for use...                            */
/*------------------------------------------------------------*/

void init_queue( void )
{
    b_head = b_tail = 0;
    q_head = q_tail = 0;
}

/*------------------------------------------------------------*/
/* Return count of fmt tokens in queue...                     */
/*------------------------------------------------------------*/

int  token_cnt( void )
{
    int cnt;

    if( q_head > q_tail )
    {
        cnt = Q_SIZE - q_head;
        cnt += q_tail;
    }
```

Listing 6.6   continues

Listing 6.6 continued

```
    else
    {
        cnt = q_tail - q_head;
    }

    return( cnt );
}

/*-----------------------------------------------------------*/
/* Get next tail record (for put_token)...                   */
/*-----------------------------------------------------------*/

static char *next_tail( void )
{
    char *tail;

    tok_queue[q_tail] = tok_buffer+b_tail;
    tail = tok_queue[q_tail++];
    if( q_tail >= Q_SIZE )
        q_tail = 0;

    return( tail );
}

/*-----------------------------------------------------------*/
/* Get next head record (for get_token)...                   */
/*-----------------------------------------------------------*/

static char *next_head( void )
{
    char *head;

    head = tok_queue[q_head++];
    if( q_head >= Q_SIZE )
        q_head = 0;

    return( head );
}

/*-----------------------------------------------------------*/
/* Put a token in queue from passed string...                */
/*-----------------------------------------------------------*/

char *put_token( char *str )
{
    int   i;

    /* count chars in token */
    i = 0;
    while( (str[i] != 0) && (str[i] != END_FMT) )
        i++;
    if( str[i] == END_FMT )
        i++;

    /* If token will fit at current end of buffer */
    /* then it goes there, otherwise we wrap back */
    /* to start of buffer.  This is to keep the   */
    /* token in physically contiguous memory.     */
```

Listing 6.6 continues

Listing 6.6 continued

```
        if( b_tail + i >= B_SIZE )
            b_tail    = 0;

        /* reserve next queue pointer */
        next_tail();

        /* buffer the token */
        while( i-- )
        {
            tok_buffer[b_tail++] = *str++;
        }
        tok_buffer[b_tail++] = 0;

        /* return pointer to char following token */
        return( str );
}

/*--------------------------------------------------------*/
/* Get a token from queue...                              */
/*--------------------------------------------------------*/

char *get_token( void )
{
    char *head;

    head = next_head();
    return( head );
}

/*--------------------------------------------------------*/
/* Unqueue the last token placed in queue...              */
/*--------------------------------------------------------*/

char *unput_token( void )
{
        q_tail--;
        if( q_tail < 0 )
            q_tail = Q_SIZE - 1;
        return( tok_queue[q_tail] );
}

/*--------------------------------------------------------*/
/* Restore the last token read from the queue....         */
/*--------------------------------------------------------*/

void unget_token( void )
{
        q_head--;
        if( q_head < 0 )
            q_head = Q_SIZE - 1;
}

/*--------------------------------------------------------*/
/* The following reads the queue without disturbing it... */
/*--------------------------------------------------------*/

char *rd_tail( void )  /* last item put into queue */
{
```

Listing 6.6 continues

Listing 6.6 continued

```
    int i;

    i = q_tail - 1;
    if( i < 0 )
        i = Q_SIZE - 1;
    return( tok_queue[i] );
}

char *rd_head( void )  /* next item to be removed */
{
    return( tok_queue[q_head] );
}

/*---------------- End of File TOKEN.C ----------------*/
```

LISTING 6.7 PRTDOC.C, Program to Illustrate Use of LJ Text Toolkit

```
/*-----------------------------------------------------------*/
/* FILE:   PRTDOC.C                                          */
/* DESC:   Program to illustrate use of LJ text toolkit.     */
/* NOTE:   Tested under MS/DOS with the following:           */
/*         Zortech 2.1 and Turbo C 2.0+                      */
/*-----------------------------------------------------------*/
#include "stdlib.h"
#include "stdio.h"
#include "string.h"
#include "ctype.h"

/* define the following for MS-DOS systems */
#define MSDOS 1

#if MSDOS
#include "dos.h"
#endif

#include "ljfont.h"
#include "fntmgmt.h"
#include "docmgmt.h"
#include "token.h"

/* Fonts to use in printing... In actual practice these    */
/* would be read from a "config" file or would somehow be   */
/* specified by the program user.                           */

char *fonts_d[] =
{
    "PA010R.SFP",    /* Palatino 10pt regular */
    "PA010RI.SFP",   /* Palatino 10pt regular italic */
    "PA010B.SFP",    /* Palatino 10pt bold */
```

Listing 6.7 continues

Listing 6.7 continued

```
      "PA010BI.SFP"      /* Palatino 10pt bold italic */
};

char *fonts_r[] =
{
      "PA010R.WTL",     /* Palatino 10pt regular */
      "PA010RI.WTL",    /* Palatino 10pt regular italic */
      "PA010B.WTL",     /* Palatino 10pt bold */
      "PA010BI.WTL"     /* Palatino 10pt bold italic */
};

#define FNT_CNT ( sizeof(fonts_d) / sizeof(char *) )

FILE *docf;

#define BUF_SIZE 256

char buf[BUF_SIZE];

/*------------------------------------------------------------*/
/* Function to read a line without adding <cr> to string. */
/*------------------------------------------------------------*/

int read_ln( char *buf, int len, FILE *fp )
{
      int i, ch;

      i = 0;
      while( 1 )
      {
         ch = fgetc(fp);
         if( feof(fp) ) break;
         if( ch == 0x0D ) continue;
         if( ch == 0x0A ) break;
         if( i >= len-1 ) break;
         buf[i++] = ch;
      }
      buf[i] = 0;

      return( i );
}

/*------------------------------------------------------------*/
/*                        M A I N                             */
/*------------------------------------------------------------*/

void main( int argc, char *argv[] )
{
      int i, dload;

      if( argc < 2 )
      {
         printf( "Usage:  PRTDOC doc_file  [ r ]\n" );
         exit( 0 );
      }

      /* open file to print... */
      docf = fopen( argv[1], "rt" );
```

Listing 6.7 continues

Listing 6.7 continued

```c
    if( docf == NULL )
    {
        printf( "Could not find '%s'\n", argv[1] );
        exit( 8 );
    }

    /* open the printer... */
    if( open_printer( "LPT1" ) == 0 )
    {
        printf( "Error opening printer\n" );
        exit( 8 );
    }

    /* download or register? */
    dload = 1;
    if( (argc  2) && ((*argv[2]=='r') || (*argv[2]=='R')) )
        dload = 0;

    /* download the fonts... */
    for( i=0; i<FNT_CNT; i++ )
    {
        if( dload )
        {
            printf( "Downloading %s...", fonts_d[i] );
            download_font( fonts_d[i], i+1 );
        }
        else
        {
            printf( "Registering %s...", fonts_r[i] );
            register_font( fonts_r[i], i+1 );
        }
        printf( "done\n" );
    }

    /* setup the default environment */
    select_font( 1, 1 );
    set_doc_font( 1 );
    set_just( J_LEFT );
    set_ln_spacing( LS_AUTO );

    /* and print the document */
    printf( "Printing %s...", argv[1] );
    read_ln( buf, BUF_SIZE, docf );
    while( ! feof( docf ) )
    {
        process_ln( buf );
        read_ln( buf, BUF_SIZE, docf );
    }
    flush_txt();

    /* finish up */
    fclose( docf );
    close_printer( 1 );
    printf( "done\n" );

}

/*--------------- End of File PRTDOC.C ------------------*/
```

LISTING 6.8 SAMPLE.DOC, Sample File for Input to PRTDOC Program

```
This line prints left justified (the default justification).

{C}This line prints centered.{c}

{R}This line prints right justified.{r}

{J}Starting with this line, text is fully justified.  All lines
are adjusted so that both the left and right margins are
uniform down the page.  This adjustment is not made to the
final printed line of a paragraph.  The final line is printed
with normal left justification.

Note that this line
begins
a new paragraph.
This is signaled by the occurrence of the blank
line between this paragraph and the previous one.

Finally, we can apply face changes.  For example, {B}this is Bold
face{b} while {I}this is Italic face{i}.  There is also {BI}Bold
Italic{n}.  Any of these can be {U}Underlined as you see here{u}.
```

7
Font Modification
and Synthesis

Introduction

Once you have a good understanding of the HP font format, the next logical step is to ponder font file alterations. A font file's character images are easy to get at, and you now have the tools you need to read and modify a file's character descriptors. In this chapter we consider a number of useful modifications that can easily be applied to font files.

Scaling Bitmapped Fonts

Virtually all commercially available font generators that will emit the HP font format start with a stroked outline definition of a typeface. A font of a requested size is then created by scaling the typeface outlines to that size and then generating character bitmaps by rasterizing the filled outlines. With this kind of tool it is always possible to obtain a font of a given size. If your application does not have this kind of resource then it probably utilizes a fixed set of font files in predetermined sizes. When it requires a font in a size that is not provided for, then it is forced to substitute a near match or abandon its task—neither of which is satisfactory. The ability to resize a given font file on an as-needed basis is a useful feature.

Resizing a font file requires scaling its character bitmaps, a process that does not provide uniformly useful results. For one thing, the apparent resolution of the output varies inversely with the scaling factor. Thus, if we take a 300-dpi font and scale it to twice its original size, the effective resolution of the scaled font will be only 150 dpi. A different problem arises with scaling factors less than one: since the scaled bitmap will contain fewer pixels than the source bitmap, small image features apparent in the source bitmap may be missing in the scaled bitmap. This problem is more obvious in highly ornate typefaces such as a gothic or script font. A typical sans serif face, such as a Helvetica, does not suffer as much from this effect when scaled to smaller sizes. Note that I use the term "gothic" as it applies to architecture and language, where it in fact implies ornateness. In the United States the term has been erroneously used in the field of typography to indicate a "sans serif" or "plain" typestyle. The incorrect usage persists to the extent that typefaces such as Avant Garde Gothic are in fact sans serif.

In practice, these problems can be minimized by limiting scaling factors to some neighborhood around 1.0, say, 0.75 to 1.5. It is also possible to apply an antialiasing (smoothing) filter to the scaled bitmaps. This technique extends the useful scaling range but with a cost of significantly longer execution times.

The Scaling Algorithm

Let us suppose that we have an existing character bitmap (the source bitmap), the dimensions of which are are Ws pixels wide by Hs pixels high, and that we wish to scale this to a new size (the destination bitmap) of Wd pixels wide by Hd pixels high. This corresponds to scaling factors of

$Sx = Wd / Ws$

and

$Sy = Hd / Hs$

Conceptually, each destination pixel will correspond to a fractional source pixel if we are scaling up in size, or to a range of 1 or more source pixels if we are scaling down in size.

In the simplest implementation, using integer arithmetic for speed, the destination pixel takes the value of the source pixel in the first case (scaling up) and the average value of the range of source pixels in the second case (scaling down). The calculation to determine the range of source pixels for each destination pixel is illustrated in Figure 7.1. Note that the figure shows the calculations for width only. The same process is used to calculate height to obtain both a range of rows and a range of columns for each destination pixel.

Using the calculations from Figure 7.1 for each destination pixel, we obtain a range of source rows, say, $i1$ to $i2$, and a range of source columns, $j1$ to $j2$. Note that the number of source pixels in that area is

```
pixel_cnt = (i2 - i1 + 1) * (j2 - j1 + 1)
```

We write a function to sum pixel values in the source area, in which a sum variable is initialized to zero. Then, if a source pixel is **on** we increment sum, and if a source

FIGURE 7.1   Image of Destination Pixel on Source Bitmap

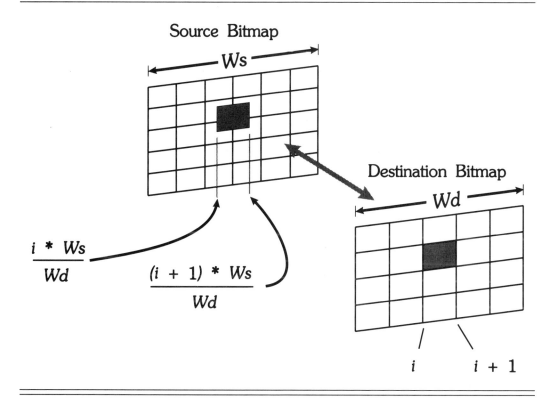

pixel is **off** we decrement sum. If the final value of sum is greater than zero we set the corresponding destination pixel.

In order to set a pixel we must compute which byte contains the pixel and a bit mask to isolate the bit corresponding to that pixel. Recall that character bitmaps in HP font files are stored as a sequence of rows, or scan lines, proceeding from the top row of the image to the bottom row of the image. Each row is padded with 0 to 7 unused bits at its end so that the row is an integral number of bytes.

Given that the destination bitmap is *Wd* pixels wide by *Hd* pixels high, the number of bytes per row is

```
rowbytes = (Wd + 7) / 8
```

and the offset to the byte containing pixel (x,y) is

```
offset = (rowbytes * y) + (x / 8)
```

The bit mask to isolate the bit corresponding to (x,y) is

```
        mask = 80h >> (x % 8)
```

Then, to set pixel (*x*,*y*) we do

```
        buffer[offset] |= mask
```

The source code for the C implementation of the algorithm is given in Listing 7.1.

LISTING 7.1 Code to Scale a Character Bitmap

```
/*----------------------------------------------------------*/
/* FILE:   SCLBMAP.C                                        */
/* DESC:   Functions to scale a bitmap.  This version uses  */
/*         integer-only arithmetic for the sake of speed.   */
/*----------------------------------------------------------*/

/* function to compute (p + n*m) and normalize */
extern char *p_normal( char *p, int n, int m );

/*----------------------------------------------------------*/
/* function to scale an int without overflow...             */
/*----------------------------------------------------------*/

int iscl( int v, int m, int d )
{
    long i;

    i = v;   i *= m;   i += d >> 1;   i /= d;

    return( (int) i );
}

/*----------------------------------------------------------*/
/* scan pixel area, return average pixel value...           */
/*----------------------------------------------------------*/

int pxl_on( char *row, int rb, int nrows, int col1, int col2 )
{
    int             i, j, sum;
    unsigned char   mask;
    char            *p;

    sum = 0;
    for( i=0; i<=nrows; i++ )
    {
        p = row + (col1 > 3);
        row += rb;
        mask = 0x80 >> (col1 & 7);
        for( j=col1; j<=col2; j++ )
        {
            if( *p & mask )
                sum++;
            else
                sum--;
            mask >>= 1;
```

Listing 7.1 continues

Listing 7.1 continued

```
            if( mask == 0 )
            {
                p++;
                mask = 0x80;
            }
        }
    }

    return( (sum > 0) ? 1 : 0 );
}

/*-----------------------------------------------------------*/
/* scale source bitmap to dest...                            */
/*-----------------------------------------------------------*/

void scl_bitmap( char *src, int ws, int hs,
                 char *dst, int wd, int hd )
{
    int             i, j, i1, i2, j1, j2, srb, drb;
    unsigned char   mask;
    char            *d, *s;
    /* note: dst assumed cleared to zeroes */

    srb = (ws + 7) / 8;
    drb = (wd + 7) / 8;

    i2 = 0;
    for( i=0; i<hd; i++ )
    {
        d = dst;
        dst = p_normal( dst, drb, 1 );
        mask = 0x80;

        i1 = i2;
        i2 = iscl( i+1, hs, hd );
        s  = p_normal( src, srb, i1 );

        j2 = 0;
        for( j=0; j<wd; j++ )
        {
            j1 = j2;
            j2 = iscl( j+1, ws, wd );

            if( pxl_on( s, srb, i2-i1, j1, j2 ) )
                *d |= mask;

            mask >>= 1;
            if( mask == 0 )
            {
                d++;
                mask = 0x80;
            }
        }
    }
}

/*--------------- End of File SCLBMAP.C ------------------*/
```

Image Quality

The algorithm we just discussed—using integer-only arithmetic and dealing with pixel counts—produces reasonable results in a reasonable amount of time. Note that we could perform the computations using real arithmetic and then accommodate fractional pixels. In effect, this treats each pixel as a square area of 1.0 units on each side, and the sum variable discussed previously would correspond to pixel area rather than pixel count.

Unfortunately, the increase in image quality that results from considering pixel area rather than pixel count does not justify the increased computational time. In trials conducted for this discussion a 10-point font was scaled to 14 points on a 386SX without a math coprocessor. The integer method took approximately fifteen seconds, while the area method required approximately five minutes for the same operation. And, while the area method produced noticably better image quality, neither scaled font was precise enough to replace the output of a commercial font generator where publication quality is the goal.

Finally, it should be noted that the code for the `scl_bitmap()` function was written from the perspective of clearly illustrating the algorithm rather than optimizing performance. If speed is paramount then scaling should probably be implemented in assembly language.

Font Rotation

Both the LaserJet III and later versions of the Series II printers can rotate a portrait font for use in landscape mode. The need for an application to be able to rotate a font is therefore less important than it once was. Nonetheless, we discuss the technique here, since it is still useful for older models in the LaserJet family.

The most common situation requiring rotation is a portrait font that needs to be rotated for landscape use. This requires rotation by 90 degrees counterclockwise (mathematically, rotation by a positive angle). If we impose a left-handed coordinate system on each character bitmap, with an upper left origin, X increasing to the right, and Y increasing down, then the relationship of a rotated point (xr, yr) to the corresponding source point (x, y) is

$$xr = y \text{ and } yr = w - x$$

where w is the source bitmap's width in pixels.

If we consider the opposite case, rotation by a negative angle (which occurs when a landscape font is rotated for portrait use), then the transformation is expressed by

$$xr = h - y \text{ and } yr = x$$

where *h* is the source bitmap's height in pixels. Note that rotation by 90 degrees can be implemented without performing any of these calculations. It is only necessary to adjust the order (row major or column major) and direction (start to end or end to start) with which the source and destination bitmaps are scanned in order to obtain the desired rotation. This is presented in Listing 7.2, which implements the rotation algorithm.

LISTING 7.2 Code to Rotate a Character Bitmap

```
/*-----------------------------------------------------------*/
/* FILE:   ROTBMAP.C                                         */
/* DESC:   Functions to rotate a bitmap by +90 or -90 deg. */
/*-----------------------------------------------------------*/

/* function to compute (p + n*m) and normalize */
extern char *p_normal( char *p, int n, int m );

/*-----------------------------------------------------------*/
/* function to rotate -90 (landscape to portrait)           */
/*-----------------------------------------------------------*/

void rot_minus_90( char *src, char *dst, int ws, int hs )
{
    int             i, j, srb, drb;
    unsigned char   sm, dm;
    char            *s, *d;

    srb = (ws + 7) / 8;
    drb = (hs + 7) / 8;

    /* each source row becomes a dest column */

    dm  = 0x01;
    if( hs & 7 )
        dm <<= 8 - (hs & 7);
    dst += drb - 1;
    for( i=0; i<hs; i++ )
    {
        sm  = 0x80;
        s   = src;
        src = p_normal( src, srb, 1 );
        d   = dst;

        for( j=0; j<ws; j++ )
        {
            if( *s & sm )
                *d |= dm;
            sm >>= 1;
            if( sm == 0 )
            {
                s++;
                sm = 0x80;
            }
            d = p_normal( d, drb, 1 );
        }
    }
```

Listing 7.2 continues

Listing 7.2 continued

```
        dm <<= 1;
        if( dm == 0 )
        {
            dst--;
            dm = 0x01;
        }
    }
}

/*----------------------------------------------------------*/
/* function to rotate +90 (portrait to landscape)         */
/*----------------------------------------------------------*/

void rot_plus_90( char *src, char *dst, int ws, int hs )
{
    int             i, j, srb, drb;
    unsigned char   sm, dm;
    char            *s, *d;

    srb = (ws + 7) / 8;
    drb = (hs + 7) / 8;

    /* each source row becomes a dest column */

    dm   = 0x80;
    for( i=0; i<hs; i++ )
    {
        sm   = 0x01;
        if( ws & 7 )
            sm <<= 8 - (ws & 7);
        s    = src + srb - 1;
        src  = p_normal( src, srb, 1 );
        d    = dst;

        for( j=0; j<ws; j++ )
        {
            if( *s & sm )
                *d |= dm;
            sm <<= 1;
            if( sm == 0 )
            {
                s--;
                sm = 0x01;
            }
            d = p_normal( d, drb, 1 );
        }

        dm >>= 1;
        if( dm == 0 )
        {
            dst++;
            dm = 0x80;
        }
    }
}

/*----------------------------------------------------------*/
/* function to rotate a character bitmap...               */
/*----------------------------------------------------------*/
```

Listing 7.2 continues

Listing 7.2 continued

```
void rot_bitmap( char *src, char *dst, int ws, int hs, int sgn )
{
    if( sgn < 0 )
        rot_minus_90( src, dst, ws, hs );
    else
        rot_plus_90( src, dst, ws, hs );
}

/*--------------- End of File ROTBMAP.C -----------------*/
```

Character Modifications

Up to this point we have considered scaling and rotation, which by themselves do not alter the basic look of a font. We now turn to modifications that do alter the look of a font. Perhaps the two most basic alterations that can be performed on a font are conversion of the face to bold or italic. Commercial font generators will normally create bold and italic fonts from separate outlines defined for this purpose. In this sense a bold or italic version of a face is not so much a face alteration as a face substitution. Here, however, we are considering true alterations. Although we discuss creating bold and italic forms of a face, remember that these are synthetic alterations, resulting in a "pseudo-bold" or "pseudo-italic" face.

Bold Synthesis

Virtually every printer can produce bold type. This is most commonly achieved by printing character images multiple times while applying a slight horizontal offset to successive images. The resulting image is a thicker version of the original image. This same technique can be implemented in software by successively "or-ing" a character image with a right-shifted copy of itself. The degree of boldness is controlled by the number of repetitions of the process. Note that each repetition increases the image's nominal width by one dot. If the technique is applied to an HP Soft Font then each character descriptor's `char_wid` and `delta_x` members must be appropriately modified.

This discussion applies to a font in portrait orientation. If the technique is to be performed for a landscape font, then no bit shifting is involved. Rather, each row in the character image is or-ed with the succeeding row, and each character descriptor's `char_hgt` and `delta_x` members are incremented.

Finally, note that the alteration cannot be applied in place, but requires a working copy of the unmolested image. Also note that the modified copy will normally require a larger buffer, since each source row can potentially grow by one or more bytes. Refer to Listing 7.3 for a typical implementation.

The degree of boldness obtained with this method varies with the number of iterations of the algorithm. Generally speaking, the larger the font, the larger the number of iterations required to obtain an appropriate visual effect. However, note that the algorithm also has the tendency to fill in holes in the source image, so you must sometimes limit iterations to avoid loss of character features. A good number for a 10-point font is two or three. Listing 7.3 gives the source code for the synthetic bold character modifier.

LISTING 7.3 Code to Bold a Character Bitmap

```
/*---------------------------------------------------------*/
/* FILE:   BOLDCHR.C                                        */
/* DESC:   Functions for synthetic bold char modification. */
/*---------------------------------------------------------*/

#include "ljfont.h"
#include "fontutl.h"
#include "fontmod.h"

/*---------------------------------------------------------*/
/* bold the character horizontally...                      */
/*---------------------------------------------------------*/

static void hbold_chr( char *src, char *dst, int ws,
                       int hs, int nreps )
{
    int           n, i, j, srb, drb;
    char          *s, *d, *p;
    unsigned char m;

    srb = (ws + 7) / 8;
    drb = (ws + nreps + 7) / 8;

    for( n=0; n<=nreps; n++ )
    {
        for( i=0; i<hs; i++ )
        {
            s = p_normal( src, srb, i );
            d = p_normal( dst, drb, i );

            /* shift this dest row right */
            p = d + drb - 1;
            for( j=0; j<drb; j++ )
            {
                m   = (*(p-1) & 1) < 7;
                if( j == drb-1 )
                    m = 0;
                *p = (*p >> 1) | m;
                p--;
            }
        }
```

Listing 7.3   continues

Listing 7.3 continued

```c
            /* or in the source row */
            for( j=0; j<srb; j++ )
            {
                *d |= *s;
                d++;
                s++;
            }
        }
    }
}

/*------------------------------------------------------------*/
/* bold the character vertically...                          */
/*------------------------------------------------------------*/

static void vbold_chr( char *src, char *dst, int ws,
                       int hs, int nreps )
{
    int         n, i, j, rb;
    char        *s, *d;

    rb = (ws + 7) / 8;

    for( n=0; n<=nreps; n++ )
    {
        s = src;
        d = p_normal( dst, rb, n );

        for( i=0; i<hs; i++ )
        {
            for( j=0; j<rb; j++ )
                d[j] |= s[j];

            s = p_normal( s, rb, 1 );
            d = p_normal( d, rb, 1 );
        }
    }
}

/*------------------------------------------------------------*/
/* primary entry point...                                    */
/*------------------------------------------------------------*/

void bold_chr( char *src, char *dst, int ws, int hs,
               int dir, int nreps )
{
    if( dir == IS_LAND )
        vbold_chr( src, dst, ws, hs, nreps );
    else
        hbold_chr( src, dst, ws, hs, nreps );
}

/*---------------- End of File BOLDCHR.C ------------------*/
```

Italic Synthesis

Many people think of an italic face as a slanted form of the root typeface, since italic type is generally slanted. Strictly speaking this is not true; the correct terminology for a slanted form of a typeface is **oblique**. However, both italic and oblique letters are used for the same purpose, which is to emphasize text visually, so we will ignore the distinction here.

Mathematically, obliqueness is like rotation, except that only one axis (that is, one dimension) is rotated. Thus, given a point (x,y) and an angle θ, which is used to rotate the Y axis, then the corresponding point in the oblique coordinate system, (xo,yo) is given by

$$yo = y \text{ and } xo = x + y*\tan(\theta)$$

Figure 7.2 illustrates this and shows a typical oblique letter.

Conceptually, we can create an oblique form of a character bitmap as follows: set n to zero; proceeding from the bottom of the bitmap to the top, right-shift each row by n positions; after every m rows, increment n. This produces an angle of obliqueness (measured from the vertical) whose tangent is $1/m$. The angles for the first few values of m follow. The most useful values for m are 3 through 5.

FIGURE 7.2 Example of an Oblique Letter

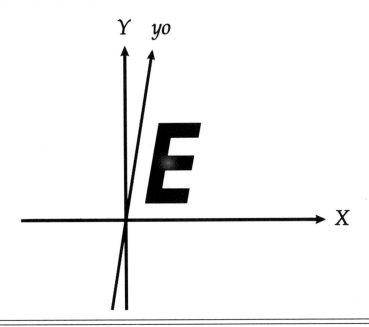

m	1/m	θ
1	1.00	45
2	0.50	30
3	0.33	18
4	0.25	14
5	0.20	11

Note that a font modified in this fashion will have a smaller pitch than the unmodified form. That is, each character cell increases in width, so that fewer characters will fit in a given width on the page. The code to create an oblique bitmap is given in Listing 7.4. As with scaling and bolding, the synthesized italic font is not generally suitable for publication-quality use. However, it does provide reasonable results for use in draft printing or document preview mode.

Patterned Text

One of the easier font effects to implement is patterned text, in which each character in a font is combined with a repeating geometric pattern. Only where a pattern and

LISTING 7.4 Code to Produce a Synthetic Italic Font

```
/*---------------------------------------------------------*/
/* FILE:   ITALCHR.C                                       */
/* DESC:   Functions for synthetic italic (oblique) chars. */
/*---------------------------------------------------------*/

#include "ljfont.h"
#include "fontutl.h"
#include "fontmod.h"


/*---------------------------------------------------------*/
/* copy (src>>obits) to dst...                             */
/*---------------------------------------------------------*/

static void rshift_buf( char *src, char *dst,
                        int nbits, int obits )
{
   unsigned char sm, dm;
   int           obytes;

   /* obits can be greater than 8 - if so, compute a */
   /* byte offset and a bit offset in range 0..7.    */
   obytes = obits >> 3;
   obits  &= 7;

   sm = 0x80;
   dm = (obits > 0) ? 0x80 >> obits : 0x80;
   dst += obytes;

   while( nbits-- )
```

Listing 7.4 continues

Listing 7.4 continued

```
    {
        if( *src & sm )
            *dst |= dm;
        sm >>= 1;
        if( sm == 0 )
        {
            src++;
            sm = 0x80;
        }
        dm >>= 1;
        if( dm == 0 )
        {
            dst++;
            dm = 0x80;
        }
    }
}

/*------------------------------------------------------------*/
/* obliquely copy src to dst...                               */
/*------------------------------------------------------------*/

static ocopy( char *src, char *dst, int ws,
              int wd, int ncols )
{
    unsigned char mask;
    int           srb, drb, n;

    srb  = (ws + 7) / 8;
    drb  = (wd + 7) / 8;
    mask = 0x80;
    n    = 0;
    while( ws-- )
    {
        if( *src & mask )
            *dst |= mask;
        n++;
        if( n == ncols )
        {
            n = 0;
            dst += drb;
        }
        mask >>= 1;
        if( mask == 0 )
        {
            mask = 0x80;
            src++;
            dst++;
        }
    }
}

/*------------------------------------------------------------*/
/* italicize the character horizontally...                    */
/*------------------------------------------------------------*/

static void hital_chr( char *src, char *dst, int ws,
              int hs, int wd, int hd, int mcnt )
```

Listing 7.4 continues

Listing 7.4 continued

```
{
   int   i,  m, dy, srb, drb;
   char *s, *d;

   srb = (ws + 7) / 8;
   drb = (wd + 7) / 8;
   dy  = (hs - 1) / mcnt;
   m   = 0;

   for( i=0; i<hs; i++ )
   {
      rshift_buf( src, dst, ws, dy );
      m++;
      if( m == mcnt )
      {
         m = 0;
         dy--;
      }
      src = p_normal( src, srb, 1 );
      dst = p_normal( dst, drb, 1 );
   }
}

/*------------------------------------------------------------*/
/* italicize the character vertically...                     */
/*------------------------------------------------------------*/
static void vital_chr( char *src, char *dst, int ws,
                int hs, int wd, int hd, int mcnt )
{
   int   i, srb, drb;
   char *s, *d;

   srb  = (ws + 7) / 8;
   drb  = (wd + 7) / 8;

   for( i=0; i<hs; i++ )
   {
      ocopy( src, dst, ws, wd, mcnt );
      src = p_normal( src, srb, 1 );
      dst = p_normal( dst, drb, 1 );
   }
}

/*------------------------------------------------------------*/
/* primary entry point...                                    */
/*------------------------------------------------------------*/

void ital_chr( char *src, char *dst, int ws, int hs,
                int wd, int hd, int dir, int mcnt )
{
   if( dir == IS_LAND )
      vital_chr( src, dst, ws, hs, wd, hd, mcnt );
   else
      hital_chr( src, dst, ws, hs, wd, hd, mcnt );
}

/*---------------- End of File ITALCHR.C ------------------*/
```

character coincide is color actually deposited on the page. This is achieved by bit-wise "and-ing" a character bitmap with a pattern bitmap.

Each pattern is implemented as a square pixel array, typically 8 by 8 or 16 by 16. The pattern is repeated as necessary to cover the full area of a character bitmap. Here is an example of a pattern of 8 bytes notated in binary:

```
1 1 1 1 1 1 1 1
0 0 0 0 0 0 0 0
1 1 1 1 1 1 1 1
0 0 0 0 0 0 0 0
1 1 1 1 1 1 1 1
0 0 0 0 0 0 0 0
1 1 1 1 1 1 1 1
0 0 0 0 0 0 0 0
```

When this pattern is and-ed with a character bitmap, the interior of each character is filled in with a pattern of horizontal lines. However, because the pattern's intrinsic resolution is at the limit of the printer's resolution of 300 dpi, the effect to the eye will be more of a texture than a pattern of lines. Indeed, because of the tendency of adjacent dots on the page to appear to blend into each other, the gap between adjacent lines in the pattern might not be apparent, rendering the pattern unintelligible. This problem can be remedied by decreasing the spatial frequencies in the pattern, as in the following example:

```
1 1 1 1 1 1 1 1
1 1 1 1 1 1 1 1
0 0 0 0 0 0 0 0
0 0 0 0 0 0 0 0
1 1 1 1 1 1 1 1
1 1 1 1 1 1 1 1
0 0 0 0 0 0 0 0
0 0 0 0 0 0 0 0
```

As a general rule, the patterned effect should be used in moderation and then only on fonts in larger point sizes, such as 16 and up. For very large point sizes, say, 60 and up, at least a 16-by-16-bit pattern cell should be used. This effect, combined with outlining, which is discussed in the next section, produces some interesting results.

Listing 7.5 presents the source code for a function to implement 8-by-8 patterns. To modify it for a larger cell size, such as 16 by 16, you increase the number of bytes in each cell from 8 to 32, yielding 2 bytes per row for 16 rows.

LISTING 7.5　Code to Produce Patterned Character Images

```
/*------------------------------------------------------*/
/* FILE:   BOLDCHR.C                                     */
/* DESC:   Functions for synthetic bold char modification. */
/*------------------------------------------------------*/

#include "ljfont.h"
#include "fontutl.h"
#include "fontmod.h"


/*------------------------------------------------------*/
/* 8x8 pattern cells for patterned fonts                */
/*------------------------------------------------------*/

#define P_MAX 16

static int npat = P_MAX;

static unsigned char fntpat[P_MAX][8] =
{
    /* 1 - "half-toned" */
    { 0xAA, 0x55, 0xAA, 0x55, 0xAA, 0x55, 0xAA, 0x55 },

    /* 2 - fine horizontal stripes */
    { 0xFF, 0x00, 0x00, 0x00, 0xFF, 0x00, 0x00, 0x00 },

    /* 3 - fine vertical stripes */
    { 0x11, 0x11, 0x11, 0x11, 0x11, 0x11, 0x11, 0x11 },

    /* 4 - diagonal stripes */
    { 0x01, 0x02, 0x04, 0x08, 0x10, 0x20, 0x40, 0x80 },

    /* 5 - horz/vert weave - fine */
    { 0x11, 0x11, 0x11, 0xFF, 0x11, 0x11, 0x11, 0xFF },

    /* 6 - horz/vert weave - coarse */
    { 0x10, 0x10, 0x10, 0xFF, 0x10, 0x10, 0x10, 0x10 },

    /* 7 - horz candy stripes */
    { 0xFF, 0xFF, 0xFF, 0x00, 0x00, 0xFF, 0x00, 0x00 },

    /* 8 - checkerboard */
    { 0xF0, 0xF0, 0xF0, 0xF0, 0x0F, 0x0F, 0x0F, 0x0F },

    /* 9 - curves */
    { 0x60, 0x90, 0x90, 0x90, 0x09, 0x09, 0x09, 0x06 },

    /* 10 - bricks */
    { 0x04, 0x04, 0x04, 0xFF, 0x20, 0x20, 0x20, 0xFF },

    /* 11 - ovals */
    { 0x7E, 0x81, 0x7E, 0x81, 0x7E, 0x81, 0x7E, 0x81 },

    /* 12 - diamonds */
    { 0x93, 0x39, 0x7C, 0xFE, 0x7C, 0x39, 0x93, 0xC7 },

    /* 13 - squares */
    { 0x00, 0x7E, 0x42, 0x42, 0x42, 0x42, 0x7E, 0x00 },
```

Listing 7.5　continues

Listing 7.5 continued

```
    /* 14 - crosses */
    { 0x39, 0x10, 0x52, 0x7e, 0x52, 0x10, 0x39, 0x00 },

    /* 15 - corners */
    { 0xFF, 0x80, 0x84, 0x84, 0x84, 0xBC, 0x80, 0x80 },

    /* 16 - filled corners */
    { 0x00, 0x78, 0x70, 0x62, 0x46, 0x0E, 0x1E, 0x00 },
};
/*------------------------------------------------------------*/
/* Apply a pattern to a bitmap...                             */
/*------------------------------------------------------------*/

void apply_pat( char *bmap, int w, int h, int pat )
{
    int i, j, ir, rb;

    rb = (w + 7) / 8;
    for( i=0; i<h; i++ )
    {
        ir = i & 7;
        for( j=0; j<rb; j++ )
        {
            *bmap &= fntpat[pat][ir];
            bmap++;
        }
    }
}

/*--------------- End of File PATTCHR.C -----------------*/
```

Outlined Text

Outlined, or hollowed, text is another useful effect, particularly with larger and bolder typefaces. It is implemented by removing the interior pixels from each distinct area within a charcter's bitmap, leaving behind a set of closed curves. A single pixel outline is created rather easily, as follows:

```
for each character pixel (i,j)
{
        if the pixel is set then
            if any adjacent pixel is not set then
            {
                transfer (i,j) to an output bitmap.
            }
}
```

This is essentially an edge-detection algorithm.

The thickness of the outline can be increased by increasing the size of the output pixel. Thus, to create a two-pixel-thick outline, the output pixel (i,j) is replaced by 4 pixels:

```
(i,j)        (i,j+1)
(i+1,j)      (i+1, j+1)
```

Note that in this case it is possible to write outside the destination bitmap if it is the same size as the source bitmap and if the transferred pixel is on the right or bottom edge of the source bitmap. Thus, it is necessary to check the indices being used to ensure that this does not happen.

An alternative method for increasing the outline's size is to transfer a block of source pixels where with edge pixel (i,j) at the center of the block. A two-pixel outline is generated by transferring the following set:

```
(i-1,j-1)    (i-1,j)      (i-1,j+1)
(i,j-1)      (i,j)        (i,j+1)
(i+1,j-1)    (i+1,j)      (i+1,j+1)
```

Note that this generates a two-pixel outline, not a three-pixel outline as you might think. This is because (i,j) is an edge pixel, so one side or corner of the block will contain background pixels.

The algorithm can be stated in general terms: To generate an r-pixel outline, $r > 0$, transfer all source pixels within a radius of $r - 1$ of each edge pixel (i,j). Values for r should generally be small; the range 1 through 5 is typical. The source code for the outline generator is given in Listing 7.6.

LISTING 7.6 Code to Produce Outlined Character Images

```c
/*------------------------------------------------------------*/
/* FILE:   OUTLCHR.C                                          */
/* DESC:   Functions for generating character outlines.       */
/*------------------------------------------------------------*/

#include "ljfont.h"
#include "fontutl.h"
#include "fontmod.h"

/*------------------------------------------------------------*/
/* determine if pixel (i, j) is an edge pixel...              */
/*------------------------------------------------------------*/

static int is_edge( char *bm, int w, int h, int i, int j )
{
    int          ii, jj, j0, rb;
    unsigned char  mask;
```

Listing 7.6 continues

Listing 7.6 continues

```
    char            *p;

    rb = (w + 7) / 8;
    if( i == 0 ) return( 1 );
    if( i == h-1 ) return( 1 );
    if( j == 0 ) return( 1 );
    if( j == w-1 ) return( 1 );

    j0 = j - 1;

    for( ii=i-1; ii<=i+1; ii++ )
    {
        p = p_normal( bm, rb, ii );
        p += j0 >> 3;
        mask = 0x80 >> (j0 & 7);

        for( jj=j-1; jj<=j+1; jj++ )
        {
            if( (*p & mask) == 0 )
                return( 1 );
            mask >>= 1;
            if( mask == 0 )
            {
                p++;
                mask = 0x80;
            }
        }
    }

    return( 0 );
}

/*------------------------------------------------------------*/
/* copy a rectangular block of pixels from s to d...      */
/*------------------------------------------------------------*/

static void copy_blk( char *src, char *dst, int srb, int drb,
                      int i1, int i2, int j1, int j2 )
{
    int             i, j;
    unsigned char mask;
    char            *s, *d;

    for( i=i1; i<=i2; i++ )
    {
        s = p_normal( src, srb, i );
        s += j1 >> 3;
        d = p_normal( dst, drb, i );
        d += j1 >> 3;
        mask = 0x80 >> (j1 & 7);
        for( j=j1; j<=2; j++ )
        {
            *d |= (*s & mask);
            mask >>= 1;
            if( mask == 0 )
            {
                s++;
                d++;
```

Listing 7.6 continues

Listing 7.6 continues

```
            mask = 0x80;
        }
    }
  }
}

/*------------------------------------------------------------*/
/* generate a character outline from src in dst...            */
/*------------------------------------------------------------*/

void gen_outln( char *src, char *dst, int ws, int hs,
                int wd, int hd, int r )
{
   int            i, i1, i2, j, j1, j2, srb, drb;
   char           *s;
   unsigned char mask;

   srb = (ws + 7) / 8;
   drb = (wd + 7) / 8;
   r--;

   for( i=0; i<hs; i++ )
   {
      mask = 0x80;
      s = p_normal( src, srb, i );
      for( j=0; j<ws; j++ )
      {
         if( *s & mask )
         {
            if( is_edge(src, ws, hs, i, j) )
            {
               i1 = i - r;
               if( i1 < 0 ) i1 = 0;
               i2 = i + r;
               if( i2 > hs-1 ) i2 = hs-1;

               j1 = j - r;
               if( j1 < 0 ) j1 = 0;
               j2 = j + r;
               if( j2 > ws-1 ) j2 = ws-1;
               copy_blk( src, dst, srb, drb,
                         i1, i2, j1, j2 );
            }
         }
         mask >>= 1;
         if( mask == 0 )
         {
            s++;
            mask = 0x80;
         }
      }
   }
}

/*---------------- End of File OUTLCHR.C -----------------*/
```

Drop-Shadowed Text

Drop shadows are another effect that is easy to implement. We take a copy of the character bitmap, offset it vertically and horizontally, and combine it with the original bitmap by or-ing the copy back into the original bitmap. The horizontal and vertical offsets are determined by the apparent location of the illumination source (a light source is needed to create a shadow). Thus, if the light source is above and to the left of the character, the shadow will appear below and to the right of the original character outline. This corresponds to a positive row offset and a positive column offset, which is the most straightforward to implement.

A better effect can be obtained if the shadow image is subdued relative to the character image. This can be achieved by graying the shadow, which is accomplished by removing every other pixel in the shadow as follows:

```
if( (i+j) & 1 )
    set pixel (i,j)
```

The code for the drop shadow routine is given in Listing 7.7.

Creating Fonts from Scratch

Creating a new font from scratch is an ambitious undertaking that is beyond the patience or resources of most developers. In order to achieve practical results, you need some kind of font editor. There are a number of commercial software packages that provide this tool; see Appendix E on products for more information.

Perhaps the most practical route is to start with an existing font and then modify each character image. This will generally insure stylistic unity and at least a modicum of aesthetic appeal, which are important considerations in the design of a font. Remember, typography is both a science and an art. If you are not using another font as a basis, keep in mind when creating your new font that the letters should look related. Here are some factors to consider.

Stroke weight	The individual lines and curves that make up the characters should all possess more or less the same thickness.
Line cap style	This refers to the shape of the end of a line or open arc, which can be square, rounded, serifed, or some other style. This will normally be consistent within a font.
Miters and angles	Many letters contain angles, such as those at the base of a "V" or "W." The way in which the two sides of the angle join is referred to as the miter style. These will normally be consistent from letter to letter.

LISTING 7.7 Code to Add a Drop Shadow to Character Images

```
/*-----------------------------------------------------------*/
/* FILE:   DSHWCHR.C                                         */
/* DESC:   Functions for generating drop-shadowed chars.     */
/*-----------------------------------------------------------*/

#include "ljfont.h"
#include "fontutl.h"
#include "fontmod.h"

/*-----------------------------------------------------------*/
/* generate a drop shadow...                                 */
/*-----------------------------------------------------------*/

void gen_shadow( char *src, char *dst, int ws, int hs,
                 int wd, int hd, int thk )
{
    int          i, j, di, dj, srb, drb;
    char         *s, *d;
    unsigned char sm, dm;

    srb = (ws + 7) / 8;
    drb = (wd + 7) / 8;
    dst = p_normal( dst, drb, thk );

    for( i=0; i<hs; i++ )
    {
        s  = p_normal( src, srb, i );
        sm = 0x80;
        d  = p_normal( dst, drb, i );
        d += thk >> 3;
        dm = 0x80 >> (thk & 7);

        for( j=0; j<ws; j++ )
        {
            /* use test for half-toned shadow */
            if( (i+j) & 1 )
                if( *s & sm )
                    *d |= dm;

            sm >>= 1;
            if( sm == 0 )
            {
                s++;
                sm = 0x80;
            }

            dm >>= 1;
            if( dm == 0 )
            {
                d++;
                dm = 0x80;
            }
        }
    }
}

/*--------------- End of File DSHWCHR.C ------------------*/
```

Closed curves	There are many circles and ellipses in most fonts. These should normally maintain the same eccentricity throughout. For example, the capital "O" and capital "Q" will normally overlay perfectly.
Ornateness	The ornateness of letters should be kept consistent. For example, it would be in very bad taste to combine letters from an Old English face with a Helvetica face. This is an extreme example, but it illustrates the concept.
Ascent and descent	Ascenders and descenders will normally maintain the same proportions. For example, the lower case "p" and "q" will normally extend the same distance below the baseline.
Family resemblance	We have noted that the capital "O" will normally resemble the capital "Q" and so forth. This principle should be observed throughout a font, so that similarly constructed letters resemble each other. Some examples are: OQ, VW, PR, EF, pq, bd, ij, mn.

Figure 7.3 illustrates some of these features. However, note that every rule has its exceptions; there may be situations where breaking a rule can produce a dramatic effect.

FIGURE 7.3 Examples of Font Design Considerations

Stroke Weight

Cap Styles

Angularity

Ornateness

Another matter to consider in the design of a font is its intended use. If you are creating a font for use in body text, for example, then it should be easy to read. Highly ornate faces are generally hard to read and tiring to the eye. They work best when used in small doses in appropriate contexts, for example, wedding invitations. Here, again, we are dealing with visual aesthetic concerns. Studying examples of traditional typefaces is a helpful aid to the design process.

Programming Project: A Font Modification Utility

We conclude with a utility program to implement all of the techniques described in this chapter. The program, HPMFONT.C, has the following command line syntax:

```
HPFNTMOD   fnt_in   fnt_out   swtches

    fnt_in:        font file to modify

    fnt_out:       file name of modified output

    switches:      -bn    bold by n dots
                   -dn    drop shadow n dots thick
                   -in    italicize by atan(1/n)
                   -on    gen n-dot outlines
                   -pn    apply pattern n (1-16)
                   -r     rotate (p->l or l->p)
                   -sd.d xy scale d.d
                   -xd.d x scale d.d
                   -yd.d y scale d.d
```

All the source files presented so far in this chapter (Listings 7.1 through 7.7) can be compiled and placed within a library, or they can be referenced from a make file set up for HPMFONT.C. One additional file, FONTUTL.C, is also required; it contains several functions that are used in the other source files. The remaining source and header files are presented in Listings 7.8 through 7.11. This concludes our in-depth look at fonts. The techniques covered can be used to extend the usefulness of individual fonts and to add additional capabilities to programs that deal with printer fonts. Note that all the techniques, with the exceptions of scaling and synthetic italic generation, produce results that are suitable for publication use. In the following chapters we turn to raster graphics and look at the LaserJet III's vector graphics capabilities.

LISTING 7.8 Font Modification Header File

```
/*----------------------------------------------------------*/
/* FILE:  FONTMOD.H                                          */
/* DESC:  Functions for font modification.                  */
/*----------------------------------------------------------*/

#define IS_PORT 0
#define IS_LAND 1

/* see sclbmap.c */
extern void scl_bitmap( char *src, int ws, int hs,
                        char *dst, int wd, int hd );

/* see rotbmap.c */
extern void rot_bitmap( char *src, char *dst, int ws,
                        int hs, int sgn );

/* see boldchr.c */
extern void bold_chr( char *src, char *dst, int ws, int hs,
                      int dir, int nreps );

/* see italchr.c */
extern void ital_chr( char *src, char *dst, int ws, int hs,
                      int wd, int hd, int dir, int mcnt );

/* see pattchr.c */
extern void apply_pat( char *bmap, int w, int h, int pat );

/* see outlchr.c */
extern void gen_outln( char *src, char *dst, int ws, int hs,
                       int wd, int hd, int radius );

/* see dshwchr.c */
extern void gen_shadow( char *src, char *dst, int ws, int hs,
                        int wd, int hd, int thk );

/*--------------- End of File FONTMOD.H -----------------*/
```

LISTING 7.9 Font Utility Functions Header File

```
/*-----------------------------------------------------------*/
/* FILE:   FONTUTL.H                                          */
/* DESC:   Various utility functions.                         */
/*-----------------------------------------------------------*/

int   scl_rev_word( int w, double wm, double wd );
int   scl_word( int w, double wm, double wd );
void  iswap( int *i1, int *i2 );
char *p_normal( char *p, int n, int m );
void  bitmap_or( char *src, char *dst, int ws, int hs,
                 int wd, int hd );
void  bitmap_and( char *src, char *dst, int ws, int hs,
                  int wd, int hd );
void  bitmap_clr( char *bm, int w, int h );

/*--------------- End of File FONTUTL.H ------------------*/
```

LISTING 7.10 Source Code to Font Utility Functions

```
/*-----------------------------------------------------------*/
/* FILE:   FONTUTL.C                                          */
/* DESC:   Various utility functions.                         */
/*-----------------------------------------------------------*/

#include "ljfont.h"

/*-----------------------------------------------------------*/
/* Function to scale a reversed word...                       */
/*-----------------------------------------------------------*/

int scl_rev_word( int w, double wm, double wd )
{
   int    rw;
   double drw;

   rw  = REV_WRD( w );
   drw = (rw * wm) / wd + 0.5;
   rw  = (int) drw;

   return( REV_WRD(rw) );
}

/*-----------------------------------------------------------*/
/* Function to scale a word...                                */
/*-----------------------------------------------------------*/

int scl_word( int w, double wm, double wd )
{
   int    rw;
   double drw;
```

Listing 7.10 continues

Listing 7.10 continued

```
    drw = (w * wm) / wd + 0.5;
    rw  = (int) drw;

    return( rw );
}
/*-------------------------------------------------------*/
/* Function to swap 2 ints...                            */
/*-------------------------------------------------------*/
void iswap( int *i1, int *i2 )
{
    int itmp;

    itmp = *i1;
    *i1 = *i2;
    *i2 = itmp;
}

/*-------------------------------------------------------*/
/* Function to increment and normalize a ptr...         */
/*-------------------------------------------------------*/
char *p_normal( char *p, int n, int m )
{
    char     *np;
    long      nm;
    unsigned  seg, ofs, s, o;

    nm = n;  nm *= m;
    s = nm >> 4;
    o = nm &   15;
    ofs = (((unsigned long) p) & 0xFFFF) + o;
    seg = ((((unsigned long) p) >> 16) & 0xFFFF) + s;
    seg += ofs >> 4;
    ofs &= 15;
    np = (char *) ( (((unsigned long) seg) << 16) | ofs );

    return( np );
}

/*-------------------------------------------------------*/
/* Function to OR two bitmaps : dst <- src|dst...        */
/*-------------------------------------------------------*/
void bitmap_or( char *src, char *dst, int ws, int hs,
                int wd, int hd )
{
    int   i, rb, srb, drb, h;
    char *s, *d;

    srb = (ws + 7) / 8;
    drb = (wd + 7) / 8;
    h   = (hs < hd) ? hs : hd;

    for( i=0; i<h; i++ )
    {
        s = p_normal( src, srb, i );
```

Listing 7.10 continues

Listing 7.10   continued

```
        d = p_normal( dst, drb, i );
        rb  = (srb < drb) ? srb : drb;
        while( rb-- )
            *d++ |= *s++;
    }
}

/*------------------------------------------------------------*/
/* Function to AND two bitmaps : dst  src&dst...           */
/*------------------------------------------------------------*/

void bitmap_and( char *src, char *dst, int ws, int hs,
                 int wd, int hd )
{
    int   i, rb, srb, drb, h;
    char *s, *d;

    srb = (ws + 7) / 8;
    drb = (wd + 7) / 8;
    h   = (hs < hd) ? hs : hd;

    for( i=0; ih; i++ )
    {
        s = p_normal( src, srb, i );
        d = p_normal( dst, drb, i );
        rb  = (srb < drb) ? srb : drb;
        while( rb-- )
            *d++ &= *s++;
    }
}

/*------------------------------------------------------------*/
/* Function to clear a bitmap...                           */
/*------------------------------------------------------------*/

void bitmap_clr( char *bm, int w, int h )
{
    char *row;
    int   rb, i;

    for( i=0; i<h; i++ )
    {
        rb = (w + 7) / 8;
        row = p_normal( bm, rb, i );
        while( rb-- )
            *row++ = 0;
    }
}

/*--------------- End of File FONTUTL.C -----------------*/
```

LISTING 7.11   **Program to Implement Font Modification Functions**

```
/*----------------------------------------------------------*/
/* FILE:      HPMFONT.C                                      */
/* DESC:      HP Soft Font File Modification Utility         */
/*----------------------------------------------------------*/

#include "stdlib.h"
#include "stdio.h"
#include "string.h"
#include "ctype.h"
#include "math.h"

#ifdef ZORTECH
        #include "dos.h"
#endif
#ifdef BORLAND
        #include "alloc.h"
#endif
#ifdef MICROSOFT
        #include "malloc.h"
        #define farcalloc calloc
        #define farfree   free
#endif

#include "ljfont.h"
#include "fontutl.h"
#include "fontmod.h"

#define BUF_LEN   80                 /* i/o buffer size */
#define MAX_ESEQ  80         /* largest permissible esc seq */

/*----------------------------------------------------------*/
/* global variables...                                      */
/*----------------------------------------------------------*/

char   eseq[MAX_ESEQ];           /* escape sequence buffer */

font_desc *fd = NULL;                /* a font descriptor */
char_desc cd;                        /* a char descriptor */

char   *src_file = NULL,          /* source font file name */
       *dst_file = NULL;            /* dest font file name */

char   *src = NULL,                    /* source bitmap */
       *dst = NULL,                /* destination bitmap */
       *tmp = NULL;                       /* work bitmap */

int    ws, wd,                      /* src, dst widths */
       hs, hd,                     /* src, dst heights */
       cur_ch,                   /* current character */
       bcnt = 0,                          /* bold reps */
       icnt = 0,          /* ital ang = atan(1/bcnt) */
       ipat = 0,                 /* pattern number */
       orad = 0,                 /* outline radius */
       dthk = 0,           /* drop shadow thickness */
       rsgn = 0;                  /* rotation sign */

double xscl = 1.0,                  /* scaling factors */
```

Listing 7.11   continues

Listing 7.11 continued

```
        yscl = 1.0;

char    *esc = "\033";                        /* escape character */

/*----------------------------------------------------------*/
/* explain program usage...                                 */
/*----------------------------------------------------------*/

void explain_pgm( void )
{
   printf( "HPFNTMOD  fnt_in  fnt_out  swtches\n" );
   printf( "\n" );
   printf( "fnt_in:   font file to modify\n" );
   printf( "\n" );
   printf( "fnt_out:  file name of modified output\n" );
   printf( "\n" );
   printf( "switches: -bn    -  bold by n dots\n" );
   printf( "               -dn    -  drop shadow n dots thick\n" );
   printf( "               -in    -  italicize by atan(1/n)\n" );
   printf( "               -on    -  gen n-dot outlines\n" );
   printf( "               -pn    -  apply pattern n (1-16)\n" );
   printf( "               -r     -  rotate\n" );
   printf( "               -sd.d  -  xy scale d.d\n" );
   printf( "               -xd.d  -  x scale d.d\n" );
   printf( "               -yd.d  -  y scale d.d\n" );
}

/*----------------------------------------------------------*/
/* write a message and quit...                              */
/*----------------------------------------------------------*/

void exit_pgm( char *msg )
{
   if( fd != NULL )
      farfree( fd );
   if( src != NULL )
      farfree( src );
   if( dst != NULL )
      farfree( dst );
   if( tmp != NULL )
      farfree( dst );

   printf( "%s\n", msg );
   exit( 0 );
}

/*----------------------------------------------------------*/
/* process command line args...                            */
/*----------------------------------------------------------*/

void process_args( int argc, char *argv[] )
{
   int  i;

   src_file = argv[1];
   dst_file = argv[2];

   for( i=3; i<argc; i++ )
```

Listing 7.11 continues

Listing 7.11 continued

```
    {
        /* should only find switches */
        if( *argv[i] != '-' )
            exit_pgm( "Error - switch requires leading dash" );
        switch( tolower( *(argv[i]+1) ) )
        {
            case 'b' :  bcnt = 1;
                        sscanf( argv[i]+2, "%d", &bcnt );
                        break;

            case 'd' :  dthk = 4;
                        sscanf( argv[i]+2, "%d", &dthk );
                        break;

            case 'i' :  icnt = 4;
                        sscanf( argv[i]+2, "%d", &icnt );
                        break;

            case 'o' :  orad = 1;
                        sscanf( argv[i]+2, "%d", &orad );
                        break;

            case 'p' :  ipat = 1;
                        sscanf( argv[i]+2, "%d", &ipat );
                        break;

            case 'r' :  rsgn = 1;
                        break;

            case 's' :  sscanf( argv[i]+2, "%lf", &xscl );
                        yscl = xscl;
                        break;

            case 'x' :  sscanf( argv[i]+2, "%lf", &xscl );
                        break;

            case 'y' :  sscanf( argv[i]+2, "%lf", &yscl );
                        break;
        }
    }

    /* validate values */
    if( (xscl <= 0.0) || (yscl <= 0.0) )
        exit_pgm( "Error - scale value <= 0.0" );
}

/*-----------------------------------------------------------*/
/* update an existing char descriptor...                     */
/*-----------------------------------------------------------*/

void update_cd( char_desc *cd )
{
    char_desc new_cd;
    int       itmp;

    /* scaling... */
    if( xscl != 1.0 )
    {
```

Listing 7.11 continues

Listing 7.11   continued

```
      cd->left_ofs = scl_rev_word( cd->left_ofs, xscl, 1.0 );
      cd->char_wid = scl_rev_word( cd->char_wid, xscl, 1.0 );
      cd->delta_x  = scl_rev_word( cd->delta_x, xscl, 1.0 );
   }
   if( yscl != 1.0 )
   {
      cd->top_ofs  = scl_rev_word( cd->top_ofs, yscl, 1.0 );
      cd->char_hgt = scl_rev_word( cd->char_hgt, yscl, 1.0 );
   }

   /* rotation... */
   if( rsgn > 0 ) /* rotate +90 - port to land */
   {
      memcpy( &new_cd, cd, sizeof(char_desc) );
      new_cd.char_wid = cd->char_hgt;
      new_cd.char_hgt = cd->char_wid;
      itmp = REV_WRD( cd->top_ofs );  itmp = -itmp;
      new_cd.left_ofs = REV_WRD( itmp );
      new_cd.top_ofs  = cd->char_wid+cd->left_ofs;
      new_cd.orient   = 1;
      memcpy( cd, &new_cd, sizeof(char_desc) );
   }
   else if( rsgn < 0 ) /* rotate -90 - land to port */
   {
      memcpy( &new_cd, cd, sizeof(char_desc) );
      new_cd.char_wid = cd->char_hgt;
      new_cd.char_hgt = cd->char_wid;
      itmp = REV_WRD( cd->left_ofs );  itmp = -itmp;
      new_cd.top_ofs  = REV_WRD( itmp );
      new_cd.left_ofs = cd->top_ofs - cd->char_hgt;
      new_cd.orient   = 0;
      memcpy( cd, &new_cd, sizeof(char_desc) );
   }

   /* bolding... */
   if( bcnt > 0 )
   {
      itmp = REV_WRD( bcnt );
      cd->delta_x += itmp;
      if( cd->orient )
      {
         cd->char_hgt += itmp;
         cd->top_ofs  += itmp;
      }
      else
         cd->char_wid += itmp;
   }

   /* italicize... */
   if( icnt > 0 )
   {
      if( cd->orient )
      {
         itmp = (REV_WRD(cd->char_wid) - 1) / icnt;
         itmp = REV_WRD( itmp );
         cd->char_hgt += itmp;
         cd->top_ofs  += itmp;
         cd->delta_x += itmp;
```

Listing 7.11   continues

Listing 7.11 continued

```
        }
        else
        {
            itmp = (REV_WRD(cd->char_hgt) - 1) / icnt;
            itmp = REV_WRD( itmp );
            cd->char_wid += itmp;
            cd->delta_x += itmp;
        }
    }

    /* drop shadow... */
    if( dthk > 0 )
    {
        itmp = REV_WRD( dthk );
        cd->delta_x += itmp;
        cd->char_hgt += itmp;
        cd->char_wid += itmp;
        if( cd->orient )
            cd->top_ofs  += itmp;
    }
}

/*------------------------------------------------------------*/
/* update the existing font descriptor from args...          */
/*------------------------------------------------------------*/

void update_fd( font_desc *fd )
{
    int itmp;

    fd->bl_dist     = scl_rev_word( fd->bl_dist, yscl, 1.0 );
    fd->cell_wid    = scl_rev_word( fd->cell_wid, xscl, 1.0 );
    fd->cell_hgt    = scl_rev_word( fd->cell_hgt, yscl, 1.0 );
    fd->pitch       = scl_rev_word( fd->pitch, xscl, 1.0 );
    fd->height      = scl_rev_word( fd->height, yscl, 1.0 );
    fd->xheight     = scl_rev_word( fd->xheight, yscl, 1.0 );
    fd->ul_dist     = scl_rev_word( fd->ul_dist, yscl, 1.0 );
    fd->ul_hgt      = scl_rev_word( fd->ul_hgt, yscl, 1.0 );
    fd->txt_hgt     = scl_rev_word( fd->txt_hgt, yscl, 1.0 );
    fd->txt_wid     = scl_rev_word( fd->txt_wid, xscl, 1.0 );
    fd->pitch_ext   = scl_rev_word( fd->pitch_ext, xscl, 1.0 );
    fd->height_ext  = scl_rev_word( fd->height_ext, yscl, 1.0 );

    if( rsgn != 0 ) /* rotate flag set */
    {
        if( fd->orient )  /* landscape to portrait */
        {
            fd->orient = 0;
            rsgn = -1;
        }
        else                /* portrait to landscape */
        {
            fd->orient = 1;
            rsgn = 1;
        }
    }

    if( bcnt > 0 )  /* bolding */
```

Listing 7.11 continues

Listing 7.11 continued

```
        {
            itmp = REV_WRD( bcnt );
            if( fd->orient )
                fd->cell_hgt += itmp;
            else
                fd->cell_wid += itmp;
        }

        if( icnt > 0 )   /* italicize */
        {
            if( fd->orient )
            {
                itmp = REV_WRD(fd->cell_wid) / icnt;
                fd->cell_hgt += REV_WRD(itmp);
            }
            else
            {
                itmp = REV_WRD(fd->cell_hgt) / icnt;
                fd->cell_wid += REV_WRD(itmp);
            }
        }

        if( dthk > 0 )   /* drop shadow */
        {
            itmp = REV_WRD( dthk );
            fd->cell_hgt += itmp;
            fd->cell_wid += itmp;
        }
    }

/*---------------------------------------------------------*/
/* sends a parameterized sequence...                       */
/*---------------------------------------------------------*/

void send_eseq( FILE *f_out, int pch, int gch,
                                int val, int tch )
{
    char cmd[32];

    sprintf( cmd, "%s%c%c%d%c", esc, pch, gch, val, tch );
    fwrite( cmd, strlen(cmd), 1, f_out );
}

/*---------------------------------------------------------*/
/* alloc a buffer large enough for bitmap of WxH pix...    */
/*---------------------------------------------------------*/

char *alloc_bitmap( int wid, int hgt )
{
    char *bm;
    int   rowbytes;

    rowbytes = (wid + 7) / 8;
    bm = (char *) farcalloc( hgt, rowbytes );
    if( bm == NULL )
        exit_pgm( "\nError - memory allocation failure"
                  " in function alloc_bitmap()" );
```

Listing 7.11   continues

Listing 7.11 continued

```
    return( bm );
}
/*------------------------------------------------------------*/
/* read a character bitmap...                                 */
/*------------------------------------------------------------*/

void read_src_bmap( FILE *f_in, char *bm,
                    int ncols, int nrows )
{
    int    rowbytes, n, max_b;
    long   nbytes;
    char *p;

    /* if char uses one or more continued descriptors, */
    /* bitmap size could exceed 64K, thus needs a long */
    rowbytes = (ncols + 7) / 8;
    nbytes   = ((long) rowbytes) * nrows;

    /* read the bitmap */
    p = bm;
    max_b = 32767 - sizeof(char_desc);
    while( nbytes > 0 )
    {
        n = (nbytes > max_b) ? max_b : nbytes;
        if( fread( p, n, 1, f_in ) != 1 )
            exit_pgm( "\nError - unexpected EOF reading font" );
        nbytes -= n;
        /* is this descriptor continued? */
        if( nbytes > 0 )
        {
            max_b = 32765;
            p = p_normal( p, n, 1 );
            /* skip the continuation descriptor */
            fread( &n, 2, 1, f_in );
        }
    }
}

/*------------------------------------------------------------*/
/* write a character descriptor...                            */
/*------------------------------------------------------------*/

void write_cd( FILE *f_out, char_desc *cd, char *bmap )
{
    int    rowbytes, ncols, nrows, n, max_b;
    long   nbytes;
    char *p;

    ncols = REV_WRD( cd->char_wid );
    nrows = REV_WRD( cd->char_hgt );
    rowbytes = (ncols + 7) / 8;
    nbytes   = ((long) rowbytes) * nrows;

    /* write the descriptor and bitmap */
    p = bmap;
    max_b = 32767 - sizeof(char_desc);
    n = (nbytes > max_b) ? max_b : nbytes;
    send_eseq( f_out, '(', 's', n+sizeof(char_desc), 'W' );
```

Listing 7.11 continues

Listing 7.11 continued

```
      if( fwrite( cd, sizeof(char_desc), 1, f_out ) != 1 )
         exit_pgm( "\nError - failure writing char desc" );
      if( fwrite( p, n, 1, f_out ) != 1 )
         exit_pgm( "\nError - failure writing char bitmap" );
      nbytes -= n;
      p = p_normal( p, n, 1 );
      max_b = 32765;
      cd->continued = 1;

      /* write remaing bitmap pieces with continuation desc */
      while( nbytes > 0 )
      {
         n = (nbytes > max_b) ? max_b : nbytes;
         send_eseq( f_out, '(', 's', n+2, 'W' );
         if( fwrite( &cd, 2, 1, f_out ) != 1 )
            exit_pgm( "\nError - failure writing char desc" );
         if( fwrite( p, n, 1, f_out ) != 1 )
            exit_pgm( "\nError - failure writing char bitmap" );
         nbytes -= n;
         p = p_normal( p, n, 1 );
      }
}

/*------------------------------------------------------------*/
/* gather the next escape sequence...                         */
/*------------------------------------------------------------*/

int get_eseq( FILE *f_in, char ebuf[], int esiz )
{
   int  i;
   char c;

   /* If the first byte read is not an escape character */
   /* (dec 27), then either the file is not a font file */
   /* or the file is not readable - damaged, etc. Also, */
   /* should encounter end-of-file at this point.       */

   fread( &c, 1, 1, f_in );
   if( feof(f_in) )
      return( 0 );
   if( c != 27 )
      exit_pgm( "\nError - sync error, or file not a font file." );

   i = 0;
   do
   {
      fread( &c, 1, 1, f_in );
      if( feof(f_in) )
         exit_pgm( "\nError - sync error reading escape sequence." );
      if( i >= esiz-1 )
         exit_pgm( "\nError - escape sequence buffer overflow." );
      ebuf[i++] = c;
   }
   while( ! IS_TERM_CHR( c ) );

   return( 1 );
}
```

Listing 7.11   continues

Listing 7.11 continued

```
/*------------------------------------------------------------*/
/* parse an escape sequence...                                */
/*------------------------------------------------------------*/

void parse_eseq( char eseq[], int *etyp, int *eval )
{
    int  i;
    char pchar, gchar, tchar;

    /* since we are dealing only with font-file related */
    /* sequences we limit the scope of this function as */
    /* follows: only single-valued parameterized seqs.  */
    /* also, passed buffer omits the esc char, 1B (27). */

    /* establish some initial values */
    *etyp = eUNKNOWN;
    *eval = 0;

    /* eseq[0] == parameterized character */
    /* eseq[1] == group character          */
    /* eseq[2] == start of value field     */
    /*    :                                */
    /* eseq[n] == termination character    */

    pchar = eseq[0];

    gchar = eseq[1];

    *eval = atoi( eseq+2 );

    i = 2;
    while( (! IS_TERM_CHR( eseq[i] )) && (i < MAX_ESEQ) )
        i++;
    tchar = eseq[i];

    if( (pchar==')') && (gchar=='s') && (tchar=='W') )
        *etyp = eFONTDESC;
    else if( (pchar=='(') && (gchar=='s') && (tchar=='W') )
        *etyp = eCHARDESC;
    else if( (pchar=='*') && (gchar=='c') && (tchar=='E') )
        *etyp = eCHARCODE;
}
/*------------------------------------------------------------*/
/* modify the character bitmap, leave result in src...        */
/*------------------------------------------------------------*/

void modify_char_bitmap( void )
{
    int i;

    /* scaling request? */
    if( (xscl != 1.0) || (yscl != 1.0) )
    {
        wd  = scl_word( ws, xscl, 1.0 );
        hd  = scl_word( hs, yscl, 1.0 );
        dst = alloc_bitmap( wd, hd );
        scl_bitmap( src, ws, hs, dst, wd, hd );
        farfree( src );  src = dst;  dst = NULL;
        ws = wd;  hs = hd;
```

Listing 7.11 continues

Listing 7.11   continued

```
    }

    /* rotation request? */
    if( rsgn != 0 )
    {
       dst = alloc_bitmap( hs, ws );
       rot_bitmap( src, dst, ws, hs, rsgn );
       farfree( src );  src = dst;  dst = NULL;
       iswap( &ws, &hs );
    }

    /* bold request? */
    if( bcnt > 0 )
    {
       if( fd->orient ) /* landscape */
       {
          dst = alloc_bitmap( ws, hs+bcnt );
          bold_chr( src, dst, ws, hs, IS_LAND, bcnt );
          hs += bcnt;
       }
       else              /* portrait */
       {
          dst = alloc_bitmap( ws+bcnt, hs );
          bold_chr( src, dst, ws, hs, IS_PORT, bcnt );
          ws += bcnt;
       }
       farfree( src );  src = dst;  dst = NULL;
    }

    /* italic request? */
    if( icnt > 0 )
    {
       if( fd->orient ) /* landscape */
       {
          i = (ws-1) / icnt;
          dst = alloc_bitmap( ws, hs+i );
          ital_chr( src, dst, ws, hs, ws, hs+i,
                    IS_LAND, icnt );
          hs += i;
       }
       else              /* portrait */
       {
          i = (hs - 1) / icnt;
          dst = alloc_bitmap( ws+i, hs );
          ital_chr( src, dst, ws, hs, ws+i, hs,
                    IS_PORT, icnt );
          ws += i;
       }
       farfree( src );  src = dst;  dst = NULL;
    }

    /* drop shadow request? */
    if( dthk > 0 )
    {
       dst = alloc_bitmap( ws+dthk, hs+dthk );
       gen_shadow( src, dst, ws, hs, ws+dthk, hs+dthk, dthk );
       bitmap_or( src, dst, ws, hs, ws+dthk, hs+dthk );
       ws += dthk;
       hs += dthk;
       farfree( src );  src = dst;  dst = NULL;
```

Listing 7.11   continues

Listing 7.11 continued

```
   }

   /* remaining effects are applied together */
   if( (ipat > 0) || (orad  0) )
   {
      dst = alloc_bitmap( ws, hs );
      if( orad > 0 )
         gen_outln( src, dst, ws, hs,
                        ws, hs, orad );

      if( ipat > 0 )
         apply_pat( src, ws, hs, ipat-1 );
      else
         bitmap_clr( src, ws, hs );

      bitmap_or( src, dst, ws, hs, ws, hs );
      farfree( src );  src = dst;  dst = NULL;
   }
}

/*----------------------------------------------------------*/
/* scan the font file...                                    */
/*----------------------------------------------------------*/

void scan_font( char *src_file, char *dst_file )
{
    FILE    *f_in, *f_out;
    int      eval, etyp;

    f_in = fopen( src_file, "rb" );
    if( f_in == NULL )
       exit_pgm( "Error - Font file not found." );

    f_out = fopen( dst_file, "wb" );
    if( f_out == NULL )
       exit_pgm( "Error - Could not open output file." );

    printf( "[%s -> %s]", src_file, dst_file );

    /* loop while escape sequences are found */
    while( get_eseq( f_in, eseq, MAX_ESEQ ) )
    {
       parse_eseq( eseq, &etyp, &eval );

       switch( etyp )
       {
          case eFONTDESC :

                  fd = (font_desc *) farcalloc( 1, eval );
                  if( fd == NULL )
                     exit_pgm( "Error - memory allocation failure" );
                  fread( fd, eval, 1, f_in );
                  update_fd( fd );
                  send_eseq( f_out, ')', 's', eval, 'W' );
                  fwrite( fd, eval, 1, f_out );
                  break;

          case eCHARDESC :

                  if( (cur_ch % 5) == 0 )
```

Listing 7.11 continues

Listing 7.11   continued

```
                    printf( "." );

               /* read descriptor */
               if( fread( &cd, sizeof(char_desc), 1, f_in ) != 1 )
                   exit_pgm( "Error - read on char desc failed" );
               ws  = REV_WRD( cd.char_wid );
               hs  = REV_WRD( cd.char_hgt );
               src = alloc_bitmap( ws, hs );
               read_src_bmap( f_in, src, ws, hs );

               modify_char_bitmap();

               /* write modified descriptor */
               update_cd( &cd );
               write_cd( f_out, &cd, src );
               farfree( src );   src = NULL;
               break;

           case eCHARCODE :
               cur_ch = eval;
               send_eseq( f_out, '*', 'c', eval, 'E' );
               break;
        }
    }

    printf( "done\n\n" );
    fclose( f_in );
    fclose( f_out );
}

/*------------------------------------------------------------*/
/*                        M A I N                             */
/*------------------------------------------------------------*/

void main( int argc, char *argv[] )
{
    /* sign-on */
    printf( "\nHP Soft Font Modification Utility\n\n" );

    /* help indicated? */
    if( (argc < 4) || (*argv[1] == '?') )
    {
        explain_pgm();
        exit( 0 );
    }

    /* process command line... */
    process_args( argc, argv );

    /* process the font file... */
    scan_font( src_file, dst_file );

    /* sign-off */
    printf( "end-of-pgm\n" );
}

/*---------------- End of File HPFNTMOD.C ----------------*/
```

Raster Graphics

Introduction

We have already discussed the fundamentals of LaserJet raster graphics in Chapter 3. In this chapter we explore ways to make use of those capabilities.

Evolution of Raster Graphics in the LaserJet Family

The LaserJet III offers significant improvements over the Series II's raster graphics capabilities. The main advance offers three different techniques to compress a bitmap raster image. Two of these appeared first in another member of the product line; the third is new for the LaserJet III and IIID. Each printer has included the raster graphics capabilities of its predecessors while incorporating new features. Thus, raster routines written for earlier printers may be relied on to run on later ones, but not vice versa. The programmer who wants to support the full capabilities of the LaserJet III/IIID must make a decision either to define code specifically for the LaserJet III/IIID or use global variables that must be checked at run time. In this chapter we use the #define approach, since it makes the result easier to read and since our purpose is to set out concepts in an understandable form.

The LaserJet Plus and Series II are able to send simple raster lines. The LaserJet IIP (and the DeskJet) add the ability to compress individual raster lines to achieve worthwhile space savings in the computer (and reductions in transfer time). They offer two compression techniques, one a subset of the other. The LaserJet III/IIID improves on this by allowing a raster line to be represented by its difference from its predecessor, while maintaining the compression capabilities of the IIP (and DeskJet).

Memory Considerations under MS-DOS

Most of the time when we write software for the LaserJet family, the famous MS-DOS 640K limitation on available RAM is not a concern. However, as soon as we try to build a page of raster information, we are forced to deal with this limitation. The 640K limitation can be understood in its historical context—MS-DOS came into being as an 8086 port of CP/M, a microcomputer operating system prevalent in the late 1970's, which is why software developers were able to move over so easily and develop useful applications so quickly—but this is no comfort to the programmer whose application has just hung for lack of heap space or because it can't define a one-megabyte static array.

The problem presented by raster graphics is straightforward. The LaserJet family's native resolution is 300 dots per inch. Given a printing area of 8 by 10½ inches (assuming quarter-inch margins), a full page contains 7,560,000 bits of information ($300 \times 300 \times 8 \times 10$½), or 945,000 bytes ($7,560,000/8$)—945,000 bytes into the aforementioned 640K do not go. There are three practical ways to handle this problem: **expanded memory**, **extended memory**, and **disk swapping**. We offer interfaces for all three of these possibilities; all three interfaces offer similar resources to the programmer. The concepts common to all three interfaces are discussed under the Expanded Memory section that follows; you can apply the concepts explained there even if you will be using one of the other interfaces. We put the common information where we do to entice the reluctant reader at least to look at the expanded memory approach—it's the option we prefer among the three possibilities.

Expanded Memory

The first way to get around the 640K limitation is to use expanded memory; that is, memory that is bank-switched into a portion of DOS-addressable memory. Use of expanded memory is very well standardized, thanks to formal specification developed early and promulgated by Lotus, Intel, and Microsoft (hence the LIM name commonly associated with expanded memory). The standard has evolved and is now at version 4.0. On 80386 and 80486 machines, utility software is available that will enable memory beyond the 1MB address to look like expanded memory to an application. However, the fact that an application does not have to look past the 1MB address mark means that the expanded memory approach can work even on an 8086/8088 machine.

Microsoft Windows 3.0 allows applications to use expanded memory in real mode; the documentation tells programmers to restrict themselves to the earlier LIM specification 3.2 calls, although examination of the expanded memory manager as it sits in memory suggests a full-fledged specification 4.0 manager. The restriction urged by Microsoft probably has the sensible purpose of keeping programmers from trying to use the task-switch-related functions offered by LIM

4.0. Our goals are more modest. We use what looks like a benign 4.0 function, which in some situations allows a swap area larger than the usual one.

The following routines allow the use of LIM 4.0 expanded memory. They permit only one allocation of expanded memory within an application, which makes the routines a little simpler to use and makes internal housekeeping easier.

int openEMS (int)   This function assumes an EMS version of 3.0 or later and returns an EMS **handle** in the range 1–255 if the operation is successful, or −1 if it is not. The *pages* parameter states the number of 16K chunks of memory that are needed; 16K is EMS's functional unit and is fixed.

The function takes care of the sometimes awkward problem of an over-enthusiastic EMS manager that tries to use memory below 640K as part of its swap area. The function simply refuses to use any such pages.

The handle distinguishes the memory used by the application from that used by other tasks, such as TSRs or disk caches. The handle is a hook for other functionality that the user may choose to add; the routines do not require it since they keep track of the handle internally (one benefit of allowing only a single allocation).

void closeEMS (void)   This closes the EMS interface by calling the EMS function that deallocates a handle. The programmer will never call this function, as the handle is known to the routine and the function itself is enqueued for automatic calling on termination by the ANSI C function `atexit()`, itself invoked behind the scenes by `openEMS()`.

void far *swapEMSpage (unsigned int)   This function swaps a specified logical page into a 16K swap page. This means that, if there is more than one swap page, as is almost always the case, the logical page may appear at more than one possible place. The return value of the function points to the base of the chosen swap page. The choice is based on an LRU (least recently used) algorithm to improve performance.

Listing 8.1 contains the code for managing expanded memory.

LISTING 8.1 Swapping Data to and from Expanded Memory

```
#if MSDOS
#ifdef __TURBOC__
#define _cdecl
#endif

#include <stdio.h>
#include <dos.h>
#include <limits.h>

static int EMShandle = -1 ;
static int swapPages ;
static unsigned int logicalPages ;
```

Listing 8.1   continues

Listing 8.1 continued

```c
static struct pageTableEntry
{
    unsigned int swapSegment ;
    unsigned int physicalPage ;
}
    pageTable [ 24 ], tTable [ 64 ] ;

static unsigned int swapTimes [ 24 ] ;
static int pageMap [ 24 ] ;

/* prototypes */

void            _cdecl closeEMS(void);
static int      getEMSversion(void);
int             openEMS(unsigned int);
void far *      swapEMSpage(unsigned int);

static int getEMSexist ( void )
{
    char far *p ;
    unsigned int i ;
    char namebuf [ 9 ] ;

    union REGS regs ;
    struct SREGS sregs ;

        /*------------------------------------------------------------
         * Use "second method" of checking for EMS handler authorized
         * by the LIM specification. It avoids a possible problem with
         * the "first method", namely all file handles being in use.
         *
         * Get interrupt vector for INT 67h. Prior to 6.0, Microsoft
         * did not return segment register values, so we read the
         * vector directly from the vector table.
         *------------------------------------------------------------*/

    i = *((unsigned int far *)(MK_FP(0,0x19E))) ;
    p = MK_FP(i,0) ;

        /*------------------------------------------------------------
         * To avoid possibly mixing pointer sizes in arguments
         * to strcmp(), copy to local buffer.
         *------------------------------------------------------------*/

    for ( i = 0 ; i < 8 ; ++i )
        namebuf [ i ] = *(p + i + 0x0A) ;
    namebuf [ 8 ] = '\0' ;
    return ( ! strcmp ( namebuf, "EMMXXXX0" ));
}

void _cdecl closeEMS ( void )
{
    union REGS regs ;

    if ( EMShandle > 0 )
    {
        regs.h.ah = 0x45 ;
        regs.x.dx = EMShandle ;
```

Listing 8.1 continues

Listing 8.1 continued

```
        EMShandle = -1 ;
        int86 (0x67, &regs, &regs ) ;
    }
}

/*-----------------------------------------------------------
 * Returns EMS handle (1..254) on success, -1 on failure
 *---------------------------------------------------------*/
int openEMS ( unsigned int pages )
{
    int i, j;
    union REGS regs ;
    struct SREGS sregs ;

    if ( EMShandle == -1 )
    {
        if ( getEMSexist ( ) )
        {
            regs.h.ah = 0x43 ;
            regs.x.bx = pages ;
            int86 (0x67, &regs, &regs ) ;
            EMShandle = ( regs.h.ah == 0 ) ? regs.x.dx : -1 ;

            if ( EMShandle != -1 )
            {
                logicalPages = pages ;
                for ( i = 0 ; i < 24 ; ++i )
                        pageMap [ i ] = UINT_MAX ;

                /*-----------------------------------------------------
                 * There is an EMS function to return the "version,"
                 * but this is the manufacturer's version, not the
                 * EMS version. Most vendors do track the EMS version,
                 * but not all.

                 * We will try a function that's defined under EMS 4.0.
                 * If it works we'll assume 4.0; if it fails we'll
                 * assume we have a recent enough version to support a
                 * 4-page swap area.
                 *---------------------------------------------------*/

                sregs.es = FP_SEG ( tTable) ;
                regs.x.di = FP_OFF ( tTable ) ;
                regs.x.ax = 0x5800 ;
                int86x(0x67, &regs, &regs, &sregs ) ;

                if ( regs.h.ah == 0x84 )
                {
                    /*-------------------------------------------
                     * Function failed; assume 4 pages starting
                     * at base address we're about to get.
                     *-----------------------------------------*/

                    regs.h.ah = 0x41 ;
                    int86x ( 0x67, &regs, &regs, &sregs ) ;

                    pageTable [ 0 ].swapSegment = regs.x.bx ;
                    pageTable [ 1 ].swapSegment = regs.x.bx + 0x400 ;
```

Listing 8.1   continues

Listing 8.1 continued

```
                pageTable [ 2 ].swapSegment = regs.x.bx + 0x800 ;
                pageTable [ 3 ].swapSegment = regs.x.bx + 0xC00 ;

                pageTable [ 0 ].physicalPage = 0 ;
                pageTable [ 1 ].physicalPage = 1 ;
                pageTable [ 2 ].physicalPage = 2 ;
                pageTable [ 3 ].physicalPage = 3 ;

                swapPages = 4 ;
            }
            else
            {
                swapPages = regs.x.cx ;

                /* remove any pages below 640K */

                i = 0 ;
                do
                {
                    if ( tTable [ i ].swapSegment < 0xA000 )
                    {
                        --swapPages ;
                        ++i ;
                    }
                    else break ;
                }
                while ( i < regs.x.cx ) ;

                /* copy to permanent table */

                for ( j = 0 ; j < swapPages ; ++j )
                    pageTable [ j ] = tTable [ j + i ] ;

                if ( swapPages == 0 ) EMShandle = 0 ;
            }
        }
        swapTimes [ 0 ] = UINT_MAX ;
    }
    else EMShandle = -1 ;
    }
    else EMShandle = -1 ;

    if ( EMShandle != -1 )
        atexit ( closeEMS ) ;
    return ( EMShandle ) ;
}

void far *swapEMSpage ( unsigned int pageNo )
{
    static unsigned int currentPage = UINT_MAX ;
    static unsigned int currentIndex ;
    static void far *currentPageBase = ( void far * ) NULL ;
    int i, eldestIndex ;
    unsigned int eldestTime, tTime ;
    unsigned int now ;

    union REGS regs ;
```

Listing 8.1 continues

Listing 8.1 continued

```
/*-------------------------------------------------
 * We read the time from the BIOS data area rather
 * than by using the DOS function to save time.
 *-------------------------------------------------*/

now =  *((unsigned int far *)(MK_FP(0x40,0x6C))) ;

if ( pageNo == currentPage )
{
   swapTimes [ currentIndex ] = now ;
   return ( currentPageBase ) ;
}
else
{
   if ( pageNo < logicalPages )
   {
      /* see if page is already in accessible memory */

      for ( i = 0 ; i < swapPages ; ++i )
   if ( pageNo == pageMap [ i ] )
      {
         currentPage = pageNo ;
         currentIndex = i ;
         swapTimes [ i ] = now ;
         return ( currentPageBase =
            MK_FP ( pageTable [ i ].swapSegment, 0 )) ;
      }

      /*-------------------------------
       * Find least recently used page
       * in EMS frame to swap into.
       *-------------------------------*/

      eldestTime = swapTimes [ 0 ] ;
      eldestIndex = 0 ;
      if ( ( now > eldestTime ) ||
         ( now == eldestTime && now != UINT_MAX ))
      {
         for ( i = 1 ; i < swapPages ; ++i )
         {
            tTime = swapTimes [ i ] ;
            if ( tTime < eldestTime )
            {
               eldestTime = tTime ;
               eldestIndex =  i ;
            }
         }
      }
      else

      /* initialize or re-initialize the LRU table */

      {
         for ( i = 0 ; i < swapPages ; ++i )
            swapTimes [ i ] = 0 ;
      }

      currentPage = pageNo ;
```

Listing 8.1 continues

Listing 8.1 continued

```
        swapTimes [ eldestIndex ] = now ;
        pageMap [ eldestIndex ] = pageNo ;
        currentIndex = eldestIndex ;

        /*-----------------------------------------
         * Swap desired page into EMS frame page
         * pointed to by eldestIndex.
         *------------------------------------*/

        regs.h.ah = 0x44 ;
        regs.h.al = pageTable [ eldestIndex ].physicalPage ;
        regs.x.bx = pageNo ;
        regs.x.dx = EMShandle ;
        int86 ( 0x67, &regs, &regs ) ;
        return ( currentPageBase =
            MK_FP ( pageTable [ eldestIndex ].swapSegment, 0 ));
    }
    else
        return ( void far * ) NULL ;
    }
}
#endif
```

Extended Memory

Where expanded memory is not available and cannot be emulated, we can make use of memory at addresses physically above 1MB. This memory is known as extended memory. Because the 8086 can address only 1MB, extended memory is possible only on 80286 or later processors. A machine has this memory or it hasn't; unlike expanded memory, extended memory is too tightly bound to the hardware to allow emulation.

In contrast with expanded memory, extended memory was not introduced with a specification for its use. This means the programmer must be aware of at least five different methods that are in common practice for allocating extended memory. This is necessary in order to prevent different pieces of software accessing the same chunk of extended memory. Among these five techniques, some work better than others. In other words, the extended memory world is much hairier (to use a technical term) than the expanded memory world.

Our extended memory interface conforms to the most comprehensive of the five methods of dealing with extended memory, namely, the Extended Memory Specification (XMS) (v. 2.0) promulgated by Microsoft. You will find the code in Listing 8.2. You must make sure that other software on your system does not use extended memory in a manner that conflicts with this one. The XMS specification does give error codes that an XMS manager may return on discovering the presence of VDISK (the IBM ramdisk utility), but it is not clear that a manager must use these codes and, in any case, there is no suggestion in the specification that an XMS manager will be aware of any of the other three possible uses of extended memory. This is quite understandable, since two of them did not exist when the specification was written.

If we haven't deterred you, here then is the XMS interface. There are three functions, openXMS(), closeXMS(), and swapXMSpage(). We have chosen a 16K swap-page size to allow exact analogues of the EMS functions presented earlier. The XMS interface also includes a function, openHMA(), for accessing that almost-64K area just above the 1MB address mark that is accessible in real mode on 80286 and later machines. This area is called the HMA (high memory area) and the specification for its use is part of the XMS. The user can call the function, and it will allocate the area or not; there are only those two possible outcomes. If the area is allocated, then an application can use addresses of FFFF:0010 through FFFF:FFFF by means of far pointers, just like any other addresses. However, there are two limitations: (1) DOS must not be passed these addresses, because it will normalize them (with disastrous consequences); and (2) huge pointer arithmetic must not be performed on them for the same reason. Availability of the HMA is not related to availability of memory to openXMS()—they are separate concepts.

The XMS interface did present us with some challenges that are worth discussing here, since they provide lessons that programmers may find applicable to other problems. The basis of the XMS specification is a multipurpose function whose entry point is returned to the user as a segment-offset pair by a clearly documented use of interrupt 2Fh. This presents no problem, since the major compilers offer an int86x() function. The entry point can easily be represented as a far function pointer in C. The difficulty arises because this function requires its parameters in registers. Turbo C does offer pseudo-registers, such as the ability to reference the AX register as _AX, but these are very hazardous, especially to programmers not familiar with the way their compilers generate code. As an example, the following fragment will almost certainly have the unexpected side effect of trashing the AX register.

```
static int foo = 1 ;
static int bar ;

_AX = 0 ;
foo = bar ;
```

The reason is that both foo and bar are memory addresses (unless the compiler happened to optimize one or the other variable as a register variable), and the Intel instruction set does not support the general case of a memory-to-memory move. Therefore, the assignment foo = bar is usually broken into a move of the contents of foo into a register followed a move of the register contents into bar. The register the compiler will use for this temporary assignment is almost sure to be AX, since its prominence in the instruction set plus its use to return values from C functions make it the least suitable register for such long-term duty as holding register variables, and therefore the most suitable as a scratch register.

The sanest way to handle the interface to the XMS manager is to write the core routine (`XMSfunction()`) in assembler. Both the Microsoft and the Borland compilers support in-line assembler to the extent of supporting all or most Intel instructions and supporting moves between registers and C variables. The WATCOM compiler offers a different path: the programmer can write in-line functions in assembler, actually with nothing more than byte-by-byte opcodes, but cannot access C variables directly in these functions. In compensation, the tight control that the programmer has over register usage does produce a more efficient product once the hurdles are jumped.

The Microsoft/Borland access to C variables from assembler is a great help to getting something going in a reasonable time, but, not surprisingly, there are pitfalls. For example, when we copy a global variable to a register, the memory model in use may expect that some work with segment registers will already have been done; since we're at the assembler level, we don't have the compiler to take care of the house cleaning. The best way that we have found to avoid these pitfalls is to use assembler moves between registers and C variables only if the C variable is on the stack (that is, it is a local variable). The point is that a compiler will tend to generate the same code for stack-relative operations across memory models (though of course with differing pointer sizes), while it may generate very different code for data-segment-relative (or DGROUP- or whatever-group-relative) operations.

The handling of the returned BX and DX values in `XMSfunction()` shows this principle. We want to save the returned BX value in the global variable `bx_`, and the returned DX value in `dx_`. However, to avoid segment-register problems we first move these registers to a variable on the stack and then we revert to C to move them from the stack to their global destinations, letting the compiler handle the segment registers for that move. We surround these operations with a `push ax` `pop ax` pair to preserve the function's eventual return value. If you don't see why this is done, try rereading the earlier discussion involving `foo` and `bar`; the same considerations of a memory-to-memory move in C apply here.

Note the importance of restoring DS before doing anything regarding global variables; the compiler may expect DGROUP (or some other value) to be in DS at the time a global variable is referenced. The address of the XMS handler is copied to the stack for the same reason. By passing the address on the stack we avoid the problems inherent in trying to de-reference a global function pointer in assembler, and we do it in a way that works across all memory models. If you need to shave clock cycles you can hand-optimize your compiler's assembler output, since some of the techniques we have described achieve their relative portability at the expense of efficiency.

In the WATCOM environment, the lack of access to C variables from assembler requires us to make assumptions about the positions of fields within a structure; however, these assumptions are obvious ones for the Intel architecture, and they work. The source code is inscrutable because of the embedded opcodes, but a disassembly makes things understandable. If you plan to do much of this you might want to write some macros to hide the opcodes.

We use a calling sequence for the parameters to the XMS handler that provides tolerably readable invocations. Following the function number, any parameter that is expected in DX is passed (using a dummy value if DX is not specified), and then one in BX is passed in the same manner; the exception is that a parameter in DS:SI is passed with a separate segment and offset in lieu of DX and BX respectively. Anyone wishing to use XMS functions other than those discussed here should find XMSfunction() easy to use, as long as the XMS specification is at hand. All functions defined by the 2.00 function can be handled by XMSfunction().

All three compilers will complain about the lack of a return value from XMSfunction(). This occurs because the compilers do not detect the fact that the AX register, the register that carries any returned int value, is being set. The warning may be ignored. The programmer may wish to employ a pragma or other mechanism that may be offered to suppress that particular warning in that function; the mechanism will be compiler-specific.

XMSfunction() demonstrates why you need to be knowledgeable about assembler on your target machine—assembler is sometimes the only answer, or at least the only reasonable one. For the programmer unfamiliar with 8086 assembler, reading compiler output in assembler form may be helpful, with a suitable reference book at hand. Both the Microsoft and the Borland compilers support compilations of C to assembler; WATCOM offers an object module disassembler that is equally good for study (or debugging) purposes. The Microsoft command-line switch for compilation to assembler is /Fa; the Borland switch is -S, and the WATCOM utility is wdisasm.

Listing 8.2 presents the code for the extended memory manager:

LISTING 8.2 Swapping Data to and from Extended Memory

```
#if MSDOS
#if __TURBOC__ || __WATCOMC__
#define CDECL
#else
#define CDECL _cdecl
#endif

/*-------------------------------------------------------------
 * The following #define specifies the earliest version
 * of XMS acceptable for the memory manager to operate.
 *-------------------------------------------------------*/

#define MIN_XMS_VER 0x200

struct xms_struc_type
{
   unsigned int ret_dx ;
   unsigned int ret_bx ;
   void far (*func)(void) ;
} ;

union u
{
   void far *p;
   unsigned long o;
```

Listing 8.2 continues

Listing 8.2   continued

```
} ;

/*----------------------------------------------------------
 * The definition for the following copies the definition
 * in the XMS specification, for ease of reference.
 *--------------------------------------------------------*/

static struct ExtMemMoveStruct
{
    unsigned long Length ;
    unsigned int  SourceHandle ;
    union u       SourceOffset ;
    unsigned int  DestHandle ;
    union u       DestOffset ;
} ;

static int XMShandle = -1 ;
static int HMA_exists = 0 ;
static int A20_was_enabled ;
static unsigned int bx_ ;
static unsigned int dx_ ;
static char *XMS_swap_buffer ;
static struct xms_struc_type xms_struc ;
static struct ExtMemMoveStruct XMSstruc ;

/* prototypes */

void              CDECL closeHMA(void);
void              CDECL closeXMS(void);
static int        getXMSversion(void);
int               openHMA(void);
int               openXMS(unsigned int);
void  far *       swapXMSpage(unsigned int);
unsigned int      CDECL XMSfunction(unsigned int,
                      unsigned int,unsigned int);

#if __WATCOMC__

#pragma aux get_struct_addr value [ es di ] ;
void far *get_struct_addr ( void )
{
    return ( & xms_struc ) ;
}

void funca ( void );
#pragma aux funca = 0x1e 0x8e 0xda 0x89 0xde 0x88 0xc4 ;

void funcb ( void );
#pragma aux funcb = 0x26 0xff 0x5d 0x04 0x26 0x89 0x15 0x26
                    0x89 0x5d 0x02 0x1f ;

#endif

unsigned int CDECL XMSfunction ( unsigned int func_no,
    unsigned int dx_or_ds, unsigned int bx_or_si )
{
```

Listing 8.2   continues

Listing 8.2 continued

```
    /*-------------------------------------------------
     * We _cdecl this if using MSC because MSC 6.0
     * generated incorrect code with the fastcall
     * option. The bug was fixed in 6.00a but we
     * can't assume everyone upgraded.
     *-------------------------------------------------*/
#if __WATCOMC__
#pragma aux XMSfunction parm [ax] [dx] [bx] ;
#pragma aux XMSfunction modify [si] ;
    funca() ;
    get_struct_addr() ;
    funcb() ;
#else
    unsigned int tu ;
    void far *p ;

    p = ( void far * ) xms_struc.func ;

    asm     push    ds
    asm     push    si
    asm     mov     ax,func_no
    asm     mov     ah,al
    asm     mov     bx,bx_or_si
    asm     mov     si,bx
    asm     mov     dx,dx_or_ds
    asm     mov     ds,dx
    asm     call    dword ptr [p]
    asm     pop     si
    asm     pop     ds
    asm     push    ax
    asm     mov     tu,bx
    xms_struc.ret_bx = tu ;
    asm     mov     tu,dx
    xms_struc.ret_dx = tu ;
    asm     pop     ax
#endif
}

void CDECL closeXMS ( void )
{
    if ( XMShandle != -1 )
        XMSfunction ( 0x0A, XMShandle, 0 ) ;
}

/*-------------------------------------------------
 * Returns XMS version, with major number in high 8
 * bits and minor in low 8 bits; returns 0 if no XMS
 *-------------------------------------------------*/

static int getXMSversion ( void )
{
    int i,j ;
    unsigned int u ;

    union REGS regs ;
    struct SREGS sregs ;
```

Listing 8.2 continues

Listing 8.2 continued

```c
    regs.x.ax = 0x4300 ;
    int86 ( 0x2F, &regs, &regs ) ;
    if ( regs.h.al == 0x80 )
    {
        /* XMS present */

        regs.x.ax = 0x4310 ;
        int86x ( 0x2F, &regs, &regs, &sregs ) ;

        xms_struc.func = MK_FP ( sregs.es, regs.x.bx ) ;

        /* Call XMS function 0 to get the version number */

        u = XMSfunction ( 0, 0, 0 ) ;
        HMA_exists = xms_struc.ret_dx ;
        return ( u ) ;
    }
    else return ( 0 ) ;
}

int openXMS ( unsigned int pages )
{
    union REGS regs ;
    struct SREGS sregs ;

    if ( ( XMS_swap_buffer = malloc ( 16384 ) ) != NULL )
    {
        if ( getXMSversion() = MIN_XMS_VER )
        {
            if ( XMSfunction ( 9, pages, 0 ) )
                XMShandle = xms_struc.ret_dx ;
        }
    }
    if ( XMShandle != -1 ) atexit ( closeXMS ) ;
    return ( XMShandle ) ;
}

void far *swapXMSpage ( unsigned int pageNo )
{
    static unsigned int currentPage = UINT_MAX ;

    if ( currentPage != pageNo )
    {
        if ( currentPage != UINT_MAX )
        {

            /* swap out the current page */

            XMSstruc.Length = 16384L ;
            XMSstruc.SourceHandle = 0 ;
            XMSstruc.SourceOffset.p =
                        ( void far * ) XMS_swap_buffer ;
            XMSstruc.DestHandle = XMShandle ;
            XMSstruc.DestOffset.o = 16384L * currentPage ;

            XMSfunction ( 0x0B,
                        FP_SEG (( void far * ) &XMSstruc ),
                        FP_OFF (( void far * ) &XMSstruc )) ;
```

Listing 8.2 continues

Listing 8.2 continued

```
    }

    /* swap in the new page */

    XMSstruc.Length = 16384L ;
    XMSstruc.SourceHandle = XMShandle ;
    XMSstruc.SourceOffset.o = 16384L * currentPage ;
    XMSstruc.DestHandle = 0 ;
    XMSstruc.DestOffset.p = ( void far * ) XMS_swap_buffer ;

    XMSfunction ( 0x0B, FP_SEG (( void far * ) &XMSstruc ),
        FP_OFF (( void far * ) &XMSstruc )) ;

    currentPage = pageNo ;
    }
    return ( ( void far * ) XMS_swap_buffer ) ;
}

void CDECL closeHMA ( void )
{
    if ( ! A20_was_enabled ) XMSfunction ( 4, 0, 0 ) ;
    XMSfunction ( 2, 0, 0 ) ;
}

int openHMA ( void )
{
    int gotHMA = 0 ;

    if ( ! HMA_exists ) getXMSversion ( ) ;
    if ( HMA_exists )
    {
        gotHMA = ( XMSfunction ( 1, 0xFFFF, 0 ) ) ;
        if ( gotHMA )
        {
            A20_was_enabled = XMSfunction ( 7, 0, 0 ) ;
            if ( ! A20_was_enabled ) XMSfunction ( 3, 0, 0 ) ;
            atexit ( closeHMA ) ;
        }
    }
    return ( gotHMA ) ;
}
#endif   /* end of #if MS-DOS */
```

Disk Swapping

Disk swapping is a fallback when neither expanded nor extended memory is available. The interface offers exact analogues of the EMS functions, namely `open-disk()`, `closedisk()`, and `swapdiskpage()`, again with 16K pages, but there are a couple of points worth noting. The first is that we avoid the problem of the `Abort, Retry, Ignore?` intrusion in the case of an invalid drive by using a DOS interrupt (25h) that tries to read a sector from a disk; if this function fails, it lets the programmer handle the reply. (Actually, the programmer can contrive to intercept the errors normally handled by the **Abort, Retry, Ignore?** machinery, but it is not as straightforward.) Also note that the swap file that will go to disk is opened and immediately sized to its full extent; doing this permits catching full-disk errors at the earliest possible time. Listing 8.3 presents the code for the disk swapping routines:

LISTING 8.3 Swapping Data to and from Disk

```
#if MSDOS
#include <stdio.h>
#include <limits.h>
#include <dos.h>

static int  diskhandle = -1 ;
static char *disk_swap_buffer ;
static char disk_swap_filename [13] ;
static char swap_drive ;
static char cur_drive ;

static struct packet_struc
{
    unsigned long RBA ;
    unsigned int  count ;
    void far *    buffer ;
} packet ;

/* prototypes */

void        closedisk(void);
int         opendisk(int,unsigned char);
void far *  swapdiskpage(unsigned int);

opendisk ( int pages, unsigned char drive )
{
    union  REGS regs ;
    struct SREGS sregs ;

    unsigned int ret_val = 0 ;

    if (( disk_swap_buffer = malloc ( 16384 )) == NULL )
        goto done ;

    /* make sure drive exists */

    swap_drive = regs.h.al = toupper ( drive ) - 'A' ;
    regs.x.cx = 1 ;
    regs.x.dx = 0 ;
    regs.x.bx = FP_OFF (( void far * ) disk_swap_buffer ) ;
    sregs.ds = FP_SEG (( void far * ) disk_swap_buffer ) ;
    int86x ( 0x25, &regs, &regs, &sregs ) ;
```

Listing 8.3   continues

Listing 8.3 continued

```
/* Test possibility of large partition under DOS 4.0+ */

if ( regs.x.cflag && regs.x.ax == 0x207 )
{
    regs.h.al = toupper ( drive ) - 'A' ;
    regs.x.cx = -1 ;
    packet.RBA = 0L ;
    packet.count = 1 ;
    packet.buffer = disk_swap_buffer ;
    regs.x.bx = FP_OFF (( void far * ) &packet ) ;
    sregs.ds = FP_SEG (( void far * ) &packet ) ;
    int86x ( 0x25, &regs, &regs, &sregs ) ;
}

if ( regs.x.cflag )
    goto done ;

/* drive is valid; save current drive */

regs.h.ah = 0x19 ;
intdos ( &regs, &regs ) ;
cur_drive = regs.h.al ;

/* switch to designated drive */

regs.h.ah = 0x0E ;
regs.h.dl = toupper ( drive ) - 'A' ;
intdos ( &regs, &regs ) ;

( void ) tmpnam ( disk_swap_filename ) ;

/* create file */

sregs.ds = FP_SEG (( void far * ) disk_swap_filename ) ;
regs.x.dx = FP_OFF (( void far * ) disk_swap_filename ) ;
regs.x.cx = 0 ;
regs.x.ax = 0x3C02 ;
intdosx ( &regs, &regs, &sregs ) ;

if ( regs.x.cflag )
    goto done ;

diskhandle = regs.x.ax ;

/* extend it to 16384 * pages */

regs.x.cx = pages / 4 ;
regs.x.dx = 16384 * ( pages % 4 ) ;
regs.x.bx = diskhandle ;
regs.x.ax = 0x4200 ;
intdos ( &regs, &regs ) ;
regs.x.bx = diskhandle ;
regs.x.cx = 0 ;
regs.h.ah = 0x40 ;
intdos ( &regs, &regs ) ;

/* close it */
```

Listing 8.3 continues

Listing 8.3 continued

```
    regs.x.bx = diskhandle ;
    regs.h.ah = 0x3E ;
    intdos ( &regs, &regs ) ;
    if ( regs.x.cflag ) goto done ;

    /* reopen it */

    sregs.ds = FP_SEG (( void far * ) disk_swap_filename ) ;
    regs.x.dx = FP_OFF (( void far * ) disk_swap_filename ) ;
    regs.x.ax = 0x3D02 ;
    intdosx ( &regs, &regs, &sregs ) ;
    if ( regs.x.cflag ) goto done ;
    diskhandle = regs.x.ax ;

    /* seek to EOF and make sure size is what asked for */

    regs.x.bx = diskhandle ;
    regs.x.ax = 0x4202 ;
    regs.x.cx = 0 ;
    regs.x.dx = 0 ;
    intdos ( &regs, &regs ) ;
    if ( regs.x.dx != ( pages / 4 ) ||
        regs.x.ax != ( 16384 * ( pages % 4 )))
    {
        unlink ( disk_swap_filename ) ;
        goto done ;
    }
    ret_val = diskhandle ;
    atexit ( closedisk ) ;

    /* switch back to original drive */

    regs.h.dl = cur_drive ;
    regs.h.ah = 0x0E ;
    intdos ( &regs, &regs ) ;

    done:
     return ( ret_val ) ;
}

void far *swapdiskpage ( unsigned int pageNo )
{
    union REGS regs ;
    struct SREGS sregs ;

    static unsigned int currentPage = UINT_MAX ;

    if ( currentPage != pageNo )
    {
        if ( currentPage != UINT_MAX )
        {
            /* swap out the current page */

            regs.x.ax = 0x4200 ;
            regs.x.bx = diskhandle ;
            regs.x.cx = currentPage / 4 ;
            regs.x.dx = 16384L * ( currentPage % 4 ) ;
```

Listing 8.3 continues

Listing 8.3 continued

```
        intdos ( &regs, &regs ) ;

        regs.x.bx = diskhandle ;
        regs.x.dx = FP_OFF (( void far * ) disk_swap_buffer ) ;
        sregs.ds = FP_SEG (( void far * ) disk_swap_buffer ) ;
        regs.x.cx = 16384 ;
        regs.h.ah = 0x40 ;
        intdosx ( &regs, &regs, &sregs ) ;
    }

    /* swap in the new page */

    regs.x.ax = 0x4200 ;
    regs.x.bx = diskhandle ;
    regs.x.cx = currentPage / 4 ;
    regs.x.dx = 16384L * ( currentPage % 4 ) ;
    intdos ( &regs, &regs ) ;

    regs.x.bx = diskhandle ;
    regs.x.dx = FP_OFF (( void far * ) disk_swap_buffer ) ;
    sregs.ds = FP_SEG (( void far * ) disk_swap_buffer ) ;
    regs.x.cx = 16384 ;
    regs.h.ah = 0x3F ;
    intdosx ( &regs, &regs, &sregs ) ;

    currentPage = pageNo ;
    }
    return ( ( void far * ) disk_swap_buffer ) ;
}

void closedisk ( )
{
    union REGS regs ;

    /* switch to swap drive */

    regs.h.ah = 0x0E ;
    regs.h.dl = swap_drive ;
    intdos ( &regs, &regs ) ;

    /* delete swap file */

    unlink ( disk_swap_filename ) ;

    /* switch back to original drive */

    regs.h.dl = cur_drive ;
    regs.h.ah = 0x0E ;
    intdos ( &regs, &regs ) ;
}
#endif
```

Printing a Raster Image

Now we can turn to sending a raster image to a file or to the printer. The function `print_raster()` takes care of the raster printing. Its one parameter is a pointer to a structure containing the needed information about the raster. The function is called once for each raster line in the image. On the first call, several fields are expected to contain information needed to get started: a pointer to the output file, the total horizontal and vertical extent of the graphic in pixels, the (X,Y) coordinates for the upper left corner of the graphic, the resolution in dots per inch (75, 100, 150, or 300), and if the graphic is to be forced to portrait orientation or if it is to be oriented with its longer axis parallel to the page's longer axis. Once these fields are set at the first call, all that is needed on subsequent calls is the pointer to the raster line. The first call needs the raster pointer too; it serves not only to take care of initialization but also to draw the first line. The function knows when to terminate the graphic based on the number of vertical pixels given to it at first; it will simply wait for that number of calls and then automatically invoke the terminating logic. The user may cause an early termination by calling `print_raster` with the `pix_width` field set to the artificial value of –1. This avoids the need to send empty raster lines at the end of a graphic, if it is known that only empty lines remain. However, the bounding box set initially is still in effect.

Like its predecessors, the LaserJet III/IIID can be addressed by sending it unaltered raster lines, but this doesn't make best use of its capabilities. By using compression and delta features, we can cut considerably the amount of data to be transmitted—transmission time is often the bottleneck in real-world applications. It is not possible to generalize which of the three techniques is best—uncompressed, compressed, or delta. It depends on the data.

Since transmission time to the printer is the bottleneck in many installations and since transmission time is a function of the number of bytes to be sent, we go to some effort to encode the raster image in as few bytes as possible. We compress the row and see how many bytes that takes, and we compare the row with its predecessor (even the first, which may be delta'ed against an all-zero row) and see how many bytes are required for the delta. We also remove the trailing zero bytes and see how many bytes are needed for the uncompressed row. Whichever yields the smallest quantity of data for a given line is the one we use. We do this for every raster line in the graphic. We take advantage of the fact that the compression mode that can be set at the beginning of any line remains in effect on the next line if it is not changed. For all lines after the first, the default is the compression mode of the previous line.

This code uses a number of PCL commands, which we now list for reference. We group them by the machines that support them. In each instruction, the symbol # will take a numeric value as defined by the particular instruction.

Raster Graphics Commands on the II, IID, IIP, 2000, III, and IIID

Esc * t # R   Set the resolution to # dots per inch. Allowable values are 75, 100, 150, and 300.

Esc * r # A   Switch to raster graphics mode. A value of 0 means to start at x = 0 directly to the left of the current position; a value of 1 means to start at the current position.

Esc * b # W   Transfer # bytes of raster data and move the current point to the beginning of the next raster line. The raster bytes bytes immediately follow the instruction.

Esc * r B   Exit raster graphics mode.

Raster Graphics Commands on the IID, IIP, 2000, III, and IIID

Esc * r # F   This determines whether the graphic will be presented in portrait mode regardless of the current printing orientation (3) or will be presented in the same orientation as the current printing orientation (0).

Raster Graphics Commands on the IIP, III, and IIID

Esc * b # M   Set raster graphics compression mode for the line about to be transmitted. A value of 0 means no compression (which functions like the Series II). A value of 1 means a run-length encoded compression scheme. A value of 2 means a more sophisticated compression scheme, commonly known as PackBits. These are defined in the *LaserJet Technical Reference;* we provide code for compression mode 2, and therefore an exposition of the format here is not necessary. The value remains in effect for subsequent lines until replaced by a new value.

Raster Graphics Commands on the III and IIID

Esc * b # M   On the LaserJet III a compression mode 3 is added, which adds the ability to transmit a data row by transmitting an encoding of the difference between the row and its predecessor. This compression mode is defined in the *LaserJet Technical Reference.* We provide code for it but not an exposition of the format, with one exception. The discussion on pages 14–22 through 14–24 of the *LaserJet III Technical Reference Manual* is rather unclear about something called offset; it offers more than one definition, the definitions are mutually exclusive where they are comprehensible at all, and the examples do not resolve the problem. The practical definition is that the **offset** is the number of bytes measured from the first (not last) byte of the most recent sequence of bytes to be copied, unless the immediately preceding transmission was also a compression sequence, in which case the offset no longer has anything to do with previous data but becomes 0; and the offset at the beginning of a line is defined to be 0. This is all quite sensible; it just isn't quite what the manual says. Note that a command of `Esc * b 0 W` while compression mode 3 is in effect will cause the previous line to be copied. This is not really a special case, given the definitions so far, but it needs to be pointed out because it is not obvious, especially to you who have worked with earlier LaserJets. As with the other compression modes, compression mode 3 remains in effect for subsequent lines until replaced by a new value.

Esc * r # S   Establish a raster width of **#** bits. This serves to guarantee that shorter rows are white-extended (filled with "white" bytes on their right end), which is of particular importance in the case of nontransparent operation. Transparency is discussed in Chapter 3.

Esc * r # T   Establish a raster height of **#** bits. This serves to guarantee that missing rows are white, which is of particular importance in the case of nontransparent operation. Transparency is discussed in Chapter 3.

Esc * b # Y   Move down **#** lines, filling the skipped area with white. This has the side effect of setting the seed row to zeroes.

Listing 8.4 presents the code for the raster routines.

LISTING 8.4 Sending Raster Data to the Printer

```
#include <stdio.h>
#define MIN(a, b) ((a)<(b) ? (a) : (b))

struct raster_parms
{
    char *p ;
    FILE *fp ;
    int pix_height ;
    int pix_width ;
    int x ;
    int y ;
```

Listing 8.4 continues

Listing 8.4   continued

```
   int resolution ;
   int portrait ;
} ;

/* we implement mode 2 */

static int compress ( outRow, inRow, bytes )
signed char *outRow, *inRow ;
int bytes ;
{

   /* returns the number of bytes in the compressed row */

   int same_count, diff_count ;
   signed char old_byte, new_byte, *tip, *eip, *xip, *op ;

   switch ( bytes )
   {
      case 0 : return ( 0 ) ;
      case 1 : outRow [ 0 ] = 0 ; outRow [ 1 ] = inRow [ 0 ] ;
         return ( 2 ) ;
      default :
      {
         tip = inRow ;
         eip = inRow + bytes ;
         op = outRow ;
         old_byte = *tip++ ;
         if ( ( new_byte = *tip++ ) == old_byte )
         {
            same_count = 2 ; diff_count = 1 ;
         }
         else
         {
            same_count = 0 ; diff_count = 2 ;
         }
         old_byte = new_byte ;

         while ( tip < eip )
         {
            if ( ( new_byte = *tip++ ) == old_byte )
            {
               if ( same_count ) ++same_count ;
               else same_count = 2 ;
               if ( same_count == 3 )
               /* flush bytes so far counted up as different,
                  except for the last */
               {
                  if ( diff_count > 1 )
                  {
                     --diff_count ;
                     xip = tip - diff_count - 3 ;
                     while ( diff_count >= 128 )
                     {
                        *op = 127 ;
                        memcpy ( op + 1, xip, 128 ) ;
                        op += 129 ;
                        xip += 128 ;
                        diff_count -= 128 ;
```

Listing 8.4   continues

Listing 8.4 continued

```
                    }
                    if ( diff_count > 0 )
                    {
                        *op = diff_count - 1 ;
                        memcpy ( op + 1, xip, diff_count ) ;
                        op += ( diff_count + 1 ) ;
                    }
                }
                diff_count = 0 ;
            }
        }
        else
        {
            ++diff_count ;
            /* if exactly two identical bytes,
               treat as though different */
            if ( same_count == 2 )
            {
                ++diff_count ;
                same_count = 0 ;
            }
            else
            if ( same_count > 2 )
            {
                while ( same_count >= 128 )
                {
                    *op = -127 ;
                    *(op + 1) = old_byte ;
                    op += 2 ;
                    same_count -= 128 ;
                }
                if ( same_count >= 2 )
                {
                    *op = 1 - same_count ;
                    *(op + 1) = old_byte ;
                    op += 2 ;
                }
                else
                if ( same_count == 1 ) ++diff_count ;
                same_count = 0 ;
            }
            old_byte = new_byte ;
        }
    }

    /* flush whatever remains */

    if ( same_count == 2 )
    {
        ++diff_count ;
        same_count = 0 ;
    }

    if ( diff_count > 0 )
    {
        xip = tip - diff_count ;
        while ( diff_count >= 128 )
        {
```

Listing 8.4 continues

Listing 8.4   continued

```
                *op = 127 ;
                memcpy ( op + 1, xip, 128 ) ;
                op += 129 ;
                diff_count -= 128 ;
            }
            if ( diff_count > 0 )
            {
                *op = diff_count - 1 ;
                memcpy ( op + 1, xip, diff_count ) ;
                op += ( diff_count + 1 ) ;
            }
        }

        if ( same_count > 2 )
        {
            xip = tip - same_count ;
            while ( same_count >= 128 )
            {
                *op = -127 ;
                *(op + 1) = old_byte ;
                op += 2 ;
                same_count -= 128 ;
            }
            if ( same_count >= 2 )
            {
                *op = 1 - same_count ;
                *(op + 1) = old_byte ;
                op += 2 ;
            }
            else
            if ( same_count == 1 )
            {
                *op = 0 ;
                *(op + 1) = new_byte ;
                op += 2 ;
            }
        }
        return ( op - outRow ) ;
    }
  }
}

int row_dif ( char *delta, char *old, char *new, int len )
{
    char *start_diff ;
    char *start_same ;
    char *oldp, *newp, *newendp, *deltap ;
    int last_equal, len_minus_1, bytes_now, off_now,
        off_bytes, same_bytes, diff_bytes ;
    int done_compare = 0 ;

    len_minus_1 = len - 1 ;

    oldp = old ;
    newp = new ;
    newendp = newp + len ;
    deltap = delta ;
```

Listing 8.4   continues

Listing 8.4 continued

```
start_same = start_diff = newp + 1 ;

/*-----------------------------------------------
 * Set up sentinel to ensure comparison on
 * last byte yields not equal
 *-----------------------------------------*/

last_equal = ( old [ len_minus_1 ] == new [ len_minus_1 ] ) ;
if ( !last_equal ) ++old [ len_minus_1 ] ;

for ( ;; )   /* look for match or for end of data */
{
   do
   {
      if ( newp == newendp )
      {
         done_compare = 1 ;
         break ;
      }
   }
   while ( *oldp++ != *newp++ ) ;

     /*--------------------------------------------------------
      * We have a match; send existing difference information.
      * Allow for the possibility that the difference was
      * created by the sentinel
      *-----------------------------------------------------*/

   if ( ( diff_bytes = newp - start_diff +
      ( done_compare && ! last_equal ) ) > 0 )
   {
      off_bytes = start_diff - start_same ;
      do
      {
         bytes_now = MIN ( diff_bytes, 8 ) ;
         off_now = MIN ( off_bytes, 31 ) ;
         *deltap++ = (( bytes_now - 1 ) << 5 ) | off_now ;

         /*-----------------------------------------------
          * 3 offset bytes are enough for 31 + 255 + 254
          * = 540 bytes of data, which is more than 14";
          * that's all we need.
          *-----------------------------------------*/

         if ( off_bytes >= 286 )
         {
            *deltap++ = 0xff ;
            *deltap++ = off_bytes - 286 ;
         }
         else
         if ( off_bytes >= 31 )
         {
            *deltap++ = off_bytes - 31 ;
         }
         memcpy ( deltap, start_diff - 1 , bytes_now ) ;
         deltap += bytes_now ;

         off_bytes = 0 ;
```

Listing 8.4 continues

Listing 8.4 continued

```
            start_diff += bytes_now ;
            diff_bytes -= bytes_now ;
        }
        while ( diff_bytes ) ;
    }

    if ( done_compare ) break ;

    start_same = newp ;

    /* look for difference */

    while ( *oldp++ == *newp++ ) ;
    start_diff = newp ;
  }

  return ( deltap - delta ) ;
}

int print_raster ( struct raster_parms *rp )
{
    static int h, w, zero_rows ;
    static int r = 0 ;
    static FILE *f ;
    static char *o, *d, *c, *prev_tp ;
    int i, u_ct, c_ct, d_ct, u_comp, c_comp, d_comp ;
    char *u, *tp, *ttp ;

    if ( r == 0 )
    {
        zero_rows = 0 ;
        prev_tp = NULL ;
        h = rp->pix_height ;
        w = ( rp->pix_width + 7 ) / 8 ;
        f = rp->fp ;

        /* allocate working buffers */

        o = calloc ( w, 1 ) ;
        d = calloc ( ( 9 * w + 7 ) / 8, 1 ) ;
        c = calloc ( ( 9 * w + 7 ) / 8, 1 ) ;

        /* push cursor position and set cursor to specified x,y */

        fprintf ( f, "\033&f0S\033*p%dx%dY", rp->x, rp->y ) ;

        /* set specified resolution */

        fprintf ( f, "\033*t%dR", rp->resolution ) ;

        /* set presentation type and clipping window,
           and set graphics mode */

        fprintf ( f, "\033*r%df%dt%ds1A", rp->portrait ? 3 : 0,
            h, rp->pix_width ) ;
    }

    if ( rp->pix_width != -1 )
```

Listing 8.4 continues

Listing 8.4 continued

```
{
    u = rp->p ;

    /*---------------------------------------------------
     * Determine how many bytes it would take to send
     * the row each of the three possible ways:
     * uncompressed, compressed, or delta.
     *---------------------------------------------------*/

    /* count trailing white bytes, subtract from w;
       that's uncompressed */

    /* this also detects a zero row, which is a special case */

    tp = u + w - 1 ;
    while ( *tp == 0 && tp != u ) --tp ;
    u_ct = tp - u + 1 ;
    if ( u_ct == 1 && *u == 0 ) u_ct = 0 ;

    if ( u_ct == 0 )
    {
        ++zero_rows ;
    }
    else
    {
        /* flush zero rows, if any */

        if ( zero_rows )
        {
            fprintf ( f, "\033*b%dY", zero_rows ) ;
            zero_rows = 0 ;
        }

        /* get compressed size */

        c_ct = compress ( c, u, u_ct ) ;

        /* get delta size */

        d_ct = row_dif ( d, o, u, w ) ;

        /*---------------------------------------------------
         * Determine the smallest and set a pointer to that row
         * where modes would require a switch, add 2 bytes.
         *---------------------------------------------------*/

        c_comp = ( tp == c ) ? c_ct : c_ct + 2 ;
        u_comp = ( tp == u ) ? u_ct : u_ct + 2 ;
        d_comp = ( tp == d ) ? d_ct : d_ct + 2 ;

        tp =
          ( u_comp < c_comp ) ? (( d_comp < u_comp ) ? d : u ) :
          (( d_comp < c_comp ) ? d : c ) ;

        if ( tp == d )
        {
            i = d_ct ;
            fprintf ( f, "\033*b%s%dW",
```

Listing 8.4 continues

Listing 8.4   continued

```
                            tp == prev_tp ? "" : "3m" , i ) ;
            }
            else
            if ( tp == c )
            {
                i = c_ct ;
                fprintf ( f, "\033*b%s%dW",
                            tp == prev_tp ? "" : "2m" , i ) ;
            }
            else
            {
                i = u_ct ;
                fprintf ( f, "\033*b%s%dW",
                            tp == prev_tp ? "" : "0m" , i ) ;
            }

            prev_tp = tp ;

            ttp = tp + i ;
            while ( ttp != tp )
                    fputc ( *tp++, f ) ;
        }
    }

    if ( ++r == h || rp->pix_width == -1 )
    {
        /*-----------------------------------
         * Clean up: exit raster graphics and
         * restore cursor position.
         *-----------------------------------*/

        fprintf ( f, "\033*rB\033&f1S" ) ;

        free ( o ) ;
        free ( d ) ;
        free ( c ) ;

        r = 0 ;
    }
    else
        memcpy ( o, u, w ) ;
    return ( r ) ;
}
```

Getting Raster Sources into Usable Form

Raster information can come from many sources. We discussed in Chapter 3 how the user might create a raster line from scratch. Now we look at situations where we want to print pre-existing raster information. Sometimes this information arrives as a series of bytes that can be copied to a raster line in our format. But sometimes the information arrives encoded in some nontrivial way. One source of such encoded raster information is the TIFF file, a format that is promulgated by Aldus

Corporation and by Microsoft. The TIFF format has become a de facto standard for raster interchange. It is a comprehensive raster specification that includes the ability to compress raster data.

We don't provide a complete TIFF interpreter here; what we provide are routines to decompress TIFF raster lines that have been compressed according to either of two formats supported by TIFF. (TIFF supports more than two compression formats, but the two we handle here will account for almost all real-world TIFF files.) We do not account for the special case of TIFF-encoded lines that represent more than one line in the image; that situation does not affect what we do here, and dealing with it is left to the implementor. We also do not consider gray-scale or color information.

We should stop for a moment to clear up a question that may be occurring to those who have read HP's documentation on raster graphics. HP refers to the intraline compression that we discussed above as TIFF. This is vague—they are referring to one of the two forms of TIFF-supported compression that we discuss here. The TIFF specification refers to this format as "the Macintosh PackBits scheme." When we use the term TIFF, we are referring to the TIFF specification generally, not to the one portion selected as a compression format by HP; we refer to that portion as PackBits. In this we are following the designation common in the literature.

A format like TIFF works very well in conjunction with some of the routines presented earlier; two of TIFF's fields, `ImageWidth` and `ImageLength`, map directly onto the `pix_width` and `pix_height` fields of the structure whose pointer is passed to `print_raster()`.

TIFF's PackBits Compression Format

PackBits is a run-length encoded compression format that can achieve very useful size reductions with raster lines that have large stretches of uninterrupted black or white information. A raster is compressed using this format if the TIFF header's compression field has the value 32773. The function `decompress_PackBits()` takes a raster line in PackBits format and returns an uncompressed raster line.

TIFF's CCITT Group 3 Compression Format

CCITT Group 3 is much more powerful than PackBits, though at some cost in overhead. A raster is compressed using this format if the TIFF header's compression field has the value 2. The function `decompress_CCITT3()` will take a raster line in CCITT Group 3 format and return an uncompressed raster line. Listing 8.5 presents routines for interpreting TIFF raster lines.

Starting with the foundation laid in Chapter 3, we outlined the evolution of raster graphics in the LaserJet family. We examined the advances in raster compression techniques through the delta compression in the LaserJetIII/IIID and provide code to support all compression techniques in the LaserJet family. We looked at memory management techniques to support full-page 300 dpi images, presenting orthogonal expanded memory, extended memory, and disk-swapping routines. Finally, we presented routines to decompress the two most common compression formats in the TIFF world to something we can use.

LISTING 8.5 Importing TIFF Files

```
/*------------------------------------------------------------------
 * These routines decompress raster rows in TIFF files that
 * have been compressed in TIFF format 2 ("CCITT 3") or 32773
 * ("PackBits"). The "row" parameter to the decompress_CCITT3()
 * and decompress_PackBits() functions is a pointer to the output
 * row; the input row is pointed to by the global char * "s_row".
 * The global "ImageWidth" is presumed to have been set to the
 * value of the TIFF field of the same name (the ImageWidth field
 * must be present in any TIFF file). Both functions return 0
 * on success or -1 on failure.
 *------------------------------------------------------------*/

#include <stdio.h>

/* macro for number of elements in an array */

#define ELEMENTS(a) (sizeof((a))/sizeof((a)[0]))
#define SETBIT(o,n) ((*(o)|=1<<(n)))

static struct inruns *getwhite ( unsigned int ) ;
static struct inruns *getblack ( unsigned int ) ;
static char getTifByte ( void ) ;
static int  getnibble ( void ) ;
int decompress_CCITT3 ( char * ) ;
int decompress_PackBits ( char * ) ;

/* structure for CCITT Group3 tables */

struct inruns
{
    int nbits;              /* number of codeword bits */
    unsigned int bits;      /* bits in codeword */
    int runlength;
};

/* codetable for white runs */

static struct inruns white[] =
{
    11, 0x0100,        1792,   /* "00000001000",*/
    12, 0x0120,        1984,   /* "000000010010",*/
    12, 0x0130,        2048,   /* "000000010011",*/
    12, 0x0140,        2112,   /* "000000010100",*/
    12, 0x0150,        2176,   /* "000000010101",*/
    12, 0x0160,        2240,   /* "000000010110",*/
    12, 0x0170,        2304,   /* "000000010111",*/
    11, 0x0180,        1856,   /* "00000001100",*/
    11, 0x01a0,        1920,   /* "00000001101",*/
```

Listing 8.5   continues

Listing 8.5   continued

```
    12,  0x01c0,            2368,   /* "000000011100",*/
    12,  0x01d0,            2432,   /* "000000011101",*/
    12,  0x01e0,            2496,   /* "000000011110",*/
    12,  0x01f0,            2560,   /* "000000011111",*/
     9,  0x4c00,            1472,   /* "010011000",*/
     9,  0x4c80,            1536,   /* "010011001",*/
     9,  0x4d00,            1600,   /* "010011010",*/
     9,  0x4d80,            1728,   /* "010011011",*/
     9,  0x6600,             704,   /* "011001100",*/
     9,  0x6680,             768,   /* "011001101",*/
     9,  0x6900,             832,   /* "011010010",*/
     9,  0x6980,             896,   /* "011010011",*/
     9,  0x6a00,             960,   /* "011010100",*/
     9,  0x6a80,            1024,   /* "011010101",*/
     9,  0x6b00,            1088,   /* "011010110",*/
     9,  0x6b80,            1152,   /* "011010111",*/
     9,  0x6c00,            1216,   /* "011011000",*/
     9,  0x6c80,            1280,   /* "011011001",*/
     9,  0x6d00,            1344,   /* "011011010",*/
     9,  0x6d80,            1408,   /* "011011011",*/
};

static struct inruns short_white[] =
{
    12,  0x0010,           32767,   /* "000000000001",*/
     8,  0x0200,              29,   /* "00000010",*/
     8,  0x0300,              30,   /* "00000011",*/
     8,  0x0400,              45,   /* "00000100",*/
     8,  0x0500,              46,   /* "00000101",*/
     7,  0x0600,              22,   /* "0000011",*/
     7,  0x0800,              23,   /* "0000100",*/
     8,  0x0a00,              47,   /* "00001010",*/
     8,  0x0b00,              48,   /* "00001011",*/
     6,  0x0c00,              13,   /* "000011",*/
     7,  0x1000,              20,   /* "0001000",*/
     8,  0x1200,              33,   /* "00010010",*/
     8,  0x1300,              34,   /* "00010011",*/
     8,  0x1400,              35,   /* "00010100",*/
     8,  0x1500,              36,   /* "00010101",*/
     8,  0x1600,              37,   /* "00010110",*/
     8,  0x1700,              38,   /* "00010111",*/
     7,  0x1800,              19,   /* "0001100",*/
     8,  0x1a00,              31,   /* "00011010",*/
     8,  0x1b00,              32,   /* "00011011",*/
     6,  0x1c00,               1,   /* "000111",*/
     6,  0x2000,              12,   /* "001000",*/
     8,  0x2400,              53,   /* "00100100",*/
     8,  0x2500,              54,   /* "00100101",*/
     7,  0x2600,              26,   /* "0010011",*/
     8,  0x2800,              39,   /* "00101000",*/
     8,  0x2900,              40,   /* "00101001",*/
     8,  0x2a00,              41,   /* "00101010",*/
     8,  0x2b00,              42,   /* "00101011",*/
     8,  0x2c00,              43,   /* "00101100",*/
     8,  0x2d00,              44,   /* "00101101",*/
     7,  0x2e00,              21,   /* "0010111",*/
     7,  0x3000,              28,   /* "0011000",*/
     8,  0x3200,              61,   /* "00110010",*/
```

Listing 8.5   continues

Listing 8.5 continued

```
    8,  0x3300,          62,     /* "00110011",*/
    8,  0x3400,          63,     /* "00110100",*/
    8,  0x3500,          0,      /* "00110101",*/
    8,  0x3600,          320,    /* "00110110",*/
    8,  0x3700,          384,    /* "00110111",*/
    5,  0x3800,          10,     /* "00111",*/
    5,  0x4000,          11,     /* "01000",*/
    7,  0x4800,          27,     /* "0100100",*/
    8,  0x4a00,          59,     /* "01001010",*/
    8,  0x4b00,          60,     /* "01001011",*/
    7,  0x4e00,          18,     /* "0100111",*/
    7,  0x5000,          24,     /* "0101000",*/
    8,  0x5200,          49,     /* "01010010",*/
    8,  0x5300,          50,     /* "01010011",*/
    8,  0x5400,          51,     /* "01010100",*/
    8,  0x5500,          52,     /* "01010101",*/
    7,  0x5600,          25,     /* "0101011",*/
    8,  0x5800,          55,     /* "01011000",*/
    8,  0x5900,          56,     /* "01011001",*/
    8,  0x5a00,          57,     /* "01011010",*/
    8,  0x5b00,          58,     /* "01011011",*/
    6,  0x5c00,          192,    /* "010111",*/
    6,  0x6000,          1664,   /* "011000",*/
    8,  0x6400,          448,    /* "01100100",*/
    8,  0x6500,          512,    /* "01100101",*/
    8,  0x6700,          640,    /* "01100111",*/
    8,  0x6800,          576,    /* "01101000",*/
    7,  0x6e00,          256,    /* "0110111",*/
    4,  0x7000,          2,      /* "0111",*/
    4,  0x8000,          3,      /* "1000",*/
    5,  0x9000,          128,    /* "10010",*/
    5,  0x9800,          8,      /* "10011",*/
    5,  0xa000,          9,      /* "10100",*/
    6,  0xa800,          16,     /* "101010",*/
    6,  0xac00,          17,     /* "101011",*/
    4,  0xb000,          4,      /* "1011",*/
    4,  0xc000,          5,      /* "1100",*/
    6,  0xd000,          14,     /* "110100",*/
    6,  0xd400,          15,     /* "110101",*/
    5,  0xd800,          64,     /* "11011",*/
    4,  0xe000,          6,      /* "1110",*/
    4,  0xf000,          7,      /* "1111",*/
};

/* codetable for black runs */

static struct inruns black[] =
{
    11, 0x0100,          1792,   /* "00000001000",*/
    12, 0x0120,          1984,   /* "000000010010",*/
    12, 0x0130,          2048,   /* "000000010011",*/
    12, 0x0140,          2112,   /* "000000010100",*/
    12, 0x0150,          2176,   /* "000000010101",*/
    12, 0x0160,          2240,   /* "000000010110",*/
    12, 0x0170,          2304,   /* "000000010111",*/
    11, 0x0180,          1856,   /* "00000001100",*/
    11, 0x01a0,          1920,   /* "00000001101",*/
    12, 0x01c0,          2368,   /* "000000011100",*/
```

Listing 8.5   continues

Listing 8.5   continued

```
12, 0x01d0,      2432,    /* "000000011101",*/
12, 0x01e0,      2496,    /* "000000011110",*/
12, 0x01f0,      2560,    /* "000000011111",*/
10, 0x0200,      18,      /* "0000001000",*/
12, 0x0240,      52,      /* "000000100100",*/
13, 0x0250,      640,     /* "0000001001010",*/
13, 0x0258,      704,     /* "0000001001011",*/
13, 0x0260,      768,     /* "0000001001100",*/
13, 0x0268,      832,     /* "0000001001101",*/
12, 0x0270,      55,      /* "000000100111",*/
12, 0x0280,      56,      /* "000000101000",*/
13, 0x0290,      1280,    /* "0000001010010",*/
13, 0x0298,      1344,    /* "0000001010011",*/
13, 0x02a0,      1408,    /* "0000001010100",*/
13, 0x02a8,      1472,    /* "0000001010101",*/
12, 0x02b0,      59,      /* "000000101011",*/
12, 0x02c0,      60,      /* "000000101100",*/
13, 0x02d0,      1536,    /* "0000001011010",*/
13, 0x02d8,      1600,    /* "0000001011011",*/
11, 0x02e0,      24,      /* "00000010111",*/
11, 0x0300,      25,      /* "00000011000",*/
13, 0x0320,      1664,    /* "0000001100100",*/
13, 0x0328,      1728,    /* "0000001100101",*/
12, 0x0330,      320,     /* "000000110011",*/
12, 0x0340,      384,     /* "000000110100",*/
12, 0x0350,      448,     /* "000000110101",*/
13, 0x0360,      512,     /* "0000001101100",*/
13, 0x0368,      576,     /* "0000001101101",*/
12, 0x0370,      53,      /* "000000110111",*/
12, 0x0380,      54,      /* "000000111000",*/
13, 0x0390,      896,     /* "0000001110010",*/
13, 0x0398,      960,     /* "0000001110011",*/
13, 0x03a0,      1024,    /* "0000001110100",*/
13, 0x03a8,      1088,    /* "0000001110101",*/
13, 0x03b0,      1152,    /* "0000001110110",*/
13, 0x03b8,      1216,    /* "0000001110111",*/
10, 0x03c0,      64,      /* "0000001111",*/
11, 0x0500,      23,      /* "00000101000",*/
12, 0x0520,      50,      /* "000001010010",*/
12, 0x0530,      51,      /* "000001010011",*/
12, 0x0540,      44,      /* "000001010100",*/
12, 0x0550,      45,      /* "000001010101",*/
12, 0x0560,      46,      /* "000001010110",*/
12, 0x0570,      47,      /* "000001010111",*/
12, 0x0580,      57,      /* "000001011000",*/
12, 0x0590,      58,      /* "000001011001",*/
12, 0x05a0,      61,      /* "000001011010",*/
12, 0x05b0,      256,     /* "000001011011",*/
10, 0x05c0,      16,      /* "0000010111",*/
10, 0x0600,      17,      /* "0000011000",*/
12, 0x0640,      48,      /* "000001100100",*/
12, 0x0650,      49,      /* "000001100101",*/
12, 0x0660,      62,      /* "000001100110",*/
12, 0x0670,      63,      /* "000001100111",*/
12, 0x0680,      30,      /* "000001101000",*/
12, 0x0690,      31,      /* "000001101001",*/
12, 0x06a0,      32,      /* "000001101010",*/
12, 0x06b0,      33,      /* "000001101011",*/
```

Listing 8.5   continues

Listing 8.5 continued

```
    12,  0x06c0,           40,        /* "000001101100",*/
    12,  0x06d0,           41,        /* "000001101101",*/
    11,  0x06e0,           22,        /* "00000110111",*/
     9,  0x0c00,           15,        /* "000011000",*/
    12,  0x0c80,          128,        /* "000011001000",*/
    12,  0x0c90,          192,        /* "000011001001",*/
    12,  0x0ca0,           26,        /* "000011001010",*/
    12,  0x0cb0,           27,        /* "000011001011",*/
    12,  0x0cc0,           28,        /* "000011001100",*/
    12,  0x0cd0,           29,        /* "000011001101",*/
    11,  0x0ce0,           19,        /* "00001100111",*/
    11,  0x0d00,           20,        /* "00001101000",*/
    12,  0x0d20,  .        34,        /* "000011010010",*/
    12,  0x0d30,           35,        /* "000011010011",*/
    12,  0x0d40,           36,        /* "000011010100",*/
    12,  0x0d50,           37,        /* "000011010101",*/
    12,  0x0d60,           38,        /* "000011010110",*/
    12,  0x0d70,           39,        /* "000011010111",*/
    11,  0x0d80,           21,        /* "00001101100",*/
    12,  0x0da0,           42,        /* "000011011010",*/
    12,  0x0db0,           43,        /* "000011011011",*/
    10,  0x0dc0,            0,        /* "0000110111",*/
};

static struct inruns short_black[] =
{
    12,  0x0010,        32767,        /* "000000000001",*/
     8,  0x0400,           13,        /* "00000100",*/
     8,  0x0700,           14,        /* "00000111",*/
     7,  0x0800,           10,        /* "0000100",*/
     7,  0x0a00,           11,        /* "0000101",*/
     7,  0x0e00,           12,        /* "0000111",*/
     6,  0x1000,            9,        /* "000100",*/
     6,  0x1400,            8,        /* "000101",*/
     5,  0x1800,            7,        /* "00011",*/
     4,  0x2000,            6,        /* "0010",*/
     4,  0x3000,            5,        /* "0011",*/
     3,  0x4000,            1,        /* "010",*/
     3,  0x6000,            4,        /* "011",*/
     2,  0x8000,            3,        /* "10",*/
     2,  0xc000,            2,        /* "11",*/
};

static unsigned char white_lookup[] =
{
    0x00, 0xff, 0x01, 0x02, 0x03, 0x04, 0x05, 0x05,
    0x06, 0x06, 0x07, 0x08, 0x09, 0x09, 0x09, 0x09,
    0x0a, 0x0a, 0x0b, 0x0c, 0x0d, 0x0e, 0x0f, 0x10,
    0x11, 0x11, 0x12, 0x13, 0x14, 0x14, 0x14, 0x14,
    0x15, 0x15, 0x15, 0x15, 0x16, 0x17, 0x18, 0x18,
    0x19, 0x1a, 0x1b, 0x1c, 0x1d, 0x1e, 0x1f, 0x1f,
    0x20, 0x20, 0x21, 0x22, 0x23, 0x24, 0x25, 0x26,
    0x27, 0x27, 0x27, 0x27, 0x27, 0x27, 0x27, 0x27,
    0x28, 0x28, 0x28, 0x28, 0x28, 0x28, 0x28, 0x28,
    0x29, 0x29, 0x2a, 0x2b, 0xff, 0xff, 0x2c, 0x2c,
    0x2d, 0x2d, 0x2e, 0x2f, 0x30, 0x31, 0x32, 0x32,
    0x33, 0x34, 0x35, 0x36, 0x37, 0x37, 0x37, 0x37,
    0x38, 0x38, 0x38, 0x38, 0x39, 0x3a, 0xff, 0x3b,
```

Listing 8.5 continues

Listing 8.5 continued

```
    0x3c, 0xff, 0xff, 0xff, 0xff, 0xff, 0x3d, 0x3d,
    0x3e, 0x3e, 0x3e, 0x3e, 0x3e, 0x3e, 0x3e, 0x3e,
    0x3e, 0x3e, 0x3e, 0x3e, 0x3e, 0x3e, 0x3e, 0x3e,
    0x3f, 0x3f, 0x3f, 0x3f, 0x3f, 0x3f, 0x3f, 0x3f,
    0x3f, 0x3f, 0x3f, 0x3f, 0x3f, 0x3f, 0x3f, 0x3f,
    0x40, 0x40, 0x40, 0x40, 0x40, 0x40, 0x40, 0x40,
    0x41, 0x41, 0x41, 0x41, 0x41, 0x41, 0x41, 0x41,
    0x42, 0x42, 0x42, 0x42, 0x42, 0x42, 0x42, 0x42,
    0x43, 0x43, 0x43, 0x43, 0x44, 0x44, 0x44, 0x44,
    0x45, 0x45, 0x45, 0x45, 0x45, 0x45, 0x45, 0x45,
    0x45, 0x45, 0x45, 0x45, 0x45, 0x45, 0x45, 0x45,
    0x46, 0x46, 0x46, 0x46, 0x46, 0x46, 0x46, 0x46,
    0x46, 0x46, 0x46, 0x46, 0x46, 0x46, 0x46, 0x46,
    0x47, 0x47, 0x47, 0x47, 0x48, 0x48, 0x48, 0x48,
    0x49, 0x49, 0x49, 0x49, 0x49, 0x49, 0x49, 0x49,
    0x4a, 0x4a, 0x4a, 0x4a, 0x4a, 0x4a, 0x4a, 0x4a,
    0x4a, 0x4a, 0x4a, 0x4a, 0x4a, 0x4a, 0x4a, 0x4a,
    0x4b, 0x4b, 0x4b, 0x4b, 0x4b, 0x4b, 0x4b, 0x4b,
    0x4b, 0x4b, 0x4b, 0x4b, 0x4b, 0x4b, 0x4b, 0x4b,
};

unsigned char black_lookup[] =
{
    0x00, 0xff, 0xff, 0xff, 0x01, 0xff, 0xff, 0x02,
    0x03, 0x03, 0x04, 0x04, 0xff, 0xff, 0x05, 0x05,
    0x06, 0x06, 0x06, 0x06, 0x07, 0x07, 0x07, 0x07,
    0x08, 0x08, 0x08, 0x08, 0x08, 0x08, 0x08, 0x08,
    0x09, 0x09, 0x09, 0x09, 0x09, 0x09, 0x09, 0x09,
    0x09, 0x09, 0x09, 0x09, 0x09, 0x09, 0x09, 0x09,
    0x0a, 0x0a, 0x0a, 0x0a, 0x0a, 0x0a, 0x0a, 0x0a,
    0x0a, 0x0a, 0x0a, 0x0a, 0x0a, 0x0a, 0x0a, 0x0a,
    0x0b, 0x0b, 0x0b, 0x0b, 0x0b, 0x0b, 0x0b, 0x0b,
    0x0b, 0x0b, 0x0b, 0x0b, 0x0b, 0x0b, 0x0b, 0x0b,
    0x0b, 0x0b, 0x0b, 0x0b, 0x0b, 0x0b, 0x0b, 0x0b,
    0x0b, 0x0b, 0x0b, 0x0b, 0x0b, 0x0b, 0x0b, 0x0b,
    0x0c, 0x0c, 0x0c, 0x0c, 0x0c, 0x0c, 0x0c, 0x0c,
    0x0c, 0x0c, 0x0c, 0x0c, 0x0c, 0x0c, 0x0c, 0x0c,
    0x0c, 0x0c, 0x0c, 0x0c, 0x0c, 0x0c, 0x0c, 0x0c,
    0x0c, 0x0c, 0x0c, 0x0c, 0x0c, 0x0c, 0x0c, 0x0c,
    0x0d, 0x0d, 0x0d, 0x0d, 0x0d, 0x0d, 0x0d, 0x0d,
    0x0d, 0x0d, 0x0d, 0x0d, 0x0d, 0x0d, 0x0d, 0x0d,
    0x0d, 0x0d, 0x0d, 0x0d, 0x0d, 0x0d, 0x0d, 0x0d,
    0x0d, 0x0d, 0x0d, 0x0d, 0x0d, 0x0d, 0x0d, 0x0d,
    0x0d, 0x0d, 0x0d, 0x0d, 0x0d, 0x0d, 0x0d, 0x0d,
    0x0d, 0x0d, 0x0d, 0x0d, 0x0d, 0x0d, 0x0d, 0x0d,
    0x0d, 0x0d, 0x0d, 0x0d, 0x0d, 0x0d, 0x0d, 0x0d,
    0x0d, 0x0d, 0x0d, 0x0d, 0x0d, 0x0d, 0x0d, 0x0d,
    0x0e, 0x0e, 0x0e, 0x0e, 0x0e, 0x0e, 0x0e, 0x0e,
    0x0e, 0x0e, 0x0e, 0x0e, 0x0e, 0x0e, 0x0e, 0x0e,
    0x0e, 0x0e, 0x0e, 0x0e, 0x0e, 0x0e, 0x0e, 0x0e,
    0x0e, 0x0e, 0x0e, 0x0e, 0x0e, 0x0e, 0x0e, 0x0e,
    0x0e, 0x0e, 0x0e, 0x0e, 0x0e, 0x0e, 0x0e, 0x0e,
    0x0e, 0x0e, 0x0e, 0x0e, 0x0e, 0x0e, 0x0e, 0x0e,
    0x0e, 0x0e, 0x0e, 0x0e, 0x0e, 0x0e, 0x0e, 0x0e,
    0x0e, 0x0e, 0x0e, 0x0e, 0x0e, 0x0e, 0x0e, 0x0e,
};
```

Listing 8.5 continues

Listing 8.5 continued

```
static int ImageWidth ;
static struct inruns *runp ;
static int havenibble ;
static char *s_row ;
static int s_row_ptr ;

/*------------------------------------------------------------
 * The binary search routines in the following code return
 * a pointer to the array element that is equal to or nearest
 * below the key, or to the zeroth element if all elements are
 * greater than the key. The last shouldn't happen in the
 * context of this program. The point is that the key will
 * match the pointed-to element for nbit bits, meaning that we
 * have the run length.
 *----------------------------------------------------------*/

static struct inruns *getwhite ( unsigned int x )
{
   unsigned int i, j, mid ;

   if ( ( i = white_lookup [ x / 256 ] ) != 0xFF )
      return ( &(short_white[i] ) ) ;
   else
   {
      i = 0 ;
      j = ELEMENTS ( white ) - 1 ;

      do
      {
         mid = ( i + j + 1 ) / 2 ;
         if ( white[mid].bits > x )
            j = mid - 1 ;
         else
            i = mid ;
      }
      while ( i < j ) ;
      return ( &(white[i] ) ) ;
   }
}

static struct inruns *getblack ( unsigned int x )
{
   unsigned int i, j, mid ;

   if ( ( i = black_lookup [ x / 256 ] ) != 0xFF )
      return ( &(short_black[i] ) ) ;
   else
   {
      i = 0 ;
      j = ELEMENTS ( black ) - 1 ;

      do
      {
         mid = ( i + j + 1 ) / 2 ;
         if ( black[mid].bits > x )
            j = mid - 1 ;
         else
            i = mid ;
```

Listing 8.5 continues

Listing 8.5 continued

```
        }
        while ( i < j ) ;
        return ( &(black[i] ) ) ;
    }
}

static char getTifByte ( void )
{
    return ( s_row [ s_row_ptr++ ] ) ;
}

static int  getnibble ( void )
{
    static int  ch ;
    int    ret ;

    if ( havenibble )
    {
        ret = ch & 0xF ;
    }
    else
    {
        ch = getTifByte ( ) ;
        ret = ( ch >> 4 ) & 0xF ;
    }
    havenibble = ! havenibble ;
    return ( ret ) ;
}

int decompress_CCITT3 ( char *out_row )
{
    int    i, x, c, out_len ;
    int    extraBits ;
    int    totalbits, blackk, livebits, bitsread,
    startrun, endrun;
    unsigned int    theword ;

    s_row_ptr = 0 ;

    out_len = ( ImageWidth + 7 ) / 8 ;
    extraBits = ( ( out_len * 8 ) - ImageWidth ) ;

    totalbits = blackk = 0 ;
    endrun = -1 ;

    for ( i = out_len - 1 ; i >= 0 ; --i )
        out_row [ i ] = 0 ;

    havenibble = theword = 0 ;
    livebits = 16 ;
    for ( i = 0 ; i < 4 ; ++i )
    {
        theword <<= 4 ;
        theword |= getnibble() ;
    }

    bitsread = 0 ;
```

Listing 8.5 continues

Listing 8.5 continued

```
for ( ;; )
{
    runp = blackk ? getblack ( theword & 0xFFFF ) :
    getwhite ( theword & 0xFFFF ) ;
    bitsread += runp->nbits ;
    startrun = endrun + 1 ;
    endrun = startrun + runp->runlength - 1 ;
    if ( blackk )
    {
        i = startrun ;
        while ( i <= endrun )
        {
            if ( i % 8 || endrun - i < 7 )
            {
                SETBIT ( &(out_row[i/8]), 7 - (i % 8)) ;
                ++i ;
            }
            else
            {
                out_row[i/8] = 0xFF ;
                i += 8 ;
            }
        }
    }
    if ( runp->runlength <= 63 ) blackk = !blackk ;
    totalbits += runp->runlength ;

    for ( i = runp->nbits ; i > 0 ; --i )
    {
        theword <<= 1 ;
        --livebits ;
        if ( livebits == 12 )
        {
            theword |= getnibble() ;
            livebits = 16 ;
        }
    }
    if ( totalbits >= ImageWidth && runp->runlength <= 63 )
        break ;
}

if ( totalbits > ImageWidth ) return ( -1 ) ;

if ( extraBits )
{
    c = out_row [ x ] ;
    switch ( extraBits )
    {
    case 1:
        c &= 0xFE ;
        break ;
    case 2:
        c &= 0xFC ;
        break ;
    case 3:
        c &= 0xF8 ;
        break ;
    case 4:
```

Listing 8.5 continues

Listing 8.5 continued

```
            c &= 0xF0 ;
            break ;
        case 5:
            c &= 0xE0 ;
            break ;
        case 6:
            c &= 0xC0 ;
            break ;
        case 7:
            c &= 0x80 ;
            break ;
        }
        out_row [ x ] = c ;
    }
    return ( 0 ) ;
}

int decompress_PackBits ( char *out_row )
{
    int    i, j, c, out_len ;
    int    bytes, Control ;

    s_row_ptr = 0 ;

    bytes = 0 ;

    while ( bytes < out_len )
    {
        Control = getTifByte ( ) ;

        /* to handle 32-bit ints in some operating systems */
        if ( Control > 128 )
            Control |= 0xFFFFFF00 ;

        if ( Control <= -1 )
        {
            c = getTifByte ( ) ;
            j = -Control + 1 ;
            for ( i = 0 ; i < j ; ++i )
                out_row [ bytes++ ] = ( char ) c ;
        }
        else if ( Control <= 127 )
        {
            j = Control + 1 ;
            for ( i = 0 ; i < j ; ++i )
            {
                c = getTifByte ( ) ;
                out_row [ bytes++ ] = ( char ) c ;
            }
        }
    }
    if ( bytes > out_len ) return ( -1 ) ;
    return ( 0 ) ;
}
```

9
Vector Graphics

Introduction

The most dramatic improvement in the LaserJet's graphics capabilities is LaserJet III's support of the HP Graphics Language (HP-GL). Various versions of this language have been used to drive HP's line of pen plotters, but with the LaserJet III's HP-GL support, HP finally offers a serious alternative to PostScript as a page description language that can incorporate vector graphics (graphics that consist of drawing instructions rather than bit maps).

HP-GL in a PCL Environment

The LaserJet III supports HP-GL by embedding a version of the HP-GL language within the PCL language that users of earlier LaserJet products already know; we call it HP-GL/2. In order for HP-GL to exist within it, an enhanced version of the PCL language is used. There is a PCL command to indicate that the information following it is to be understood as a HP-GL instruction, and there is a complementary command to turn this interpretation off. The nature of the instruction set makes this switching necessary; it is not always possible for the HP-GL/2 interpreter to determine PCL versus HP-GL based on context alone.

There is an important difference between an HP-GL file prepared instruction by instruction by the user and one created elsewhere and then imported. In the first case, the user has control over what HP-GL instructions are used and what ones are not. In the second case, the user must take the HP-GL instruction mix as it comes. Because classic HP-GL describes jobs rather than graphic objects, a traditional HP-GL file does not contain all the information needed to render the graphic independently of the plotter device it was meant for. Because of this, some extra machinations may be needed to import such files. We describe this process later in the chapter. First, we show how to create HP-GL/2 information from scratch, in a form optimal for the LaserJet III's interpreter.

Locally Produced HP-GL/2

The most generic form of HP-GL sets out the user's coordinate system, followed by drawing instructions that specify graphic operations with respect to one or more points in that coordinate system. We present here a subset of the HP-GL/2 language that will enable the programmer to produce respectable graphics. To describe the complete HP-GL/2 language requires a book in itself. (See *The HP-GL/2 Reference Guide*, Hewlett-Packard Press, 1990, and the Bibliography in this book for additional references on the subject.)

Leaving the PCL Environment

Assume that we have been working to create a traditional PCL page, and now we suddenly want to insert a vector graphic object. We save the cursor position, move to where we are going to work, do the work, and restore the cursor position. This may sound familiar; the differences show up when we get to the doing-the-work phase. The other phases are essentially the same. As we do with raster graphics, we start by saving the cursor position, defining the drawing area, and moving to one corner of it. However, some of the mechanics are different from those we used in raster graphics. We have to introduce the following new PCL commands for this.

    Esc * c # X

sets the width of the HP-GL/2 drawing area to # decipoints, and

    Esc * c # Y

sets the height of the drawing area to # decipoints. We move to the upper left corner of the picture frame exactly as we would change position for any other reason in PCL; the mechanics do not need to be repeated here. The next command

    Esc * c 0 T

sets the anchor point of the picture to the current active cursor position, providing the link between our world and the PCL's.

   With this set-up done, we enter the world of vector graphics by telling the interpreter that we are switching from PCL to HP-GL commands. This is done by the command

    Esc % 1 B

which enters HP-GL mode at the current PCL cursor position. The interpreter from now on reads what it sees as HP-GL, until it sees the corresponding command to exit HP-GL mode. (We will show that at the appropriate time.)

Each HP-GL command consists of a unique pair of upper-case letters. Some commands take parameters and some do not. Now that we are in HP-GL mode, we must think only in HP-GL terms and set aside PCL thinking. The most important mental adjustment to make is to accept that the PCL coordinate system has effectively ceased to exist and will not return to existence until we are back in PCL mode (or it is explicitly created in the HP-GL/2 environment).

The first command we use is

```
BPSP1
```

which stands for begin plot and select pen 1. (If you are an experienced HP-GL user, note that `BP` is merely the logical equivalent of `PG` followed by `IN`; you can substitute this combination if you desire. As we go along, you will see that the new HP-GL instruction set is just the old one with some additions.) HP-GL instructions sometimes require semicolon separators, but as a rule they do not require them when there is no ambiguity. Since interpreting the separator just bogs down the interpreter, we omit separators wherever permissible, losing nothing but a small measure of readability. We could have encoded begin plot just as well with

```
BP;SP1;
```

if we had wanted to. (The LaserJet III does not actually require `BP`, but it is good practice for portability of data.)

The function `execute_hpgl()` will do the things described so far to get ready for HP-GL; it will then pass a string containing HP-GL commands to the interpreter and return to PCL mode with the reference point where it was. We give a number of examples in the following material.

Establishing the HP-GL/2 Coordinate System

Now we tell the interpreter what our coordinate system will be. As we noted, the PCL coordinate system is no longer in effect. HP-GL uses a Cartesian coordinate system with X values increasing to the right across the page and Y values increasing *up* the page. Our next decision cannot be made in a way best for all cases, so we offer a general-purpose solution. Although we can specify noninteger values, we choose not to because integers are simpler to work with and produce a more compact and hence more quickly transmitted output file. The interpreter can also handle integers more quickly. A minor side benefit is that, if we are able to avoid real arithmetic altogether, our program may be smaller because a sensible compiler will not link in run-time floating-point support if it is not needed. We choose values that make some simple calculations easy to do mentally when we are trying to visualize what the effect of instructions will be. Our suggestion for complex work is a coordinate system of ±32000 on each axis, assuming a square work area. This provides adequate precision for most purposes, while staying within the range of 16-bit arithmetic, making things easy for our own software and also making it easy to bisect our drawing area several times if necessary while retaining round base-10 numbers. The command for this is

```
SC-32000,32000,-32000,32000
```

where the arguments are minimum *X*, maximum *X*, minimum *Y*, and maximum *Y* respectively. There are further possible arguments to SC, but this is enough to show how to produce a graphic from scratch. Since the other parameters do not benefit us here, we will not discuss them.

Line Widths, Patterns, and Intersections

HP-GL is a language for pen plotters, so from time to time the commands make reference to pens. On an actual plotter, selection of a pen may have an effect on line width simply because one pen has a wider or a narrower tip than another. HP-GL/2 incorporates an enhancement that is made necessary by the fact that there are no actual pens, so "pen widths" must be controlled artificially. As with SC, we will discuss this instruction, PW, only as far as we need to in order to get some basic work done. For our purposes, PW takes one parameter, width. Although there is another command that determines the units in which the width is expressed, we will use the default of millimeters. As a special case, a parameter of 0 calls for the thinnest line available, or $\frac{1}{300}$ of an inch on the LaserJet III. For a line width of 5 mm the command is

```
PW5
```

The width remains in effect until changed.

The default line type is solid. HP-GL/2 provides several other line types, designated by integers 1 through 8. The integer alone establishes a **fixed** line type, for example, LT2. The negation of the same integer, LT-2, makes it **adaptive**. The pattern length of an adaptive line type is adjusted so that only complete cycles of the pattern appear in any line segment. The fixed line type has a fixed pattern size that may or may not exactly fit a line segment; it it does not, the portion that fits is drawn and the rest is carried over to the next line segment. At any time the previous line type may be selected by LT99; the solid line type may be selected by LT with no parameter. The command LT0 draws a single point at the origin of the line segment. The eight types are

1   a dotted line
2   a dashed line with 50% fill
3   a dashed line with 70% fill

4	a long-dash–dot pattern
5	a long-dash–short-dash pattern
6	a long-dash–short-dash–short-dash pattern
7	a long-dash–dot–dot pattern
8	a long-dash–dot–short-dash–dot pattern

The line type remains in effect until changed.

On a pen plotter, line ends and joins take care of themselves as the pen changes direction. A digital device offers more flexibility, so the HP-GL/2 instruction set includes control over line intersections. The command is

LA

It takes pairs of integer arguments; within each pair, the first integer specifies which of three items is being set (1 = line ends, 2 = line joins, and 3 = miter limit) and the second argument makes the choice. Line ends can be of four types: 1 = butt (the default), 2 = square, 3 = triangular, and 4 = round. Line joins can be of six types: 1 = mitered (the default), 2 = mitered/beveled, 3 = triangular, 4 = round, 5 = beveled, and 6 = as is. The miter limit determines how far the mitered join can extend, which can be important when two lines intersect at a very small angle. This number, which need not be an integer, is the ratio of the distance, from the inner intersection point to the outer one, to the line width. The number must be between 0 and 32767; any value less than 1 is converted to 1. For example, to set round line ends and round line joins, mimicking a plotter, the command is

LA1,4,2,4

Pen Up and Pen Down

Now that we know how to change the pen width, we need to distinguish between pen up and pen down. (There is a resemblance here to turtle graphics seen in other environments; pen up is analogous to hideturtle.) Pen up simply means that movements of the pen are made without anything being drawn—exactly what happens on a pen plotter when the pen is raised from the paper, that is, up. The pen up command is

PU

The pen down command is

PD

Drawing Straight Line Segments

With the pen up or down, the pen can be moved to coordinates of, for example, (1000,2000) with the command

```
PA1000,2000
```

or to the coordinates displaced 1000 horizontally and 2000 vertically from the current position with

```
PR1000,2000
```

where PA is plot absolute and PR is plot relative. In either case, successive coordinate pairs can be appended without instructions. For example, if the cursor is at 0,0, an approximately equilateral triangle can be drawn with

```
PA 1000,0,500,866,0,0
```

PA or PD can be combined with drawing instructions. For example, if the pen is at 0,0 in the up position, the same triangle can be drawn by

```
PD 1000,0,500,866,0,0
```

In this and the following sections we present figures that illustrate the commands we discuss. The code to produce the figures is shown in Listing 9.1. We use the following code to invoke the program for each figure:

```
hpgl x <figure number> <HP-GL commands>
```

The source code shows how to set the appropriate fields in the structure whose pointer is passed to either of the working functions. In our case, the drawing area was set to 6 by 6 inches, with an origin of 300,300 for each figure.

LISTING 9.1 Using the LaserJet III's HP-GL/2 Capabilities

```
#include <stdio.h>

struct hpgl_parms
{
    void    *p ;
    FILE    *fp ;
    int     pix_height ;
    int     pix_width ;
    int     x ;
    int     y ;
    double  original_height ;
    double  original_width ;
```

Listing 9.1 continues

Listing 9.1 continued

```
   int      resolution ;
   int      portrait ;
} ;

void execute_hpgl ( struct hpgl_parms *hp )
{
   fputs ( "\033&f0S", hp->fp ) ;
   fprintf ( hp->fp, "\033*p%dx%dY", hp->x, hp->y ) ;
   fprintf ( hp->fp, "\033*c%dx%dy0T",
            hp->pix_width * 12 / 5, hp->pix_height * 12 / 5 ) ;
   fputs ( "\033%1BBPSP1", hp->fp ) ;
   fputs ( ( char *)hp->p, hp->fp ) ;
   fputs ( ";\033%0A\033&f1S", hp->fp ) ;
}

void encapsulate_hpgl ( struct hpgl_parms *hp )
{
   int ch ;

   fputs ( "\033&f0S", hp->fp ) ;
   fprintf ( hp->fp, "\033*p%dx%dY", hp->x, hp->y ) ;
   fprintf ( hp->fp, "\033*c%dx%dy%1.1fk%1.1flOT",
      hp->pix_width * 12 / 5 , hp->pix_height * 12 / 5 ,
      hp->original_width, hp->original_height );
   fputs ( "\033%1BINLA1,4,2,4SP1PA0,0;", hp->fp ) ;
   while (( ch = fgetc (( FILE * ) hp->p )) != EOF )
      fputc ( ch, hp->fp ) ;
   fputs ( ";\033%1A\033&f1S", hp->fp ) ;
}

void main ( int argc, char **argv )
{
   struct hpgl_parms hpp ;
   int execute ;
   FILE *f ;

   if ( argc != 4 )
      exit ( -1 ) ;

   execute = ( argv [ 1 ][ 0 ] == 'x' ) ;

   hpp.fp = fopen ( argv [ 2 ], "wb" ) ;

   if ( ! execute )
   {
      f = fopen ( argv [ 3 ], "rb" ) ;
      hpp.p = f ;
   }
   else
      hpp.p = argv [ 3 ] ;

   hpp.pix_height = 1800 ;
   hpp.pix_width = 1800 ;
   hpp.x = 300 ;
   hpp.y = 300 ;
   hpp.original_width = 6.5 ;
   hpp.original_height = 6.5 ;
   hpp.resolution = 300 ;
```

Listing 9.1 continues

Listing 9.1 continued

```
hpp.portrait = 1 ;

fprintf ( hpp.fp, "\033E" ) ;
if ( execute )
{
    fprintf ( hpp.fp, "Figure 9-%02d\r\n", atoi ( argv[2] )) ;
    fputs ( argv [ 3 ], hpp.fp ) ;
}

if ( execute )
    execute_hpgl ( & hpp ) ;
else
    encapsulate_hpgl ( & hpp ) ;

fprintf ( hpp.fp, "\033E" ) ;
fclose ( hpp.fp ) ;
}
```

Figure 9.1 shows what happens when we set the coordinate system to 0,1000,0,1000. From 0,0 to 1000,0 we draw a wide line, which the interpreter correctly places on the center of the coordinate points. What happens, though, is that part of the line falls outside the drawing area and gets clipped. To compensate for this we alter the SC specification to include a little extra room. Figure 9.2 shows the improved version. If you are concerned about precise sizing of graphics and are using wide lines, you must be aware of this problem.

FIGURE 9.1 A First Attempt at a Triangle

FIGURE 9.2   An Improved Triangle

For rectangles there is a special command. It produces a rectangle from the current point at one corner to a specified point at the diagonally opposite corner. Like **PA** and **PR**, the rectangle command is either absolute or relative. To draw a rectangle with one corner at 0,0 and its opposite corner at 2000,1000 the command is

```
EA 2000,1000
```

To draw a rectangle with its lower left corner at the current point and dimensions of 2000 by 1000, the command is

```
ER 2000,1000
```

Pen down is implicit in the rectangle commands. Making one or both dimensions negative reverses the direction the rectangle is drawn from the originating point. Try visualizing this by noting that **PR X,Y** produces a diagonal of the rectangle that is drawn with **ER X,Y**. **EA** and **ER** each have a counterpart for filling (rather than outlining) a rectangle; they are **RA** and **RR** respectively. The syntax is identical to that of **EA** and **ER**. (Before you use **RA** or **RR** in a particular case, however, you may want to consider treating the rectangle as a rule in PCL mode. Rules are described in Chapter 2.) Figure 9.3 illustrates use of the rectangle commands.

Drawing Circles and Ellipses

We are not restricted to straight lines. We can also draw circles or ellipses and circular or elliptical arcs and wedges. We will illustrate circles and ellipses only, since

FIGURE 9.3   Examples of Rectangles

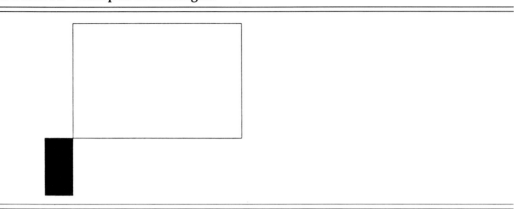

the arcs and wedges are easily derived from them. To draw a circle we move the pen (using the PU instruction) to the center of the circle. We call the circle instruction with two parameters: one to specify the radius and one to specify in degrees the arc subtended by each of the chords with which the circle will be approximated. The smallest available chord, 0.5 degrees, will give a very good approximation of a circle indeed: the error is less than .001 percent. However, the smaller the chord, the longer the interpretation time. The command for a circle of radius 1000 drawn as accurately as possible, with an 0.5-degree chord, is

```
CI1000,0.5
```

No PD is needed here because it is implied by the CI command. Specifying PD will add a dot to the center of the circle.

Drawing an ellipse requires a bit more input, since there is not a specific command to do it. We rely on the fact that a circle drawn on an anisotropic grid will appear as an ellipse with reference to an isotropic grid. What we do to accomplish this is to change the horizontal or vertical scaling and proceed with our circle. We need to adjust all dimensions in the changed direction. This is best illustrated by example. In Figure 9.4 we drew a circle with a radius of 80, placed its center three-quarters of the way from the left edge of the drawing area, and centered it vertically. We then drew an ellipse to the same specification concentric with the circle and stretched it horizontally by 25 percent.

To do this we start by setting the scaling to –320,320,–320,320. We use the following command sequence to draw the circle:

```
PU160,0CI80,0.5
```

In order to produce the ellipse we rescale the horizontal axis (leaving the vertical unchanged) so that each increment of movement is 25 percent greater than the orig-

FIGURE 9.4   Drawing a Circle and an Ellipse

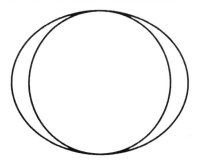

inal scale. To do this we reduce the number of increments in the given space (the bounding box on the paper stays the same) by 25 percent divided by (1 + 25 percent), or 20 percent. Now 320 becomes 256. We go to the point that was 160,0 but is now 128,0 and specify the circle as before. What appears is an ellipse. The command sequence is as follows:

```
SC-256,256,-320,320PU128,OCI80,0.5
```

Note that the new coordinate system stays in effect until changed again.

Drawing Bezier Cubics

The Bezier cubic is a staple today in computer-aided drawing and font design. Its omission from HP-GL/2 is a shame, especially given the simplicity of the Bezier's computational method. We discuss the Bezier in detail in Chapter 10. Perhaps if the LaserJet III's designers had represented a circle by using the closest fitting Bezier cubic rather than by the polygon representation, it would have allowed supporting the general Bezier cubic. The LaserJet III designers faced a dilemma common enough in the software (or in this case firmware) trade, that of functionality versus compatiblity. They opted for maximum compatibility with existing plotter technology by choosing to approximate a circle with a many-sided polygon. This is also the method used on pen plotters, but for a totally different reason, namely, the constraints of mechanical devices. The Bezier approximation of a circle does yield an error—.06 percent for a quarter-circle—greater than the .001 percent approximation resulting from the method chosen. It does have other, cosmetic advantages, as in the case of an arc that is part of a circle that is larger than the page—the curve has no doglegs. (If the circle fits on the page, there is generally no visible error attributable to the use of chords.) The Bezier approximation is the one that PostScript uses.

Whatever the history, the programmer cannot ask the HP-GL/2 interpreter to draw a Bezier cubic. In the next chapter we discuss how to represent a Bezier curve in the raster world, thus giving a solution in the PCL environment that the programmer can use if need be. A solution within the HP-GL/2 environment would entail approximating a Bezier cubic by means of elliptical arcs, a task whose magnitude is beyond the scope of this book.

Drawing and Filling Polygons

There is one more capability of HP-GL that we want to touch on in our overview of the language—its ability to specify and fill a polygon. (The special case of the rectangle has already been covered.) A polygon is a series of line segments that are connected end to end. HP-GL will treat a series of line segments as a polygon if it is put in polygon mode. Once a polygon is created it can be treated as an object that can be filled.

In geometry there is a distinction between open polygons, where the last line segment does not come back to the first, and closed polygons, where it does. If you are planning to create only open polygons, or if you have no need to fill a closed polygon, you don't need to use polygon mode—you simply create them using the drawing commands already discussed. In polygon mode, an open polygon is treated as a closed polygon with the final segment implied.

To enter polygon mode, use the following command:

    PM

To exit polygon mode use

    PM2

In between the two commands you can use any normal normal arc or line drawing commands. They are not executed right away. Instead, they are stored in a polygon buffer for future processing. After you exit polygon mode, the polygon defined by the commands stored in the buffer can be edged, or traced, around its perimeter with the command

    EP

or the polygon can be filled with the command

    FP

Using both commands produces both the outline and the fill.

It is possible to draw a subpolygon, that is, a polygon inside another polygon, and even to nest several subpolygon layers. Filling such nested polygons follows an odd-even rule: an area is filled if and only if a ray from any point in it crosses an odd number of polygon edges. The command

    PM1

causes the current polygon (or subpolygon) to be closed and signals the start of a subpolygon. A circle is a special case. In polygon mode a circle is considered a complete subpolygon. This means that any existing subpolygon is automatically closed when CI is encountered in polygon mode.

In addition, a polygon can be filled solidly (the default) or with a pattern. The pattern is specified with the FT instruction, which takes at least one parameter (the fill type) and possibly more, depending on what the first parameter is. A fill type of 1 is the default solid fill. A fill type of 3 specifies parallel lines and takes two further parameters; the first gives the spacing between lines in user units (for us, the unit implied in the SC command), and the second specifies the angle of the lines, in degrees, counterclockwise from the X-axis. Fill type 4 is the same as 3, but specifies cross-hatching (which is basically the same as filling with parallel lines and then filling again with the same type of parallel lines rotated 90 degrees). Figure 9.5 illustrates nested polygons showing the alternating filled and white feature.

As an esoteric point, the command string fails if the −9,−6 that concludes the PD command is omitted, although the documentation implies that this subpolygon should be closed automatically. It is not clear to us why this happens. To be safe we recommend closing all subpolygons explicitly.

FIGURE 9.5 Nested Polygons with Solid Fill Specified

Returning to the PCL Environment

To finish our plot, we must send a semicolon (or we must be sure the last HP-GL/2 instruction ended with one) and then command a return to PCL mode. This is done with

```
; Esc % 0 A
```

after which we are back in PCL mode with the current point where we left it. A redundant semicolon, should it occur, is harmless.

Externally Produced HP-GL Files

Externally produced HP-GL files may have been designed using the techniques discussed so far, but it is just as likely they weren't. The drawing commands will be more or less the same, but the framing of the HP-GL commands will probably have been done with a specific plotter in mind. In such a situation the coordinate system is probably not the one we would have chosen, but rather a plotter's coordinate system. Unfortunately, HP plotter models each have different coordinate systems, and there is nothing in an HP-GL file to tell us which one is used. In interpreting an HP-GL file, any plotter will assume its own coordinate system by default. This is one of two characteristics of HP-GL that limit traditional HP-GL as a graphics interchange language. (The specification of pens by carousel position rather than by drawing characteristics is the other.)

Faced with this problem, the programmer must know the coordinate system of the original plotter if the drawing is to be scaled successfully. The user needs to produce what we will call encapsulated HP-GL. (We chose this name because of its analogy to encapsulated PostScript.) We offer a function by which HP-GL information can be encapsulated to print within a document at a user-specified size and position. The function `encapsulate_hpgl()` will do its best to allow a freestanding HP-GL file to be imported and interpreted the way `execute_hpgl()` interprets our locally produced files. It is limited by the fact that some information in the file is plotter-specific. It works much as `execute_hpgl()` does and, by specifying round line ends and joins, attempts to produce output that resembles that produced on a plotter.

The programmer may be able to avoid some of the difficulty of device dependence if the file happens to satisfy one particular set of conditions: If an `IP` command, along with its parameters, appears and is followed by an `SC` command with its parameters, all before any drawing instructions appear, *and* if no other `IP` instruction appears in the file, it *may* be possible to remove the IP instruction and parameters and get some device independence. We say may because some HP-GL commands rely on the `IP` command to set some values. Still, using files that meet these criteria might be worth the effort involved.

In this chapter we examined the most important advance of the LaserJet III over its predecessors as far as graphics is concerned—the incorporation of the HP-GL plotter language in its updated HP-GL/2 form. We explored the various HP-GL/2 commands to create various graphic elements and showed how to create ellipses from circles by using an anisotropic scaling environment. Finally, we provided a way to import an existing HP-GL file and render it on the LaserJet III.

10
Advanced Raster Graphics: Lines and Curves

Introduction

In this chapter we examine three kinds of objects: straight lines, ellipses, and Bezier cubics, in a raster environment. (Chapter 9 discussed graphics in the HP-GL/2 environment.) Ellipses, of course, include circles as a special case. Bezier curves are commonly created by freehand drawing programs because of some special properties that we will discuss later, and they are important enough that PostScript defines Bezier curves as a primitive type. Any of these objects can be created in any width, not necessarily just one pixel wide. We discuss straight lines in both one pixel and wider widths. We also treat ellipses and Bezier cubics, but limit them to one pixel wide.

All code presented in this chapter will be able to produce raster lines that can be passed to the `print_raster()` function given in Chapter 8. The large objects in the routines presented in this chapter can possibly exhaust DOS memory. Refer to Chapter 8 if you need to enhance your memory capabilities.

Polygons

Our first subject is polygons and how to fill them. We start with this because we will need to fill polygons in order to take care of one of the objects that are the subject of this chapter. There are many ways to represent a polygon internally in a program, and there are also many ways to fill one. Since the two topics are interdependent we discuss them together. Filling a polygon can be a treacherous operation, but it becomes much easier if the representation of the polygon is planned with due care in the first place. For our purposes a polygon is defined as a closed series of line segments. For any line segment that is not parallel to the X-axis, a traversal along its length yields exactly one x for each point y on the line between the

287

starting and ending y's. This is a good start; each such point will clearly be one end of a horizontal raster line that will need to be drawn to fill the polygon, and each raster line will equally clearly be represented by a pair of the (x,y) points thus generated.

It is handy to represent the polygon in such a way that the array of points contains series of starting and end points for all the required raster lines sorted in y order, leaving us only to connect each pair of points in the array (zero to first, second to third, fourth to fifth, and so on) to fill the polygon. This turns out to be an interesting exercise. As we said, entering one x for each y for each line segment is a start, but care is needed at the end points of a line segment. Since the ending point of one line segment is the beginning point of the next, we want to consider what to do with line segment end points before we proceed further.

Note that there must always be an even number of points in the array for each y value, regardless of the complexity of the polygon, if our plan of connecting successive pairs of points is to work. With an odd number, an attempt to connect two points having different y values causes the process to fail. Consider a polygon whose edge is moving downward vertically, and which suddenly changes to a slope of, say, 10 degrees off the vertical, but still moving downward. Clearly in this case the duplicate end point—where the vector changes—should be entered only once; there is no conceptual difference between this case and one of an unbroken line segment. This is a **cross** of the relevant $y = k$ (current x) line. But now suppose that the same initial line almost reverses itself, say to 10 degrees off the vertical but now moving upward. This is no longer the case of a downward line that will be matched by an upward line on the other side of the polygon, giving the second x for the y; rather, the matching line is right in view, so the x value must be entered twice into the array. This is called a **graze**. Horizontal lines further complicate the situation. If the horizontal line merely delays a graze (giving, for example, down-horizontal-up) nothing is changed; both x's are entered. A horizontal line between two lines both going downward or both going upward is like the earlier case of the downward line followed by another downward line of a different slope; the common end point is represented only once. But this time, which of the two available points should be used? If we are filling a polygon whose outline has already been traced, it doesn't matter; but if the outline has not been traced, it is critical to determine which of the points is at the vertex of the reflex exterior angle and which is at the vertex of the nonreflex exterior angle (there must be one of each in the case described). Figure 10.1 shows the difficulty. It depicts a polygon composed of straight line segments. In the figure, a count of both vertices within the circle-inscribed area produces an odd number of x's for the y once the crossing on the far side of the polygon (indicated by the arrow) is added; the algorithm as described so far will fail. We could solve this problem efficiently by introducing the concepts of inside and outside in relation to the polygon. However, a simpler approach is only slightly less efficient, so we will use it here. We simply trace the polygon as a separate step and then fill it. This may seem clumsy, but it makes life much easier and introduces a run-time penalty only when the polygon is being filled, which is likely to take much more time than the tracing anyway.

FIGURE 10.1   The Problem of Three X's for One Y in a Polygon

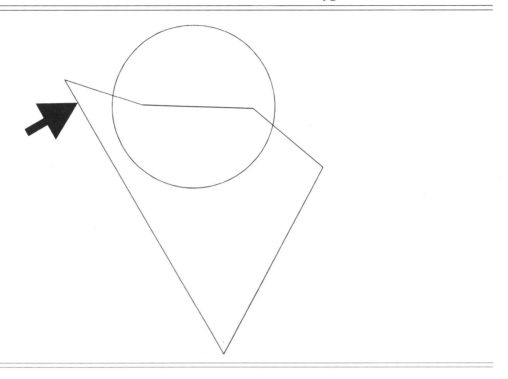

You have some choices to make when you have a self-intersecting polygon, such as the common five-pointed star drawn with five lines. Self-intersection produces subpolygons that can be filled or not. The five-pointed star drawn with five lines is a good illustration of the general case. Here we choose not to fill the internal pentagon. The reason for this choice is that the five-pointed star is structurally similar enough to nested polygons (imagine the internal pentagon shrunk slightly) that it seems consistent to treat it in the same way. In the case of nested polygons, to fill an internal polygon with the same color as the polygon surrounding it would be to attribute no significance to it.

The fact that the computational method for the choice we prefer is much easier than the alternative is mere coincidence, of course. A pleasant consequence of this method of filling polygons is that nested polygons, or the similar self-intersecting polygons, can be handled with no problem whatsoever. The two (or more) polygons are simply represented all in the same array, and the connecting of successive pairs of points will automatically leave the interior polygon empty while filling one interior to that, and so forth. This approach will handle nested polygons and the polygons artificially produced by self-intersection in the same way. The function `fill_poly()` in Listing 10.1 contains the code to fill a polygon, given the array of points.

LISTING 10.1   Filling a Polygon Given an Array of X,Y Coordinates

```
/*----------------------------------------------------------
 * Each of these listings represents code that can be compiled
 * and executed independently, with the exception of line.c,
 * which requires an object module consisting of everything
 * in fillpoly.c except for main().
 *
 * As stated in the text, the routines in these listings yield
 * raster lines that can be passed to print_raster. For demon-
 * stration, we define main_arr as 72 pixels wide x 25 high,
 * allowing the examples to be displayed on a standard PC screen
 * in 80x25 text mode. For practical work, the reader will want
 * to redefine XSIZE, YSIZE, and (where it appears) MAX_POLY_-
 * POINTS appropriately.
 *----------------------------------------------------------*/

#include <stdio.h>
#include <stdlib.h>

#define XSIZE 72
#define YSIZE 25

#define MAX_POLY_POINTS 200

char main_arr [ ( XSIZE + 7 ) / 8 ][ YSIZE ] ;

struct point
{
    int x, y ;
};

struct point g_pointArray [ MAX_POLY_POINTS ] ;
int array_ptr ;

static void  poly_point(int, int );
static int   komp(const void *, const void *);
static void  blacken(int, int, int );
void         fill_poly(struct point *, int );

static void poly_point ( int x, int y )
{
    g_pointArray [ array_ptr ].x = x ;
    g_pointArray [ array_ptr++ ].y = y ;
}

/*----------------------------------------------------------
 * Comparison function for use by qsort() below
 * The variables which simply recast the pointers passed to
 * the function are required for strict ANSI adherence, where
 * the pointers must be const void *. Turbo C/C++ is especially
 * picky on this point.
 *----------------------------------------------------------*/
static int komp ( const void *va, const void *vb )
{
    struct point *a, *b ;
    a = (struct point *) va ;
    b = (struct point *) vb ;
```

Listing 10.1   continues

Listing 10.1 continued

```
    return ( a->y == b->y ? a->x - b->x : a->y - b->y ) ;
}

/*------------------------------------------------------------
 * Blacken the pixels from x_start to x_end in row y.
 *----------------------------------------------------------*/
static void  blacken ( int y, int x_start, int x_end )
{
    static unsigned char SB[8] =
    {
        0xFF, 0x7F, 0x3F, 0x1F, 0xF, 7, 3, 1
    };
    static unsigned char EB[8] =
    {
        0x80, 0xC0, 0xE0, 0xF0, 0xF8, 0xFC, 0xFE, 0xFF
    };

    int i, sByte, eByte ;

    if ( x_start > x_end )
    {
        i = x_start ;
        x_start = x_end ;
        x_end = i ;
    }

    sByte = x_start / 8 ;
    eByte = x_end / 8 ;

    if ( sByte == eByte )
    {
        main_arr [ sByte ][ y ] |= ( SB [ x_start % 8 ] &
            EB [ x_end % 8 ] ) ;
    }
    else
    {
        main_arr [ sByte ][ y ] |= ( SB [ x_start % 8 ] ) ;
        main_arr [ eByte ][ y ] |= ( EB [ x_end % 8 ] ) ;
        for ( i = sByte + 1 ; i < eByte ; ++i )
            main_arr [ i ][ y ] = 0 ;
    }
}

/*------------------------------------------------------------
 * This sorts the array of points and fills each consecutive pair.
 *----------------------------------------------------------*/

void fill_poly ( struct point *g_pointArray, int array_ptr )
{
    int i ;

    ( void ) qsort ( g_pointArray, ( size_t ) array_ptr,
                    sizeof ( struct point ), komp ) ;

    for ( i = 0 ; i < array_ptr ; i += 2 )
    {
        blacken ( g_pointArray[i].y, g_pointArray[i].x ,
```

Listing 10.1 continues

Listing 10.1 continued

```
          g_pointArray[i+1].x );
    }
}

/*-----------------------------------------------------------
 * We will artificially create and fill a diamond-shaped
 * polygon and subpolygon by specifying the points for each,
 * and then print them to the screen.
 *------------------------------------------------------*/
void main ()
{
    int x, y ;

    array_ptr = 0 ;

    /* outer polygon: */
    for ( y = 0 ; y <= 11 ; ++y )
    {
        poly_point ( 11 - y, y ) ;
        poly_point ( 11 + y, y ) ;
    }
    for ( y = 12 ; y <= 22 ; ++y )
    {
        poly_point ( y - 11, y ) ;
        poly_point ( 33 - y, y ) ;
    }

    /* inner polygon: */
    for ( y = 4 ; y <= 11 ; ++y )
    {
        poly_point ( 15 - y, y ) ;
        poly_point ( 7 + y, y ) ;
    }
    for ( y = 12 ; y <= 18 ; ++y )
    {
        poly_point ( y - 7, y ) ;
        poly_point ( 29 - y, y ) ;
    }

    fill_poly ( g_pointArray, array_ptr ) ;

    for ( y = YSIZE - 1; y >= 0 ; --y )
    {
        for ( x = 0 ; x < XSIZE ; ++x )
        {
            printf ( "%c", ( main_arr [ x / 8 ][ y ] &
                ( 1 << ( 7 - x % 8 ))) ? '#' : ' ' ) ;
        }
        printf ( "\n" ) ;
    }
}
```

Lines

The technique of representing a thin straight line on a raster device was presented some time ago by J. E. Bresenham, and we use his work. We also use his work in representing wider lines, though in a way he may not have anticipated.

If a straight line is more than one pixel wide, it is really a rectangle and should be treated as such. Handling a wide line that is not parallel to either axis as a group of parallel one-pixel lines is inadvisable (except perhaps for draft work) since pixels are almost certain to be missed in a repetitive pattern because of rounding errors. The visual effect of this is very much like moire patterns. The routine to draw and fill rectangles of any dimension and orientation— and hence to represent any fat line—is given in `line()` in Listing 10.2. This routine draws the four sides as a polygon and then uses `fill_poly()` to fill it. The rectangle used to represent a fat straight line segment is the one that has the end points of the line segment as the midpoints of two nonadjacent sides and whose dimension perpendicular to the line segment is the specified line width.

A right rectangle is a simple process on the LaserJet and doesn't need the polygon treatment; its handling is discussed in Chapter 2. Nonright rectangles are based on a simple one-pixel-wide line-drawing algorithm for each of the four edges, followed by a fill of the resulting polygon. Where Bresenham's algorithm works for us, we use it; however, in many cases it does not do what we need and we use something else. The reader who is familiar with Bresenham's algorithm may wonder why another routine is necessary. Remember the logic of polygon filling and think what happens when all points on a line making an angle of less than 45 degrees with the X-axis are used in defining an edge of a polygon. There are multiple x's for some (or all) y's, and chaos results when it comes time to draw the raster lines.

The routine presented in Listing 10.2 does not handle line ends. That is, no points are filled that are outside the rectangle that we have defined. This is all right for many situations, but not for all; drawing and CAD software in particular may need line ends. If a situation calls for square ends, the routine should be called with the line extended in each direction by one-half the line width (preferably before any rounding of floating point values, where such are used). If it calls for round ends, the ellipse- (and hence circle-) drawing code that is discussed next can be employed to provide them.

LISTING 10.2   Drawing a Line or a Polyline

```
/*-------------------------------------------------------------
 * This code references the following items from Listing 10-1:
 * blacken(), fill_poly(), main_arr, g_pointArray.
 *-------------------------------------------------------*/

#include <stdio.h>
#include <limits.h>

#define ROUND(x)    ((long)floor((x)+0.5))
```

Listing 10.2   continues

Listing 10.2 continued

```
int i, fillingPoly = 0 ;
int arrayPtr, xx1, xx2, xx3, xx4,
               yy1, yy2, yy3, yy4 ;
static int  prev_dy, prev_prev_dy,
            firstX,  firstY,
            secondX, secondY,
            thirdX,  thirdY,
            polyX,   polyY ;
static int  first_X, prev_X, prev_Y ;

#define XSIZE 72
#define YSIZE 25

#define MAX_POLY_POINTS 200

extern char main_arr [ ( XSIZE + 7 ) / 8 ][ YSIZE ] ;

struct point
{
   int x, y ;
};

extern  struct point g_pointArray [ MAX_POLY_POINTS ] ;
extern  int array_ptr ;

extern  void blacken ( int, int, int );
extern  void g_openPoly ( void );
extern  void g_closePoly ( void );
extern  void line ( int, int, int, int, int );
static  void addRule ( int, int, int, int );
extern  void fill_poly ( struct point *, int );
static  void write_dot ( int, int );
static  void bline ( int, int, int, int, int, int );
static  void fill_line (int, int, int, int );
static  void rite (int, int );
static  void flush ( void );

void g_openPoly()
{
   fillingPoly = 1 ;
   prev_prev_dy = prev_dy = INT_MAX ;
   arrayPtr = 0 ;
}

/*-----------------------------------------------------------
 * This procedure flushes the polygon buffer.
 *-----------------------------------------------------------*/
void g_closePoly()
{
   if ( prev_dy != INT_MAX )
   {
      if ( polyX != firstX || polyY != firstY )
      {
         line ( polyX, polyY, firstX, firstY, 0 ) ;
      }
      line ( firstX, firstY, secondX, secondY, 0 ) ;
      line ( secondX, secondY, thirdX, thirdY, 0 ) ;
```

Listing 10.2 continues

Listing 10.2 continued

```c
        fill_poly ( g_pointArray, arrayPtr ) ;
    }
    fillingPoly = 0 ;
}

/*-----------------------------------------------------------
 * Draws a fat line.
 *-------------------------------------------------------*/
void line ( int x1, int y1, int x2, int y2, int width )
{
    int filled, i, dx, dy ;
    double  hw, sine, cosine, tangent ;

    if ( fillingPoly )
    {
        dy = ( y2 > y1 ? -1 : ( y2 < y1 ? 1 : 0 ) ) ;
        polyX = x2 ;
        polyY = y2 ;
        if ( prev_dy == INT_MAX )
        {
            firstX = x1 ;
            firstY = y1 ;
            secondX = x2 ;
            secondY = y2 ;
        }
        else if ( prev_prev_dy == INT_MAX )
        {
            if ( prev_dy == 0 && dy == 0 )
            {
                secondX = x2 ;
                secondY = y2 ;
                goto lineret ;
            }
            else
            {
                thirdX = x2 ;
                thirdY = y2 ;
            }
        }
        else if ( dy != 0 )
        {
            bline ( x1, y1, x2, y2, 0, 0 ) ;
            if ( !( prev_dy == 0 && dy == prev_prev_dy ) )
            {
                /*-----------------------------------------------
                 *  The condition fails if and only if we have a
                 *  non-zero dy following one or more zero dy's
                 *  following a dy of the same sign as the current
                 *  one. In this case alone, it is an error to write
                 *  (x1, y1), as to do so would have the effect of
                 *  writing both endpoints of the zero-dy line --
                 *  giving an odd (i.e. wrong) number of points on
                 *  the raster line for the closed polygon. The fact
                 *  that we separately trace the edge of the polygon
                 *  means that it doesn't matter which end point we
                 *  ignore; any error here, which can only be a
                 *  failure to write the zero-dy segment, is exactly
                 *  covered by the edge trace.
                 *-----------------------------------------------*/
```

Listing 10.2 continues

Listing 10.2 continued

```
            write_dot ( x1, y1 ) ;
        }
        if ( dy + prev_dy == 0 )
        {
            /* grazing, so we need to write this point twice */
            write_dot ( x1, y1 ) ;
        }
    }
    else
    {
        if ( prev_dy != 0 )
            write_dot ( x1, y1 ) ;
        else
            goto lineret ;
        /*-------------------------------------------------------
         *  So as to leave prev's as they were--this takes
         *  care of the "...or more..." at the start of the
         *  second preceding comment
         *-----------------------------------------------------*/
    }
    prev_prev_dy = prev_dy ;
    prev_dy = dy ;
}
else
{
    arrayPtr = 0 ;

    /*-----------------------------------------------------------
     * Amount to add on either side of line to get desired width.
     * The 0.5 is because we assume that the line itself is 1
     * pixel wide, which is roughly true on a LaserJet.
     *---------------------------------------------------------*/
    hw = ( double ) width / 2.0 - 0.5 ;

    /* we need y2 >= y1 */

    if ( y2 < y1 )
    {

        i = x1 ;
        x1 = x2 ;
        x2 = i ;

        i = y1 ;
        y1 = y2 ;
        y2 = i ;

    }

    dy = y2 - y1 ;
    dx = x2 - x1 ;

    if ( dx == 0 ) /* vertical line */
    {
        if ( width )
            addRule ( x1 - width / 2, y1, x2 +
                ( width - 1 ) / 2, y2 ) ;
    }
```

Listing 10.2 continues

Listing 10.2 continued

```
else if ( dy == 0 ) /* horizontal line */
      {
        if ( width )
           addRule ( x1, y1 - width / 2, x2,
              y2 + ( width - 1 ) / 2 ) ;
      }
      else
      {
        tangent = ( ( double ) ( y2 - y1 ) /
           ( double ) ( x2 - x1 ) ); /* by definition */
        sine = tangent /
        sqrt ( 1.0 + tangent * tangent ); /* standard identity */
        if ( y2 < y1 ) sine = -sine ;
        cosine = sine / tangent ;

        xx1 = x1 + ( ROUND ( ( double ) hw * sine ) ) ;
        xx2 = x2 + ( ROUND ( ( double ) hw * sine ) ) ;
        xx3 = x2 - ( ROUND ( ( double ) hw * sine ) ) ;
        xx4 = x1 - ( ROUND ( ( double ) hw * sine ) ) ;

        yy1 = y1 - ( ROUND ( ( double ) hw * cosine ) ) ;
        yy2 = y2 - ( ROUND ( ( double ) hw * cosine ) ) ;
        yy3 = y2 + ( ROUND ( ( double ) hw * cosine ) ) ;
        yy4 = y1 + ( ROUND ( ( double ) hw * cosine ) ) ;

        filled = 0 ;

        /*-------------------------------------------------
         * In the following, care is taken with crossing
         * vs. grazing vertices, just as with polygons.
         * That is the reason for the two booleans passed
         * to bline().
         *-------------------------------------------------*/

        if ( yy2 == yy3 )
        {
           if ( xx2 == xx3 )
           {
              filled = 1 ;
              fill_line ( xx1, yy1, xx2, yy2 ) ;
           }
           else
           {
              bline ( xx1, yy1, xx2, yy2, 1, 1 ) ;
              bline ( xx4, yy4, xx3, yy3, 1, 1 ) ;
           }
        }
        else if ( yy3 == yy4 )
        {
           if ( xx3 == xx4 )
           {
              filled = 1 ;
              fill_line ( xx2, yy2, xx3, yy3 ) ;
           }
           else
           {
              bline ( xx2, yy2, xx3, yy3, 1, 1 ) ;
              bline ( xx1, yy1, xx4, yy4, 1, 1 ) ;
```

Listing 10.2 continues

Listing 10.2 continued

```
              }
           }
           else
           {
              bline ( xx1, yy1, xx2, yy2, 1, 1 ) ;
              bline ( xx2, yy2, xx3, yy3, 0, 1 ) ;

              bline ( xx1, yy1, xx4, yy4, 1, 1 ) ;
              bline ( xx4, yy4, xx3, yy3, 0, 1 ) ;
           }

           if ( !filled )
              fill_poly ( g_pointArray, arrayPtr ) ;
        }
     }
   lineret:
        return ;
}

/*-----------------------------------------------------------
 *  This blackens the area specified by a rule (in other
 *  words, a rectangle) by getting the parameters in the
 *  relation expected by blacken() and then calling that
 *  function.
 *-------------------------------------------------------*/
void addRule ( int x_start, int y_start,
               int x_end,   int y_end )
{
   int a, b, y ;

   if ( y_start <= y_end )
   {
      a = y_start ;
      b = y_end ;
   }
   else
   {
      a = y_end ;
      b = y_start ;
   }
   for ( y = a; y <= b; ++y )
      blacken ( y, x_start, x_end ) ;
}

static void  write_dot ( int x, int y )
{
   g_pointArray [ arrayPtr ].x = x ;
   g_pointArray [ arrayPtr++ ].y = y ;
}

static void bline ( int x1, int y1,
                    int x2, int y2,
                    int botpix, int toppix)
{
   int x, y, endY, startY ;
   long int    x2mx1 ;
   int y2my1, hy2my1 ;
```

Listing 10.2 continues

Listing 10.2 continued

```
    if ( y2 == y1 )
    {
        if ( botpix && toppix )
        {
            write_dot ( x1, y1 ) ;
            if ( x1 != x2 )
                write_dot ( x2, y2 ) ;
        }
        return;
    }

    if ( y2 < y1 )
    {

        i = x1 ;
        x1 = x2 ;
        x2 = i ;

        i = y1 ;
        y1 = y2 ;
        y2 = i ;

    }

    startY = botpix ? y1 : y1 + 1 ;
    endY = toppix ? y2 : y2 - 1 ;

    y2my1 = y2 - y1 ;

    /*-------------------------------------------------------
     * This being integer arithmetic, rounding in division
     * is best handled by adding or subtracting half the divisor
     * to/from the dividend in the first place. The variable
     * hy2my1 will do that.
     *-----------------------------------------------------*/

    hy2my1 = ( x2 < x1 ) ? -y2my1 / 2 : y2my1 / 2 ;
    x2mx1 = ( long ) x2 - x1 ;

    for ( y = startY ; y <= endY ; ++y )
    {
        x = ( ( long ) ( y - y1 ) * ( x2mx1 ) + hy2my1 )
            / y2my1 + x1 ;
        write_dot ( x , y ) ;
    }
}

static void  fill_line ( int x1, int y1,
                         int x2, int y2)
{
    /*-------------------------------------------------------
     * This is an implementation of Bresenham's line-drawing
     * algorithm. Explanations are widely available in the
     * literature.
     *-----------------------------------------------------*/

    int inc1, inc2, inc3, xend, yend, d, x, y, dx, dy ;
    prev_Y = 0 ;
```

Listing 10.2   continues

Listing 10.2   continued

```
dx = abs(x2 - x1);
dy = abs(y2 - y1);

if (dy <= dx)
{
   if (x1 > x2)
   {
      x = x2;
      y = y2;
      xend = x1;
      dy = y1 - y2;
   }
   else
   {
      x = x1;
      y = y1;
      xend = x2;
      dy = y2 - y1;
   }
   inc1 = dy << 1;
   inc2 = (dy - dx) << 1;
   inc3 = (dy + dx) << 1;
   d = (dy >= 0) ? inc1 - dx : inc1 + dx ;
   while (x < xend)
   {
      rite(x, y);
      /* plot point */
      x++;
      if (d >= 0)
      {
         if (dy <= 0)
            d += inc1 ;
         else
         {
            y++;
            d += inc2 ;
         }
      }
      else
      {
         if (dy >= 0)
            d += inc1;
         else
         {
            y--;
            d += inc3 ;
         }
      }
   }
}
else
{
   if (y1 > y2)
   {
      y = y2;
      x = x2;
      yend = y1;
      dx = x1 - x2;
```

Listing 10.2   continues

Listing 10.2 continued

```
        }
        else
        {
            y = y1;
            x = x1;
            yend = y2;
            dx = x2 - x1;
        }
        inc1 = dx << 1;
        inc2 = (dx - dy) << 1;
        inc3 = (dx + dy) << 1;
        d = (dx >= 0) ? inc1 - dy : inc1 + dy ;
        while (y < yend)
        {
            rite(x, y);
            /* plot point */
            y++;
            if (d >= 0)
            {
                if (dx <= 0)
                    d += inc1;
                else
                {
                    x++;
                    d += inc2;
                }
            }
            else
            {
                if (dx >= 0)
                    d += inc1;
                else
                {
                    x--;
                    d += inc3;
                }
            }
        }
    }
    rite(x, y);
    flush() ;
    /* plot point */
}

static void rite ( int x, int y )
{
    if ( y != prev_Y )
    {
        if ( prev_Y != 0 )
            addRule ( first_X, prev_Y, prev_X, prev_Y ) ;
        first_X = x ;
        prev_Y = y ;
    }
    prev_X = x ;
}

static void flush ( )
{
```

Listing 10.2   continues

Listing 10.2 continued

```
    addRule ( first_X, prev_Y, prev_X, prev_Y ) ;
}

void main ()
{
    int x, y ;

    g_openPoly ( ) ;
    line ( 10, 0, 35, 23, 1 ) ;
    line ( 35, 23, 70, 0, 1 ) ;
    line ( 70, 0, 0, 17, 1 ) ;
    line ( 0, 17, 70, 17, 1 ) ;
    line ( 70, 17, 10, 0, 1 ) ;
    g_closePoly ( ) ;

    for ( y = YSIZE - 1; y >= 0 ; --y )
    {
        for ( x = 0 ; x < XSIZE ; ++x )
        {
            printf ( "%c", ( main_arr [ x / 8 ][ y ] &
                ( 1 << ( 7 - x % 8 ) ) ) ) ? '#' : ' ' ) ;
        }
        printf ( "\n" ) ;
    }
}
```

Ellipses

Ellipses can be handled with no loss of precision in the digitized environment other than what the digitization requires in the first place. We use an algorithm based on the same principles as Bresenham's algorithm for straight lines and circles, but adapted for the more complex conic section. This algorithm was first presented by J. L. V. Pitteway in 1967 and was further developed in a magazine article in 1988 (David Weber, "Ellipses, Parabolas, and Hyperbolas," *Computer Language,* November 1988), which cleaned up a rough spot that Pitteway had acknowledged. However, that article had a flaw that was resolved by one of the present authors (Babcock) in an article in 1989. We present the 1989 work here and add further improvements.

Most notably, we improve execution time by employing reflections, taking advantage of the fact that an ellipse is point-symmetrical about its center. This cuts the computational work by nearly half and yields a measurable improvement in performance. The routine is `ellipse()` found in Listing 10.3.

We attach a front end to the Pitteway algorithm that converts a much more common representation of an ellipse to the general conic form ($ax^2 + bxy + cy^2 + dx + ey = 0$) that Pitteway used. The ellipse representation that we use specifies the center of the ellipse and the coordinates of one of the end points of each of a conjugate pair of diameters not necessarily coincident with the axes. (This is the way ellipses are specified in the Computer Graphics Metafile (CGM) format, which is gaining acceptance as a standard file representation for vector graphics. In addition, anyone having to handle Interleaf graphics may be pleased to learn that Interleaf's ellipse representation uses the same basic format except for specifying the corners of the parallelogram instead of the conjugate diameter endpoints. The transformation from the Interleaf to the CGM representation is trivial.) The real appeal of this format is that it supports the sorts of transformations likely to be required in CAD/CAM, since a conjugate diameter pair remains a conjugate diameter pair across any graphic transformation. The interested reader may care to work out mappings from other practical representations, such as both-foci-plus-major-axis, to this one (hint: the major and minor axes of an ellipse are a conjugate diameter pair). Note that the listing contains a number of multiplications and divisions by two or four such as the one on the line of code commented by "compiler should optimize this to shift". If necessary, these can be changed to shifts in the 8086 environment, though any decent compiler will do this optimization automatically. Where the compiler does not do this and clock cycles are critical, the programmer may implement shifts by hand. It has not been done here in order to keep the code as portable as possible.

We make use of reflections by tracing the ellipse only as far as the point on the ellipse that is directly across the ellipse from the starting point. As we plot each point, we also record in a buffer the point that is directly across from that point; the arithmetic to determine that point is simpler and more quickly performed than the arithmetic that would be required to determine that point if we traversed the entire ellipse. When we have reached the point across from the starting point, we then plot the points that we have saved in the buffer, completing the ellipse. You may wonder why we don't just plot the reflection point at the time of determining it rather than saving first and then plotting it. It would be simpler, but it would also be more time consuming in many cases. The reason is that each point plotted would be so distant from the point previously plotted that any mechanism used to provide virtual memory—such as the EMS, XMS, and disk routines discussed in Chapter 8—would be doing much more page-switching than it would have to do if it were fed a series of points in which each point was adjacent to the previous point, making page-switching relatively unlikely in each case. The time cost in page-switching is considerable, whereas the time cost in buffering is relatively small. With that in mind, we have incorporated the buffered approach in the code presented in Listing 10.3 even though it does not specifically incorporate any virtual memory techniques: the penalty is very small where there is a penalty at all, while the gain is great where there is a gain.

LISTING 10.3   Drawing an Ellipse Given the Center and a Conjugate Diameter Pair

```c
#include <stdio.h>
#include <math.h>

#define ROUND(x)                ((long)floor((x)+0.5))
#define SQUARE(x)               ((double)((x))*(double)((x)))

#define XSIZE 72
#define YSIZE 25

static char main_arr [ ( XSIZE + 7 ) / 8 ][ YSIZE ] ;

#if XSIZE > YSIZE
static int xarr [ XSIZE + 1 ] ;
static int yarr [ XSIZE + 1 ] ;
#else
static int xarr [ YSIZE + 1 ] ;
static int yarr [ YSIZE + 1 ] ;
#endif

static int g_2x0 ;
static int g_2y0 ;
static int *xp, *yp ;

void  write_dot ( int, int );
void  record_dot ( int, int );
void  ellipse ( int, int, int, int, int, int );

static void write_dot ( int x, int y )
{
   main_arr [ x / 8 ][ y ] |= ( 1 << ( 7 - x % 8 ) ) ;
}

static void record_dot ( int x, int y )
{
   write_dot ( x, y ) ;
   *xp++ = g_2x0 - x ;
   *yp++ = g_2y0 - y ;
}

void ellipse ( int x0, int y0,
               int x1, int y1,
               int x2, int y2 )
{
   double      xp2, yp2, maxabs, scale ;
   double      cosine, sine, cr1, cr2alt, m ;
   double      aa, bb, cc, dd, ee ;
   double      oneovrcr2altsqr,
               x0mx1, x2mx1,
               y2my1, y0my1,
               oneovrcr1;
   double      temp1, temp2 ;
   long int    pa, pb, pc, pd, pe ;
   long int    k1, k2, k3, a, b, d, w;
   int         xpt, ypt, octant;
   int         xend, yend ;
   long int    x, y, askip, bskip;

   g_2x0 = x0 + x0 ;
```

Listing 10.3   continues

Listing 10.3 continued

```
g_2y0 = y0 + y0 ;

xp = xarr ;
yp = yarr ;

x0mx1 = ( double ) ( x0 - x1 ) ;
x2mx1 = ( double ) ( x2 - x1 ) ;
y0my1 = ( double ) ( y0 - y1 ) ;
y2my1 = ( double ) ( y2 - y1 ) ;

oneovrcr1 =
 1.0 / ( cr1 = sqrt(SQUARE(x0mx1) + SQUARE(y0my1))) ;

/* translate so that (x1,y1) is at (0,0) and y0 is 0 */

xp2 = ( x0mx1 * x2mx1 + y0my1 * y2my1 ) * oneovrcr1 ;
yp2 = (-y0my1 * x2mx1 + x0mx1 * y2my1 ) * oneovrcr1 ;

cr2alt = yp2 ;

/* if 0.0, we have colinear points */
if ( cr2alt != 0.0 )
{
   oneovrcr2altsqr = 1.0 / SQUARE(cr2alt) ;
   cosine = x0mx1 * oneovrcr1 ;
   sine   = y0my1 * oneovrcr1 ;

   m = ( cr1 - xp2 ) / yp2 ;

   temp1 = ( cosine - m * sine ) * oneovrcr1 ;
   temp2 = ( sine + m * cosine ) * oneovrcr1 ;

   dd = -2 * temp1 ;
   ee = -2 * temp2 ;
   aa = SQUARE ( temp1 ) +
        SQUARE ( sine ) * oneovrcr2altsqr ;
   bb = 2 * ( temp1 * temp2 - sine * cosine *
        oneovrcr2altsqr ) ;
   cc = SQUARE ( temp2 ) +
        SQUARE ( cosine ) * oneovrcr2altsqr ;

   /* scale aa, bb, cc, dd, ee to fit range */

   maxabs = fabs(aa);
   if ( fabs ( bb ) > maxabs )
      maxabs = fabs ( bb );
   if ( fabs ( cc ) > maxabs )
      maxabs = fabs ( cc );
   if ( fabs ( dd ) > maxabs )
      maxabs = fabs ( dd );
   if ( fabs ( ee ) > maxabs )
      maxabs = fabs ( ee );

   scale = fabs(( 0x20000000 - 2 ) / maxabs );

   pa  = ROUND ( aa * scale ) ;
   pb  = ROUND ( bb * scale ) ;
   pc  = ROUND ( cc * scale ) ;
```

Listing 10.3 continues

Listing 10.3 continued

```
        pd  = ROUND ( dd * scale ) ;
        pe  = ROUND ( ee * scale ) ;

        xpt = x1 ;
        ypt = y1 ;

        xend = 2 * ( x0 - x1 ) ;
        yend = 2 * ( y0 - y1 ) ;

        /* start from origin */
        x = y = 0L;

        /* find initial octant; try first octant */
        k1 = 2 * pa;
        k2 = k1 + pb;
        k3 = k2 + 2 * pc + pb;
        b = -pd - pa - pb / 2; /* compiler should
                                  optimize this to shift */
        a = -b + pe;
        d = b - pe / 2 - pc / 4;
        octant = 1;

        if ((a < 0) || (b < 0))
        {                       /* try second octant */
           k1 = -2 * pc;
           k2 = k1 - pb;
           k3 = k2 - 2 * pa - pb;
           b = pe + pc + pb / 2;
           a = -b - pd;
           d = b + pd / 2 + pa / 4;
           octant = 2;
        }
        if ((a < 0) || (b < 0))
        {                       /* try third octant */
           k1 = 2 * pc;
           k2 = k1 - pb;
           k3 = k2 + 2 * pa - pb;
           b = -pe - pc + pb / 2;
           a = -b - pd;
           d = b + pd / 2 - pa / 4;
           octant = 3;
        }
        if ((a < 0) || (b < 0))
        {                       /* try fourth octant */
           k1 = -2 * pa;
           k2 = k1 + pb;
           k3 = k2 - 2 * pc + pb;
           b = -pd + pa - pb / 2;
           a = -b - pe;
           d = b + pe / 2 + pc / 4;
           octant = 4;
        }
        if ((a < 0) || (b < 0))
        {                       /* try fifth octant */
           k1 = 2 * pa;
           k2 = k1 + pb;
           k3 = k2 + 2 * pc + pb;
           b = pd - pa - pb / 2;
```

Listing 10.3 continues

Listing 10.3 continued

```
            a = -b - pe;
            d = b + pe / 2 - pc / 4;
            octant = 5;
        }
        if ((a < 0) || (b < 0))
        {                            /* try sixth octant */
            k1 = -2 * pc;
            k2 = k1 - pb;
            k3 = k2 - 2 * pa - pb;
            b = -pe + pc + pb / 2;
            a = -b + pd;
            d = b - pd / 2 + pa / 4;
            octant = 6;
        }
        if ((a < 0) || (b < 0))
        {                            /* try seventh octant */
            k1 = 2 * pc;
            k2 = k1 - pb;
            k3 = k2 + 2 * pa - pb;
            b = pe - pc + pb / 2;
            a = -b + pd;
            d = b - pd / 2 - pa / 4;
            octant = 7;
        }
        if ((a < 0) || (b < 0))
        {                            /* try eighth octant */
            k1 = -2 * pa;
            k2 = k1 + pb;
            k3 = k2 - 2 * pc + pb;
            b = pd + pa - pb / 2;
            a = -b + pe;
            d = b - pe / 2 + pc / 4;
            octant = 8;
        }

        /* smooth gradients at first */
        askip = bskip = 0;

        /* for each point in quadrant */
        for ( ;; )
        {                                   /* draw */
            (void) record_dot((int)x + xpt, (int)y + ypt);
            if (d < 0)
            {               /* move horizontal or vertical */
                switch (octant)
                {
                case 1 :
                case 8 :
                    x++;
                    break;
                case 2 :
                case 3 :
                    y++;
                    break;
                case 4 :
                case 5 :
                    x--;
                    break;
```

Listing 10.3 continues

Listing 10.3 continued

```
      case 6 :
      case 7 :
          y--;
          break;
      }
      b -= k1;
      a += k2;
      d += b;
  }
  else
  {                            /* move diagonal */
      switch (octant)
      {
      case 1 :
      case 2 :
          x++;
          y++;
          break;
      case 3 :
      case 4 :
          x--;
          y++;
          break;
      case 5 :
      case 6 :
          x--;
          y--;
          break;
      case 7 :
      case 8 :
          x++;
          y--;
          break;
      }
      b -= k2;
      a += k3;
      d -= a;
  }

  if ( x == xend && y == yend )
  {
      for ( --xp, --yp ; xp >= xarr ; --xp, --yp )
          write_dot ( *xp, *yp ) ;
      return ;
  }

  if (b < 0)                   /* square octant change */
  {
      if (bskip == 0)
          (octant == 1) ? (octant = 8) : (octant--);
      /* if (octant == start) return; */
      w = k2 - k1;
      k1 = -k1;
      k2 = w + k1;
      k3 = 4 * w - k3;
      b = -b - w;
      d = b - a - d;
      a = a - 2 * b - w;
```

Listing 10.3 continues

Listing 10.3   continued

```
            askip = bskip = 0;
            if (b < 0)
                bskip = 1;     /* steep gradients */
        }
        if (a < 0)              /* diagonal octant change   */
        {
            if (askip == 0)
                (octant == 1) ? (octant = 8) : (octant--);

            w = 2 * k2 - k3;
            k1 = w - k1;
            k2 = k2 - k3;
            k3 = -k3;
            b = b + a - k2 / 2;
            d = b - a / 2 - d + k3 / 8;
            a = w / 2 - a;
            askip = bskip = 0;
            if (a < 0)
                askip = 1;     /* steep gradients */
        }
    }
}

void main ( void )
{

    int x, y ;

    ellipse ( 36, 12, 40, 18, 60, 13 ) ;

    for ( y = YSIZE - 1; y >= 0 ; --y )
    {
        for ( x = 0 ; x < XSIZE ; ++x )
        {
            printf ( "%c", ( main_arr [ x / 8 ][ y ] &
                ( 1 << ( 7 - x % 8 ) ) ) ? '#' : ' ' ) ;
        }
        printf ( "\n" ) ;
    }
}
```

Bezier Cubics

Bezier cubics have become increasingly common with the ongoing improvement
of freehand drawing capabilities in CAD and other software. The Bezier curve is
the tool of choice nowadays for the common task of joining one end of each of two
nonparallel and nonintersecting line segments. The Bezier method is ideal for this
because the curve can be forced to be tangent to a specified line at each end (and
not necessarily the same line). In practice, it is in terms of such tangents that the
curve is normally created in drawing work. Figure 10.2 shows the screen presented

by a PC-based drawing package after the program has serviced two requests to draw a Bezier cubic. The four identifiable points on the screen that are not on the curve are the control points, two for each of the two curves. Of those points, the two to the left are for one curve and the remaining two are for the other curve. The curves meet at the arrow. For each of the four points, it can be seen that the curve starts off in the direction of that point from the point to which the control point is anchored by the dotted line. We see from this example that Beziers can be placed end-to-end with no break in the curve as long as the common end point and the two associated control points, one for each curve, are collinear. A further refinement, shown in this case, is that if two control points are not only collinear with an end point but equidistant from it, the curvatures on either side of the point will be equal in magnitude, thus giving a further impression of smoothness. Since the Bezier routine given here is recursive, the user may want to pay appropriate attention to stack size. The code appears in `bezier()` in Listing 10.4.

Building on the foundation of Chapter 3 and 8 we discussed the handling of geometric objects using the raster graphics capabilities offered by all LaserJet family

FIGURE 10.2   Screen Showing a Commercial Drawing Program Manipulating a Bezier Cubic

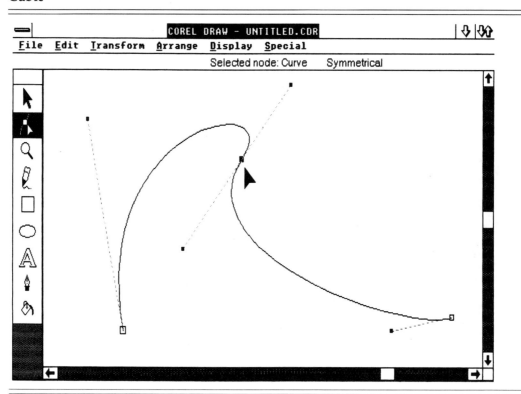

members. We showed how to fill an arbitrary polygon as well as nested polygons.
We showed how to handle straight lines of any width, as well as circles, ellipses,
and Bezier cubes. We discussed the theory of our ellipse-drawing algorithm in
enough depth to allow a developer to expand on it to draw other conic sections.

LISTING 10.4 Drawing a Bezier Cubic Given the Four Control Points

```
#include <stdio.h>

#define XSIZE 72
#define YSIZE 25

static char main_arr [ ( XSIZE + 7 ) / 8 ][ YSIZE ] ;

void  bezier( int, int, int, int, int, int, int, int );
static void _bezier(long, long, long, long,
                    long, long, long, long );

static void  write_dot(int  x,int  y);

static void write_dot ( int x, int y )
{
   main_arr [ x / 8 ][ y ] |= ( 1 << ( 7 - x % 8 ) ) ;
}

void bezier ( x1, y1, x2, y2, xc1, yc1, xc2, yc2 )
int x1, y1, x2, y2, xc1, yc1, xc2, yc2 ;
{
    /*----------------------------------------------------------
     * We expand to longs because that gives better accuracy
     * and avoids problems with the terminating condition.
     *----------------------------------------------------------*/
    _bezier ( ( long ) x1 << 16, ( long ) y1 << 16,
        ( long ) x2 << 16, ( long ) y2 << 16,
        ( long ) xc1 <<16, ( long ) yc1 << 16,
        ( long ) xc2 << 16, ( long ) yc2 << 16 ) ;
}

static void _bezier ( long x1,  long y1,
                      long x2,  long y2,
                      long xc1, long yc1,
                      long xc2, long yc2 )
{
    long    xm1, ym1, xm2, ym2, xm3, ym3,
            xm4, ym4, xm5, ym5, xm6, ym6 ;

    xm1 = ( x1 + xc1 ) / 2 ;
    ym1 = ( y1 + yc1 ) / 2 ;

    xm2 = ( x2 + xc2 ) / 2 ;
    ym2 = ( y2 + yc2 ) / 2 ;

    xm3 = ( xc1 + xc2 ) / 2 ;
    ym3 = ( yc1 + yc2 ) / 2 ;

    xm4 = ( xm1 + xm3 ) / 2 ;
```

Listing 10.4 continues

Listing 10.4 continued

```c
    ym4 = ( ym1 + ym3 ) / 2 ;

    xm5 = ( xm2 + xm3 ) / 2 ;
    ym5 = ( ym2 + ym3 ) / 2 ;

    xm6 = ( xm4 + xm5 ) / 2 ;
    ym6 = ( ym4 + ym5 ) / 2 ;

    if ( labs (((x1 + 32768) >> 16 ) -
        ((x2 + 32768) >> 16 )) > 1L ||
        labs ( ( (y1 + 32768) >> 16 ) -
        ((y2 + 32768) >> 16 )) > 1L )
    {
        _bezier ( x1, y1, xm6, ym6, xm1, ym1, xm4, ym4 ) ;
        _bezier ( xm6, ym6, x2, y2, xm5, ym5, xm2, ym2 ) ;
    }
    else
    {
        write_dot ( (int) ( (x1 + 32768) >> 16 ),
            (int) ((y1 + 32768) >> 16 )) ;
        write_dot ( (int) ( (x2 + 32768) >> 16 ),
            (int) ((y2 + 32768) >> 16 )) ;
    }
}

void main ( void )
{
    int x, y ;

    bezier ( 20, 1, 58, 1, 88, 26, -10, 26  ) ;

    for ( y = YSIZE - 1; y >= 0 ; --y )
    {
        for ( x = 0 ; x < XSIZE ; ++x )
        {
            printf ( "%c", ( main_arr [ x / 8 ][ y ] &
                ( 1 << ( 7 - x % 8 ) ) ) ) ? '#' : ' ' ) ;
        }
        printf ( "\n" ) ;
    }
}
```

11
File Formats

Introduction

We have now examined the principal capacities of the LaserJet, and we can consider some issues that LaserJet programmers might encounter over and above the problems and solutions presented in Chapters 1 through 10. The problems we examine in this chapter concern the manipulation of files frequently encountered in the LaserJet environment. Two such files are PCX (and PCC) graphics files and WordPerfect documents.

Each of these two examples presents difficulties that are typical of other files in its category. For example, the PCX file, which is used to store multicolored graphics, must be converted for printing on a monochrome device such as the LaserJet. The WordPerfect file format, product of the world's most popular word processor, shows how text files carry ancillary information and how this information can be put to use creatively in the LaserJet environment. We hope that our discussion of these two examples will help you deal with other file formats you will undoubtedly encounter in the field of printer software.

PCX Format

The popularity of the PCX format is not so much a reflection of the format's utility as it is a testament to Microsoft's marketing prowess. The format originated with ZSoft's PC Paintbrush program, and almost every developer has a box full of Paintbrush disks from purchases of Microsoft products that included a free copy of Paintbrush. It remains an important format, and it is useful for developers to be able to deal with it. In this section we discuss printing a PCX file on an HP LaserJet or compatible printer.

An Overview of the PCX File Format

A PCX file contains a 128-byte header record followed by scan lines that are compressed using run-length encoding. The header contains a 48-byte buffer suitable for storing 16 RGB (red-green-blue) triples; that is, 16 sets of three bytes, one each for the red, green, and blue settings. These triples are used to record the palette of the display on which the PCX file was created.

With the introduction of the VGA (Video Graphics Array) display adapter and 256-color video modes, the creators of the PCX format were faced with a dilemma: what to do with the 768 bytes of palette data required by a 256-color image. They elected to leave the existing PCX header intact and append the 256-color palette to the end of the file. In actual practice, 769 bytes are appended: a palette identification byte with the value 10 (0Ah), followed by 768 bytes of RGB information. The palette ID byte simply duplicates the value of the first byte of the header.

The PCX header, which is a binary data structure, contains many fields, four of which are words that give the screen pixel-coordinate extents of the file's image (see Listing 11.1). They are the four values 0, 0, `screen_width - 1`, and `screen-_height - 1`. Thus, for a mode 12h VGA image (640 × 480), these values are 0, 0, 639, and 479. If the image is a subset of the full screen, then some other set of values will be present and the file's extension should properly be .PCC instead of .PCX. The .PCC extension indicates a **clipped image**. However, the convention of using .PCC for images smaller than a full screen is only loosely followed, so don't rely on the file extension; instead, rely on the header values.

The PCX Header

Listing 11.1 illustrates a C structure suitable for reading or writing a PCX header record. The following list defines the terms used in Listing 11.1.

`manuf`	This is a byte value that indicates the manufacturer. It always has the value 10 decimal.
`vers`	A byte value indicating the format version. This can generally be ignored.
`rle`	A flag that is set to 1 if the image is compressed (using run-length encoding). This is normally the case.
`bitpx`	The number of bits per pixel. For 256-color images, it is 8. For monochrome and 16-color images, it is 1. For 4-color CGA images (modes 4 and 5), it is 2.
`x1, y1, x2, y2`	The upper left and lower right corners of the image in screen pixel coordinates. For example, a full-screen EGA image has the values 0, 0, 639, and 349, respectively.

LISTING 11.1 PCX Header File

```
/*-----------------------------------------------------------------*
 *    PCX File Header Structure                                     *
 *-----------------------------------------------------------------*/

typedef struct
_pcx_header
    {
    char            manuf;        /* Always is 10 for Paintbrush */
    char            vers;         /* Version information         */
    char            rle;          /* Run-length encoding (=1)    */
    char            bitpx;        /* Bits per pixel              */
    unsigned        x1;           /* Picture bounds- left        */
    unsigned        y1;           /*                 top         */
    unsigned        x2;           /*                 right       */
    unsigned        y2;           /*                 bottom      */
    unsigned        hres;         /* Display horiz resolution    */
    unsigned        vres;         /* Display vert  resolution    */
    unsigned char   rgb[48];      /* Palette                     */
    char            vmode;        /* (ignored)                   */
    char            nplanes;      /* Number of planes (v2.5=0)   */
    unsigned        bplin;        /* Bytes per line              */
    unsigned        palinfo;      /* Palette Info (1=clr,2=gray) */
    unsigned        shres;        /* Scanner resolution          */
    unsigned        svres;        /*                             */
    char            xtra[54];     /* Extra space (filler)        */
    }
pcx_header;
```

`hres, vres`	The resolution of the screen display on which the image was created. Resolution is somewhat of a misnomer, since the values stored here are the dimensions of the screen in pixels. For example, values for mode 10h of an EGA are 640 and 350.
`rgb`	A 48-byte array containing 16 RGB triples that define the image's default palette. The bytes are ordered as r0, b0, g0, r1, b1, g1, and so on. The actual values are somewhat hardware dependent and are used as follows:

- For an EGA, each array byte is right-shifted 6 bits to obtain a two-bit value in the range 0–3. Each set of three bytes is then used to format an EGA palette register value of eight bits in the form `00RGBrgb` (which is the format employed by the EGA BIOS) where `RGB` comprises the high-order bits from each of the three shifted bytes, and `rgb` comprises the corresponding low-order bits.

- For 256-color VGA modes, each byte is right-shifted 2 bits to generate a 6-bit quantity in the range 0–63. Three such bytes are combined to form the 18-bit palette values used by the VGA. Note that on the VGA the EGA's 8-bit palette registers are used as an index register to select one of 256 18-bit DAC palette registers. This is how the VGA maintains backward compatibility with the EGA.

vmode	This is supposed to contain the BIOS video mode number, but most programs ignore this field, so it is not safe to make any assumptions from its value.
nplanes	The number of planes in the image. For 16-color images it is 4; for all other video modes it is 1.
bplin	The number of bytes in a scan line. This value can be used by the decoding algorithm to determine when a full scan line has been decoded.
palinfo	A flag indicating a color image (1) or a gray-scale image (2).
shres, svres	These fields are used by scanner software to indicate the horizontal and vertical resolutions at which an image was scanned.
xtra	Padding bytes that are not used for anything. Presumably, fields added to the header in the future will be placed here, so it is wise to leave this area free.

The Image Data

The encoded (or compressed) image data immediately follows the file header. The image is presented one scan line at a time. If the image is multiplane, each plane of each scan line is listed. Thus, for a full screen image from an EGA display the data are as follows:

Scan line 0, Plane 0 (80 bytes)
Scan line 0, Plane 1 (80 bytes)
Scan line 0, Plane 2 (80 bytes)
Scan line 0, Plane 3 (80 bytes)
Scan line 1, Plane 0 (80 bytes)

.
.
.

The byte values in parentheses represent the original data sizes. Since the data is compressed, the actual number of bytes read will be different.

The image data is compressed using a simple run-length encoding scheme. The decoding algorithm is as follows: (1) Read a byte, V, from the file; (2) if the two high-order bits of V are set, then `RepeatCount` equals low-order 6 bits and `ImageByte` equals next byte from file; (3) otherwise, `RepeatCount` = 1 and `ImageByte` = V. Some notes regarding the algorithm are in order. First, repeated runs can span planes and can also span scan lines. Thus, the code should not depend upon a forced break at the ends of these items. Second, scan lines are stored as an integral number of bytes, so if the image width is not a multiple of 8, then each line is padded with unused bits to a multiple of 8. Third, most software encodes a scan line as a run of bytes, so the last few unused bits contain whatever followed the image at that location on the screen. Therefore, you should mask off the last byte of each scan line with the following code:

```
w = x2 - x1 + 1;
...
if( w & 7 )
{
    mask = 0xFF << (8 - (w & 7));
    last_byte &= mask;
}
```

Fourth, the maximum repeat count is 3Fh, or 63. A repeated run of more than 63 bytes must therefore be split into two or more repeating elements. For example, to encode 80 bytes of zeroes, the following 4 bytes are used: FFh 00h D1h 00h. If the top two bits are removed, this translates to 3Fh 00h 11h 00h, which in decimal is 63 00 17 00. Encoding a single byte whose two high-order bits are set requires a two-byte sequence: C1h followed by the data byte being encoded. This represents a sequence with a repeat count of 1.

LaserJet Graphics

Printing rectangular bitmapped images on the LaserJet is a straightforward proposition that entails sending a mixture of escape sequences and image scan lines. An overview of the process, with the escape sequence syntax, is as follows:

- Set the cursor position (X, Y), to determine the image's upper left corner on the page. (Positioning was discussed in Chapter 1.)
- Specify the print resolution of the graphic. This can be 75, 100, 150, or 300 dpi. For the typical screen image, 100 dpi works well:

    Esc * t 1 0 0 R

- Enter raster graphics mode by sending:

  Esc * r 1 A

- Send each scan line in the image.

  Esc * b # W [Raster Data]

- Then terminate LaserJet raster graphics mode by sending:

  Esc * r B

These escape codes were presented in detail in Chapter 3.

Rendering Color Images

If we are printing a monochrome graphic, then each 1 in the image corresponds to a black dot on the page, and each 0 corresponds to white (or no dot). On the other hand, if we are printing a 16- or 256-color image, we must find some way to render colors so that they have some variation. Otherwise, all nonzero pixel values will be rendered as black and the resulting printed image will probably be unintelligible.

This problem is solved by printing each pixel value using a shading pattern or gray-scale pattern that is distinct for each possible pixel value. To render a 16-color image, we set up an 8-bit by 8-bit pattern cell for each pixel value. For example, we can render one of the colors using a pattern consisting of closely spaced horizontal lines. The pattern cell in Figure 11.1 does this. We set up a 16-by-8 `char` array, say pat[16][8], and use a pixel's value as the first index, its Y position modulo 8 as the second index, and its X position modulo 8 as the bit offset within the selected byte. The printed monochrome pixel takes the value of this bit. (Refer to the source code implementation if you are confused, Listing 11.2.)

With a 256-color image it is not practical to extend the method just described—how could we discern 256 shading patterns! What we do is retain the 16 shading

FIGURE 11-1. A Pattern Cell for Gray Scaling

```
FFh        1 1 1 1 1 1 1 1
00h        0 0 0 0 0 0 0 0
FFh        1 1 1 1 1 1 1 1
00h        0 0 0 0 0 0 0 0
FFh        1 1 1 1 1 1 1 1
00h        0 0 0 0 0 0 0 0
FFh        1 1 1 1 1 1 1 1
00h        0 0 0 0 0 0 0 0
```

patterns for indices 0–15 and then determine the closest index in the range 0–15 for the indices 16–255. This is easily implemented as a lookup table, an array T[256] where T[i] is a value in the range 0–5, which replaces i as a pixel's value.

The algorithm for finding the closest index utilizes the RGB palette values. We treat the RGB triples as points in 3-space and use the distance between points as a measure of how closely one index resembles another. Then, for each triple (r_i, g_i, b_i), where 16 <= i <= 255, we find the triple (r_j, g_j, b_j), 0 <= j <= 15 that is closest, and use pattern j to represent color i. Recall that distance is calculated as

$$dist = \sqrt{(x_2 - x_1)^2 + (y_2 - y_1)^2 + (z_2 - z_1)^2}$$

Note that since we are concerned with relative values only, it is not necessary to take the square root. Thus, we use distance squared for the comparison.

The PCX Print Program

Listing 11.2 provides the source code for the PCX print program, PRTPCX.C. The program is controlled via command-line switches and has the following syntax:

```
PRTPCX pcx_file  [prt_port]  [switches]
```

The syntax elements are defined as follows:

pcx_file	The full path and name of file to be printed
prt_port	The printer port, which defaults to LPT1

switches is one of the following:

-i	Invert the image data. This is useful for printing files from programs that treat white as the background color.
-rnnn	Set printer resolution to nnn. The default value is 100 and possible values are 75, 100, 150, and 300 dpi.
-xd.d	Set left edge of image at d.d inches from the left. The default value is 0.0.
-yd.d	Set top edge of image at d.d inches from the top. The default value is 0.0.

This is a bare-bones print program; there are a number of useful features that can be added including support for landscape output and image scaling. Many extras can be added using PCL escape sequences.

LISTING 11.2 Printing PCX Files on the LaserJet

```
/*------------------------------------------------------------*
 * Prints PCX files on an HP LaserJet.                        *
 *------------------------------------------------------------*/

#include <stdlib.h>
#include <stdio.h>
#include <string.h>
#include <ctype.h>
#include <dos.h>
#include <io.h>

#include "pcx.h"

typedef struct _rgb_triple {
        unsigned char r;                                /* red */
        unsigned char g;                                /* green */
        unsigned char b;                                /* blue */
} rgb_triple;

#define TYP_MASK 0xC0          /* mask top 2 bits of a byte */
#define CNT_MASK 0x3F          /* mask bot 6 bits of a byte */

char pcx_file[80] = "\0",                    /* file to print */
     prt_port[80] = "LPT1";         /* printer destination */

int   res  = 100,                             /* resolution */
      inv  = 0,                               /* invert flag */
      xorg = 0,                               /* xorg in dots */
      yorg = 0;                               /* yorg in dots */

char  pat[16][8] =                    /* shading pattern set */
{
    { 0xFF, 0xFF, 0xFF, 0xFF, 0xFF, 0xFF, 0xFF, 0xFF },
    { 0xFF, 0xAA, 0xFF, 0xAA, 0xFF, 0xAA, 0xFF, 0xAA },
    { 0xAA, 0x55, 0xAA, 0x55, 0xAA, 0x55, 0xAA, 0x55 },
    { 0xAA, 0x41, 0xAA, 0x14, 0xAA, 0x41, 0xAA, 0x14 },
    { 0x88, 0x22, 0x88, 0x22, 0x88, 0x22, 0x88, 0x22 },
    { 0x80, 0x08, 0x80, 0x08, 0x80, 0x08, 0x80, 0x08 },
    { 0x80, 0x00, 0x08, 0x00, 0x80, 0x00, 0x08, 0x00 },
    { 0x00, 0x00, 0x00, 0x00, 0x00, 0x00, 0x00, 0x00 },
    { 0xFF, 0xFF, 0xFF, 0xFF, 0xFF, 0xFF, 0xFF, 0xFF },
    { 0xFF, 0xAA, 0xFF, 0xAA, 0xFF, 0xAA, 0xFF, 0xAA },
    { 0x55, 0xAA, 0x55, 0xAA, 0x55, 0xAA, 0x55, 0xAA },
    { 0x14, 0xAA, 0x41, 0xAA, 0x14, 0xAA, 0x41, 0xAA },
    { 0x22, 0x88, 0x22, 0x88, 0x22, 0x88, 0x22, 0x88 },
    { 0x80, 0x08, 0x80, 0x08, 0x80, 0x08, 0x80, 0x08 },
    { 0x08, 0x00, 0x80, 0x00, 0x08, 0x00, 0x80, 0x00 },
    { 0x00, 0x00, 0x00, 0x00, 0x00, 0x00, 0x00, 0x00 },
};

/*------------------------------------------------------------*/
/* Explain program usage...                                   */
/*------------------------------------------------------------*/

void explain_pgm( void )
{
   printf( "\n" );
```

Listing 11.2 continues

Listing 11.2 continued

```
    printf( "usage:     PRTPCX  pcx_file  [prt_port] [sw...]\n" );
    printf( "\n" );
    printf( "pcx_file : file to print\n" );
    printf( "\n" );
    printf( "prt_port : printer port (def = LPT1)\n" );
    printf( "\n" );
    printf( "switches : -i    : invert image\n" );
    printf( "          -rnnn : resolution nnn dpi (def=100)\n" );
    printf( "          -xd.d : x origin d.d inches (def=0.0)\n" );
    printf( "          -yd.d : y origin d.d inches (def=0.0)\n" );
    printf( "\n" );
}

/*------------------------------------------------------------*/
/* Write a message and quit...                                */
/*------------------------------------------------------------*/

void exit_pgm( char *msg )
{
    printf( "%s\n", msg );
    exit( 0 );
}

/*------------------------------------------------------------*/
/* Process command line args...                               */
/*------------------------------------------------------------*/

void process_args( int argc, char *argv[] )
{
    double v;
    int    i;
    char   c;

    /* look at command line args */
    for( i=1; i<argc; i++ )
    {
        if( (*argv[i] == '/') || (*argv[i] == '-') )
        {
            c = *(argv[i] + 1);
            switch( tolower(c) )
            {
                case 'i' : /* resolution */
                        inv = 1;
                        break;

                case 'r' : /* resolution */
                        sscanf( argv[i]+2, "%d", &res );
                        if( (res != 75)  && (res != 100) &&
                            (res != 150) && (res != 300) )
                            exit_pgm( "Invalid resolution" );
                        break;

                case 'x' : /* x org */
                        sscanf( argv[i]+2, "%lf", &v );
                        v *= 300.0;   v += 0.5;
                        xorg = (int) v;
                        break;
```

Listing 11.2 continues

Listing 11.2   continued

```
                case 'y' : /* y org */
                            sscanf( argv[i]+2, "%lf", &v );
                            v *= 300.0;   v += 0.5;
                            yorg = (int) v;
                            break;

                default :   /* error */
                            exit_pgm( "Invalid switch" );
                            break;
            }
        }
        else if( pcx_file[0] == 0 )
        {
            strcpy( pcx_file, argv[i] );
            /* add .PCX extension if none provided */
            if( strchr( pcx_file, '.' ) == NULL )
                strcat( pcx_file, ".pcx" );
        }
        else
        {
            strcpy( prt_port, argv[i] );
        }
    }

    /* do we have a file name? */
    if( pcx_file[0] == 0 )
        exit_pgm( "No PCX file name given." );
}

/*----------------------------------------------------------*/
/* Initialize the LaserJet...                               */
/*----------------------------------------------------------*/

void init_prt( FILE *fptr, int xo, int yo, int resolution )
{
    char cmd[24];

    /* set cursor position */
    sprintf( cmd, "\033*p%dx%dY", xo, yo );
    fwrite( cmd, strlen(cmd), 1, fptr );

    /* set resolution */
    sprintf( cmd, "\033*t%dR", resolution );
    fwrite( cmd, strlen(cmd), 1, fptr );

    /* enter raster graphics mode */
    fwrite( "\033*r1A", 5, 1, fptr );

    /* check that it all happened */
    if( ferror(fptr) )
        exit_pgm( "Error in init_prt" );
}

/*----------------------------------------------------------*/
/* Terminate on the LaserJet...                             */
/*----------------------------------------------------------*/

void term_prt( FILE *fptr )
```

Listing 11.2   continues

Listing 11.2 continued

```
{
    /* end raster graphics mode */
    fwrite( "\033*rB", 4, 1, fptr );

    /* eject a page */
    fwrite( "\014", 1, 1, fptr );
}

/*-----------------------------------------------------------*/
/* Print a monochrome image...                               */
/*-----------------------------------------------------------*/
void print_mono( FILE *f_in, FILE *f_out, pcx_header *pH )
{
    int             bytecnt, rowcnt, done;
    int             nrows, ncols, endmask;
    unsigned char   hdr, cnt, dat;
    char            cmd[24];

    bytecnt = rowcnt = done = 0;
    nrows = pH->y2 - pH->y1 + 1;
    ncols = pH->x2 - pH->x1 + 1;
    endmask = ( ~(255 >> (ncols & 7)) ) & 255;
    sprintf( cmd, "\033*b%dW", pH->bplin );

    while( ! done )
    {
        /* get a byte */
        hdr = fgetc( f_in );

        /* decode it */
        if ( (hdr & TYP_MASK) == TYP_MASK )
        {
            cnt = hdr & CNT_MASK;
            dat = fgetc( f_In );
        }
        else
        {
            cnt = 1;
            dat = hdr;
        }

        /* if invert selected, bitwise invert */
        if( inv )
            dat = ~dat;

        /* send the byte(s) */
        while( cnt-- )
        {
            /* if bytecnt is zero, start a row */
            if( bytecnt == 0 )
                fwrite( cmd, strlen(cmd), 1, f_out );

            /* update counter, send byte */
            bytecnt++;
            if( bytecnt == pH->bplin )
            {
                fputc( dat&endmask, f_out );
```

Listing 11.2   continues

Listing 11.2 continued

```
            bytecnt = 0;
            rowcnt++;
            if( rowcnt == nrows )
                done = 1;
        }
        else
            fputc( dat, f_out );
    }
  }
}

/*------------------------------------------------------------*/
/* Output 16-color scanline...                                */
/*------------------------------------------------------------*/

void lineout_16( FILE *f_out, int *scanline, int npix, int rm8 )
{
    int  i, mask, curb, nbytes;
    char cmd[24];

    nbytes = (npix + 7) / 8;
    sprintf( cmd, "\033*b%dW", nbytes );
    fwrite( cmd, strlen(cmd), 1, f_out );

    curb = 0;
    mask = 0x80;

    for( i = 0; i < npix; i++ )
    {
        curb |= pat[scanline[i]][rm8] & mask;
        mask >>= 1;
        if( mask == 0 )
        {
            mask = 0x80;
            fputc( curb, f_out );
            curb = 0;
        }
    }
    if( npix & 7 )
        fputc( curb, f_out );
}

/*------------------------------------------------------------*/
/* Print a 16-color image...                                  */
/*------------------------------------------------------------*/

void print_color_16( FILE *f_in, FILE *f_out, pcx_header *pH )
{
    int  bytecnt, rowcnt, planecnt, done, hdr, cnt, dat;
    int  i, nrows, ncols, *scanline, sclen, curpx, plmask;

    bytecnt = rowcnt = planecnt = done = 0;
    curpx  = 0;
    plmask = 0x08;
    nrows = pH->y2 - pH->y1 + 1;
    ncols = pH->x2 - pH->x1 + 1;

    /* scanline will hold a full row of pixels, including */
```

Listing 11.2 continues

Listing 11.2   continued

```
    /* unused padding pixels.  padding will be ignored.   */
    sclen = pH->bplin * 8 * sizeof(int);
    scanline = (int *) malloc( sclen );
    if( scanline == NULL )
        exit_pgm( "Out of memory in print_color_16" );
    memset( scanline, 0, sclen );

    while( ! done )
    {
        /* get a byte */
        hdr = fgetc( f_in );

        /* decode it */
        if ( (hdr & TYP_MASK) == TYP_MASK )
        {
            cnt = hdr & CNT_MASK;
            dat = fgetc( f_in );
        }
        else
        {
            cnt = 1;
            dat = hdr;
        }

        /* if invert selected, bitwise invert */
        if( inv )
            dat = ~dat;

        /* accumulate pixels in scanline buffer */
        while( cnt-- )
        {
            /* isolate 8 pixels in current byte */
            for( i=128; i>0; i>>=1 )
            {
                if( dat & i )
                    scanline[curpx] |= plmask;
                curpx++;
            }

            /* update counters */
            bytecnt++;
            if( bytecnt == pH->bplin )
            {
                bytecnt = 0;
                curpx = 0;
                planecnt++;
                plmask >>= 1;
                if( planecnt == pH->nplanes )
                {
                    lineout_16( f_out, scanline, ncols, rowcnt & 7 );
                    memset( scanline, 0, sclen );
                    planecnt = 0;
                    plmask = 0x08;
                    rowcnt++;
                    if ( rowcnt == nrows )
                        done = 1;
                }
            }
        }
```

Listing 11.2   continues

Listing 11.2 continued

```c
        }
    }
}

/*-----------------------------------------------------*/
/* Fill in pixel lookup table for 256-color images     */
/*-----------------------------------------------------*/

void init_lu_256( rgb_triple *rgb, int *lutbl )
{
    int          i, j, ic;
    unsigned int ri, gi, bi;
    long         d, dc;

    /* set base palette */
    for( i = 0; i < 16; i++ )
    {
        lutbl[i] = i;
    }

    /* compute indexes above 15 */
    for( i = 16; i < 256; i++ )
    {
        ri = rgb[i].r;
        gi = rgb[i].g;
        bi = rgb[i].b;
        ic = 0;

        /* dc is "distance" from rgb[i] to rgb[0] */
        dc  = (rgb[0].r - ri) * (rgb[0].r - ri);
        dc += (rgb[0].g - gi) * (rgb[0].g - gi);
        dc += (rgb[0].b - bi) * (rgb[0].b - bi);

        for( j = 1; j < 16; j++ )
        {
            /* d is "distance" from rgb[i] to rgb[j] */
            d  = (rgb[j].r - ri) * (rgb[j].r - ri);
            d += (rgb[j].g - gi) * (rgb[j].g - gi);
            d += (rgb[j].b - bi) * (rgb[j].b - bi);

            if( d < dc )
            {
                dc = d;
                ic = j;
            }
        }

        lutbl[i] = ic;
    }
}

/*-----------------------------------------------------*/
/* Print a 256-color image...                          */
/*-----------------------------------------------------*/

void print_color_256( FILE *f_in, FILE *f_out, pcx_header *pH )
{
    rgb_triple *rgb;
```

Listing 11.2 continues

Listing 11.2 continued

```
int          *lutbl, *scanline;
int           bytecnt, rowcnt, done, hdr, cnt, dat;
int           nrows, ncols, sclen;

/* allocate palette variables */
rgb = (rgb_triple *) malloc( sizeof(rgb_triple) * 256 );
if( rgb == NULL )
   exit_pgm( "Out of memory in print_color_256" );
lutbl = (int *) malloc( sizeof(int) * 256 );
if( lutbl == NULL )
   exit_pgm( "Out of memory in print_color_256" );

/* read palette info from end of file */
if( fseek( f_in, -768L, SEEK_END ) )
   exit_pgm( "Error seeking to palette" );
if( fread( rgb, sizeof(rgb_triple), 256, f_in ) != 256 )
   exit_pgm( "Error reading palette" );

/* construct lookup table */
init_lu_256( rgb, lutbl );

/* reposition file ptr to start of image */
if( fseek( f_in, 128, SEEK_SET ) )
   exit_pgm( "Error seeking to image" );

/* allocate scanline buffer */
sclen = pH->bplin * sizeof(int);
scanline = (int *) malloc( sclen );
if( scanline == NULL )
   exit_pgm( "Out of memory in print_color_16" );

bytecnt = rowcnt = done = 0;
nrows = pH->y2 - pH->y1 + 1;
ncols = pH->x2 - pH->x1 + 1;

while( ! done )
{
   /* get a byte */
   hdr = fgetc( f_in );

   /* decode it */
   if ( (hdr & TYP_MASK) == TYP_MASK )
   {
      cnt = hdr & CNT_MASK;
      dat = fgetc( f_in );
   }
   else
   {
      cnt = 1;
      dat = hdr;
   }

   /* if invert selected, bitwise invert */
   if( inv )
      dat = ~dat;

   /* accumulate pixels in scanline buffer */
   while( cnt-- )
```

Listing 11.2 continues

Listing 11.2 continued

```
        {
            /* put pixel into scanline buffer */
            scanline[bytecnt] = lutbl[dat];

            /* update counter */
            bytecnt++;
            if( bytecnt == pH->bplin )
            {
                lineout_16( f_out, scanline, ncols, rowcnt & 7 );
                bytecnt = 0;
                rowcnt++;
                if( rowcnt == nrows )
                    done = 1;
            }
        }
    }
}

/*-----------------------------------------------------------*/
/* Print the specified PCX file...                           */
/*-----------------------------------------------------------*/

void print_pcx( char *pcxf, char *prtf, int xo, int yo, int r )
{
    FILE          *f_in, *f_out;
    pcx_header    pcxH;

    /* set up */
    if (( f_in = fopen( pcxf, "rb" )) == NULL )
        exit_pgm( "Error opening PCX file" );
    if (( f_out = fopen_laserjet ( prtf )) == NULL )
        exit_pgm( "Error opening printer" );
    set_binary_mode( f_out );

    /* read the pcx header */
    if ( fread(&pcxH, sizeof(pcx_header), 1, f_in) != 1 )
        exit_pgm( "Error reading PCX header" );

    /* initialize the printer */
    printf( "\nPrinting '%s'...", pcxf );
    init_prt( f_out, xo, yo, r );

    /* indicate image dimensions */
    printf( "%d W x %d H, %d bytes/line, ",
            pcxH.x2-pcxH.x1+1, pcxH.y2-pcxH.y1+1, pcxH.bplin );

    /* determine the image type, call the appropriate */
    /* image processing function...                   */

    /* monochrome bitmap */
    if( (pcxH.nplanes == 1) && (pcxH.bitpx == 1) )
    {
        printf( "monochrome..." );
        print_mono( f_in, f_out, &pcxH );
    }

    /* 16-color bitmap */
    else if( pcxH.nplanes == 4 )
```

Listing 11.2 continues

Listing 11.2   continued

```c
    {
        printf( "16 color..." );
        print_color_16( f_in, f_out, &pcxH );
    }

    /* 256-color bitmap */
    else if( pcxH.bitpx == 8 )
    {
        printf( "256 color..." );
        print_color_256( f_in, f_out, &pcxH );
    }

    /* unsupported image type */
    else
        printf( "Unsupported image type, skipping print!" );

    /* finish up on the printer */
    term_prt( f_out );
    printf( "done" );

    /* clean up */
    fclose( f_in );
    fclose( f_out );
}

/*-----------------------------------------------------------*/
/*                        M A I N                            */
/*-----------------------------------------------------------*/

void main( int argc, char *argv[] )
{
    /* sign-on */
    printf( "\nPrint PCX File on LaserJet\n" );

    /* help indicated? */
    if( (argc < 2) || (*argv[1] == '?') )
    {
        explain_pgm();
        exit( 0 );
    }

    /* process command line... */
    process_args( argc, argv );

    /* print the file */
    print_pcx( pcx_file, prt_port, xorg, yorg, res );

    /* sign-off */
    printf( "\nend-of-pgm" );
}
```

WordPerfect Documents

During the last half of the 1980s a company called SSI took a little-known word processor called WordPerfect and developed it into one of the most capable text handling packages available. Renaming itself after the product, WordPerfect Corp.
eventually became the industry leader in sales due to aggressive product development, adept marketing, and a reputation for excellent technical support. As a result,
WordPerfect documents are encountered in all arenas where the PC is likely to be
found. Any text package that is intended for professional use is expected to be able
to process WordPerfect files.

The WordPerfect document format is loaded with hundreds of data items that
control text formatting as it appears on the screen and on paper. Processing these
files means knowing how to get at the text and how to interpret the formatting
data. The definitive source of information on WordPerfect files is the *DOS
Developer's Toolkit for WordPerfect Corporation Products*, which is available directly
from WordPerfect Corp. for a nominal fee. The ensuing discussion relies on information from this Toolkit as well as on direct analysis of the files themselves.

The program developed in Listing 11.3 (presented at the end of this section)
reads a WordPerfect file and prints it on the LaserJet. It is not a substitute for
WordPerfect's own printing capabilities. Rather, it allows you to print draft copies
of a document quickly without having to load WordPerfect. The program uses only
fonts that are already downloaded or resident in the LaserJet. In this manner, the
long delay caused by downloading fonts to the LaserJet is avoided.

Because the objective is to use a minimum of formatting, many of the advanced
document features supported by WordPerfect are simply ignored. Others are entirely implemented using PCL commands. The implementation of these features
and the format of WordPerfect files are the topics we cover in the rest of this section.

WordPerfect File Format

WordPerfect documents are divided into two parts: a header, called the **prefix area**,
and the **document area**. The prefix area contains basic identifying information and
a considerable amount of information about the word-processing environment.
The identifying information is contained in the first 16 bytes of the file. Its layout is
given in `struct prefix` at the start of `process_header()` in Listing 11.3. The
tests in this function show that these bytes mostly serve to confirm that the file is in
WordPerfect format, to test whether it is encrypted, and to identify which version
of WordPerfect created the file. We have limited ourselves to using version 5.1. The
field `text_offset` is of particular importance. It is a *long int* (32-bit signed integer) that gives the offset, in bytes, at which the document area begins. The offset is
measured from the start of the file. In the function `process_body()` we use this
value to `fseek()` to the start of the document area.

The rest of the header area, which often accounts for 2000 bytes, consists of index blocks that point to a wide variety of data packets. These packets contain information about the environment in which the document was created: default printers and printer options, fonts, display attributes, serial/license number, keyboard maps, location of thesaurus and dictionary, and so forth. None of this information is used by us, so it is simply skipped.

WordPerfect Document Area

Using `text_offset`, we jump to the document area, which contains the text of the document liberally interspersed with multibyte function codes. These codes are the primary source of formatting information. They are broken down into four categories depending on their format: single-byte codes, single-byte functions, fixed-length multibyte functions, and variable-length multibyte functions. All four categories will be explored shortly. Text consists of the data between codes. It comprises characters from the ASCII character set with values between 20h (space) and 7Eh (tilde), inclusive. The effects obtained by use of the upper 128 characters in the IBM-PC alphabet, characters that differ widely in their effect depending on printer and character set, must be emulated using the many features of WordPerfect.

Single-byte Codes and Functions   Single-byte codes are codes whose values fall between 01h and 1Fh, inclusive. Bytes in this range are often referred to as **control characters** and are processed in Listing 11.3 by the function `process_-ctl_char()`. Most of these codes are used by WordPerfect as merge codes—where mail-merged files hook into the document. The few codes of importance here are hard and soft carriage returns (0Ah and 0Dh, respectively) and hard and soft page (0Ch and 0Bh). The qualifier *hard* here means that the associated action must occur at the specified location; *soft* means that the location of the action can be changed (or even eliminated) depending on the formatting performed by WordPerfect.

Single-byte functions are codes whose values fall between 80h and BFh, inclusive. They generally consist of one-byte toggle switches that either enable or disable a specific feature. They are also used to print specific characters (such as hyphens) the presence of which may be influenced by a variety of factors. Examples of toggles are 81h and 82h, which respectively turn right justification on and off, and 9Fh and 9Eh, which turn hyphenation on and off.

We perform nothing as ambitious as hyphenation or right justification, but we are interested in codes that identify the location of two specific characters, namely the hyphen and the solitary space. The presence of spaces and hyphens is influenced by context: they are printed as such when they occur in the middle of a line, but when they occur at the end of a line, page, or document, they acquire special characteristics that must be dealt with when a document is reformatted. Not only are there hard and soft hyphens (and spaces) to think of, but deletable spaces, deletable end-of-line, and so forth. For our purposes, all variations are treated as printable: any kind of hyphen or space is printed. Single-byte codes not related to printing these characters are simply ignored.

Fixed-length Multibyte Functions Functions in this category have a leading byte in the range C0h to CFh, inclusive. As of WordPerfect version 5.1, only C0h through C7h have been implemented. These codes are processed in Listing 11.3 by the function `process_fixed_len_func()`. Fixed-length functions have the following format: a 1-byte identifying code in the range stated above, one or more data bytes, and a terminating byte that simply duplicates the leading byte. Hence, these functions have a minimum length of three bytes. Their length is set by WordPerfect and hard-coded into our program.

The most important function in this class is C3h, turn-on attribute (and its complement C4h, turn-off attribute). Attribute here refers to a font attribute. WordPerfect selects fonts on the basis of size and stroke weight. The selection is communicated by the second byte in the C3h function. The values for each range from 0 to 15 and are explained in the body of the function. Mostly, these values change the font size. They are implemented on the LaserJet by the family of PCL commands with the prefix **Esc (s**. These commands allow selection of a font by stroke weight, size, and orientation. When a selection is made, the LaserJet reads through the attributes stored with each built-in or downloaded font and searches for the best match. If no close match is found, no change of font takes place. For example, to change stroke weight the command is

```
Esc ( s # B
```

where **#** ranges from −7 (ultrathin) to 0 (normal) to 7 (ultrablack). To switch a courier font to its bold counterpart, the command is **Esc (s 3 B**; to switch back to normal in courier is **Esc (s 0 B**.

The one unusual attribute is strike-out, which prints a dash across every printed letter. In our implementation this simply sets a global variable, imaginatively called `strike_out`, which will cause a backspace and a hyphen to be printed after every printed character. Consult the function `process_ascii_char()` in Listing 11.3.

The remaining fixed-length functions should be understandable from the comments in the listing.

Variable-length Functions These functions have a leading byte in the range D0h through FFh, inclusive. They all have the following form: a leading identifying byte, a byte to identify the subfunction, a two-byte word giving the length of the data, the data, a copy of the two-byte word stating the length of the data, a copy of the subfunction identification byte, and a copy of the leading identification byte. For example, code D3h, subfunction 01h, establishes the underline mode. Its form is

Number of Bytes	Code	Explanation
1	D3h	Identifying byte (called the set group, it sets variables)
1	01h	Set underline mode subfunction
2	06	Length of the data in bytes
1	?	Old underline value (unused)
1	?	New underline value:
		bit 0: 1 = underline spaces
		bit 1: 1 = underline other white space
2	06	Copy of length of the data in bytes
1	01h	Copy of subfunction byte
1	D3h	Copy of identifying byte

Did you notice that only two bytes of data appeared for the six bytes promised? The missing bytes come from the data-length bytes themselves. In other words, the six data bytes are: two bytes for data length, two individual data bytes, and the repetition of the two bytes for data length. This means that the data length is always four bytes less than the length of the complete function. At the point where you have read the data length, you will have read exactly four bytes (the two ID bytes and the data length); hence if you skip over the number of bytes in the data length you arrive at the first byte after the function. This technique of reading the length and skipping that distance is often employed in Listing 11.3 to ignore unsupported variable-length functions. Note that the data length is stored in Intel byte order with the low-order byte first. Hence it can be read as a regular 16-bit integer. This is frequently performed in the function `process_var_len_func()` by the following code:

```
int i;
...
fread ( &i, 2, 1, fin); /* read 2 bytes into i */
```

All variable-length functions are handled in `process_var_len_func()`. This function makes up the bulk of Listing 11.3. There are literally hundreds of subfunctions and each one must be entered into—some to implement, some to ascertain how far to skip. Each subfunction is explained in the comments along with details of its implementation on the LaserJet.

The only unusual processing comes in handling WordPerfect's units of measure. With few exceptions, the fundamental unit of distance for printing is the **wpu**, which stands for WordPerfect unit. It measures $\frac{1}{1200}$ of an inch. At various junctures, notably when margins need to be calculated, these units must be converted into units suitable for the LaserJet. For horizontal motion, we use columns of $\frac{1}{10}$ of an inch in width; for vertical motion, we use VMI (vertical motion index) units of $\frac{1}{48}$ of an inch. These conversions are included in Listing 11.3. (For more information on VMI, consult Chapter 1.)

In its final form, `wpdoc.c`, the program created by Listing 11.3, reads a WordPerfect document and quickly prints the text with a modicum of formatting. Because the program relies on the monospaced courier fonts (built into the LaserJet), printing frequently extends past the right margin of the page. At present, these lines are simply truncated. This choice means that the document will retain the same pagination and paragraph depth as the final WordPerfect document. If you would like the excess text to wrap around to the next line rather than be truncated, you should use the following PCL command early in the program:

Esc & s # C

where **#** is: **1** = end-of-line wrap disabled (truncation will occur); **0** = end-of-line wrap enabled (no truncation). The LaserJet defaults to end-of-line-wrap disabled (truncation will occur).

LISTING 11.3 Read and Quickly Print WordPerfect Documents

```
/*-------------------------------------------------------------
 * WPDOC.C --- Reads a WordPerfect 5.1 document and prints
 *             it emulating WP formatting but relying only
 *             on built-in or already downloaded fonts.
 *             Usage:
 *
 *                     wpdoc infile [outfile]
 *
 *             If outfile not specified, it defaults to PRN.
 *
 *             This implementation presumes:
 *                 1) LaserJet printer
 *                 2) Portrait orientation
 *                 3) Sheet size: 8.5" x 11"
 *-------------------------------------------------------*/

#include <stdio.h>
#include <stdlib.h>
#include <string.h>

#include "ljmain.h"

FILE *fin, *fout;

/*-------------------------------------------------------
 * Globals which affect formatting
 *-----------------------------------------------------*/
int strike_out;       /* toggle: ON or OFF      */
```

Listing 11.3 continues

Listing 11.3 continued

```c
int line_height;      /* in VMI units of 1/48" */
int top_margin;       /* in VMI units of 1/48" */
int line_spacing;     /* in full lines         */

/*-------------------------------------------------------------
 * Prototypes for functions defined in this program
 *-----------------------------------------------------------*/
int  eat_bytes               ( int );
void left_indent             ( int );
void process_ascii_char      ( int );
void process_body            ( long );
void process_ctl_char        ( int );
void process_fixed_len_func  ( int );
long process_header          ( void );
void process_single_byte_func ( int );
void process_var_len_func    ( int );

/*-------------------------------------------------------------
 * Main line starts here
 *-----------------------------------------------------------*/
main ( int argc, char *argv[] )
{
    long text_offset;                /* offset to WP document text */

    char out_filename [14];

    if ( argc < 2 )
    {
        fputs ( "File to be printed/converted not specified\n", stderr );
        exit ( EXIT_FAILURE );
    }

    if (( fin = fopen ( argv[1], "rb" )) == NULL )
    {
        fprintf ( stderr, "Error! Cannot find/open %s\n", argv[1] );
        exit ( EXIT_FAILURE );
    }

    if (( fout = fopen_laserjet ( argc > 2 ? argv[2] : "PRN" )) == NULL )
    {
        fputs ( "Error opening printer/output file", stderr );
        exit ( EXIT_FAILURE );
    }

    text_offset = process_header();

    line_height  = 8;   /* initialize to 6 lpi        */
    top_margin   = 48;  /* initialize top margin to 1" */
    line_spacing = 1;   /* lines to space at line-feed */

    fputs ( "\033E", fout ); /*Init LaserJet: EscE */

    process_body ( text_offset );

    process_ctl_char ( 0x0C );  /* Final form-feed     */

    return ( EXIT_SUCCESS );
}
```

Listing 11.3   continues

Listing 11.3 continued

```c
long process_header ( void )
{
    struct prefix {        /* WP actually refers to this as a prefix  */
        signed char neg_one;                /* must contain -1         */
        char        wpc [3];                /* must contain "WPC"      */
        long        text_offset;            /* where text starts       */
        char        prod_type;              /* = 1 for WordPerfect     */
        char        file_type;              /* = 0x0A for document     */
        char        maj_version;            /* = 0                     */
        char        min_version;            /* = 1 for WP5.1           */
        short int   encryption;             /* 0 = not encrypted       */
        short int   filler;                 /* reserved                */
    }
        wp_prefix;

    if ( fread ( &wp_prefix, 1, 16, fin ) != 16 )
    {
        fputs ( "Error reading input file\n", stderr );
        exit ( EXIT_FAILURE );
    }

    if (( wp_prefix.neg_one      != -1  ) ||
        ( wp_prefix.wpc[0]       != 'W' ) ||
        ( wp_prefix.wpc[1]       != 'P' ) ||
        ( wp_prefix.wpc[2]       != 'C' ) ||
        ( wp_prefix.maj_version  != 0   ) ||
        ( wp_prefix.min_version  != 1   ))
    {
        fputs ( "Input file is not a WP5.1 document\n", stderr );
        exit ( EXIT_FAILURE );
    }

    if ( wp_prefix.encryption != 0 )
    {
        fputs ( "Input file is encrypted\n", stderr );
        exit ( EXIT_FAILURE );
    }

    fputs ( "Header done. File is unencrypted WP5.1 document\n", stderr );

    return ( wp_prefix.text_offset );
}

void process_body ( long text_offset )
{
    int c, r;

    if ( fseek ( fin, text_offset, SEEK_SET ) != 0 )
    {
        fputs ( "Error finding start of text area\n", stderr );
        exit ( EXIT_FAILURE );
    }

    for (;;)
    {
        if (( c = fgetc ( fin )) == EOF )
```

Listing 11.3 continues

Listing 11.3 continued

```
            break;

        if ( c >= 0x01 && c <= 0x1F )
            process_ctl_char ( c );
        else
        if ( c >= 0x20 && c <= 0x7E )
            process_ascii_char ( c );
        else
        if ( c >= 0x80 && c <= 0xBF )
            process_single_byte_func ( c );
        else
        if ( c >= 0xC0 && c <= 0xCF )
            process_fixed_len_func ( c );
        else
        if ( c >= 0xD0 && c <= 0xFF )
            process_var_len_func ( c );
        else
        {         /* can only be 00 or 0x7F */
            fprintf ( stderr, "Error: Illegal character %x found\n", c );
            exit ( EXIT_FAILURE );
        }
    }
}

void process_ascii_char ( int letter )
{
    fputc ( letter, fout );

    if ( strike_out == YES )
    {
        fputs ( "\033&a-1C", fout );    /* back up 1 letter     */
        fputc ( '-', fout );            /* and strike it out    */
    }
}

void process_ctl_char ( int ctl_char )
{
    int i;

    static int page_no = 1;

    /* Skip merge codes */

    if (( ctl_char >= 0x03 && ctl_char <= 0x07 ) ||
        ( ctl_char >= 0x0E && ctl_char <= 0x16 ))
            return;

    /* Skip "reserved" (i.e., unused) bytes */

    if (( ctl_char == 0x01 || ctl_char == 0x08 || ctl_char == 0x09 ) ||
        ( ctl_char >= 0x17 && ctl_char <= 0x1F ))
            return;

    /* Process carriage returns */

    if ( ctl_char == 0x0A ||        /* Hard return */
         ctl_char == 0x0D )         /* Soft return */
        for ( i = 0; i < line_spacing; i++ )
```

Listing 11.3 continues

Listing 11.3 continued

```
            fprintf ( fout, "%c%c", 0x0D, 0x0A );

    if ( ctl_char == 0x0B ||          /* Soft page    */
         ctl_char == 0x0C )           /* Hard page    */
    {
        fputc ( 0x0C, fout );
        fputc ( '\r', fout ); /* LaserJet does not move printhead back */
                              /* so we must, using a carriage-return.  */
        fprintf ( stderr, "Page %d done\r", page_no );
        page_no += 1;
    }

    if ( ctl_char == 0x02 )           /* Print page # */
        fprintf ( fout, "%d", page_no );
}

void process_single_byte_func ( int code )
{
    switch ( code ) /* most of these have no printable effect  */
    {
        case 0xA9:                /* Hard hyphens                */
        case 0xAA:
        case 0xAB:
        case 0xAD:                /* Soft hyphen at EOL          */
        case 0xAE:                /* Soft hyphen at page end     */
        case 0x94:                /* Invisible return at EOF     */
                fputc ( '-', fout );  break;

        case 0xA0:                /* Hard space                  */
        case 0x93:                /* Invisible return in line    */
                fputc (( strike_out == YES ? '-' : ' '), fout );
                break;

        case 0x8C:                /* Hard Return / Soft Page     */
        case 0x95:                /* Invisible return at pg end  */
                process_ctl_char ( 0x0C );  /* = form-feed       */
                break;

        default:                  /* Ignore all the rest         */
                break;
    }
}

void process_fixed_len_func ( int code )
{
    switch ( code )
    {
        case 0xC0:     /* 4 bytes - print an extended character   */
            fputc ( '*', fout );  /* so, just print an asterisk: */
            eat_bytes ( 3 );      /* boring, but effective       */
            break;

        case 0xC1:     /* Center/Align/Tab/Left margin release    */
        {
            unsigned short int flags, i;

            flags = fgetc ( fin );
```

Listing 11.3   continues

Listing 11.3   continued

```
/*-----------------------------------------------------
 * bits 6 and 7 (counting from 0) in flags:
 *  if = 0, setting is a tab
 *     = 1, setting is an alignmet
 *     = 2, setting is left margin release
 *     = 3, setting is center
 *
 * We will only handle tabs here.
 *-----------------------------------------------------*/

if (( flags & 0x00C4 ) == 0 )  /* If bits 6 & 7 off,  */
{                              /*    it is a tab.     */
    eat_bytes ( 2 );
    fread ( &i, 2, 1, fin );

    /*-------------------------------------------------
     * The following code performs the same calculations
     * that are carefully explained in the function
     * left_indent() which appears near the end of this
     * program. The only difference is that rather than
     * resetting the left margin, we are simply tabbing,
     * that is, moving the cursor. Look to the afore-
     * mentioned routine for explanation of the follow-
     * ing calculations.
     *-------------------------------------------------*/

    i = i / 4;    /* Convert WPU to dots */
    i -= 50;      /* LJII: physical left edge less
                         left edge of logical page. */

    i += 15;      /* To prepare for rounding */
    i /= 30;      /* Column to move to.*/

    /* Finally, we set the cursor in column units */

    fprintf ( fout, "\033&a%dC", i );

    eat_bytes ( 3 );
}
else
    eat_bytes ( 7 );   /* Not a tab, so ignore.      */
}
    break;

case 0xC2:                 /* Left and right indent    */
{                          /* We'll worry only about left */
    int c;
    eat_bytes ( 8 );       /* 9th byte has indent level   */
    fread ( &c, 2, 1, fin );
    left_indent ( c );
    eat_bytes ( 1 );
}
    break;

case 0xC3:    /* Turn on attribute  */
case 0xC4:    /* Turn off attribute */
{
```

Listing 11.3   continues

Listing 11.3 continued

```
int c = fgetc ( fin );
switch ( c )
{
    case 0:         /* extra large */
    case 1:         /* very large  */
    case 2:         /* large       */
        if ( code == 0xC3 )                     /* turn it on   */
            fputs ( "\033(s13V", fout );   /* font >= 13pts */
        else                                    /* turn it off  */
            fputs ( "\033&k0S", fout );    /* std. 10pt font*/
        break;

    case 3:         /* small       */
    case 4:         /* fine        */
    case 5:         /* superscript */
    case 6:         /* subscript   */
        if ( code == 0xC3 )                     /* turn it on   */
            fputs ( "\033&k2S", fout );    /* line-printer */
        else
            fputs ( "\033&k0S", fout );    /* std. 10pt font*/

        if ( c == 5 )  /* superscript */
        {
            if ( code == 0xC3 )  /* turn on superscript   */
                fputs ( "\033*p-25Y", fout ); /* go back up*/
            else
                fputs ( "\033*p+25Y", fout ); /* go down   */
        }

        if ( c == 6 )  /* subscript */
        {
            if ( code == 0xC3 )  /* turn on subscript     */
                fputs ( "\033*p+25Y", fout ); /* go down   */
            else
                fputs ( "\033*p-25Y", fout ); /* go up     */
        }
        break;

    case 8:             /* italic   */
        if ( code == 0xC3 )                     /* turn on italic */
            fputs ( "\033(s1S", fout );
        else
            fputs ( "\033(s0S", fout );    /* back to normal */
        break;

    case 9:             /* shadow   */
        if ( code == 0xC3 )                     /* turn on shadow */
            fputs ( "\033(s128S", fout );
        else
            fputs ( "\033(s0S", fout );    /* back to normal */
        break;

    case 10:            /* redline */
    case 11:            /* double underline */
    case 14:            /* underline */
        if ( code == 0xC3 )                 /* turn on underline */
            fputs ( "\033&d0D", fout );
        else
```

Listing 11.3 continues

Listing 11.3 continued

```
                            fputs ( "\033&d@", fout );     /* underline off */
                        break;

                case 12:            /* bold */
                    if ( code == 0xC3 )             /* select a bold font */
                        fputs ( "\033(s3B", fout );
                    else
                        fputs ( "\033(s0B", fout );  /* select normal  */
                    break;

                case 13:            /* strike out */
                    /* sets a global for use by process_ascii   */
                    strike_out = ( code == 0xC3 ? YES : NO );
                    break;

                default:            /* no other printable actions */
                    break;
            }
            eat_bytes ( 1 );
        }
            break;

    case 0xC5:      /* protect a block -- ignored here */
        eat_bytes ( 4 );
        break;

    case 0xC6:      /* end of indent */
    {
        int c;
        eat_bytes ( 2 );        /* 4th byte has old indent level    */
        fread ( &c, 2, 1, fin );
        left_indent ( c );
        eat_bytes ( 1 );
    }
        break;

    case 0xC7:      /* display when hyphenated-- ignored here */
        eat_bytes ( 6 );
        break;

    default:        /* no other functions currently defined */
        break;
    }
}

void process_var_len_func ( int code )
{
    int c, len;

    switch ( code )
    {
    case 0xFE:      /* unknown (per WP documentation) function */
    {
        int i;

        eat_bytes ( 1 );
        fread ( &i, 2, 1, fin );
        fseek ( fin, (long) i, SEEK_CUR );
```

Listing 11.3 continues

Listing 11.3 continued

```
    }
        return;

    case 0xD0:        /* Page format group                        */
    {
        int i;
        switch ( c = fgetc ( fin ))
        {
        case 0x00:  /* line height */

            /*-----------------------------------------
             * WP specifies line height in WP units of
             * 1/1200". These are converted to LaserJet
             * VMI units of 1/48" (divide by 25). If WP
             * line height is 0, use default, which we
             * arbitraily set at 6 lpi (= 8 VMI units).
             *-----------------------------------------*/

            eat_bytes ( 4 );
            fread ( &i, 2, 1, fin ); /* get the height */
            if ( i > 0 )
                line_height = i / 25;
            else
                line_height = 8;

            fprintf ( fout, "\033&l%dC", line_height);
            eat_bytes ( 4 );
            break;

        case 0x01:  /* left-right margin set. We only use left*/
            eat_bytes ( 6 );
            fread ( &i, 2, 1, fin ); /* i = left margin in    */
            left_indent ( i );
            eat_bytes ( 6 );
            break;

        case 0x02: /* set spacing -- lines per LF      */
            eat_bytes ( 4 );            /* skip over      */
            fread ( &i, 2, 1, fin ); /* line spacing */

            /* Line spacing integer:
                high-order byte = full lines
                low-order byte  = line / 256
            We'll only worry about full lines.  */

            line_spacing = ( i > 8 );

            eat_bytes ( 4 );
            break;

        case 0x03: /* set hyphenation zone -- ignore*/
            eat_bytes ( 10 );
            break;

        case 0x04: /* tab stops -- ignore */
            eat_bytes ( 212 );
            break;
```

Listing 11.3   continues

Listing 11.3 continued

```
            case 0x05: /* top and bottom margins */
            {
                int i, lines;

                eat_bytes ( 6 );
                fread ( &i, 2, 1, fin ); /* i = top margin in WPU */
                top_margin = i /= 25;    /* change to VMI units   */
                i /= line_height;        /* convert to lines       */
                fprintf ( fout, "\033&l%dE", i ); /* set top marg.*/

                fread ( &i, 2, 1, fin ); /* i = bottom margin     */
                i /= 25;                 /* change to VMI units   */
                /* lines in form = page - top - bottom */
                lines =
                (( 11 * 48 ) - top_margin - i ) / line_height;
                fprintf ( fout, "\033&l%dF", lines );
            }
                eat_bytes ( 4 );
                break;

            case 0x06:  /* justification -- ignore      */
                eat_bytes ( 8 );
                break;

            case 0x07:  /* header-footer printing -- ignore */
                eat_bytes ( 8 );
                break;

            case 0x08:  /* page number position -- ignore */
                eat_bytes ( 12 );
                break;

            case 0x0B:  /* form description -- ignore    */
                eat_bytes ( 250 );
                break;

            default:
                fprintf ( stderr,
                    "Error bad group %X in 0xD0 function\n", c );
                break;
            }
            return;
        }
        case 0xD1:      /* Font group -- implemented only to know*/
        {               /*               how many bytes to skip  */
            int c;

            switch ( c = fgetc ( fin ))
            {
            case 0x00:      /* font color -- ignore      */
                    eat_bytes ( 12 );
                    break;

            case 0x01:      /* switch WP fonts -- ignore */
                    eat_bytes ( 37 );
                    break;

            case 0x02:      /* font color (again!) -- ignore */
```

Listing 11.3 continues

Listing 11.3   continued

```
                eat_bytes ( 8 );
                break;

        case 0x03:      /* font pattern -- ignore    */
                eat_bytes ( 12 );
                break;

        default:
                fprintf ( stderr,
                    "Error: bad group %x in 0xD1 function", c );
                break;
        }
        return;
}
case 0xD2:  /* Definition Group -- All ignored.          */
{           /* Implemented here to know how many bytes to skip */

        int c, i;

        switch ( c = fgetc ( fin ))
        {
        case 0x00:  /* define math columns          */
            eat_bytes ( 214 );
            break;

        case 0x01:  /* define print columns         */
            eat_bytes ( 200 );
            break;

        case 0x02:  /* paragraph number definition  */
            eat_bytes ( 142 );
            break;

        case 0x03:  /* footnote options             */
        case 0x04:  /* end note options             */
            eat_bytes ( 162 );
            break;

        case 0x05:  /* graph box for figures        */
        case 0x06:  /* graph box for tables         */
        case 0x07:  /* graph box for text boxes     */
        case 0x08:  /* graph box for user-defined boxes */
        case 0x09:  /* graph box for equations      */
            eat_bytes ( 130 );
            break;

        case 0x0B:  /* define tables                */
        case 0x0D:  /* define link start            */
        case 0x0E:  /* define link end              */
            fread ( &i, 2, 1, fin ); /* length to skip  */
            eat_bytes ( i + 2 );
            break;

        case 0x11:  /* Border options */
                eat_bytes ( 59 );
                break;
        default:
                fprintf ( stderr,
```

Listing 11.3   continues

Listing 11.3   continued

```
                        "Error: bad group %x in 0xD2 function", c );
                   break;
        }
        return;
}
case 0xD3:   /* Set Group -- All of these can be ignored.*/
{
        /*-----------------------------------------------------
         * Implemented here to know how many bytes to skip.
         * Since these are all fixed length, the bytes to skip
         * are determined from a look-up table. A value of
         * 0 in the table means an unsupported function.
         *-----------------------------------------------------*/

        int c, i;

        static int skip [] = {
             14,   /* 0x00:  set alignment character  */
              8,   /* 0x01:  set underline mode       */
             10,   /* 0x02:  set footnote number      */
             10,   /* 0x03:  set endnote number       */
             12,   /* 0x04:  set page number          */
             16,   /* 0x05:  set line numbering       */
             11,   /* 0x06:  advance to page position */
              9,   /* 0x07:  force odd/even page      */
              8,   /* 0x08:  character at baseline    */
              0,   /* 0x09:  unsupported function!    */
             14,   /* 0x0A:  character/space width    */
             14,   /* 0x0B:  space expansion          */
             10,   /* 0x0C:  graph box # for figures  */
             10,   /* 0x0D:  graph box # for tables   */
             10,   /* 0x0E:  graph box # for text box */
             10,   /* 0x0F:  graph box # for user box */
             10,   /* 0x10:  graph box # for equation */
             10,   /* 0x11:  set language             */
             66    /* 0x12:  page number style        */
        };

        c = fgetc ( fin );

        if ( c < 0 || c > 0x12 || skip[c] == 0 )
            fprintf ( stderr,
                    "Error: bad group %x in 0xD3 function", c );
        else
            eat_bytes ( skip[c] );
}
        return;
case 0xD4:   /* Format Group -- Most of these can be ignored.   */
{            /* Implemented here to know how many bytes to skip */

        int c, i;

        switch ( c = fgetc ( fin ))
        {
        case 0x00:   /* end of page specs. */
                   fread ( &i, 2, 1, fin ); /* get length word */
                   eat_bytes ( i );
                   break;
```

Listing 11.3   continues

Listing 11.3 continued

```
                case 0x01:  /* end of line specs */
                        fread ( &i, 2, 1, fin ); /* get length word */
                        eat_bytes ( i );
                        break;

                case 0x02:  /* graph box specs */
                        fread ( &i, 2, 1, fin ); /* get length word */
                        eat_bytes ( i );
                        break;

                case 0x03:  /* repositioning marker */
                        eat_bytes ( 8 );
                        break;

                case 0x04:  /* hidden text in table cells */
                        fread ( &i, 2, 1, fin ); /* get length word */
                        eat_bytes ( i );
                        break;

                case 0x05:  /* decimal justification specs */
                        eat_bytes ( 10 );
                        break;

                default:
                        fprintf ( stderr,
                            "Error: bad group %x in 0xD4 function", c );
                        break;
                }
        }
        return;
case 0xD5:  /* Header /Footer Group. Ignored here.       */
case 0xD6:  /* Footnote/Endnote Group. Ignored here.     */
case 0xD7:  /* Generate Group. Ignored here.             */
{
    int i;

    fgetc ( fin );              /* All options ignored.     */
    fread ( &i, 2, 1, fin ); /* i = length to skip.         */
    eat_bytes ( i );            /* Do it.                   */
}
        return;

case 0xD8:  /* Display group. All but date item ignored.*/
{
    int i, c;
    c = fgetc ( fin );

    if ( c == 0x00 )
        fputs ( "[Date here]", fout );

    fread ( &i, 2, 1, fin ); /* i = length to skip.         */
    eat_bytes ( i );            /* Do it.                   */
}
        return;

case 0xD9:  /* Miscellaneous group.                      */
{               /* All but printer commands ignored.     */
    int i, c;
```

Listing 11.3 continues

Listing 11.3 continued

```
c = fgetc ( fin );
fread ( &i, 2, 1, fin ); /* i = length to skip.      */

switch ( c )
{
case 0x00:  /* printer command string */
    if (( fgetc ( fin )) == 0x00 ) /*it's a command */
    {
        int j;
        for ( j = 0; j < i - 3; j++ )
            fputc ( fgetc ( fin ), fout );
        eat_bytes ( 3 );
    }
    else                            /* it's a filename */
    {
        FILE *fspecs;
        char filename [127];
        int j;

        /* copy the filename / open the file */

        memset ( filename, '\0', 127 );
        for ( j = 0; j < i -  3; j++ )
            filename[j] = fgetc ( fin );
        fspecs = fopen ( filename, "rb" );

        /* copy the file right out */

        if ( fspecs != NULL )
            while (( c = fgetc ( fspecs )) != EOF )
                fputc ( c, fout );

        fclose ( fspecs );
        eat_bytes ( 3 );
    }
    break;

case 0x01:  /* conditional end of page     */
    eat_bytes ( 7 );
    break;

case 0x02:  /* comment records            */
    fread ( &i, 2, 1, fin ); /* i = length */
    eat_bytes ( i );
    break;

case 0x03:  /* kerning                    */
    eat_bytes ( 8 );
    break;

case 0x04:  /* turn outline on            */
    eat_bytes ( 22 );
    break;

case 0x05:  /* leading adjustment         */
    eat_bytes ( 14 );
    break;
```

Listing 11.3 continues

Listing 11.3   continued

```
            case 0x06:  /* more kerning               */
                eat_bytes ( 8 );
                break;

            case 0x07:  /* even more kerning           */
                fread ( &i, 2, 1, fin ); /* i = length  */
                eat_bytes ( i );
                break;
        }
    }
        return;

    case 0xDA:  /* Box group. Ignored here.           */
    {
        int i;

        switch ( fgetc ( fin ))
        {
        case 0x00:     /* Figure definition            */
        case 0x01:     /* Table definition             */
        case 0x02:     /* Text box                     */
        case 0x03:     /* User-defined box             */
        case 0x04:     /* Equation definition          */
                fread ( &i, 2, 1, fin ); /* i = length */
                eat_bytes ( i );
                break;

        case 0x05:     /* Horizontal line              */
        case 0x06:     /* Vertical line                */
                eat_bytes ( 123 );
                break;
        }
    }
        return;

    case 0xDB:  /* Style group. Ignored here.         */
    {
        int i;

        switch ( fgetc ( fin ))
        {
        case 0x00:     /* Begin style on               */
        case 0x01:     /* End style on                 */
        case 0x02:     /* Global (open) style on       */
                fread ( &i, 2, 1, fin ); /* i = length */
                eat_bytes ( i );
                break;

        case 0x03:     /* Style Off                    */
                eat_bytes ( 7 );
                break;
        }
    }
        return;

    case 0xDC:  /* Table end-of-line group. Ignored here.   */
    {
```

Listing 11.3   continues

Listing 11.3 continued

```
            int i;

            fgetc ( fin );  /* All options ignored      */
            fread ( &i, 2, 1, fin );  /* i = length      */
            eat_bytes ( i );
        }
            return;

        case 0xDD:  /* Table end-of-page group. Ignored here.   */
        {
            int i;

            fgetc ( fin );  /* All options ignored      */
            fread ( &i, 2, 1, fin );  /* i = length      */
            eat_bytes ( i );
        }
            return;

        case 0xDE:  /* Merge codes command group. Ignored here. */
            eat_bytes ( 6 );
            return;

        case 0xDF:  /* Nested functions group. Ignored here.    */
        {
            int i;

            fgetc ( fin );               /* All options ignored    */
            fread ( &i, 2, 1, fin ); /* i = length               */
            eat_bytes ( i );
        }
            return;
    }
}

void left_indent ( int wpu )          /* indent left margin */
{

    int i;

    /*-------------------------------------------------------
     * We are converting WPU units of 1/1200" to dots.
     * Each dot (1/300") = 4 WPU.
     *-------------------------------------------------------*/

    i = wpu / 4;

    /*-------------------------------------------------------
     * We deduct the distance between the left edge of the
     * physical page and the left edge of the logical page.
     * This distance varies by model. We set it up for the
     * LaserJet II. Modify as needed.
     *
     *      LaserJet II        50 dots
     *      LaserJet IIP       75 dots
     *      LaserJet III       75 dots
     *
     *-------------------------------------------------------*/
```

Listing 11.3   continues

Listing 11.3 continued

```
    i -= 50;

    /*------------------------------------------------------
     * Convert dots to columns. Columns at 10 cpi are 30 dots
     * wide. Since we are using integers, rounding is done by
     * truncation. To compensate, we add a half-column (15 dots)
     * before the division.
     *----------------------------------------------------*/

    i += 15;
    i /= 30;

    /* Finally, we set the margin in column units */

    fprintf ( fout, "\033&a%dL", i );
}

int eat_bytes ( int munch_count )   /* gobble up bytes that aren't used */
{
    int i;

    for ( i = 0; i < munch_count; i++ )
        fgetc ( fin );

    return ( munch_count );
}
```

Appendix A

PCL 5 Escape Codes and Sequences (Alphabetical)

This appendix contains a complete list of PCL escape sequences and codes. It is divided into two parts: two-byte escape codes, and escape sequences (which always exceed two bytes). The leading `Esc` character is not presented here since it precedes every one of the listed codes and sequences. Within each section the listing is in alphabetical order. This permits the reader to quickly look up a sequence or code. For a listing sorted by function, use the manuals that come with the LaserJet printer. If an escape sequence is followed by a small letter in parentheses, this indicates that the sequence can be part of a combined command, in which case the escape sequence ends with the parenthesized letter.

Two-Byte Escape Codes

=	Half-line Feed
9	Clear Horizontal Margins
E	Reset LaserJet
Y	Display Functions On
Z	Display Functions Off

Escape Sequences

(

(#X	(x)	Select Font # as Primary Font
(0D	(d)	Primary Symbol Set: ISO 60, Norwegian 1

(0F	(f)	Primary Symbol Set: ISO 25, French (obsolete)
(0G	(g)	Primary Symbol Set: HP German (obsolete)
(0I	(i)	Primary Symbol Set: ISO 15, Italian
(0K	(k)	Primary Symbol Set: JIS ASCII (obsolete)
(0N	(n)	Primary Symbol Set: ECMA-94 Latin 1
(0S	(s)	Primary Symbol Set: ISO 11, Swedish
(0U	(u)	Primary Symbol Set: ISO 6, ASCII
(10U	(u)	Primary Symbol Set: PC-8
(11U	(u)	Primary Symbol Set: PC-8 D/N
(12U	(u)	Primary Symbol Set: PC850
(1D	(d)	Primary Symbol Set: ISO 61, Norwegian 2 (obsolete)
(1E	(e)	Primary Symbol Set: ISO 4, United Kingdom
(1F	(f)	Primary Symbol Set: ISO 69, French
(1G	(g)	Primary Symbol Set: ISO 21, German
(1S	(s)	Primary Symbol Set: HP Spanish (obsolete)
(2K	(k)	Primary Symbol Set: ISO 57, Chinese (obsolete)
(2S	(s)	Primary Symbol Set: ISO 17, Spanish
(2U	(u)	Primary Symbol Set: ISO 2, IRV (obsolete)
(3@		Font Default: Primary Font
(3S	(s)	Primary Symbol Set: ISO 10, Swedish (obsolete)
(4S	(s)	Primary Symbol Set: ISO 16, Portuguese (obsolete)
(5S	(s)	Primary Symbol Set: ISO 84, Portuguese (obsolete)
(6S	(s)	Primary Symbol Set: ISO 85, Spanish (obsolete)
(8U	(u)	Primary Symbol Set: Roman-8
(s-1B		Primary Font Stroke Weight: Semi Light
(s-2B		Primary Font Stroke Weight: Demi Light
(s-3B		Primary Font Stroke Weight: Light
(s-4B		Primary Font Stroke Weight: Extra Light
(s-5B		Primary Font Stroke Weight: Thin
(s-6B		Primary Font Stroke Weight: Extra Thin
(s-7B		Primary Font Stroke Weight: Ultra Thin
(s#H	(h)	Primary Pitch (# = characters/inch)
(s#V	(v)	Primary Height of Font (# = height in points)
(s#W[Data]		Soft Font Creation: Download Character (# = bytes to download)
(s0B		Primary Font Stroke Weight: Medium (normal)

(s0P	(p)	Primary Spacing: Fixed
(s0S	(s)	Primary Font Style: Upright
(s0T	(t)	Primary Typeface: Line Printer
(s1B		Primary Font Stroke Weight: Semi Bold
(s1P	(p)	Primary Spacing: Proportional
(s1S	(s)	Primary Font Style: Italic
(s2B		Primary Font Stroke Weight: Demi Bold
(s3B		Primary Font Stroke Weight: Bold
(s3T	(t)	Primary Typeface: Courier
(s4101T	(t)	Primary Typeface: CG Times
(s4148T	(t)	Primary Typeface: Univers
(s4B		Primary Font Stroke Weight: Extra Bold
(s5B		Primary Font Stroke Weight: Black
(s6B		Primary Font Stroke Weight: Extra Black
(s7B		Primary Font Stroke Weight: Ultra Black

)		

)#X	(x)	Select Font # as Secondary Font
)3@		Font Default: Secondary Font
)s#W[Data]		Soft Font Creation: Font Header/Descriptor (# = number of bytes)

*		

*b#W[Data]		Send Raster Data (# = number of bytes to follow)
*b#Y	(y)	Raster Vertical Offset (# = lines of vertical movement)
*b0M	(m)	Set Raster Compression Mode: Uncoded
*b1M	(m)	Set Raster Compression Mode: Run-Length Encoded
*b2M	(m)	Set Raster Compression Mode: TIFF
*b3M	(m)	Set Raster Compression Mode: Delta Row
*c#A	(a)	Rectangle Width (# = number of dots)
*c#B	(b)	Rectangle Height (# = number of dots)
*c#D	(d)	Assign Font ID #
*c#E	(e)	Soft Font Creation: Character Code (# = code in decimal)

`*c#G`	(g)	Select Shading % or Pattern to Fill Area.
		If shading has previously been selected, # = %.
		Values rounded to: 2, 10, 15, 30, 45, 70, 90, 100% shading.
		If cross-hatch has previously been selected, # can equal:

                1   Horizontal Lines
                2   Vertical Lines
                3   Diagonal Lines (lower left to upper right)
                4   Diagonal Lines (upper left to lower right)
                5   Square Grid
                6   Diagonal Grid

`*c#H`	(h)	Rectangle Width (# = number of decipoints)
`*c#K`		HP-GL/2 Horizontal Plot Size (# = inches)
`*c#L`		HP-GL/2 Vertical Plot Size (# = inches)
`*c#V`	(v)	Rectangle Height (# = number of decipoints)
`*c#X`		HP-GL/2 Picture Frame Horiz. Size (# = decipoints)
`*c#Y`		HP-GL/2 Picture Frame Vert. Size (# = decipoints)
`*c0F`	(f)	Delete All Fonts
`*c0P`		Fill Rectangular Area: Solid Black
`*c0T`		HP-GL/2 Set Anchor Point to CAP
`*c1F`	(f)	Delete All Temporary Fonts
`*c1P`		Fill Rectangular Area: Solid White (same as Erase)
`*c2F`	(f)	Delete Last Font ID Specified
`*c2P`		Fill Rectangular Area: Shaded Fill
`*c3F`	(f)	Delete Last Character Specified
`*c3P`		Fill Rectangular Area: Cross-Hatch Fill
`*c4F`	(f)	Make Font Temporary
`*c4P`		Fill Rectangular Area: User-Defined
`*c5F`	(f)	Make Font Permanent
`*c5P`		Fill Rectangular Area: Current Pattern
`*c6F`	(f)	Copy/Assign the Currently Invoked Font as Temporary
`*p#X`	(x)	Horizontal Position (# = dots)
`*p#Y`	(y)	Vertical Position (# = dots)
`*r#S`	(s)	Raster Width (# = pixels at specified resolution)
`*r#T`	(t)	Raster Height (# = raster rows)
`*r0A`	(a)	Start Raster Graphics at Left Raster Margin
`*r0F`	(f)	Rotate Raster Image
`*r1A`	(a)	Start Raster Graphics at Current Cursor Position
`*r3F`	(f)	LaserJet Landscape Compatible Raster Presentation

*rB	(b)	End Raster Graphics
*t#R	(r)	Raster Resolution (# = 75, 100, 150, or 300 dots/inch)
*v0N		Source Transparency Mode: Transparent
*v0O		Pattern Transparency Mode: Transparent
*v0T		Select Pattern: Solid Black (default)
*v1N		Source Transparency Mode: Opaque
*v1O		Pattern Transparency Mode: Opaque
*v1T		Select Pattern: Solid White
*v2T		Select Pattern: HP-Defined Shading Pattern
*v3T		Select Pattern: HP-Defined Cross-Hatch Pattern

%

%0A		Enter PCL Mode Using Previous PCL Cursor Position
%0B		Enter HP-GL/2 Using Previous HP-GL/2 Pen Position
%1A		Enter PCL Mode Using Current HP-GL Pen Position
%1B		Enter HP-GL/2 Using Current PCL CAP

&

&a#C	(c)	Horizontal Position (# = columns)
&a#H	(h)	Horizontal Position (# = decipoints)
&a#L	(l)	Left Margin (# = number of columns)
&a#M	(m)	Right Margin (# = number of columns)
&a#P		Degrees of Rotation (# = 90° increments)
&a#R	(r)	Vertical Position (# = rows)
&a#V	(v)	Vertical Position (# = decipoints)
&d@		Disable Underline
&d0D	(d)	Enable Fixed Underline
&d3D	(d)	Enable Floating Underline
&f#Y	(y)	Macro ID (# = ID)
&f0S	(s)	Push Position
&f0X	(x)	Start Macro Definition
&f10X	(x)	Make Macro Permanent
&f1S	(s)	Pop Position
&f1X	(x)	Stop Macro Definition

`&f2X`	`(x)`	Execute Macro
`&f3X`	`(x)`	Call Macro
`&f4X`	`(x)`	Enable Overlay
`&f5X`	`(x)`	Disable Overlay
`&f6X`	`(x)`	Delete Macros
`&f7X`	`(x)`	Delete Temporary Macros
`&f8X`	`(x)`	Delete Macro ID
`&f9X`	`(x)`	Make Macro Temporary
`&k#H`	`(h)`	Horizontal Motion Index (HMI), (# = $\frac{1}{120}$")
`&k0G`	`(g)`	Line Termination: CR=CR, LF=LF, FF=FF
`&k0S`	`(s)`	Set Pitch to 10 cpi
`&k1G`	`(g)`	Line Termination: CR=CR+LF, LF=LF, FF=FF
`&k2G`	`(g)`	Line Termination: CR=CR, LF=CR+LF, FF=CR+FF
`&k2S`	`(s)`	Set Pitch to 16.5-16.7 cpi (compressed)
`&k3G`	`(g)`	Line Termination: CR=CR+LF, LF=CR+LF, FF=CR+FF
`&k4S`	`(s)`	Set Pitch to 12 cpi (elite)
`&l#C`	`(c)`	Vertical Motion Index (VMI), (# = $\frac{1}{48}$")
`&l#D`	`(d)`	Lines per Inch (# = 1, 2, 4, 6, 8, 12, 16, 24, 48)
`&l#E`	`(e)`	Top Margin (# = number of lines)
`&l#F`	`(f)`	Text Length (# = number of lines)
`&l#P`	`(p)`	Page Length (# = number of lines)
`&l#U`	`(u)`	Long-Edge (Left) Registration (# = decipoints)
`&l#X`	`(x)`	Number of Copies (# = 1–99)
`&l#Z`	`(z)`	Short-Edge (Top) Registration (# = decipoints)
`&l0H`	`(h)`	Eject Page
`&l0L`	`(l)`	Disable Perforation Skip
`&l0O`	`(o)`	Portrait Orientation
`&l0S`		Print in Simplex Mode
`&l1A`	`(a)`	Executive Paper Size
`&l1H`	`(h)`	Paper Tray Auto Feed
`&l1L`	`(l)`	Enable Perforation Skip
`&l1O`	`(o)`	Landscape Orientation
`&l1S`		Print in Duplex Mode, Long-Edge Binding
`&l26A`	`(a)`	A4 Paper Size
`&l2A`	`(a)`	Letter Paper Size
`&l2H`	`(h)`	Manual Feed

&12O	(o)	Reverse Portrait
&12S		Print in Duplex Mode, Short-Edge Binding
&13A	(a)	Legal Paper Size
&13H	(h)	Manual Envelope Feed
&13O	(o)	Reverse Landscape
&180A	(a)	Monarch Envelope Size
&181A	(a)	COM 10 Envelope Size
&190A	(a)	DL Envelope Size
&191A	(a)	C5 Envelope Size
&p#X[Data]		Transparent Print Data (# = number of bytes)
&s0C	(c)	End-of-Line Wrap Enabled
&s1C	(c)	End-of-Line Wrap Disabled

Appendix B
Header Files

The programs that have been presented in the foregoing chapters have relied on two header files, which are presented in this appendix. The first file, ljmain.h, is used by many of the programs and simply contains manifest constants that are convenient when working with LaserJet printers. It also makes a good attempt to test the compiler in use in order to ascertain whether compilation is occurring in an MS-DOS environment. Since almost all popular C compilers under MS-DOS use some distinguishing manifest constant, we assume that if confirmation of MS-DOS is not found, then compilation is taking place under UNIX.

```
/*--------------------- LJMAIN.H -----------------------
 *        Manifest constants used in LaserJet work
 *        Version 1.4
 *-------------------------------------------------*/
#ifndef LJMAIN                       /* Only #include this once */
#define LJMAIN        1


#ifndef MSDOS                        /* Microsoft #defines this.*/
#if ( __MSDOS__ )                    /* Turbo C and TopSpeed C. */
#define MSDOS         1
#endif                               /* Zortech and MetaWare do */
#endif                               /*  not #define for MS-DOS */

#if MSDOS
#include <dos.h>
#undef UNIX

#else
#define UNIX 1
#endif

#pragma pack(1)                      /* Byte-alignment of fields */

#define ESC           0x1B
#define FormFeed      0x0C
```

```
#define ON            1
#define OFF           0

#define YES           1
#define NO            0

/* Units of Measure         */
#define POINTS        1
#define DECIPOINTS    2
#define COLUMNS       4
#define ROWS          8

/* Edges                    */
#define TOP           'T'
#define BOTTOM        'B'
#define LEFT          'L'
#define RIGHT         'R'

/* Directions               */
#define HORIZ         'H'
#define VERT          'V'

#endif
/*--------------- End of File LJMAIN.H ------------------*/
```

The work on LaserJet soft fonts as presented in Chapters 4–7 of this book relies heavily on a number of complex structures, unusual values, and manifest constants. Since all programming of soft fonts requires these items, they have been gathered together in the header file ljfont.h:

```
/*--------------------- LJFONT.H  ------------------------
 *         Header file for HP Soft Fonts
 *         version 1.1
 *----------------------------------------------------------*/

#ifndef LJFONT                    /* Only #include this once */
#define LJFONT    1

/* these define structures within an HP font file */

typedef struct _font_desc                /* font descriptor */
{
    unsigned short fd_size;              /* descriptor size */
    unsigned char  fd_fmt;            /* descriptor format */
    unsigned char  font_type;                /* font type */
    unsigned char  style_msb;          /* style word msb */
             char  resv_1;                    /* reserved */
    unsigned short bl_dist;        /* baseline distance */
    unsigned short cell_wid;              /* cell width */
    unsigned short cell_hgt;             /* cell height */
    unsigned char  orient;          /* 0=por, 1=land */
    unsigned char  spacing;       /* 0=fixed, 1=propnl */
    unsigned short sym_set;              /* symbol set */
    unsigned short pitch;                    /* pitch */
    unsigned short height;                  /* height */
```

```
        unsigned short  xheight;                        /* x height */
                 char   wid_typ;                         /* width type */
        unsigned char   style_lsb;               /* style word lsb */
                 char   stk_wgt;                         /* stroke weight */
        unsigned char   typeface;                       /* typeface */
        unsigned char   vendor;                  /* vendor-version */
        unsigned char   serif;                         /* serif style */
        unsigned char   quality;                        /* quality */
                 char   placement;                      /* placement */
                 char   ul_dist;                 /* underline dist */
        unsigned char   ul_hgt;                  /* underline height */
        unsigned short  txt_hgt;                        /* text height */
        unsigned short  txt_wid;                        /* text width */
        unsigned short  min_ch;                  /* 1st ADE in font */
        unsigned short  max_ch;                  /* last ADE in font */
        unsigned char   pitch_ext;                /* pitch extended */
        unsigned char   height_ext;               /* height extended */
        unsigned short  cap_hgt;                  /* cap letter hgt */
        unsigned long   font_id;                  /* font ID code  */
                 char   font_name[16];                  /* font name */
        /*      vendor-dependent data follows...   (optional)     */
}
font_desc;

typedef struct _char_desc          /* character descriptor */
{
        unsigned char   format;                          /* LJII=4 */
                 char   continued;               /* 0=cd, 1=data */
        unsigned char   cd_size;                  /* des+data size */
        unsigned char   cd_class;                        /* LJII=1 */
        unsigned char   orient;                  /* 0=por, 1=land */
                 char   resv_1;                          /* reserved */
                 short  left_ofs;                        /* left offset */
                 short  top_ofs;                         /* top offset */
        unsigned short  char_wid;                 /* char wid in dots */
        unsigned short  char_hgt;                 /* char hgt in dots */
                 short  delta_x;                  /* cur pos change */
        /*      character bitmap data follows...   (required)     */
}
char_desc;

/*------------------------------------------------------------*/

/* these define structures used within the book's code */

typedef int width_tbl[256];        /* array of char widths */

typedef struct _font_hdr           /* font file data structure */
{
        char       name[18];                    /* name of font */
        short      family;                      /* typeface family */
        short      orient;               /* portrait or landscape */
        short      spacing;              /* proportional or fixed */
        short      posture;                     /* upright or italic */
        short      weight;               /* light, med, bold, etc */
        short      pitch;                        /* default pitch */
        short      height;                      /* default leading */
        short      bldist;               /* cell top to baseline */
        width_tbl  wtbl;                 /* array of char widths */
}
```

```c
font_hdr;

typedef struct _string_metric       /* string measurements */
{
        double  width;                      /* full width, inches */
        double  height;                     /* max height, inches */
        double  nb_width;               /* width excluding blanks */
        double  ascent;                          /* max ascent */
        double  descent;                        /* max descent */
}
string_metric;

/*-----------------------------------------------------*/

/* macros... */

/* reverse the two bytes in a word */
#define REV_WRD(w)    ( ((w >> 8) & 255) | (w << 8) )

/* a two-character, non-parameterized seq begins with... */
#define IS_SMPL_SEQ(c)  (((c >= 48) && (c <= 126)) ? 1 : 0)

/* a parameterized escape seq begins with... */
#define IS_PARM_SEQ(c)  (((c >= 33) && (c <= 47)) ? 1 : 0)

/* a parameter character is from this range... */
#define IS_PARM_CHR(c)  (((c >= 96) && (c <= 126)) ? 1 : 0)

/* termination character (end-of-sequence) */
#define IS_TERM_CHR(c)  (((c >= 64) && (c <= 94)) ? 1 : 0)

/*-----------------------------------------------------*/

/* constants... */
/* escape sequence identifiers */
#define  eUNKNOWN      0                      /* anything else */
#define  eFONTDESC     1            /* define font descriptor */
#define  eCHARDESC     2            /* define char descriptor */
#define  eCHARCODE     3                    /* specify char ADE */

/* units */
#define  uDPI        300                    /* dots per inch */
#define  uQDPI      1200             /* quarter-dots per inch */

/* spacing */
#define  sFIXED        0                     /* fixed width */
#define  sPROPORTIONAL 1              /* proportional width */

/* orientation */
#define  oPORTRAIT     0             /* portrait orientation */
#define  oLANDSCAPE    1            /* landscape orientation */

/* font formats */
#define  fBITMAP       0                   /* bitmapped font */
#define  fSCALABLE    10                    /* outlined font */

#endif
/*--------------- End of File LJFONT.H ---------------*/
```

Other header files can be profitably constructed so that reliance on complex escape codes and unintuitive values can be minimized. This is especially true if LaserJet work consists primarily of one kind of application. For example, a header file for graphics work is not uncommon. The two files presented here were the only ones used sufficiently in this work to warrant formal codification. Extending them for new applications is greatly encouraged.

Appendix C

Compatibility Parameters

This appendix presents a list of parameters that vary by LaserJet model. These parameters should be consulted any time programs must be able to generate identical output across various models of the LaserJet printer. This list is not comprehensive; rather, it presents the items most likely to affect the portability of PCL commands.

Raster Compression

Only available on models IIP, III, and IIID (and presumably models thereafter).

Internal Units of Measure

LaserJet, LaserJet+, LaserJet series II	$\frac{1}{3600}$"
LaserJet 2000, IIP, IID, III, IIID	$\frac{1}{7200}$"

Margins

Unprintable Areas:

LaserJet, LaserJet+, Series II,	Left:	50 dots
	Right:	100 dots
	Top/Bottom:	60 dots

LaserJet 2000, IID, IIP, III, IIID	Left:	50 dots
	Right:	50 dots
	Top/Bottom:	50 dots

Logical Page:

LaserJet, LaserJet+, Series II	Left:	50 dots
	Right:	100 dots
LaserJet 2000, IID, IIP, III, IIID	Left:	75 dots
	Right:	75 dots

First Line Location

Top Margin +

LaserJet, LaserJet+, Series II	72/100 VMI
LaserJet 2000, IID, IIP, III, IIID	75/100 VMI

Page-Size Command: Esc &l#A

Not available on LaserJet or LaserJet+.

Appendix D

Function Cross-Reference

The following Appendix lists all functions presented in this book. The first number after the function name is the listing number in which the function is first defined. The second number is the page on which the actual definition begins. Some functions occur more than once; this is indicated by several page number references. In many cases, the functions present identical or nearly identical code. In such cases, only the first few occurrences are listed. An example of such a function is `set_binary_mode`, which appears in almost every program in chapters 4 through 7. It is only listed a few times in the index, thus indicating to the reader the common use of the function without suggesting multiple look-ups of the same code.

Function	Listing	Page
addRule	10.2	298
alloc_bitmap	7.11	223
apply_pat	7.5	206
assert_error	6.2	146
bezier	10.4	311
_bezier	10.4	311
bitmap_and	7.10	217
bitmap_clr	7.10	217
bitmap_or	7.10	216
blacken	10.1	291
bline	10.2	298
bold_chr	7.3	199
call_macro	3.2	75

Appendix E

Reviews

This appendix discusses some of the many third-party tools available to users of the LaserJet series of printers. This list is by no means comprehensive; rather, it is a list of tools the authors have used, along with perceptions about their use.

This appendix is divided into two parts. The first covers items other than the high-resolution hardware and software from LaserMaster Corp.; the second part deals exclusively with LaserMaster's products, along with detailed code relating to their use. This emphasis on one company's product is not a recommendation per se, but an acknowledgment that being able to access and program the LaserJet at an effective resolution of 1200 dpi requires special techniques and tools.

Soft Fonts

Bitstream Inc.
Athenaeum House
215 First Street
Cambridge, MA 02142
(617) 497-7514

Bitstream is a type foundry specializing in the development of very high-quality soft fonts. Bitstream products are available in many computer stores and through many mail-order vendors. A set of font outlines, generally representing a single family of typefaces, come on one diskette. These are then used to develop fonts of a user-selected size through a program called Fontware. Fontware is available separately from Bitstream; it also comes bundled with some products such as Ventura Publisher. Generating fonts from the outlines is a slow, disk-intensive exercise. The Fontware software, the outlines, and the generated fonts can eat up vast tracts of disk space, so only the needed fonts should be built.

The fonts themselves, however, are the best commercially available. Letters are perfectly round and well proportioned. They appear to have been custom-made for every point size. They are also expensive. A typical disk offering two or three variations of a typeface will list at around $200, with street prices of about $100 available after considerable searching. However, for desktop publishing applications or for documents where print quality must be of the highest order, Bitstream fonts are the best bet. If you do not need the very best fonts, or simply cannot afford to spend so much money to build a font library, the fonts from Digi-Fonts (reviewed next) will provide an excellent solution.

Digi-Fonts, Inc.
528 Commons Drive
Golden, CO 80401
(303) 526-9435

Digi-Fonts is a type foundry that offers an outstanding collection of typefaces for the LaserJet family at very attractive prices. Typefaces are sold by the disk or as a complete set. In addition, Digi-Fonts offers a number of accessory programs for installing fonts into your favorite word processor. There is also a special effects utility that implements effects similar to the ones described in Chapter 7.

The Digi-Fonts font file generator program, called Digi-Duit, can generate bitmapped font files for the entire LaserJet family, including the DeskJet. For LaserJet III owners, a separate utility is available that will download typefaces in the AGFA Compugraphic scalable outline format. This is especially useful, as the printer can then generate a font in any size. It also allows the printer to utilize its resolution enhancement technology, which is not available with a downloaded bitmapped font.

A typeface disk generally contains eight sets of scalable outlines that can represent from one to eight typestyles or typeface families. Disks sell for $79.95 each. By contrast, the entire typeface library is also available, and comes on 33 5¼" disks packaged in their own floppy storage box. The library contains 264 typestyles and sells for a reasonable $599.95. Digi-Fonts also has an extensive set of foreign language fonts that are available separately.

Overall, the typeface quality is very good. In most cases it is impossible to distinguish Digi-Fonts' print from that of premium vendors such as Bitstream without resorting to the use of a magnifying glass. On the other hand, your pocketbook will have no trouble telling the two apart: Digi-Fonts typefaces are substantially less expensive.

Digi-Fonts also has a reasonable licensing policy for redistribution of individual bitmapped font files. If you are developing a commercial application for the LaserJet and would like to include a basic set of fonts you might consider this option.

A good deal of the font-related code for this book was developed and tested using Digi-Fonts typefaces. Digi-Fonts graciously gave their consent to include several font files on the source code disk for this book, which are intended to provide sample fonts for testing the program code.

SWFTE International Ltd.
Stone Mill Office Park
724 Yorklyn Road #150
Hockessin, DE 19707
(302) 234-1740

SWFTE fonts are good quality, inexpensive fonts distinguished by the fact that they are created as needed. They are stored on disk strictly as outlines. When it comes time to download to the LaserJet, they are created then and there. This process is quick except on fonts over about 18 points. The fonts themselves are of good (but not *very* good) quality. They are entirely sufficient for interoffice communication, drafts, and typical correspondence where top-notch appearance is not critical.

In addition to the substantial disk savings they provide, the typefaces are much cheaper than the other fonts reviewed here. Foundry fonts (typefaces that come with true italic and true bold) sell for $49.95 each; decorative fonts (which generally have no bold or italic options) sell for $24.95 each. Software interfaces to the leading word processors are provided separately. These allow for the generation of fonts on-the-fly from within the word processor. For non-critical applications, the savings of space and money make the SWFTE products attractive indeed.

PostScript Generation

GoScript v. 3.0
LaserGo Inc.
9369 Carroll Park Drive #A
San Diego, CA 92121
(619) 450-4600

LaserGo markets a software Postscript interpreter. The interpreter can display the results of a postscript file to the screen, or it can send the image to the printer using one of many printer drivers (including the LaserJet). The product comes in two versions: GoScript, which has 13 built-in scalable fonts, and GoScript Plus, which has 35 fonts. The prices are $149 and $299, respectively.

While the output from GoScript is of good quality, the product is difficult to use and has a number of significant rough edges. The biggest issue is that the images needed to generate PostScript files take up considerable space, which GoScript finds on the PC in expanded and/or extended memory. If the program runs out of memory it aborts without cleaning up any temporary files it may have created. If the program is restarted then recognizes the presence of its previous work files, it aborts again rather than erasing the files. The files must be manually deleted.

Its ability to interpret Postscript is not ensured either. There are many instances where Postscript files cannot be interpreted correctly. This does not generate erroneous images; it simply aborts the program.

Finally, when everything works correctly, images were generated slowly on the printer (as much the fault of the LaserJet as the software) and poorly (although much faster) on the display. Overall, this is a product with a lot of unfulfilled potential.

Adobe PostScript Cartridge
Adobe Systems Inc.
1585 Charleston Road
Mountain View, CA 94039
(415) 961-4400

This is a PostScript cartridge that plugs into the front of the LaserJet printer (different cartridges are required for different models). Along with the software that comes with it, the cartridge traps files sent to the LaserJet. If the file is straight text or PCL, it is sent through to the LaserJet untouched. If it is a PostScript file, it is processed by the cartridge. The cartridge interprets the commands and renders the image and text as a raster image for the LaserJet. The quality of the printed image as well as the faithful execution of PostScript commands are assured due to the fact that the cartridge is manufactured by Adobe Systems, the designers of PostScript.

The PostScript translation works reasonably quickly (these things are always slow on the LaserJet) and makes use of memory on the printer itself. A standard size sheet requires 1.5MB, and a legal size sheet ($8\frac{1}{2}$" × 14") requires 2.5MB. For optimal performance, 2.5MB is recommended. The cartridge contains the standard 35 PostScript fonts, which saves having all the printer fonts on disk. To see the document in its final form, however, it may be necessary to create display fonts for your video hardware. Software to do this comes with the cartridge. Software is also provided to set up a convenient interface to standard word-processing and desktop-publishing software. Overall, a solid and usable way of adding PostScript facilities to the LaserJet, priced at $495 retail, $249 typical street price.

The LaserMaster Series III Professional and Its C Toolkit
LaserMaster Corp.
7156 Shady Oak Road
Eden Prairie, MN 55344
(612) 944-9330

The LaserMaster Series III Professional is an add-on board for ISA-bus PC-family machines that greatly increases print quality on the LaserJet III, even in comparison with the LaserJet III's built-in "resolution enhancement." It has been extensively reviewed in the trade press (see, for example, "Add-In Laser Boards," *PC Magazine*, April 24, 1990). The board comes with an assortment of drivers, and it can do a good deal of work out of the box, but its attraction for the C programmer is the developer's kit available separately. A special version of the board is available for the LaserJet IIID.

The Series III Professional can function with 2-, 4-, or 6MB of memory. It installs straightforwardly into the PC, with an attachment going into the "Optional I/O" slot on the back of the LaserJet III. 4MB of memory provides the maximum 800 DPI "TurboRes" on a stock LaserJet III. For the IIID version of the board, 6MB are required to get the maximum 600 DPI "TurboRes" in the printer's duplex mode. We completed installation of our 4MB board into our LaserJet III and the subsequent testing in about a half hour, after which the host machine, a no-name AT clone, functioned as before in its accustomed jobs, including some that addressed the printer in the traditional way. This implied no unhappy side effects from the installation. LaserMaster has anticipated most of the likely problems by making the board's port addresses user-selectable. The default of 100 hex is likely to work in most systems. The board requires 16 contiguous addresses.

The Series III Professional is one in a line of LaserJet enhancement products released by LaserMaster during its short lifetime since it started as a skunk works at Intran Corporation, once a player in publishing workstations. LaserMaster products take an idiosyncratic approach to enhancing the LaserJet III in that they ignore the LaserJet III's native language, PCL 5. Instead, LaserMaster boards support LaserMaster's own protocol, DDPI. LaserMaster announced in November, 1990 that it will be incorporating Microsoft's TrueImage PostScript-compatible technology in its product line, including a software-based implementation for the Series III Professional. The prospective user has to decide whether the lack of PCL 5 and the clone-only PostScript support represent real problems. If they do not, the Series III Professional is a remarkable product. It is not cheap, but for what it does, this should be expected. DDPI is a rich protocol, servicing just about every sensible task that one could want to perform with fonts or with graphics. It is comparable to PostScript in the extent of its instruction set and exceeds PostScript in some areas. In particular, it is much more sophisticated than PostScript in its handling of raster graphics. In vector graphics work, it provides the Bezier curve support omitted from the LaserJet's native language. In the area of fonts it supports LaserMaster's own outline font format plus the Adobe Type 1 and Bitstream formats, the latter two by one-time conversions using utilities provided. The Series III Professional does not support bitmap fonts. LaserMaster has always featured its support of Ventura Publisher, but the Series III Professional is capable of much more.

The lack of adherence to existing standards does imply programming of some sort if one is to use the board with an application that is not already supported. The C developer's toolkit, in version 3.20a at this writing, includes subroutine libraries supplied as .obj files for each of the four main memory models (small, compact, medium, and large) that are meant to be linked with Microsoft C 5.1 or 6.0, source for these .obj files, a group of header files, and substantial documentation. The granularity of the largest subroutine library is on the coarse side, all 156 functions being in one module. Fortunately, that module is only 22K for the large memory model.

The Series III Professional can be addressed in either of two ways. A program can address a supplied TSR presumed to have been already loaded, or it can load the equivalent of the TSR while running. The second method avoids wasting 34K of conventional memory. The documentation refers to the second method as the "overlay" method because it makes use of the DOS overlay function (AX=4B03 hex). This is transparent to the programmer; it has nothing to do with the Microsoft linker's overlay facility. The application doesn't care whether the TSR is loaded or not, since DDPI takes care of such housekeeping.

There is some implication in the READ.ME file that DDPI should be expected to support Turbo C. At this moment, it does not, at least not reliably. A test program that compiles with Turbo C++ yielded an .exe file that simply hung, even with the TSR installed. The same .exe file functioned correctly when produced with the Microsoft compiler. This program, DEMOLM, is shown in Listing E.1 and its output is shown in Figure E.1. (Listings having to do with the DDPI protocol are for demonstration purposes only, since proprietary header files would be required to compile them.) The READ.ME file states that an .exe file produced with Turbo C/C++ will not work in the overlay mode, thereby limiting access.

LISTING E.1 Program to Generate Sample Output in Figure E.1 on the LaserMaster Series III Professional.

```
/*------------------- DEMOLM.C -------------------------
 * Program to generate sample output in Figure E.1
 *---------------------------------------------------*/

On Microsoft, compile with

cl /c /AL /Fm /Gs /J /Oecigt demolm.c
link demolm+ddpi+ddpiinit+ddpilib,,,, /STACK:5120

*/

#include <conio.h>
#include <stdio.h>
#include <stdlib.h>
#include <string.h>
#include "ddpilib.h"
#include "ddpi.h"

static card16 device = 0;   /* 0=printer, 1=display, 2=network */
static card16 error;        /* error code returned by fSetup
                               --see DDPIDEFS.H */
/*--------------------------------------------------------
 * This function will print a simple text string in two
 * point sizes. There is a full range of commands to mani-
 * pulate fonts.
 *--------------------------------------------------------*/
void text (void)
```

Listing E.1 continues

Listing E.1 continued

```
{
    byte    aString[50]; /* array for the string to be imaged    */
    card32 status2 = 0; /* ReportPrinterStatus2 status field      */
    card16 ch;

    lSetOrientation(PORTRAIT,device);
    lSetTextImageMode(FILL,device);

    lDefineFont("PLTNR",1,device);

    strcpy (aString, "We say more than HELLO WORLD.");

    lSetFont(1,24.0,device);
    lPutString(aString,10, 3000,0,ALIGNLEFT,NOJUSTIFY,device);

    if (device != 1)
    {
        lReportPrinterStatus2(&status2,device);
        while (status2)
        {
            printf("\nThe Printer is not ready for printing.");
            printf("\nPlease correct, then press any key to continue...");
            while (!kbhit());
            if ((ch=getch()) == 0)
                ch=getch();
            printf("\n");
            lReportPrinterStatus2(&status2,device);
        }
    }
}

#define RADSPERDEGREE 3.141592765 / 360.0

/*-----------------------------------------------------------
 * This function will print some simple vectors.
 *-----------------------------------------------------------*/
void vectors ( void )
{
    struct      /* our own structure, so we have an array
    {               larger than DDPIDEFS.H */
        card16 count;
        int16  pairs[350];
    } vector1;

    struct      /* our own structure, so we have an array
    {               larger than DDPIDEFS.H */
        card16 count;
        int16  baseline;
        int16  initial_x;
        byte   y_val[2401];
    } vector2;

    int16  x,y;
    card32 status2 = 0; /* ReportPrinterStatus2 status field  */
    card16 ch;
```

Listing E.1 continues

Listing E.1 continued

```
/*-----------------------------------------------------
 * Multivector 1 takes an array of co-ordinate pairs,
 * x and y. The first value in the array is the number
 * of vector pairs.
 *------------------------------------------------------*/

y = 0;
for (x = 1; x < 2400; x += 30)
{
    vector1.pairs[y++] = -x;
    vector1.pairs[y++] = 2300;
    vector1.pairs[y++] = x;
    vector1.pairs[y++] = 2900;
}

vector1.count = y / 2;
vector1.pairs[0] = 1;

lMultiVector1(&vector1,device);

y = 0;
for (x = 2300; x <= 2900; x+=30)
{
    vector1.pairs[y++] = -1;
    vector1.pairs[y++] = x;
    vector1.pairs[y++] = 2370;
    vector1.pairs[y++] = x;
}
vector1.count = y / 2;

lMultiVector1(&vector1,device);

/*-----------------------------------------------------
 * Multivector2 takes a starting co-ord (x,y) and an array
 * of y's, with x increasing automatically by 1 for each y
 * data point.
 *
 * MAX range for the array of y's is -128 to 127 from the
 * baseline.
 *------------------------------------------------------*/

for (x=0; x < 2370; x++)                 /* fill in the y values */
{
    vector2.y_val[x] = (byte)(sin(x * RADSPERDEGREE) * 127);
}

vector2.count = --x;
vector2.baseline = 2600;
vector2.initial_x = 0;

lMultiVector2(&vector2,device);

if (device != 1)
{
    lReportPrinterStatus2(&status2,device);
    while (status2)
    {
        printf("\nThe Printer is not ready for printing.");
```

Listing E.1 continues

Listing E.1 continued

```
        printf("\nPlease correct, then press any key to continue...");
        while (!kbhit());
        if ((ch=getch()) == 0)
            ch=getch();
        printf("\n");
        lReportPrinterStatus2(&status2,device);
    }
  }
}

/*-----------------------------------------------------------
 * This is a small function that will print some very simple
 * graphics. Since the coordinates are fixed, the size of the
 * graphics will vary, depending on the resolution of the output
 * device.
 *---------------------------------------------------------*/

void graphics (void)
{
    card32 status2 = 0; /* ReportPrinterStatus2 status field  */
    card16 ch;

    /*-----------------------------------------------------------
     * Draw a line from the lower left area to the upper right area.
     *---------------------------------------------------------*/

    lDrawLine(600, 400, 2000, 2200, device);

    /*-----------------------------------------------------------
     * Draw a small box in the lower left hand corner of the page.
     *---------------------------------------------------------*/

    lInitPath(device);
    lMoveTo(200, 200, device);
    lLineTo(200, 400, device);
    lLineTo(400, 400, device);
    lLineTo(400, 200, device);
    lClosePath(device);    /* draws a line between the
                              last MoveTo and LineTo */
    lOutlinePath(device); /* shows the path           */

    /*-----------------------------------------------------------
     * Draw a vertical line on the left side of the page.
     *---------------------------------------------------------*/

    lInitPath(device);
    lMoveTo(1,1,device);
    lLineTo(1,2200, device);
    lOutlinePath(device);

     /*-----------------------------------------------------------
      * Draw a small arc with ends connected by line segment.
      *---------------------------------------------------------*/

    lInitPath(device);
    lMoveTo(800, 1200, device);
    lCurveTo(800, 1900, 1800, 1900, 1800, 1200, device);
```

Listing E.1 continues

Listing E.1 continued

```
    lClosePath(device);  /* draws a line between the
                            last MoveTo and CurveTo */
    lOutlinePath(device);/* shows the path  */

    if (device != 1)
    {
        lReportPrinterStatus2(&status2,device);
        while (status2)
        {
            printf("\nThe Printer is not ready for printing.");
            printf
            ("\nPlease correct, then press any key to continue...");
            while (!kbhit());
            if ((ch=getch()) == 0)
                ch=getch();
            printf("\n");
            lReportPrinterStatus2(&status2,device);
        }
    }
}

/*-----------------------------------------------------
 * Main line starts here.
 *-------------------------------------------------*/
void main ( void )
{

  /*-----------------------------------------------------
   * Check to see if DDPI is loaded as a TSR, if it is, use the
   * int 17h calls. If it is not, load DDPI as an overlay and
   * use the far * calls.
   *-------------------------------------------------*/

    if ((error=fSetup(device)) != 0 )
    {
        printf
        ("\nWe had trouble initializing DDPI.  ERROR=:%d\n",error);
                        exit (error);
            }

            lSetPrintingMode(LORES,device);
            lClearFrameBuffer(device);

            text ( ) ;
            vectors ( ) ;
            graphics ( ) ;

    lPrintPage(1, device);

    fOut(device);
}
```

FIGURE E.1

We say more than HELLO WORLD.

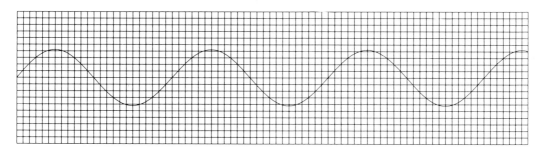

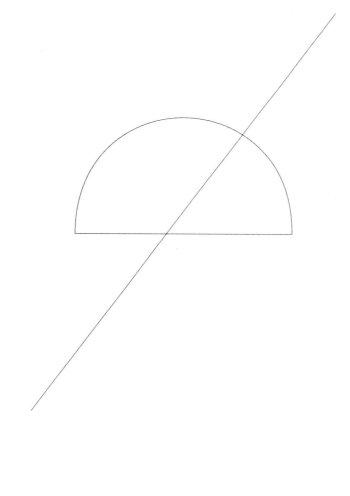

The Series III Professional takes over the printer interrupt, 0x17. Normal BIOS calls pass through unhindered. LaserMaster assigns a range of normally undefined register values in conjunction with the interrupt to awaken itself when the DDPI's services are required. A potential for conflict exists here if the machine happens to have other software that does something similar, but we are not aware of anything likely to be functional on the same system that would raise this problem.

Programmers are given a high-level interface to call if they wish. In this mode, the 156 available functions are normal-looking C functions. Each is documented adequately, with each function's description starting on the top of a page in the reference manual, which is the civilized way to lay out a library reference. Alternatively, the programmer may use lower-level functions, calling the BIOS routine directly. This usage is documented, and LaserMaster recommends use of those functions for time-critical applications. There may be no alternative to them if the development environment is something other than Microsoft C or Turbo C. However, the high-level functions appear to offer everything the low-level ones do, and readability with them is better, so we suggest staying with them if possible.

One mental adjustment that the programmer has to make in dealing with the DDPI, as compared with the raw LaserJet, is to remember that it is possible to get information from it. One can get font metric information, as well as information on the capabilities of the output machine. Both of these can be useful if one is going to do page formatting in software and use the Series III Professional as a dumb output device. That is a valid use for the Series III Professional, and we use ours that way as an output device for the TeX typesetting system. Here, a little bit of handiwork was needed, since DDPI will return character metrics but not kerning information. For the basic 35 fonts, the font metrics, like the fonts, are the same as Adobe's. For the other 100 fonts, all that is available is what DDPI tells you, and the kerning information, if needed, has to be developed separately. The character set available to the DDPI is shown in Figure E.2, and is generated by Listing E.2. This is the output of a LaserMaster-supplied utility that will show the DDPI character set (or the Ventura or Windows character set) for any LaserMaster font. For our main purpose—taking TeX output—the character set was slightly better than the PostScript character set in mapability from Computer Modern Roman, since some of the Greek letters are available; however, the `ffi` and `ffl` ligatures are missing, just as they are in PostScript. Listing E.2 shows a program that will give the font metrics for the current font at the current point size. The function called appears to work only for characters in the range 1 to 255, but that is enough for most needs, although in our TeX mapping it misses the angstrom symbol and the Greek letters.

In summary, the Series III Professional is worth looking at where the highest possible output quality is needed on a LaserJet III, whether buyers intend to use the supplied drivers or intend to roll their own. The cost is $1995 for resolution of 400 dpi, and $2995 for 800 dpi.

LISTING E.2   Program to Dump a LaserMaster Character Set; Output Appears in Figure E.2

```
/*-------------------- TEXWID.C --------------------
 * Program to dump a LaserMaster character set.
 *--------------------------------------------------*/

On Microsoft, compile with:

cl /c /AL /Fm /Gs /J /Oecigt textwid.c
link textwid+ddpi+ddpiinit+ddpilib,,,, /STACK:5120

*/

#include <conio.h>
#include <stdio.h>
#include <stdlib.h>
#include <string.h>
#include "ddpilib.h"
#include "ddpi.h"

static card16 device = 0;  /* 0=printer, 1=display, 2=network   */
static card16 error;       /* error code ret'd by fSetup
                                    --see DDPIDEFS.H */
static struct CHARWIDTHS cwid ;

/*--------------------------------------------------------------
 * This is a small function that will print a simple text
 * string in point sizes. There is a full range of
 * commands to manipulate fonts.
 *--------------------------------------------------*/
void text (void)
{
    byte    aString[50]; /* array for the string to be imaged */
    card32 status2 = 0; /* ReportPrinterStatus2 status field */
    card16 ch;
    int i;

    lSetOrientation(PORTRAIT,device);
    lSetTextImageMode(FILL,device);

    lDefineFont("PLTNR",1,device);

    lSetFont(1,24.0,device);

    printf ( "\nchr  r_wid  p_wid    l/EM    p/EM rel_ht bas_ht\n" ) ;
    for ( i = 1; i < 255 ; ++i )
    {
            cwid.charcode = i ;
            lReportCharWidth ( &cwid, device ) ;
            printf ( "\n%3u%7u%7u%7u%7u%7u",
            cwid.charcode, cwid.relative_width,
            cwid.pixel_width, cwid.lines_per_EM,
            cwid.pixels_per_EM,
            cwid.relative_height,cwid.baseline_height ) ;
    }
```

Listing E.2   continues

Listing E.2 continued

```
    if (device != 1)
    {
        lReportPrinterStatus2(&status2,device);
        while (status2)
        {
            printf("\nThe Printer is not ready for printing.");
            printf
            ("\nPlease correct, then press any key to continue...");
            while (!kbhit());
            if ((ch=getch()) == 0)
                ch=getch();
            printf("\n");
            lReportPrinterStatus2(&status2,device);
        }
    }
}

/*-----------------------------------------------------------
 * Main line starts here.
 *---------------------------------------------------------*/

void main ( void )
{
    /*-------------------------------------------------------
     * Check to see if DDPI is loaded as a TSR. If it is, use the
     * int 17h calls. If it is not, load DDPI as an overlay and
     * use the far * calls.
     *-----------------------------------------------------*/

    if ((error=fSetup(device)) != 0 )
    {
        printf
        ("\nWe had trouble initializing DDPI.   ERROR=:%d\n",error);
        exit (error);
    }

    lSetPrintingMode(LORES,device);
    lClearFrameBuffer(device);

    text ( ) ;

    fOut(device);
}
```

FIGURE E.2 The Lasermaster Character Set

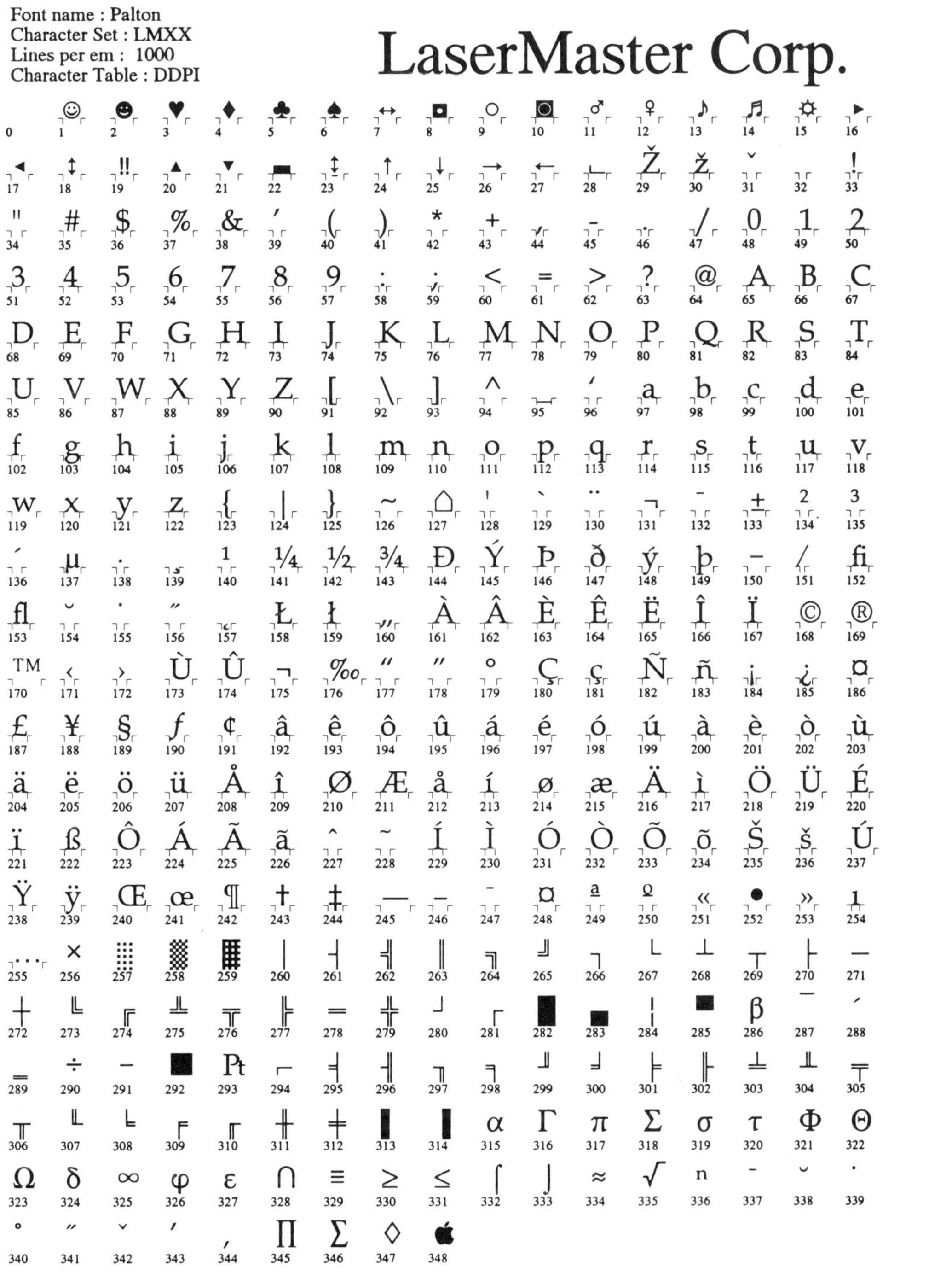

Font name : Palton
Character Set : LMXX
Lines per em : 1000
Character Table : DDPI

LaserMaster Corp.

Bibliography

Aldus Corporation and Microsoft Corporation. *Tagged Image File Format Specification.* Revision 5.0 Final. 1988. Available from the Developer's Desk at Aldus Corporation, 411 First Avenue South, #200, Seattle, WA 98104. (206) 622-5500.

Babcock, David. "Advanced graphics on the HP LaserJet II and DeskJet." *C Gazette,* Summer 1989.

Binstock, Andrew. "Graphics on the HP LaserJet, part I." *C Gazette,* March 1988.

Binstock, Andrew. "Graphics on the HP LaserJet, part II." *C Gazette,* Summer 1988.

Binstock, Andrew. "Postal barcodes." *C Gazette,* Winter 1990.

Bresenham, J. E. "Algorithm for computer control of a digital plotter." *IBM Systems Journal,* 4 (1965). This article was the first presentation of the now-famous Bresenham algorithm.

Casciola, Guilio. "Basic concepts to accelerate line algorithms." *Computers & Graphics,* 12 (3/4, 1988).

Chandler, Richard E. "A tracking algorithm for implicitly defined curves." *IEEE Computer Graphics & Applications,* March 1988.

Farin, Gerald. *Curves and Surfaces for Computer Aided Geometric Design.* 2d ed. San Diego: Academic Press, 1990. This book is notable for its presentation of many examples in C and for its detailed discussion of the nonuniform rational b-spline (NURB).

Harrington, Steven. *Computer Graphics: A Programming Approach.* New York: McGraw-Hill, 1987.

Hewlett-Packard. *LaserJet III Printer Developer's Guide.* Hewlett-Packard, 1990.

Hewlett-Packard. *LaserJet III Technical Reference Manual.* Hewlett-Packard, 1990. The reader should be warned that the sample C code appearing on page 15-15 of the *LaserJet Technical Reference* is faulty. The % literals in the format arguments to `fprintf()` should be `%%`. Also, the code overlooks the difference between opening a DOS device and opening a DOS file in binary mode. That subject is covered in Chapter 1 of the present book.

Hewlett-Packard. *The HP-GL/2 Reference Guide.* Reading, Mass.: Addison-Wesley, 1990.

Knuth, Donald E., *The METAFONTbook*. Reading, Mass.: Addison-Wesley, 1986. Gives a good introduction to the Bezier cubic, in the context of font design.

Lotus Development Corporation, Intel Corporation, and Microsoft Corporation. *Lotus/Intel/Microsoft Expanded Memory Specification*. Version 4.0. 1987. The definitive explanation of the expanded-memory standard. Available free of charge from Intel Corporation. Comes with manual and MS-DOS format diskettes bearing code and linkable libraries. Intel Corp., 5200 NE Elam Young Parkway, Hillsboro, OR 97124. (503) 629-7854.

Luse, Marv. "Downloading fonts to LaserJet printers." *C Gazette*, Autumn 1989.

Luse, Marv. "Resizing bitmapped fonts." *C Gazette*, Summer 1989.

Luse, Marv. "Converting proportional LaserJet fonts to fixed width." *C Gazette*, Autumn 1990.

Luse, Marv. "Printing PCX files." *C Gazette*, Winter 1990.

McCown, Rainer, and Heeth Clark. "Laser metrics." *PC Tech Journal*, September 1987. One of the earliest articles to offer in-depth discussion of PCL 4 and the LaserJet II.

Microsoft Corporation, Lotus Development Corporation, Intel Corporation, and AST Research, Inc. *eXtended Memory Specification (XMS)*. Version 2.0. 1988.

Pitteway, M. L. V. "Algorithm for drawing ellipses or hyperbolae with a digital plotter." *Computer Journal* (U.K.), November 1967.

Rimmer, Steve. *Bit-Mapped Graphics*. Blue Ridge Summit, Pa.: Windcrest Books, 1990.

Rogers, David F., and J. Alan Adams. *Mathematical Elements for Computer Graphics*. New York: McGraw-Hill, 1976.

Van Aken, Jerry, and Mark Novak. "Curve-drawing algorithms for raster displays." *ACM Transactions on Graphics*, April 1985.

Weber, David. "Ellipses, parabolas, and hyperbolas." *Computer Language*, November 1988.

WordPerfect Corporation. *DOS Developer's Toolkit for WordPerfect Corporation Products*. Orem, Utah: WordPerfect Corp, 1990. The definitive source of information on WordPerfect file formats. The 1990 version (which covers WordPerfect version 5.1) is available for $75 from WordPerfect Corporation, 1555 N. Technology Way, Orem, UT 84057. (801) 222-7178.

Index

Source Code Disk Order Form

Please send me _____ copies of the source code disk for *HP LaserJet Programming*. I have enclosed $25.00 for each disk. (Foreign orders please add $3.00 for Canada and Mexico; $7.00 for all other countries. Foreign orders may send cash by registered mail, use a credit card, or use a check. If a check is used, it must bear the name of *only one bank,* which must be a U.S. bank.) Make checks payable to Pacific Data Works.

Name _____

Address _____

_____

City _____   State _____

Country _____

IBM PC diskette size: 5.25" _____   3.5" _____

Send to:

HP LaserJet Disk
Pacific Data Works
1341 Ocean Ave. #257
Santa Monica, CA 90401
U.S.A.

If using a credit card:

Credit Card Type: Visa   MasterCard   American Express

Card# _____

Cardholder Name _____

Expiration Date _____

Signature _____

Comments to authors: